Social Work with Children and Families

Developing advanced practice

Penelope Welbourne

Routledge
Taylor & Francis Group

LONDON AND NEW YORK

First published 2012
by Routledge
2 Park Square, Milton Park, Abingdon, Oxon, OX14 4RN

Simultaneously published in the USA and Canada
by Routledge
711 Third Avenue, New York, NY 10017

Routledge is an imprint of the Taylor & Francis Group, an informa business

British Library Cataloguing in Publication Data
A catalogue record for this book is available from the British Library

Library of Congress Cataloging-in-Publication Data
Welbourne, Penelope.
Social work with children and families : developing advanced practice /
Penelope Welbourne. — 1st ed.
    p. cm.
    1. Social work with children. 2. Family social work. I. Title.
    HV713.W45 2012   362.82'53—dc23
    2011045070

ISBN13: 978-0-415-56379-6 (hbk)
ISBN13: 978-0-415-56380-2 (pbk)
ISBN13: 978-0-203-11965-5 (ebk)

Typeset in Goudy
by Bookcraft Ltd, Stroud, Gloucestershire

Printed and bound in Great Britain by
CPI Antony Rowe, Chippenham, Wiltshire

There is an increasing emphasis on post-qualifying training for social workers, especially in the complex and demanding area of working with children and families. This essential textbook is especially designed for practitioners studying at this level.

Accessible and thorough, the text focuses on a mixture of conceptual and organisational topics, skills, law, policy and key practice issues. It includes chapters on:

- social work values and ethics
- risk, uncertainty and accountability
- direct work with children and young people
- promoting security and stability
- working with reluctant service users
- assessment of parenting
- working with poverty, drugs and alcohol
- going to court and the legal framework
- children and young people going home
- supporting others in their professional development.

Using case studies and activities to link research, theory and practice, *Social Work with Children and Families* takes a wider look at the role and tasks of an experienced social work practitioner, and at the skills and knowledge needed to develop professionally from this point.

Penelope Welbourne is Programme Lead for the MA in social work at the University of Plymouth, UK. She has research interests in the areas of child protection, child law and children's rights and the development of social work as a profession.

Post-qualifying Social Work

The General Social Care Council (GSCC) requires all social workers to take responsibility for maintaining and improving their knowledge and skills to maintain registration. Post-qualifying Social Work is a series designed to support social workers, as they work towards their GSCC post-qualifying award, and to enhance and develop their practice as they continue within their professional careers.

Featuring highly accessible texts, packed with pedagogical features, this series will be invaluable for students undertaking post-qualifying training, as well as equipping practitioners to deal with the current and future challenges of social work.

Available titles:

Professional Development in Social Work
Complex issues in practice
Janet Seden, Sarah Matthews, Mick McCormick and Alun Morgan

Social Work with Children and Families
Developing advanced practice
Penelope Welbourne

Contents

List of illustrations

Figures

Tables

Acknowledgements

My particular thanks are due to those who read drafts, commented on the work in progress and otherwise offered their support. I am very grateful for their help, and especially grateful for their valuable time and expertise. Needless to say, any omissions and errors are all my own work. The people I would like to thank are Michael Sheppard, Naomi Knott, Bill Jordan, Avril Bellinger, Diane Garrard and Stephen Trahair.

Introduction

Social work with children and families, and child protection social work in particular, is under review (Munro, 2010a; 2010b; 2011). One theme that has emerged strongly from that review process is the need to maintain a focus on the child throughout all social work interventions, to be 'child centred'. This is not new; indeed it is arguable that social work has reached a point in its development where we are seeing many themes repeated (Dickens, 2011). The most significant of these recurring themes is perhaps the tension between the need for social work to contribute effectively to early intervention services for children in need and their families, and pressure to focus on the most vulnerable children, because of limited resources and high levels of demand for child protection services. This tension is played out at the level of the individual practitioner, who also needs to be skilled in balancing their work to support families with more assertive interventions to protect children when appropriate. While the preventive and protective roles are not incompatible, the heavy demands of protecting children mean that developing skills in preventive work have sometimes made it appear so. Negotiating this tension is a core skill for child and family social workers, and the organisations that employ them.

Social work is a relatively new profession, and is still working to define aspects of its special remit and expertise. At the same time, social work in Britain is facing additional challenges related to high turnover of staff, high levels of stress, and a challenging economic climate, which has an impact on the numbers of families under pressure, as well as the resources available to respond to the effects of that pressure on children and young people. This book cannot offer any panacea for these challenges.

What it does aim to do is to identify some of the key areas in which it is important for children and families that social workers have a good level of expertise, and explore ways in which social workers who already have some familiarity with these areas of practice can develop their competence. Competence in listening to children, reflecting on what they and other key people have to say, and helping to create a shared understanding as to how to achieve desired and improved outcomes are the bases for everything that child and family social workers do.

In Part I, I have also included a section on poverty. So many people who receive services from child and family social workers are affected by poverty. The relationship between social work and poverty is not a straightforward one. Social work is not primarily aimed at the alleviation of poverty, yet so many of the problems with which it deals are bound up with families' experience of coping with daily 'hassles' that are in one way or another linked to the limited resources available to them. Money would not solve all the problems that the families face, but lack of it makes life harder for the children who live in them.

The second part of the book addresses situations in which social workers need to be more aware of their statutory powers as well as their duties. Any experienced or newly qualified child and family social worker reading this book will be conscious of the importance of awareness of risk in assessment and in ongoing work with children and young people. This book cannot cover more than a fraction of the diversity of situations in which risk is an issue in social work – probably no book could. What I have sought to do is consider how we might think about risk in general, and how it links to another dominant theme in social work at present: that of prevention.

Thinking about risk perhaps inevitably leads to the idea of resistance: service users who are assessed as presenting a risk to their families, and sometimes to professionals too, but who do not choose to engage with services. Resistance to engagement is a recurring feature in inquiries into child deaths and perhaps a major source of stress for social workers. Parents who use illicit drugs and alcohol and who become users of social work services present particular issues because the of nature of their problems: stigmatised and – except in the case of alcohol – illegal. This book considers ways in which social workers might reflect on these professional challenges and keep the best interests of children at the forefront in doing so.

The last two chapters specifically consider supporting people: first, parents and children, when living at home has not been an option and, second, colleagues who are engaged in social work with children and families to whom more experienced colleagues might offer their support.

Munro (2010: 31) suggests that there is a

> ... need for a practice and policy framework which acknowledges the complexity of the social work task, the emotional and intellectual demands on individuals making highly complex and emotionally charged decisions concerning the lives of children and young people, and the need for this work to be housed within an explicit space for critical reflection.

This book aims to explore some of that complexity and uncertainty in social work. It starts from the position that the demands placed on practitioners by this combination of complexity and uncertainty are the aspects of social work that make it a most interesting and rewarding profession. They are arguably what make it a unique profession in its field of supporting people and promoting well-being and independence. Social work as a profession engages with people's lives at all levels, from the practical to the deeply personal. It is the reflective ability, polished in practice, that enables social workers to do the work they do, across the breadth of human experience: empathetically, respectfully and reflectively. This book is intended to offer ideas and material to support the ongoing development of reflective skills, and to support social work professionals working to offer the quality of help that children and young people deserve.

Part 1

Child- and family-centred
social work

1 Hearing children's voices and respecting children's wishes and feelings, part 1

Trust, communication and support

This chapter:

- considers what we mean when we talk about 'listening to children';
- reviews the legal basis for listening to children;
- encourages thought about the way children and young people are viewed, in society and in social work practice.

Not everyone is impressed with the idea that children's best interests, let alone their wishes and feelings, should influence what adults do. Guggenheim has argued that '[a] significant number of adults who ought to know better have taken far too seriously the importance of furthering the child's best interests. ... Indeed, it is astonishing to observe how much the best interests and child-centered rhetoric is taken seriously by countless children's advocates' (Guggenheim 2005: 157). Munro (2011: 135) reminds us that, given 'the depressing evidence on outcomes for looked after children in adult life, humility about our ability to know what is in children's best interests seems to be the appropriate emotion.' It is the latter position that is central to social work with children and young people: avoiding rhetoric and practising with care.

Ofsted (2011) lists five 'main messages' for practice with regard to the voice of the child (see box on page 6). These messages come from studies of cases in which there was child death or other serious incident relating to a child, so the material they draw on is not, one hopes, representative of all child care cases. On the other hand, there is at present no research that tells us if cases in which children came to serious harm or died are atypical cases in many respects, or atypical solely with reference to what happened to the child. Using Reason's (2000) model of active and latent errors (see Chapter 7), it is possible that many of the 'errors'[1] identified in Serious Case Reviews are common in social work practice with children and young people, although few come to harm as a result because other factors prevent it from happening. Equally, it may be that 'typical' practice avoids such mistakes. In either event, we cannot afford *not* to learn from analysis of cases in which things went wrong, so that the important things that are discovered about good practice can be consolidated, and areas in which practice needs to be developed are improved. Children's social care agencies, and those who work in them, should consider how practice can be made proof against making these particular mistakes.

Box 1.1 Five main messages from the 2011 Ofsted review of the voice of the child in Serious Case Reviews

- The child was not seen frequently enough by the professionals involved, or was not asked about their views and feelings.
- Agencies did not listen to adults who tried to speak on behalf of the child and who had important information to contribute.
- Parents and carers prevented professionals from seeing and listening to the child.
- Practitioners focused too much on the needs of the parents, especially on vulnerable parents, and overlooked the implications for the child.
- Agencies did not interpret their findings well enough to protect the child.

Ofsted 2011: 6

The report notes that often the children involved were too young to speak for themselves, but some practitioners found ways of being responsive to their expressed feelings and wishes, even though those wishes and feelings were expressed non-verbally. Verbal communication is only one aspect of communication. Young children and those who find it difficult to say what they would like to say in words may have become adept at finding other ways of expressing their feelings and their wishes. Behaviour as diverse as clinginess, running away from home, self-harm and social withdrawal may all be ways of expressing things that it is hard for the child or young person to put into words. Once a wider definition of 'expressed wishes and feelings' is brought into use, the scope for hearing children's wishes becomes very broad.

One thing that is essential for hearing children's wishes and feelings is actually spending time with the child. Parents, teachers, relatives and others who know a child well may be able to give a good account of the child's wishes and feelings as they see them. People who know the child well may be able to discuss difficult issues with them more easily than the social worker – but children may also be reluctant to speak openly, about abuse, neglect or feelings of despair, with people who they think may have a stake in thinking well of the people who care for them, or thinking badly of them, or who might be shocked and distressed to hear what they think. Information from 'third parties' is not a substitute for seeing and speaking to a child directly, however helpful and well-intentioned the friends, relatives and other informants may be. Both sources of information about children's wishes and feelings are important. Listening to adults who speak on behalf of the child is important (Ofsted 2011), but not everyone who speaks on behalf of a child will be representing the child's experiences, wishes and feelings accurately.

Social workers may reflect on the ways they 'see' children, not on a practical day-to-day basis, but conceptually. One's own experiences in childhood, and experience of being with children as an adult – as a parent, a professional, a relative or a friend, for example – may shape the way one thinks about children as a social worker. James describes four ways of seeing children:

- **The developing child:** incomplete, lacking in status and competence: voice not to be taken (too) seriously.
- **The tribal child:** living in a conceptually different world from adults, separate from adults and having their own rules and agendas: part of an independent culture, worthy of study in its own right.
- **The adult child:** competent participants in a shared but adult-centred world: socially competent in ways comparable to adults.
- **The social child:** children have different but not necessarily inferior competences from adults: affords them the same status as adults. (James 1995 cited in Mantle *et al.* 2007: 790)

Box 1.2 Exercise: ways of 'seeing' children

Think about three or four children who you know of different ages and in different contexts. Do you recognise any of the above ways of seeing children in the way you think about your own relationships with those children? When you relate to them, is it consistently according to one of the 'ways of seeing', or does the way you see and relate to the children vary? What determines which 'mode of seeing' dominates at any one time?

Keeping the focus on the child, not the tasks

Social workers carry out bureaucratic functions such as reviews of care plans. They are also called on to act as an 'agent of social control', for example when a Secure Accommodation Order is being considered for a young person. They assess need and risk. While these are core tasks, relationships with children and young people are all too readily structured around these tasks, rather than making the relationship with the young person or child a matter of importance in its own right because of what it contributes to understanding the child's needs. Social work is particularly easily adapted to accommodate the demands of bureaucratic elements such as 'form-filling'. Such pressures undermine capacity for developing meaningful relationships with children and young people. For children in care, in particular, there is a danger that *minimum* expectations in terms of frequency of contact easily become 'normalised' into baseline standards for frequency of visits. If meeting children in care happens because there is a schedule to be followed, not because the child needs or merits a visit in themselves, the child is likely to understand this and this will affect how they view you.

What do adults mean by 'listening' to children, and what do children mean when they say they want to be listened to?

Listening is a term that is understood differently by adults in different contexts. At its most basic, it is a matter of hearing what someone has to say, or paying attention to communication that may be non-verbal, such as written information or thoughts expressed through specialist communication systems. It is different from 'hearing' in that it implies a purposeful activity: one may hear without intending to do so; listening requires attention and an effort to understand what is being expressed. Social work arguably uses the idea of 'listening' in a very particular way, and ideas about 'active listening' and body language may be stressed. Children may have quite a different understanding. The potential for miscommunication about communication is great.

It is unlikely that children think of listening as a *skill*: research indicates they consider listening is associated with paying attention and taking what is said seriously. It means more than just hearing, or even paying attention: it may mean listening *and* paying attention to what is said, and doing something differently as a result. Many children in care felt well listened to, but there is scope for improvement. Roger Morgan, Children's Rights Director for England, found that:

> Most children (65%) said they are asked usually or a lot about things that matter to them, and 63% said their views are taken as seriously as an adult's views. A majority (60%) said their views make quite a bit or a lot of difference; 77% are usually or always told what changes are going to happen in their lives.
>
> Morgan 2007: 5

For the trained social worker, active listening has the specialist meaning of demonstrating that the other person has been heard and listened to with care and attention during the conversation. Body language on the part of the listener is important, as it helps to show that one has understood what has been said. For children, the manner in which one listens may be very important, giving messages to the child about the value being placed on what they say, but what happens next is really important: carrying the message away and, the child hopes, acting on it. The children in McLeod's (2010) study had very different ideas from the social workers about what constitutes good 'listening'. For them, listening was definitely not about the attitude of the listener so much as the listener's willingness to take action on what they heard. One child described her social worker as sitting, apparently listening and nodding, but because nothing changed as a result, she felt the social worker was not really listening at all.

This is not surprising given the way parents often use 'listening', as in: 'If you had listened to me you would have done your homework already'. *Listening* as used in families frequently means: 'Do something you would not otherwise have done, as a result of listening to me'. It is not surprising if children sometimes use the term this way themselves. Social workers need to be able to do both kinds of listening: conveying a sense of interest and respect for the child's views and wishes; and follow through, when this is what the child reasonably expects to happen. Being clear with the child about what will happen as a result of the conversation is important to build trust and make speaking to social workers seem worthwhile.

McLeod (2006) studied social workers' own accounts of what it means to 'listen' as an *attitude*: a receptive process. They used the term in a way that was consistent with an ethic of openness and respect – paying attention and taking what is said seriously. They also wanted to find out about children's feelings, consistent with the requirement that they should take children's 'wishes and feelings' into account. The social workers in McLeod's study had an expectation that they should find out about children's feelings, even hidden and painful ones, but McLeod notes 'none of the workers made reference to any theoretical base; it just seemed to be taken for granted as practice wisdom' (McLeod 2006: 48). This raises the question of how social workers *think* about the personal information they ask children, and indeed adults, to provide them with.

Sometimes it will be clear why the information is needed: perhaps to help a court decide on the best residence and contact arrangements for a child when her parents are divorcing. On other occasions, it may be less clear to the child and even perhaps to the worker why information is being sought, and the purpose to which it may be put. Children in care sometimes complain about an expectation that they will tell their story over again to every new social worker allocated to them. For the social worker, this may be a way of getting to hear the child's authentic view of what has happened to them to support the development of a working relationship. However, if nothing appears to change as a result of this sharing of information, which is often deeply personal and highly significant to the child, the reluctance to go through the process again with a new worker is understandable.

If the object of a discussion with a child is to find out from the child his or her views on what has happened in the past, and much of this is already recorded on file, it may be better to find out from the child or young person how they feel about telling their story again. Repeated telling of the same story may be therapeutic, as each new telling brings out different features of the story and helps to create a coherent narrative. On the other hand, for some children, it may feel like an imposition or evidence that what they say is not really taken seriously: why else would they need to keep repeating it? The purpose of the conversation with the child makes a difference. A belief that the worker cares enough to treat the information with care and respect is also very important to children (Staller 2007). Trust in the worker, a safe place to talk in, and a belief that something positive will ensue – effective action will be taken – are all important.

If we can increase our understanding of children's thoughts, feelings and hopes for the future, this will 'contribute to a more accurate assessment of the likely outcomes of different care plan options' (Schofield 2005: 29). Having chosen an option for a child, McLeod (2006) notes that the children in her study who had been the subject of the most extensive efforts at direct work and eliciting feelings when they were younger tended to be making better progress than those who had not been. Persevering in gaining trust appears to have a positive effect on children's well-being.

Some practitioners writing reports for courts use the report they write after talking to children to check that they have 'got it right' for the child. They also sometimes re-phrase children's views in ways they judge they will be less likely to cause embarrassment for the child or anger to be directed at the child. This may not always be possible, however. Sometimes children's views are both important and likely to cause someone else – perhaps a parent – distress or anger (Mantle *et al.* 2007). The implications of the desire to protect them from the consequences of discussing their true wishes and feelings should be considered carefully.

> With older children, maybe eleven and above, I will show them the piece of the report that relates to them. ... I will make a further appointment to go back and check with them, that what I've written is an accurate reflection of what they intended, because I'm always conscious that I may have interpreted wrongly. Also, by the third visit I'll

have checked out – *I think last time you told me this, is that right?* – or – *I understand that this is how you feel, tell me if I'm wrong* – so, you've tried to confirm it along the way.'

Children's Guardian, quoted in Mantle *et al.* 2007: 797

The child's right to privacy in child protection enquiries

Ofsted (2011) highlights the importance of considering where to meet a child to talk to them. A 'safe and trusting environment' is important. For some children, home is a good place to talk but, if this is a place in which they are being abused, it may be very difficult for children to speak of abuse there. Similarly, it is important to consider who is present, since the presence of an abuser, or someone who might talk to the abuser about what was said, would be a barrier to talking about abuse. 'The emphasis on sharing information with parents must not override the rights of a child to privacy and a safe way to discuss their concerns with professionals' (Ofsted 2011: 7).

This raises a delicate question; how far does one respect the child's right to privacy,[2] when parents have a prima facie right to 'private and family life' too, also under the Human Rights Act 1998 Article 8. This arguably gives them a reasonable expectation that their children will *not* usually be interviewed about their private family life without the parents' knowledge or consent. In which situations might it be appropriate to set aside that right and see the child alone, to talk about 'private' matters, without parents' knowledge and therefore without their consent?

In the case of serious concern about a child when parents know that social workers want to see and speak to a child and are not co-operating, there are two alternative legal routes to follow. One is to obtain an Emergency Protection Order – in urgent cases; the second is to obtain a Child Assessment Order – in less urgent cases. However, most section 47 enquiries do not involve overt disputes about whether or not the child may be seen, possibly because government guidance apparently gives social workers wide discretion over when to see children alone without parental knowledge or consent. *Working Together* does not invoke children's 'right to privacy', but 'appropriate' social work judgement:

> Section 47 enquiries should always involve interviews with the child who is the subject of concern. The child should be seen by the lead social worker and communicated with alone when appropriate.

DCSF 2010: para. 5.64

This raises the question of what is meant by 'appropriate'. The urgency and seriousness of the concerns; the strength of the justification for the need for privacy; the right of the child to be seen alone; any needs the child has that mean they should not be seen alone but with a carer – for example, if they are very young and would be distressed if a carer were not present – or with an interpreter, or similar, if they need support with communication; and whether or not there is consent from a parent or person with parental responsibility, or from a child of sufficient understanding who is able to give valid consent for him or herself, appear to be the main issues that are relevant in judging appropriateness. It will have to be judged on a case-by-case basis using those criteria.

In another section, the wording is slightly stronger: the child should be seen alone unless it is 'inappropriate' for the child. The implication is that the default position in child protection cases is that the child should be seen alone. *Working Together* states that a function of strategy discussions is:

> ... agreeing, in particular, when the child will be seen alone (unless to do so would be inappropriate for the child) by the lead social worker ... and the methods by which the child's wishes and feelings will be ascertained so that they can be taken into account when making decisions under section 47.
>
> DCSF 2010 para. 5.58

The principle of working in partnership with parents means that obtaining consent from parents prior to interviewing children is the preferred approach, but, in some child protection cases, the child's right to protection from harm justifies overriding the parents' right to 'private and family life', and justifies interviewing the child without parents' consent.[3] The guiding principle is the necessity of safeguarding the child. Children's voices may still be a 'faint cry' (MacDonald 2008) in many settings, but in child protection there is a legal basis for making the child's voice the one most clearly heard. However, the bar is high. If the child is not judged competent to decide for him or herself that he or she does not wish the parents to be involved at this stage, the justification needs to be that the child might be threatened or coerced into silence, or evidence destroyed if the parents are alerted to the interview.[4]

Children have structural difficulties in making themselves heard, but the overriding and absolute right to protection from cruelty and neglect means that other rights have to be granted too, including the right to speak in private or away from those who might silence the child, to someone able to act on their behalf to protect them. The role of the social worker is to be the person to whom the child can speak, confident that they will act in the best interests of the child. Ofsted (2011: 18) adds that practitioners should not only listen to what children say, but also recognise behaviour as a means of communication, and understand behavioural indicators of abuse. 'Listening' in this context is also a matter of looking carefully at what children do, and thinking critically about what one sees and hears.

Sometimes seeing children on their own is difficult because parents intimidate social workers (see Chapter 9 on working with resistant and aggressive service users). In such cases, one thing to consider is the likely impact on the child of living in a family in which hostility and aggression may be used as a strategy for controlling others: 'When professionals ... have concerns about their own personal safety, they must always consider the implications for children [of] exposure to the same risk factors' (Ofsted 2011: 11). The behaviour that prevents social workers from speaking to parents may also be preventing the child from speaking, too. Even if the hostility is presented as 'protecting' the child and family from unwarranted interference, it may be indicative of regular abuse of adult power within the family.

Narratives and trust

While it is important to form trusting relationships with parents wherever possible, the effort to do so should not prevent workers from taking action that does not increase parental trust, but may increase the trust of the child, and at least afford them the opportunity to speak. Ofsted (2011: 12) notes that: 'Too much attention has been paid to forming a trusting relationship with the adults at the expense of considering whether good enough care was being provided for the child.'

Listening to what children have to say may be the focus of work undertaken with the child to develop and understand his or her own narrative account of what has happened to him or her. Making sense of the past is not something the adult 'does to' the child, but is done through the medium of a co-produced narrative (see Chapter 5 on 'questions and stories'). The social worker will often hold a lot of information about the child's life history even before they meet the child, and will have a professional view based on information from file records, and their own personal frame for interpreting this account – their professional ethics and values; their own cultural norms and their knowledge about the culture, religion and social environment in which the child grew up/is living; their views about matters such as adult responsibilities towards children; their own experiences; and possibly bias from things other people have told them about the child.

The child, on the other hand, has direct experience of these events, and his or her own narrative that explains the way different factors have shaped his or her life. Having an adult listening to him is an opportunity for the child to explore his identity and his story about the way the world works and how this affects him, and to develop his own narrative account of his life. This in turn underpins the child's wishes and feelings about what they would like to happen to them next, and what they see as the right way for things to happen. Children may feel that the right thing is for an adult to make the decision for them on certain things: they may feel the responsibility for the decision should not fall to them. Children in divorce cases may feel uncomfortable about being asked to express views about their parents because they know they are already being 'judged' by the court. Children in care may not feel able to say that they do not feel it is time for them to go back to a parent who they think is not ready to care for them.

Children need to have some discretion *not* to say what they want, which means social workers need to be skilled in asking questions, identifying resistance to answering questions, and consider who the child might be protecting if they are unwilling to answer. There is a qualitative difference between the kinds of decisions that *all* children routinely address and the kinds of decisions being faced by many children who are abused or in other challenging family situations (Schofield 2005). This other kind of decision may involve stark alternatives: disclosure versus keeping abuse a secret; or returning home when remaining in care is a safer option, for example. Children may choose not to participate in choosing, and want adults to make the choices because it is too difficult. That also is a choice, and represents decision making.

Asking questions to find out about 'feelings' and other personal matters may be experienced as being intrusive, reflecting Bell's (2002) suggestion that children's most common criticism of social workers carrying out child protection investigations is that the questioning is perceived as invasive and threatening. If children in care are to have their voices heard clearly, one of the most important things is the quality of relationship between the child and their social worker. High staff turnover is a barrier to developing good relationships. This may be a symptom of another problem: the exhausting nature of child and family social work has led to high levels of job dissatisfaction, work overload, decreased time to spend with service users, and an increase in bureaucratic control over social work activities, which has not favoured activities that can only be measured through qualitative assessment, rather than quantitative audit (Broadhurst *et al.* 2010a; Le Grand 2007; Parton 2008).

Children in care do not always feel that they have good relationship with their social workers, nor is participation a felt reality for many children (Leeson 2007; Morgan 2011a). The tension between the different roles of social workers can undermine positive use of time spent with children, taking the focus away from the child's agenda (Winter 2009a). They do not see their social workers often enough; children say that social workers do not always keep appointments, nor do they have enough power to make decisions. They change too often; they are too difficult to get hold of; they need to be more effective on behalf of the children whose interests they represent, and they need to 'keep their promises'. (Winter 2009b). Winter (2009a: 450) notes that: 'At the heart of [*the implementation plan for* Care Matters, *is*] the centrality of social workers building consistent, long-term relationships with children in care, listening to their views and taking these views seriously.'

The social worker should be clear to the child that their first priority is the protection of the child. It is a matter of professional judgement in each case as to how much a child should be encouraged to speak about their family life, especially when there are concerns about their safety, but it is never ethical to make promises that one cannot keep; for example, that certain people will not know what has been said, if it is possible that they will find out. It is not ethical to place pressure on children to speak when they are hesitant about doing so, but nor is it ethical to abandon too easily efforts to reassure a child that they can disclose abuse, if the alternative is to return the child to a probably abusive situation.

Families create their own stories, too, which the child may share. An interview with a child is an opportunity to find out information, but not all that information is 'hard facts'. Implicit in any child's account of events, or description of family life, will be assumptions: those assumptions are important information, although they may never be spoken about directly. Assumptions that might be important to listen for in children's communication include:

- What does the child think a 'good' parent, or a 'good' family, is like?
- What is a 'good' child like?
- What situations make a child feel safe?
- Why do adults sometimes abuse children?
- What should society do to help parents and children when there are problems in a family, for example parental mental illness or drug abuse?

The purpose of a conversation, or a conversation with a purpose

Conversations cover a range of purposes, including:

1   establishing a trusting relationship between the child or young person and their social worker;
2   carrying out a statutory duty: checking that they are being cared for adequately; following up a report that they may be at risk of harm; having their welfare and developmental needs met, or planning next steps for the young person, for example;

3   exploring their history and the path that brought them to where they are now, with a view to helping them make sense of their life story and help free them to focus on their plans for the future.

These different functions require different but overlapping skills. The kinds of skills needed for the first point are more general communication skills, of which a genuine expressed professional concern for the well-being of the child or young person; warmth; active listening; judgement about how far one explores personal information and what is 'private'; empathy; and a confident professional identity are all important. The ability to establish genuine shared interest is helpful, but children and young people are aware that social workers have a professional role and expect the focus to be on matters of professional concern as well as being a 'friend' (McLeod 2010). Although adult service users have said they prefer social workers to be 'friendly', showing warmth, empathy, respect and listening to them, they are able to differentiate between the qualities they seek in a friend and friendship itself (Beresford *et al.* 2008). Children are likely to be able to make a similar distinction between 'friendliness' and friendly professionalism, and look for the latter quality in their social worker, especially older children and young people.

For the second type of conversation there may be a 'script' that determines part of the conversation at least. Completing forms for reviews, for example, involves following a set agenda, but the skilled practitioner will be able to use the review framework, as a trigger and aide-memoire rather than going through the process question by question. Giving the young person the review format in advance so they can complete sections of it themself may free up time for more free-ranging conversation about their responses. Software is available in many authorities to make forms accessible and user friendly for children with a range of communication needs, languages and developmental stages.

Conversations need to be purposeful; otherwise they are a waste of the young person's time. While they focus on inviting the child or young person to share information with the aim of making professional judgements about need and welfare, they should be open enough to allow children and young people to determine aspects of the agenda and to ask questions about the social worker's or agency's objectives in providing services for them and promoting their welfare, as seen by the agency. And the child or young person should always know to whom they are talking, why the conversation is taking place, how far they can rely on confidentiality, and what might happen after the conversation is over as a consequence of things discussed. At the end, they should know what is going to happen next, or what might happen, and when they will know, and how to contact their social worker to discuss it.

For the third objective of a conversation, more therapeutic skills are required, including a high level of sensitivity to the young person's feelings and emotional needs. The worker needs to be confident of his or her own boundaries and sensitive to those of the young person: when to ask for more information; when to express an opinion; when to validate the perceptions and interpretations of the young person and when to challenge them, for example, when a young person expresses a negative view of themselves based on emotionally abusive experiences or racist views. Talking about painful things is important: children who have had an opportunity to make sense of what has happened to them are more likely to cope with the demands of the present.

Within all three types of conversation there are levels or degrees of structure versus openness, and of engagement with difficult emotional issues versus focus on practical issues. Many conversations will have a mixed purpose, and end up fulfilling different functions. While they should be *purposeful* – not wasteful of the time of children and young people – they should not be cut short by organisational demands that do not prioritise relationship-based help and support. The purpose should be clear for both worker and child, so that any potential for empowerment of the child/young person is also clear: through the administrative actions or through exploring ideas about the young person's worth, positive qualities and potential future development.

While social skills were important to the social workers in McLeod's (2010) study, they were less important to the children, who judged the interaction on the basis of what was achieved for them. Social workers were concerned to be respectful, children and young people wanted to be empowered. This challenges the view that listening is *primarily* about giving and receiving information, facilitating communication, offering explanations or exploring feelings, although all these things are important components of a successful meeting with a child or young person. For the children and young people, listening was primarily about what was *done* once they had said what they felt and thought.

Ferguson (2010) describes the value that the 'in between space' of a car journey can offer for communication with children and young people. He also notes the risks that can go with confinement in a small space, travelling at speed between places that may have strong emotional charge associated with them. They offer a 'protected' space in which there is no pressure to make eye contact and few distractions if people wish to talk, but also the danger of talking while travelling at speed in a metal box. Different places have different advantages and disadvantages in terms of privacy, comfort, familiarity or neutrality, and 'ownership': is it a professional space, or one in which the child or young person feels most at home?

Making space to listen, and support for social workers too

McLeod (2006: 44) analyses 'listening' into four different activities with different aims:

- **Communication:** setting up a dialogue with child, answering their questions and explaining to them the situation and their options.
- **Consultation:** seeking the child's views of choices facing them.
- **Participation:** promoting the child's involvement in planning and decision-making.
- **Redress:** providing opportunities to complain and seek recompense for grievances.

Some children may find questions intrusive (Bell 2002), others may find it hard to tell their stories even when they would like to do so. Certain things may inhibit them from being open about their stories, one of which is concern about the social workers' management of their feelings when children have very difficult stories to tell. Children who lack confidence that the worker is able to hear what they say may keep information to themselves. Possible reasons for this include:

- the child perceiving that the worker is uncomfortable listening to their account of what has happened to them or what they have witnessed;

- the child believing that the worker may judge them for their involvement in abuse, although they were without control over the situation.

Children who have been exposed to abusive situations may have more developed skills in assessing adult emotional states than other children, and may be particularly likely to avoid engaging in discussions which raise levels of stress and anxiety in adults. Reassuring the child that the worker has had experience of talking with children and young people about difficult things will be helpful, but only if it is credible. Workers who have themselves experienced frightening and disempowering situations may find discussing abusive situations triggers memories and responses from their past; but workers with no such history may, equally, find the experience of hearing about situations that they have no personal strategies for managing very difficult. Each worker involved in discussing painful, difficult histories with children needs to consider what support and preparation they may need in order to be able to engage in discussion of abuse with children and young people. Social work courses will have offered space for reflection on one's own self and identity, but, once in practice, it is inevitable that the demands of the social work role reveal areas for further reflection and professional development. Access to supervision is important for workers dealing with high levels of distress, but social work management structures are generally not oriented to the provision of emotional support and personal development, nor to engage with the emotional labour of social work (Leeson 2010; Morrison 2007).

Box 1.3 Exercise: preparing to hear what abused children may have to say

Everyone encounters difficulties and stress, and most people have traumatic experiences of one kind or another at some time in their lives. The impact of such experiences may be positive, supporting insight and empathy; or it may interfere with the capacity to listen to other people's experience. How do you think your personal history of any of the following:

- childhood attachments to parents, siblings, grandparents, close friends;
- disempowering and frustrating situations;
- stress or trauma;
- feeling responsible for someone else, with limited power to help them;

impacts on your practice when talking with children and young people? What do you do to manage the feelings when an interview with a young person has left you upset or anxious? Do you have the opportunity to talk to someone – your manager, your partner, a friend, a counsellor – about these feelings? Does your employer/team provide support for you in such situations, in work time and without making you feel you should be 'getting on with the job'?

Consider a) how you use the experiences you have had in a positive way to talk with children and young people who have experienced distressing events, and b) what support you might have a reasonable expectation of receiving from your employer to address the 'emotional labour' of the work? Would peer supervision, or some other strategy for developing your practice help you to cope with the demands of the social work role, in addition to supervision?

All social workers working with children and families are entitled to supervision that addresses distressing and stressful aspects of the work, and supervision needs to be geared towards identifying those aspects of the workers' skills that need to be developed in order to promote the provision of continuously improving services.

> Working to ensure children are protected from harm requires sound professional judgements to be made. It is demanding work that can be distressing and stressful. All of those involved should have access to advice and support from, for example, peers, managers, named and designated professionals. Those providing supervision should be trained in supervision skills and have an up to date knowledge of the legislation, policy and research relevant to safeguarding and promoting the welfare of children. Supervision can be defined as: 'an accountable process which supports, assures and develops the knowledge, skills and values of an individual, group or team. The purpose is to improve the quality of their work to achieve agreed outcomes.'
>
> DCSF 2010: 23

Good quality supervision is not a standard regular occurrence. It rarely happens as frequently or for as long as recommended, and managers often get less supervision themselves than they need. Supervisors tend to focus on process issues and case management rather than skills development (Unison 2008a; Laming 2009; SWTF 2009). *Working Together* (DCSF 2010: 23) expresses the aims of supervision: 'Through it, social workers review their day-to-day practice and decision-making, plan their learning and development as professionals, and work through the considerable emotional and personal demands the job often places on them.' Engaging with the emotional demands of hearing the voices of children and understanding their perspective calls for high quality support from a competent supervisor:

> Research into 'what works' consistently points to the need for relationship-based practice built on a sound understanding of the service user's perspective, history and current circumstances. The limited research that exists into the impact of supervision on outcomes for service users indicates that supervision also needs to be grounded within a secure professional relationship where the supervisor takes time to understand and assess the supervisee's strengths and weaknesses. Professional practice, and worker/service user dynamics need to be critically analysed, and the impact of the worker's emotions on thoughts and actions is explored. This is the basis by which reflective but authoritative social work/care practice is developed.
>
> Morrison and Wonnacott 2010: 1

Supervisors need to take time with those they supervise to understand their professional development needs, as social workers need to spend time with children and young people to understand their wishes and feelings. Professionals displaying intense emotion may be seen as problematic, unprofessional, and as displaying signs of over-involvement and failure to cope (Winter 2009a). Maintaining distanced relationships is a self-protective strategy, but this 'avoidant' style of coping may create additional stress, increasing rather than reducing emotional exhaustion (Anderson 2000).

Engaging directly with children and building relationships that support meaningful conversations about their wishes and feelings is time consuming and emotionally demanding, but may in the longer term be less emotionally demanding and more rewarding than the style of work that is characterised by a task-oriented approach driven by organisational pressures. As well as being in keeping with best practice and the social work values of respect and empowerment, standing up for spending time with looked after and other vulnerable children may make social work a viable long-term profession for individual workers, and enhance the effectiveness and standing of the profession as a whole. This empowering and child-centred approach can only be achieved through physically travelling to be where children are, spending time with them, taking responsibility for making meaningful conversations happen and seeking appropriate support.

Concluding comments

Children may think of listening rather differently from the way the term is usually used in social work. Social workers need to consider how they can involve children in discussions in such a way that they feel involved in the discussion, and that it was 'worthwhile' because their involvement brought about some change that would not have happened otherwise. If this is not realistic, children should have an opportunity to discuss the reasons that things cannot happen the way they would like, so they will at least gain an understanding as to why things are the way they are. Decisions should never appear arbitrary or motivated by something other than the best interests of the child, even if the child or young person does not agree.

In child protection cases, the need to be sensitive to the prior experiences of the child makes the task a delicate and professionally demanding one, in which social workers as well as children should feel they have someone to listen to them and support them when they need it.

2 Hearing children's voices and respecting children's wishes and feelings, part 2

The legal framework, and putting it into practice

This chapter:

- sets the duty to listen to children into a context of national and international law and other obligations;
- considers in more detail how this may be made a reality in social work practice with children and young people.

The legal basis of the duty to seek and respect children's wishes and feelings in international law

Increasingly, children have become defined as a group with rights of their own. The United Nations Convention on the Rights of the Child 1980 (UNCRC) represents an international attempt to impose duties in relation to children's welfare, participatory and autonomy rights on national governments:

> The global development of children's rights may be seen as a device within law and politics of resolving this tension [*between children's rights and adult powers over them*] by imposing some universal order, some principled values as to what children should expect from adults and the ways that adults should treat children.
>
> King 2007: 867

The UNCRC has now been ratified by all countries except the USA and Somalia (CRIC n.d.), although Somalia has announced its intentions to ratify it soon. Countries that have ratified the Convention have to submit regular reports to the Committee every five years on how the rights are being implemented. The Committee examines the country reports and responds with its own report and recommendations to the member country. This does not mean that it has been incorporated into domestic law, but it has persuasive and moral authority. Children and their representatives cannot bring cases directly in the domestic courts based on breaches of the UNCRC, but the Convention may be referred to in court, and used to inform decisions in relation to children, especially cases brought under the Human Rights Act 1998. Ministers of state have a duty to make sure that UK law reflects Britain's commitment to international treaties, including the UNCRC.

The diversity of conditions in which children live around the world, frequently involving severe and chronic breaches of UNCRC rights, illustrates the challenge involved in attempting to promote and protect children's rights on a global level. Poverty and its associated ills mean that, for many children, concerns associated with staying alive are more pressing than participation in decision making.

This has led to the idea that there are hierarchies of rights. Those from which there can be no derogation are sometimes seen as 'higher order' rights than those that are 'qualified' rights. The right to protection from inhuman and degrading treatment or punishment under the European Convention on Human Rights (ECHR) is an example of a right from which there can be no lawful derogation, even in times of national emergency. As humans, this right and all others in the ECHR apply to children, too. By contrast, under the same treaty, the right to private and family life is subject to provisions that limit its application in specified circumstances. While the right to private and family life is arguably more easily defined and enforced than some other Convention rights, rights such as the right to an adequate standard of living (UNCRC, article 27) are as, if not more, important since the child's survival may depend on them.

Many 'rights' set out in international treaties are more aspirational than statements of enforceable rights, because local circumstances do not permit their enforcement. The child's right to freedom of thought, conscience and religion (UNCRC, article 14) is an example of a children's right that may be severely limited in some societies, not least because it may not be available to adults.

It may be argued that difficulty enforcing some of these 'aspirational' rights should not mean they should be viewed *in principle* as having lower status or importance than those that can be enforced. Children have a right to be consulted and to participate in certain types of decisions that affect them (Article 12, UNCRC, see below for full text) and arguably that right is, on principle, as worthy of protection as any other right held by children or any other group of people under an international treaty.

Children's rights have become increasingly influential in law and public policy (Fortin 2009), but at the same time the rate of progress appears to be slower than the development of rights for adults. Use of the UNCRC, the Human Rights Act 1998 and the European Convention on Human Rights in children's cases is still limited:

> Unfortunately, still too few cases concerning children make use of the UN Convention on the Rights of the Child, despite the very strong ECHR Chamber judgment in the Sahin case: 'The human rights of children and the standards to which all governments must aspire in realising these rights for all children are set out in the Convention on the Rights of the Child.'[1]
>
> Children's Rights Alliance for England 2010

The Children's Rights Alliance (CRAE 2010) commented:

> We are disappointed that the UK Government has not set out any plans to incorporate the UNCRC into UK law, nor to create any new enforceable rights for children. We also remain concerned about the UK Government's proposals for more explicit links between rights and responsibilities, the implications of which still do not appear to have been fully thought through.

Box 2.1 Article 12 of the UN Convention on the Rights of the Child

1   States Parties shall assure to the child who is capable of forming his or her own views the right to express those views freely in all matters affecting the child, the views of the child being given due weight in accordance with the age and maturity of the child.

2   For this purpose, the child shall in particular be provided the opportunity to be heard in any judicial and administrative proceedings affecting the child, either directly, or through a representative or an appropriate body, in a manner consistent with the procedural rules of national law.

The most important provision of the UNCRC from the point of view of listening to children and young people is Article 12, which gives children the right to have their views and wishes taken into consideration when decisions are being made about them.

The Child Rights Information Network explains further:

> This Convention encourages adults to listen to the opinions of children and involve them in decision-making – not give children authority over adults. Article 12 does not interfere with parents' right and responsibility to express their views on matters affecting their children. Moreover, the Convention recognises that the level of a child's participation in decisions must be appropriate to the child's level of maturity. Children's ability to form and express their opinions develops with age and most adults will naturally give the views of teenagers greater weight than those of a preschooler, whether in family, legal or administrative decisions.
>
> CRIN n.d.

The less well-known European Convention on the Exercise of Children's Rights dates back to 1966, and has been signed by just over half of all EU member states, but is only in force in about a quarter of member states. The UK has neither signed nor ratified it.[2] This Convention adds to the protection of children's rights by supporting them in making their voices heard more clearly and authoritatively, by giving children access to adult support in doing so, as of right. Giving rights to children, or indeed to adults, is only of value to them when they can be exercised. The Convention on the Exercise of Children's Rights offers children the opportunity to make use of their Article 12 rights in the countries in which it has been ratified. Some of the provisions most relevant for this discussion are summarised on page 22:

While the Convention on the Exercise of Children's Rights has not, as yet, been signed by the UK, its existence in Europe is an indicator of the extent to which children's rights are part of a Europe-wide agenda, and adds weight to arguments put forward by children's rights campaigners to strengthen children's voices.

Box 2.2 Convention on the Exercise of Children's Rights 1996[3]

Council of Europe CETS No. 160

Article 5
States shall consider granting children additional procedural rights in court, including:

a)   the right to apply to be assisted by an appropriate person of their choice in order to help them express their views;
b)   the right to apply themselves, or through other persons or bodies, for the appointment of a separate representative, in appropriate cases a lawyer;
c)   the right to appoint their own representative;
d)   the right to exercise some or all of the rights of parties to such proceedings.

[Article 5 would give children rights comparable to adults in choosing their own representative and being a 'party to proceedings' – author's note]

Article 6
Courts hearing proceedings affecting children shall, before taking a decision:

a)   consider whether they have sufficient information to take a decision in the best interests of the child. Where necessary, they shall obtain further information, including from parents, and
b)   when the child has sufficient understanding:
   • ensure that the child has received all relevant information;
   • consult the child in person in appropriate cases, if necessary privately, itself or through other persons or bodies, in a manner appropriate to his or her understanding, unless this would be manifestly contrary to the best interests of the child;
   • allow the child to express his or her views;
c)   give due weight to the views expressed by the child.

[This Article would be particularly relevant for care and Section 8 proceedings, giving children enhanced rights to have relevant information about things being said about them, and to express their views in person if they choose. This right is balanced by a duty on the courts to seek additional information from parents when necessary for ascertaining the child's best interests – author's note]

Article 7 Duty to act speedily
In proceedings affecting a child the judicial authority shall act speedily to avoid any unnecessary delay and procedures shall be available to ensure that its decisions are rapidly enforced. In urgent cases the judicial authority shall have the power, where appropriate, to take decisions which are immediately enforceable.

[This Article, in light of current debate about the problem of lengthy court processes in relation to looked after children, is particularly relevant in the UK at present – author's note.]

The legal basis of the duty to seek and respect children's wishes and feelings in the UK

Social workers are required to take steps to obtain children's views on matters that concern them. Children's right to participation is a *political* right, not only a welfare right (Freeman 1999, 2000). Involving children, such as school pupils, in decision making should not be seen as an option that is 'within the gift' of adults, but a legal imperative under Article 12 (Lundy 2007: 931).

The principle that children should be 'heard' was included in the Children Act 1989 in respect of children who are the subject of care or supervision proceedings under s31 of that Act, specifically through the welfare checklist in s1 of the 1989 Act, which obliges the court to consider the wishes and feelings of the child.

The Children Act 2004 amended the 1989 Act and inserted the requirement to obtain children's wishes and feelings in relation to children in need under s17, children subject to s47 inquiries, and children accommodated under s20 of the 1989 Act, giving them something like parity with children on care orders. Having ascertained the wishes and feelings of a child, a local authority has to give them 'due consideration'. This echoes the discussion about what children might understand by 'listening', in Chapter 1. It is not enough to find out, but do nothing about, the child's wishes and feelings. The local authority, like the court, should have regard for the child's age and understanding in considering those wishes when deciding what services to provide for a child, for example under s17 of the 1989 Act. It is also under a duty to have regard to the wishes and feelings of the child's parents, and any other person they 'feel to be relevant'. They must also have regard to the child's religious persuasion, racial origin and cultural and linguistic background.

The caveat '... as far as is reasonably practicable' applies to the provision that local authorities should take children's wishes into consideration when arranging services. This creates a loophole that allows a local authority to deviate from child-centred practice if it can reasonably argue that it is not 'practicable', which in times of resource shortfall unfortunately may be rather often.

We next explore the implications of the 2004 Act provisions with reference to s20 then s31 of the Children Act 1989. Section 20 of the Children Act 1989 (accommodation of children) is '... based on co-operative working between the local authority, the young person and his or her parents because the court is not forcing the child or young person to be looked after' (Children's Legal Centre 2011). If a child is being looked after under s20, the local authority must have regard to the child or young person's views before making a decision about the proposed accommodation, having regard to the child's age and understanding. In practice, children's wishes are relevant when an older child is requesting to be accommodated against their parents' wishes, since the local authority may accommodate them at their request, but if a younger child wishes to be accommodated against a parent's wishes, or to return home against a parent's wishes, it is unlikely that this could happen. In the first case, the local authority has no power to accommodate the child and would have to apply for a care order if they wanted to do so; in the second case, if the parent is not co-operating, to return a child home against a parent's wishes would be placing the child at risk of neglect. Children may express wishes, but unless these wishes are supported by rights, this may have limited impact. Their wishes and feelings with regard to the type of placement they go into may be important for seeking a type of placement that the child will settle in, but a limiting factor is the availability of placements from which to make a choice. It is uncertain whether the provisions of the 2004 Act give children the power to exercise much influence over which services they receive, unless there are adults prepared to champion their cause.

In the case of s31, the child's wishes and feelings are one element in a decision-making process that includes issues of risk and harm, which are likely in most cases to outweigh any wishes of the child that would expose the child to harm if acted upon. The principle that the welfare of the child is paramount provides an organising rationale for courts and social workers in court. It is sometimes in tension with the principle of child empower-ment, because the wishes of the child and professional views of their best interests may be different. The professional's view may be more risk-averse than the young person's, given that many young people subject to care orders may either have little appreciation of the risks they have been exposed to, or be aware but habituated to them. 'Balancing' these may not be easy; the two perspectives may be incompatible. In this situation, the adult view of the child's welfare will always determine the outcome because of the primacy of the welfare principle; however the child's wishes and feelings are 'taken into consideration'.

One rationale for deciding not to allow children to take particular choices that would – in adult opinion – harm the child, is that allowing the child to follow their preferred course would restrict their options at a later time when they are able to make more informed and mature choices for themselves. Insisting that children go to school rather than giving them the choice of non-attendance is an example of an exercise of adult authority in the interests of safeguarding children's potential for exercising choice for themselves when they get older. To acquiesce to a child's wish not to attend school would interfere with their developmental interests because it would ultimately have the effect of restricting choice (Eekelaar 1986).

Pursuing children's best interests always involves making sure that their wishes and feelings are given due weight, even if they cannot be decisive in planning for the child. The actual influence the child's wishes have on the decision-making process may vary but, in considering them, adults may identify aspects of the child's needs that merit further consideration. If there is a clear record of the thinking process behind this, children can look back when they are older and, through the medium of case records, they may gain a better understanding as to why certain decisions were made and not others. For some children who have grown up in care, case records may take the place of the oral family history of children who have grown up with their birth families. Those records may have a later significance that exceeds the practical value that social workers tend to place upon them at the time of writing (see, for example, the Gaskin case[4]).

Section 10 of the Children and Young Persons Act 2008 inserted a new section 25A into the Children Act 1989, making it a requirement that every local authority appoint an Independent Reviewing Officer (IRO) for every looked after child: this appointment to the child's case must be done before the first 'statutory review'. It is the IRO's specific duty to ensure that 'any ascertained wishes and feelings of the child are given due considera-tion by the local authority' (Section 26B (c)), as well as to ensure the rights of the child are protected. In most authorities, this is a consolidation of existing practice.

Grimshaw and Sinclair (1997) found reviews were effective in helping children to feel consulted, but problems with the review process included a lack of familiarity with the chair of the meeting, being overawed by being expected to speak in large meetings of professionals, and a lack of preparatory work so young people did not feel able to consider the issues in a timely way and form their own views. This gives clear pointers as to what is needed to secure better participation, with 'participation' redefined as meaningful and purposeful engagement in decision making.

'Competent' children and young people

Research has shown that children frequently have the capacity to give cogent answers to questions about weighty and difficult issues concerning their future well-being, and take a responsible part in planning (Alderson 1993, 2000; Spicer and Evans 2006; Thomas 2009; Thomas and O'Kane 2009). Furthermore, 'competence' should not be seen as a 'fixed quantity' for any child at any particular time: not yet being competent to make certain decisions does not mean that children are to be regarded as non-competent in other areas of decision making. Children are not inherently 'competent' or 'not competent'. McLeod (2006: 50) cites Kjørholt *et al.* (2005), who argue that we '... should reject dichotomies and think instead of a continuum, with individuals of all ages fluctuating between vulnerability and independence, competence and incompetence'. Children's competence to make decisions for themselves depends upon the situation they are in and the support available to them as much as on the qualities of the child (Thomas 2002).

Children learn to be competent through experience: they progress through having *opportunities* to be competent and effective. They have repeatedly shown that they can effectively manage a wide range of tasks and responsibilities, given the opportunities and appropriate support (Cairns and Brannen 2005; Spicer and Evans 2006).

McLeod (2006) reports that children in care felt that the attitude of social workers to children was oppressive, from needing social workers' permission for 'everyday' decisions to placing children where they did not want to be. Children need opportunities to progress in achieving competence, so that perceived lack of competence is not a self-maintaining barrier to empowerment of children and young people. Listening without acting on what is said – and without *giving back* responsibility appropriate to the child's developmental stage and needs – is not helpful, indeed the greater the engagement in discussion, the more frustrating and disempowering the experience could be for the child.

Situations and circumstances may support a child in being competent to make a decision, or undermine that competence. Factors that affect whether or not a child or young person is competent to make a *particular decision* include:

- the child's level of maturity and cognitive ability;
- the level of preparation and support available to the child in understanding the issue and giving an informed view as to what they would like to happen;
- the way the situation is structured to engage the child: to enable or inhibit the child's ability to make a meaningful contribution to decision making. (Thomas 2002)

Children need to be offered support to become engaged with services and make their voice 'count'. Engagement shapes and supports another element in the process of empowerment – motivation: energised, directed and sustained action (Skinner and Greene 2009). There is a three-element process that can set up a virtuous cycle in engaging children and young people in decision-making:

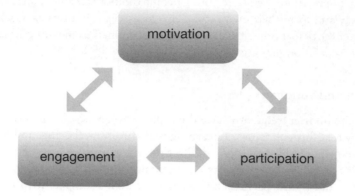

Figure 2.1 The virtuous cycle engages young people in decision making

Skinner *et al.* (2009) consider what it means to be 'engaged'. It has two main components: *initiation of motivated action* – beginning to work towards a goal – and *persistence in the face of obstacles* to achieving that goal. As well as action and persistence, engagement has three dimensions, behavioural, emotional and cognitive:

- **Behavioural engagement:** the effort, intensity and persistence the person brings to the task or project.
- **Emotional engagement:** their enthusiasm, enjoyment and sense of having fun while doing the project
- **Cognitive engagement:** their attention and focus on the task in order to achieve their goal.

Ascertaining children and young people's views

Some principles to be borne in mind when considering how to find out what children and young people think include:

- **Allow time to explain the context of the decision so the effect of the decision-making process is clear.** Children and young people need to have the significance of the decision explained clearly and honestly. The more irreversible or long-lasting the likely effect of the decision, the more professionals need to take time to explain it carefully. Is this a decision that may be reviewed and changed at the next review? The child needs all the relevant information to help them form a view as to what they think would be best for them.
- **Give the child/young person time to consider the questions they are being asked to address, and use different techniques for opening up the discussion.** The answers to these questions may have potentially life-changing importance for the child. The child may also have strong feelings of loyalty and attachment to parents and others that may make it complex for them to decide how best to answer the question. Careful use of indirect questioning – asking how others might answer the question, for example – may help separate the child's own wishes and feelings from their

perception of the views and interests of others affected by the decision. Questions may begin: 'Some people say that ...' followed by asking the child to comment (Mantle *et al.* 2007: 789). Questions need to be in age-appropriate language, and it is important to avoid unnecessarily asking questions that activate conflicting loyalties. Open-ended questions, giving children the opportunity to 'think aloud' around an issue, should be included.

- **How much responsibility and autonomy does the child/young person have in the decision-making process?** Children may welcome autonomy in some circumstances, but in other situations the weight of responsibility for decisions is such that it may be a relief to know that the final decision rests with someone else, even though their wishes and feelings are taken into consideration. In such circumstances, children may need to be reassured that any decisions taken will be with their best interests at the centre of the process, and to have explained to them what this means in practice. If they have a lot of influence over the outcome, they should know this, too. At the end of the day, the adults have the power to decide and should use this wisely. Ofsted (2011) identified instances in which children's wishes were not listened to, or taken into consideration, or were misinterpreted, but also instances where children were given too much responsibility to take decisions that were not in their interests.
- **Consider the best way of supporting the child/young person in expressing their views.** Techniques used by researchers working with children have suggested ways of supporting children in expressing themselves, especially young children. They include non-verbal techniques such as making drawings, and other visual approaches. Younger children may feel happier talking while they are drawing or playing with simple play materials such as felt shapes on a board, or modelling clay. The 'Signs of Safety' approach (Turnell 2010) encourages the use of drawing, and gives examples of its use in seeking children's views on complicated and serious matters, such as safety in the home. Spoken language may not be the way in which all children express themselves best: collage materials may be provided so the child can create a picture of how they feel about the subject (Leeson 2010). If using non-verbal materials such as drawing equipment, it is important that the worker explains to the child any use that may be made of the drawing, and that the child's permission is sought if the worker wishes to copy and use the drawing. It is suggested that children should be allowed to keep any artwork they produce if they wish to do so, which may involve copying it then returning it.
- **Children may need an opportunity to consider the issues and have a further conversation at a later point when they have had an opportunity to think things over a bit more.** This is especially important if there has been a lot to explain to the child. They should know how to contact the social worker they are speaking to if they wish to do so after the meeting. For older children, giving them a written summary of what needs to be decided and what the possibilities and issues are may help.
- **They should also know from the outset of the conversation what is going to happen to the information they give to the worker:** how it is to be recorded and what will be done with it; whether it will be included in a report and, if so, who will see it and for what purpose. Will people reading the report be able to tell from it what the child has said? (Mantle *et al.* 2007)

Box 2.3 Guidance for Education staff in ascertaining and recording the wishes and feelings of children

In ascertaining a child or young person's views, wishes and feelings staff should be mindful of and plan for:

- The age and understanding of the child or young person.
- Any communication difficulties the child/young person has.
- The child's willingness to participate in the process.

The following general principles apply:

- Consideration needs to be given to who is the most appropriate person to speak with the child/young person (and this person should be the same on each occasion wherever possible).
- The most appropriate form of communication should always be considered and discussions undertaken at a pace and using language that is consistent with the child's age and understanding.
- Where necessary specialist help should be provided (e.g. interpreter or sign language interpreter).
- It is important that the purpose of the meeting is clearly explained to the child/young person and that the [agency] is seeking to understand what the child/young person wants to happen.
- Ensure that adequate time is allowed to listen to what the child/young person is saying or thinking, even if this entails periods of silence.
- Staff should check carefully with the child/young person that they have understood and recorded their views correctly.
- Children and young people should be helped to understand the implications and issues involved in their situation, via straightforward explanation, so that they are be able to make decisions based on the fullest of information.
- The child should understand what will happen to any information they provide, who it will be shared with and why.

The child should understand how much weight will be given to their views and what other factors there are that might influence any decision to be taken:

- Where it is not in the best interests of the child/young person to accede to their wishes the reasons for this must be clearly explained to them.
- The child's/young person's views must always be recorded, as must the consideration given to these views and why decisions that conflict with them have been taken.
- The child must know who they can speak to about their views on the decisions being made and how they can be involved in future discussions/decisions.
- The views, wishes and feelings of the child or young person must be sought at regular intervals, particularly as circumstances change.

Bath and N.E. Somerset Council 2011 (abridged by the author)

Bath and North East Somerset Council have prepared detailed guidance on ascertaining children's wishes and feelings, which is reproduced in abridged form on page 28. It sets out some important general principles for all staff working with children and young people, and reflects the multi-agency nature of the requirement that professionals working with children have regard for their wishes and feelings when making decisions for and about them.

Identity, development, security, and forming an opinion

Core assessments should be unique, individualised and child-focused, but frequent use of standard or stereotypical phrases suggests that this is not always the case. Social workers do not always engage meaningfully with children's identity: case reports and records suggest that many social workers fall back on standardised accounts of children's identities, giving little space to consideration of cultural or spiritual identity, friends or interests or, perhaps most importantly, the children's view of their own identity (Thomas and Holland 2010). For an assessment to be to be valid and complete, it is essential that it reflects the child's individuality.

Assessments also need to be sensitive to the diverse ways in which children develop: they do not follow textbook patterns. Staged theories of childhood may lead to children being objectified rather than seen as individuals and do not reflect the reality of progress and achievement for many children with special needs. Winter (2009a: 456) argues that pervasive beliefs about the incapacity of younger children seem to be an 'organising principle' for some social workers. A 'developmental perspective', rigidly applied, may be an obstruction to the involvement of children, emphasising incapacity rather than capacity and suppressing children's voices (Taylor 2004). Children who have had atypical lives may have developed – or suppressed – particular capacities and sensitivities in a way that is not 'typical' of the pattern for their age. Assessments need to value both exceptional achievement in the face of adversity, and identify areas that need special support.

There needs to be a staged understanding of the child's developmental stage and needs, but this should be based on knowledge of each child's individual profile and what this tells us about their future support needs. A developmental perspective, responsively applied, may help develop practice that gives children a more effective voice (Schofield and Beek 2009).

A sense of security and having the support to manage their feelings allows children to think flexibly and be effective (Schofield 2005: 30). They may suppress expression of negative emotions because they fear it may not be safe to speak about them (Crittenden and Di Lalla 1988 cited in Schofield 2005: 32). Absence of security may limit the ability to think beyond the present, and children affected by trauma may lose hope that they can be 'rescued' (Rustin 2005).

The extraordinary nature of many of the choices and decisions that face social workers and the children with whom they work makes discussions about these choices demanding for children: there is little in children's prior experience to prepare them for such weighty discussions. Apart from the vocabulary used, the unfamiliar setting and demanding questions asked, another issue is the emotional context and content of the discussion. This adds another dimension to the complexity of the process:

> Given that trained professionals often struggle to retain all the details and ramifications of different options involved in care planning, it is hardly surprising that children frequently find this beyond their developing capacities. For children, thinking

about the risks and benefits of possible futures is not only difficult but painful. Engaging with thinking about feelings and choices in the context of survival needs requires emotional strength as well as cognitive coherence.

Schofield 2005: 39

Taking time to have more than one discussion, and working sensitively at the pace and within the limits of comfort for the child is clearly essential if any meaningful input to the decision-making process is to be made by the child.

Cameron and Maginn (2008) argue that children in care need additional support to help them adapt to a more positive situation than their previous one: one in which adults are potentially sources of support, and where achievement is possible and will be recognised. In ascertaining children's wishes and feelings, social workers need to be aware of the effect of prior experiences that may make the child or young person feel they have little intrinsic value, and that adults are unlikely to be concerned for their welfare. Their wishes, hopes and feelings may have been affected by low self-esteem and low expectations of what adults will do for them. Modest aspirations for themselves and low expectations for the future may be seen as normal. When talking to children whose self-esteem and aspirations are damaged by poor care, finding out what they think and feel is a strictly adequate response to the task of 'ascertaining children's wishes and feelings', but if the conversation is to do justice to the child's potential, the child may need support to be able to imagine a better future for themselves and validate their right to it.

Concluding comments

The legal framework for listening to children is entwined with the legal framework for protecting their rights more generally, especially their right to protection from breaches of their fundamental right not to be abused or neglected. This legal framework gives social workers the right to talk to them about private and sensitive things, but with this right goes a responsibility to consider the child holistically, as a developing person with emerging competences. The quality of the relationship the social worker is able to develop with the child is as important as the legal powers they bring to the situation and the conversation.

Winter (2009a, b) found that social workers tend to 'downplay' the social work relationship with children in care, instead of valuing it as special and unique. This saves time, relieving pressure, but also denies social workers an area of work which they find rewarding (Woodcock and Dixon 2005). Rather than relying on their own ability to form a meaningful relationship with looked after children, they often asked others, such as foster carers, to provide information for forms and review meetings (Winter 2009a). They did not give priority to relationship building, and may not have identified themselves with their distinctive role as advocates for children. Munro's (2011) review of child and family social work is premised on the belief that children should be central to the process, and services should reflect child-centredness. Using social work skills to enhance children's participation in the processes that exist to support them when they are in difficulty or in need of support is a core part of this, and this is a most timely point in the development of the profession to focus on this essential aspect of child and family social work.

3   Reflection

Theory, knowledge, identity and power in working with children and families

This chapter:

- considers different ideas about what 'reflection' means;
- provides material to support practitioners in thinking about the ways in which they currently use knowledge and theory in their practice, and ways in which they might develop this skill further.

Reflection is primarily a process of looking backwards on what has happened, to unpick the factors, conscious and unconscious, theoretical and personal, that influenced the actions taken and the way we have responded. The purpose of doing this is to make explicit the frames of reference we use, review the goodness of fit between our ideas about what good practice should be and what we actually do, and subject the ideas we have about good practice to scrutiny, to see how they stand up to rational, well-informed review. There are, it is argued, further gains from this process in that once we have experienced situations that challenge us to respond quickly, as in face-to-face communication with service users and in urgent situations, and we have reflected on what we did, we are better equipped to respond rapidly in similar 'rapid response' situations.

Another important aspect of reflection is its role in making sense of the 'here and now'. Much of the work undertaken by social workers involves working with partial information, sometimes in situations that appear chaotic. We build hypotheses and test them, and try to make sense of information that may appear to form a pattern, but often contains within it contradictory elements and conflicting stories. We have to be able to make sense of these situations in order to act but we also have to avoid imposing order on apparent chaos too quickly, and closing down avenues of exploration to satisfy our need to explain what is going on – to 'make an assessment'. The quality of reflection is important in assessment because it is this that lifts a static account of the 'facts' from a descriptive document into a professional, analytical assessment that allows for forward planning based on an understanding of the dynamic processes affecting a child and his or her family. It allows the practitioner to combine logic, knowledge, ethical principles and intuitive responses and feelings, processing them consciously to appraise the learning opportunities for the future that the situation offers, as well as reviewing the quality of work done.

Erault (1994) distinguished between *propositional knowledge*, which is that which is found in public sources such as journals and handbooks, and *personal knowledge*, gained through experience and reflection. Competence and capability come from experience, which supports the integration of propositional knowledge and personal knowledge, whereas the novice has propositional knowledge, but little personal knowledge and a limited store of learning from reflection. However, Graham Ixer suggested in 1999 that there was a problematic lack of clarity about what we mean by 'reflection': 'little is agreed about what it is, and that which is asserted is confusing and contradictory' (Ixer 1999: 513).

At the time he wrote this, the low level of understanding of the application of the concept of reflection to social work meant it was debatable whether it could reasonably be viewed as a 'measurable skill'. It was argued that reflection is not quantifiable, even if it could be defined adequately, which he also asserted was questionable:

> It claims to unlock the shackles of theory so that the learner can engage actively with praxis (theory in practice). This is called 'reflective practice'. Yet, despite the fact that the term 'reflection' is so widely used, it is equally widely misunderstood ... Indeed, a number of authors ... have claimed that everyone has their own personal understanding of what reflection is, to the extent that the term has become 'unusable'.
>
> Ixer 1999: 515

Ixer does not argue that reflective practice is not important in social work; indeed he states that:

> The challenge is in being able to access deeper thought processes, through the use of metacognitive, deliberative skills, whilst freeing oneself from the empirical constraints placed upon experience, and therefore values, by social and political influences. At the same time, language has to be shaped to act as a vehicle for conveying the ideas and thus the knowledge involved ... The relevance for social work and other professional practice, and indeed, for much of human social interaction, is self-evident.
>
> Ixer 1999: 516

Reflection is thus constructed not only as an essential attribute for the competent social worker, but as a skill without which humans generally cannot function effectively. In the decade since Ixer wrote this, there has been considerable expansion in the amount written about reflection, and its importance as a tool in training social workers and in practice has been established.

The pressured circumstances in which social work with children and families is often carried out means that there may be a need for action to be taken before the opportunity arises to leave the situation and reflect. Practitioners need to be able to make judgements rapidly, while things are happening. The social worker, therefore, accesses intuitive knowledge – or tacit knowledge, not available for scrutiny – to inform the choices taken while in the flow of a pressing process, such as a child protection investigation. Reflection arguably involves 'leaving' the situation mentally to reflect on it. The fact that the social worker does not often control the rate at which things happen means that models of reflection, such as those proposed by Dewey (1976) and Schön (1983), are not applicable to much of what happens for much of the time in the everyday experience of a child and family social worker. Reflection may be the process by which we acquire the professional competence to respond rapidly and also appropriately, based on patterns of thinking refined through past reflection which are available to be drawn on when rapid thought and action is required.

Definitions of reflection and critical best practice

Sheppard *et al.* (2000) developed the notion of 'process knowledge', which involves taking critical control of one's thought processes: a cognitive activity which lies above 'normal' patterns of thought and which is therefore described as a 'metacognitive' activity. It involves knowledge of the reasoning processes involved in decision making and, based on this, the capacity to enact that truth in the context of practice. Reflection is a core part of this process. There are at least two types of reflection:

- **reflection on action**, which is retrospective: the type of activity which is undertaken in supervision, in peer discussions, or in internal commentary and consideration such as that which happens while in the car after a social work visit, or in one of the intervals for thought offered by the unpredictable nature of social work;
- **reflection in action**, which is almost instantaneous and instinctive, and relies upon the existence of a 'bank' of knowledge and experience on which the practitioner can draw.

There are two factors that determine which type of reflection we need to, or are able to, use: time and place. While in pressured situations where action cannot be suspended for conscious, critical thinking, and where social workers cannot leave or turn aside for a discussion of events, we have to rely upon reflection in action. Reflection on action is possible when we have spatial separation from the pressure of action in the 'real world' and temporal separation so that we can 'slow the action' and consider what happened and what our role was in events on a stage-by-stage basis.

Knowledge is needed for reflection. Knowledge can be of many sorts: Trevithick (2008) lists knowledge of law, social policy, and agency policies and procedures. Knowledge of research findings and academic commentary on practice, including discussion of ethics and values in social work is another important type of knowledge. So is knowledge of theories: theories of human development and behaviour, and theories specific to social work. Trevithick adds 'knowledge of people' and 'knowledge of problems' to the list of types of factual knowledge. This type of knowledge comes from direct personal and practice experience as well as indirect sources of knowledge, the starting point being direct experience of practice (Gordon *et al.* 2009). The insights of service users and carers are also sources of knowledge about social work, from a different perspective.

Reflection, then, involves both developing the base of knowledge and experience to support rapid response in situations in which there is no time to pause to consider the next step or ponder the next thing to say, and the development of a self-critical 'metacognitive' approach in which nothing is taken for granted.

The objective of reflection is to achieve *critical best practice*. Ferguson (2003) defines this as being '... both skilful and deeply respectful of service users ... while at the same time using good judgment and authority' (cited in Jones *et al.* 2008: 15).

Figure 3.1 explores some dimensions of reflection: experience, conceptualisation, analysis and application of reflection, linking them to seeking new experiences, theory-creating, innovative practice and critical analysis. This way of thinking about reflection shows that it can happen at different levels and support different kinds of process. It may be used to ensure that practice is safe, conforms with rules and expectations, and does not violate rules of ethics or one's own personal standards for practice. It can also be used to think about the future development of one's own skills, and even the development of practice more generally.

- Experiencing the *known* – reflecting on our own experiences, interests and perspectives – or experiencing the *new* – observation of the unfamiliar, immersion in new situations, reading and recording new facts and data.
- Conceptualising by *naming* – developing categories and defining terms – or conceptualising with *theory* – making generalisations and putting the key terms together into theories.
- Analysing *functionally* – analysing logical connections, cause and effect, structure and function – or analysing *critically* – critically evaluating your own and other people's perspectives, interests and motives.
- Applying insights *appropriately* – applying insights from one's own experience to real-world situations and testing their validity in other situations/for other people – or applying them *creatively* – using insights to plan an innovative intervention which draws responsibly on one's personal interests, experiences and aspirations.

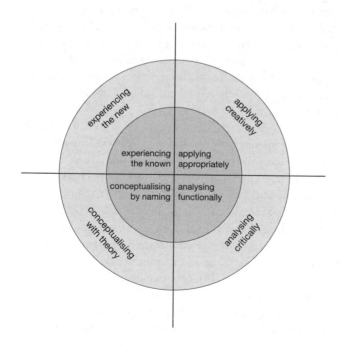

Source: Adapted from *New Learning: Transformational designs for pedagogy and assessment*, newlearningonline.com

Figure 3.1 Transformational designs for pedagogy and assessment

The Munro Review of Child and Family Social Work

In 2010, the Secretary of State for Education commissioned Professor Eileen Munro to carry out a review of child protection. One of the central questions for this review was: 'What helps professionals make the best judgements they can to protect a vulnerable child' (Munro 2011: 6). Munro is very clear that what would help support effective social work practice is the strengthening of professional expertise. Social workers need to be enabled to exercise professional judgement more, but social workers, as a group, also need to improve their expertise. They not only need to use professional judgement more, they also need to use it better. The recommendation made by Munro is that social workers should be supported in developing more expertise, in exercising judgement more and, as they develop skills and become more practiced in exercising judgement, they should become less constrained by prescriptive procedures and processes. In this context, exercising judgement includes considering the possible and likely consequences of any actions taken. It is also important, for the sake of transparency and accountability, that they should be able to describe the processes and factors that underpin such exercise of judgement.

The prescriptive context for social work in Britain in the early twenty-first century has, it is argued, undermined social workers' confidence and ability and, perhaps, motivation to exercise judgement. Social workers have become used to relying on procedural guidance, organisational norms, and processes – such as panels and other decision-making processes. Munro argues that professionalism has been undermined, to the detriment of children and families, as well as social work itself. In order to change this situation, a number of things need to happen – not all at once, but Munro argues that a process of change is needed. This should include:

- Increased commitment on the part of government and employers to support practitioners to begin to exercise more professional judgement.
- Increased commitment on the part of practitioners to take on more responsibility for complex professional decisions, and commitment to develop the expertise needed to support such professional independence.

The procedures and protocols that beset child and family social work from the 2000s onwards were developed to reduce risk – to children, to families, and to organisations. These procedures, protocols and the software to support them contribute to the problems that they were intended to address, whether they have any effect in reducing risk to children or not.[1] They were not developed to protect social workers in cases where things might go wrong, and indeed they appear to have done little to protect them. The Munro Review reflects the inevitability that some cases will 'go wrong' in the sense that one cannot expect every judgement in every complex case to be 'correct' when seen through the lens of hindsight. The Review also reflects the belief that complex organisations can inadvertently build in the conditions that make errors more likely (Broadhurst *et al.* 2010b). The experience of some social workers in Haringey in London after the deaths of Victoria Climbié and Peter Connelly suggests that procedures and protocols have done little to protect employers of social workers, either. Munro suggests that reducing bureaucracy and increasing reflective capacity and professional judgement would allow more innovation, and more responsiveness to local need. Nevertheless, freeing social workers to use professional judgement more means that they have to be prepared to take responsibility for the professional judgements they make. The quality of reflection and analysis social workers are able to bring to their work becomes of the greatest importance.

Evidence, knowledge, illusion and reflection

For Munro, improving expertise involves 'making best use of available evidence about what helps to resolve the problems in children's lives' (Munro 2011: 8). Social workers' use of the evidence base for practice has attracted considerable interest, with researchers considering how much the evidence from research actually is used to inform practice, and bring about a rapid expansion in the development of the 'what works' approach to practice in the 2000s (Sheppard and Ryan 2003; Forrester 2010).

Trevithick (2008) describes social work knowledge as having a framework with three interweaving elements:

- theoretical knowledge/theory;
- factual knowledge;
- practice/practical/personal knowledge.

Trevithick describes the range of types of theory. 'Bottom-up' theory includes 'lay theorising' and 'lay wisdom' and 'common sense' – the ordinary process of learning from experience to create explanations for the way things work. At the other end of the spectrum is 'grand' theory, which '... purports to explain more or less everything in society, such as Marxism, feminism and religious ideologies' (Trevithick 2008: 1214). In between these two extremes lies a wide span of middle-range theories, which aim to explain some things, but within a more limited range.

Trevithick (2008) argues, after Polanyi (1967),[2] that knowledge is not a uniform construct. *Knowing about* something includes scientific and abstract ideas and knowledge, whereas *knowing how* is knowledge about how to put the knowledge and understanding that one has into action. Trevithick also reminds readers that knowing about things and understanding them is not something that happens independently of the self: 'In professional circles, understanding others ... involves a degree of self-knowledge and an understanding of how we relate and come across to others' (Trevithick 2008: 1214). It is arguable that understanding anything at any level is liable to influence from aspects of the 'self': what one chooses to see and the weight one gives to the different elements of what we see, or hear, or even smell or taste, in certain contexts. It also directs what we choose to read and to whom we listen and what we remember or ignore of what we have heard and read. People perceive things differently, and understand the things they perceive differently. 'These issues can seem to be far removed from contemporary social work, yet what constitutes truth or reality lies at the heart of the assessment process, and other aspects of our work' (Trevithick 2008: 1214). Reflection is a way of making space to consider how these biases in our perception and the influences we expose ourselves to affect what we do in practice.

Sheppard and Ryan (2003) differentiate between 'product knowledge' and 'process knowledge':

Box 3.1

Product knowledge: existing knowledge that we have acquired through reading and observing and experience: research, academic knowledge, theory – for example, sociological, developmental, psychological theory.

Process knowledge: knowing how to use the information that we have, and identify what is missing: critical appraisal, hypothesising, making causal inferences, hypothesis testing, questioning information.

Process knowledge is another way of thinking about finding 'truth' or 'reality' in the assessment process. The known 'facts' of the case rarely give us a clear answer as to what a child or family needs. It is the integration of these 'facts' with each other and with a substantial body of product and process knowledge that gives us the analysis and professional judgement that is the key part of a social work assessment. Were this not the case, it would be difficult to justify social work's professional status, although professional skills are also required to ascertain what is happening in such complex systems as families. Gathering facts is also guided by professional understandings of what may be important, and how to find out about it.

Brandon *et al.* (2009), in their review of Serious Case Reviews, comment:

> Assessments are based on the systematic collection of information and evidence, including making systematic observations. An assessment needs to be made in the context of the relationship and developmental processes that have shaped children, parents and their families. ... Many assessments amounted to little more than the accumulation and presentation of disparate facts and information. The interactive and diagnostic effects of vulnerability and risk, resilience and protective factors were rarely explored.
>
> Brandon *et al.* 2009: 65

In this discussion, 'assessment' is not just about carrying out a formal assessment, such as an initial or core assessment under the Assessment Framework (DH 2000). It is an ongoing process in the sense that every encounter between a social worker and a service user and every conference or case discussion feeds into the way a 'case' – person or family – is conceptualised. Ideas about what is happening in a case are plastic: malleable and changeable, but they are also resistant to change, and we often hold on to our interpretations until substantial evidence makes us reappraise them. They have their own inertia, and it can take some significant event or information to change them.

Some optical illusions exploit our pattern recognition capacity, and those that combine more than one possible interpretation also demonstrate the tendency of our first interpretation to 'stick'. The rotating dancer is one such illusion, which can be seen at www.nobeliefs.com/puzzles/illusions.htm. While this may seem to some a long way removed from reflection in social work, some serious errors in the protection of children can be constructed as failure to recognise that a tipping point has arrived, when the child who was reasonably seen as a child in need, is more reasonably seen as a child urgently in need of protection. Reflection, especially in the context of good supervision, is a tool for looking at the way we see things, literally and in our mental construction of a child's reality.

Brandon *et al.* (2009) also comment on the importance of integration of information. The visual imagery of patterns seems useful once again: information has significance in relation to other information: context is everything in understanding human behaviour. It is the pattern that emerges from a large amount of complex information, the way it is organised, that is the outcome of the assessment, not the gathering of information of itself. The pattern is affected by factors external to the assessment, including the personal, organisational and political context for the assessment. One of the important roles that reflection plays is giving us space to consider what is influencing what when the assessment is being concluded. What contextual factors might be influencing us, and what weighting are we giving to the various factors internal and external to the assessment?

An example comes from the behaviour of local authority social workers, managers and the courts after the wide publicity following the inquiry into the death of Peter Connelly. We have attempted as a society to define the boundary between standards of behaviour that are and are not acceptable in a parent with the language of 'significant harm' and 'reasonable parents', but these definitions are subject to individual interpretation and vulnerable to a range of factors that may influence whether or not a parent is seen as sufficiently 'reasonable'. These standards should, in fairness to all parents, be applied as consistently as possible, so that parents are not judged by different standards, nor children offered different levels of safeguarding or intrusion into their family life. The surge in care applications after the death of Peter Connelly demonstrates that an event that changes the political context for child and family assessments can change the outcome of some of those assessments, although the wording of the relevant law and policy has not changed, nor has the guidance on thresholds for compulsory intervention (Mahadevan 2010).

Reflection, if it is to promote justice and fairness, needs to be directed at considering the motives behind the judgements we make. What political agendas are influencing us? How do they accord with the values of social work? How far are we protecting children, families, organisations, ourselves? If any of these people or organisations need protecting, are we doing this in a way that is true to our values as professional social workers?

Cognitive dissonance

The tendency to seek confirmatory evidence and overlook or underplay disconfirmatory evidence is a human tendency explored in the psychology of cognitive dissonance.

Cognitive dissonance theory is most closely associated with the work of Leon Festinger *et al.* (1956). It tells us about the ways people deal with a range of situations in which what they perceive challenges their beliefs. It suggests we invest in our beliefs: they are often very resistant to being overturned in the face of conflicting evidence. Festinger and colleagues discussed the extreme example of a sect of people who had 'bought into' the idea of the end of the world coming soon; to the extent they had given away all their belongings. When the world did not end, they managed this dissonant information by reframing it – to use a word from another psychological theory[3] – as evidence of the power of their faith.

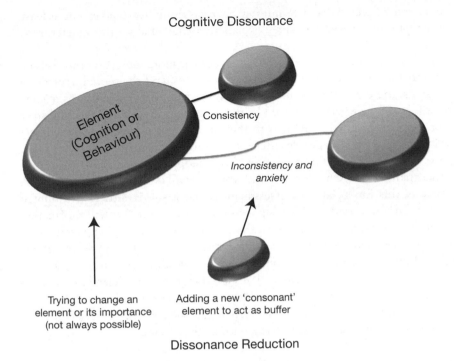

Source: Adapted from http://en.wikipedia.org/wiki/File:CognitiveDissonanceDiagram.jpg

Figure 3.2 Cognitive dissonance

When there is an established element or way of thinking about, or responding to, something, information that challenges that way of thinking gives rise to anxiety. Holding inconsistent ideas simultaneously is uncomfortable and causes stress. Consistent information, confirming what we already believe to be true, is neutral or reassuring. In order to reduce anxiety, people may provide rationalisations as buffers to protect themselves against the stress of inconsistent ideas. They change what they believe to accord with what they actually do. A classic allegory is that of the fox and the grapes: when the fox found he could not reach the grapes, he decided he would not have enjoyed them if he had been able to reach them: they were probably sour anyway. The rationalisation – 'the grapes would probably have been sour' – reduces the cognitive dissonance caused by wanting the grapes and investing effort in trying to get them, but failing – 'they are worth having and I should have them/I cannot have them however much I want them'. Another example comes from a person who buys an expensive item, such as a pair of designer shoes. Evidence that another pair of shoes would have been a better buy – more practical, cheaper, more comfortable – is managed or buffered with rationalisations – 'These will be great to wear when I get my Best Actor Award'. Evidence that the shoes were a bad buy is avoided or disregarded, but evidence they are a good buy is studied – for example, pictures of famous people wearing the same brand of shoes. The behaviour – having bought the shoes – determines what is given attention and what message is taken from it, rather than the other way around; the available evidence determining what the person thinks. In this way, what we do can be seen to be determining what we think, to some extent at least, rather than the more intuitive and accepted explanation that what we think determines what we do.

The example of the shoes is a relatively trivial one, but the more important the decision and the more difficult the choice, the more anxiety it causes, and the more important it becomes to manage the discomfort of dissonant information. If the decision is a 'close call', as when it is not clear whether it would be the best decision to remove a child from their family or support them while living with their family, cognitive dissonance theory predicts that it is more likely that people will seek reassurance that the choice they made was the right one, and will look for reassurance from people who are likely to confirm their view rather than challenge it. Dissonant information will be avoided or disregarded.

The relevance of this for social work assessment is that it suggests there is a human tendency to pay attention to evidence that supports our ideas, but to 'buffer' information that counters it. This presents a challenge to the idea that we can be completely open-minded during an assessment. We have to be prepared to abandon our initial perceptions and hypotheses. Initial perceptions may sometimes be misleading, but they can also be powerful influences on an assessment. Reflection should include considering whether the tendency to seek confirmatory evidence has influenced one's perceptions so far.

Questions to ask oneself, or another person, to challenge the tendency to seek confirmatory evidence and discount disconfirmatory evidence might include:

- What new things does the evidence from this last visit/meeting with the person/family tell you about them or their situation?
- How does what you learned during the visit/meeting accord with what you thought about the person/family at the beginning of the session? (Congruent with your developing assessment)
- What new evidence supports your assessment, and is there any that does not support it, or suggests another interpretation/assessment? (Not congruent with your developing assessment)
- What does the person least in agreement with your assessment think? Does their view have merit too?

The aim of this exercise is to encourage a self-assessment of the extent to which the existence of a pre-existing view or initial reaction to a person or situation might have given rise to a tendency to be biased. We choose which information is taken as 'signal' and given attention, and what is disregarded as 'noise'. Reflection revisits this process, considering what may have been overvalued, and what undervalued.

Reflecting on power and individual perspectives

Perspectives are described by Trevithick (2008) as a partial view of the world, which '... can involve exaggerating or overstating a particular feature, such as the racist, gender or class assumptions evident in a particular situation, at the expense of temporarily understating others' (Trevithick 2008: 1221). They add a sociological, contextual or political understanding to our perceptions of events or behaviour. Perspectives include such ways of viewing the world as an anti-discriminatory perspective, or one oriented to children's rights. They are very closely associated with social work values. Perspectives may be seen as positive or productive biases in viewing the world; ways of using contextual knowledge about oppression to understand the power dynamics of a situation, for example. However, as Trevithick notes, they involve a selective focus on certain aspects of a situation, at the expense of paying attention to others. They can lead to errors of perception, as when Victoria Climbié's over-compliance with her great-aunt's authoritarian and abusive parenting was apparently misconstrued as 'showing respect', rather than the effect of abuse of power.

Power is one aspect of social work practice that needs to be considered in reflecting on any situation or action. Reflection focused on anti-oppressive practice is concerned with the social worker's understanding of the institutions of power and his or her understanding of privilege and power, and his or her understanding of identity as being constructed within a society that creates interlocking oppressions. Some authors take a critical perspective on social work and find it inherently contradictory: committed to the idea of help and empowerment, but only able to exist as an integral part of a social system that is oppressive of those who are without power, and only able to 'help' by virtue of the professional power they hold over service users (Heron 2005). Felt pressure on social workers to challenge oppression and achieve the 'heroic' in their day-to-day practice places stress on those who work within the bounded possibilities of organisational practice (Rossiter 2005, 2011). Reflecting on power relations does not always mean that we are able to change them but, without the awareness of power relations, the possibility of challenging abuse of power is curtailed.

The object of reflection is to develop a contextualised understanding of social work, in which it is related to the pursuit of justice, or at least an understanding of individual problems that relates those problems to unjust social structures (Mandell 2008: 237). Judgements about risk may form the basis of professional actions that erode independence and may even, in some cases, be experienced as abusive by those who are the subject of those actions (Fawcett 2009). Parents may experience child protection interventions as abusive of their parental rights, their privacy, or their right to choose their own lifestyle. Families reflect the wider society in creating interlocking patters of power and vulnerability. Reflection is a space in which to focus on the way power is being used within the family, and being exerted on family members from outside the family. Personal history also affects the way we respond to others and to ethical dilemmas: '... idiosyncrasies of birth, personality, temperament, chance and life experience impact on our professional practice' (Mandell 2008: 237). At the same time, the challenge remains: professional decisions have to be made to distinguish between what is judged as tolerable and acceptable and that which is not. The experience of the child at the centre of concern must be the focus of reflection: whatever issues of power and injustice remain to be addressed, safeguarding the child has to be the first priority.

Hypothesising in reflective social work practice

The idea of hypothesising in solving human problems at the level of the individual has an established place in social work. 'Hypothesising' was one of the three principle techniques of the Milan school of family therapy (Cecchin 1987) – together with circular questioning and the neutrality of the therapist. Hypothesising may be described as a way of moving between knowing something and not knowing it: explanatory possibilities have begun to take shape, but no commitment has been made to adopting a particular one as 'the explanation' (Rober 2002). Openness to contrary evidence is clearly important in the process of establishing how well a particular explanation fits with the 'facts' as they unfold, but a hypothesis as used in a social work assessment is not the same as a hypothesis in scientific work.

Sheppard argues that the way cognitive processes of understanding and decision making are used by scientists differs from the way they are used by social workers in the *rigour* with which they are used (Sheppard and Ryan 2003). It is also arguable that tools such as hypothesising are used differently in practice from the way they are used in science, where a hypothesis is used to guide research and shape the search for confirming or disconfirming evidence. In social work, hypotheses may be used like this, to direct the attention of the social worker and direct the search for evidence, but often they are used in much less formal ways. They may shape the way a conversation runs, or influence the choice of spaces to open up in conversation. They suggest areas that are likely to be useful to explore for the creation of a narrative to describe the experiences of individuals or a family. These narratives are developed by service users with the input of the social worker influencing their shape, and are specific to the situation in which they are developed. The same person might explore an aspect of their lives in quite a different way in a different context or with a different person. This does not make one account untrue: it reflects the importance of context as a 'frame' for developing narratives. 'Hypotheses give the therapist something to hold on to in the chaos of the family session, because they offer a sense of some coherence in the constant stream of ambiguous information' (Rober 2002: 476).

Hypotheses, then, serve more varied functions in social work than they do in science. They are not applied as rigorously, but they provide added value in helping make choices at the multitude of choice points at which the social worker can decide to pick up one cue, or another, or steer the conversation onto another path, perhaps to revert to a topic introduced earlier in the conversation, or introduce one that has not been introduced and possibly avoided. They are provisional and laden with values that come from the social worker as observer. Hypotheses that are not consistent with social work values should be rejected; but not because they contemplate a 'difficult truth', such as a hypothesis that considers the possibility a child is at risk, for example. Hypotheses may be explanatory – about *why* things have happened in the way they have – as well as providing an account of *what* may have happened.

Hypotheses are sometimes discussed as if they were the property of one person, the result of the inner dialogue of the therapist or social worker, but they can be used as the focus of discussion with the service user, and developed through a dialogue. Social workers' hypotheses may be explicitly shared with service users, or used as a rationale for structuring a purposeful conversation without sharing them.

The rationale for sharing a hypothesis in Julie's case could be that Julie's marks are concrete, visible and present, which makes it more 'natural' to talk about them. Having thought about how they might have happened arguably shows concern for Julie (see Box 3.2). Julie has responded to the question about the scratches and, in sharing her concerns about the way the scratches occurred, the social worker is not challenging Julie's explanation but giving her an opening to talk further about the scratches. In George's case, the rationale for not sharing the hypothesis might be that, if he is being sexually abused,

---

Box 3.2 Julie and George

Julie (23) has scars on her arms that look like scratch marks. Her social worker thinks she may have been cutting her arms. She asks Julie how they happened. Julie says the scars come from playing with the cat. The social worker decides to tell Julie that her first thought on seeing the scratches was that Julie might have made the scratches herself.

George (6) has soiled himself at school for the fourth time this week. This is a problem that started a few weeks ago. He has a child protection plan because of a history of neglect. The social worker has an idea the soiling may be because George is being sexually abused, but has no other evidence. She sees him at home, and asks him about the people he has been spending time with, what he does after school and at the weekends, but does not tell him what she is thinking or ask any questions directly relating to sexual abuse.

---

questioning him directly might enable him to talk about it, but it might not, especially if he is in the place where abuse has taken place, or his abuser could even be in the house. Raising the possibility at this point may alert an abuser to the need to make sure George tells no one about the abuse. Asking him directly could be seen as 'leading' him and could compromise subsequent legal action. The social worker however uses the hypothesis, which may be little more than a 'gut instinct', without sharing it. She explores areas that are neutral in relation to implying suspicion of sexual abuse, but may give information that helps her test the hypothesis.

Instinct or 'gut feeling' may be useful as a pointer that an area needs closer scrutiny, but the evidence that is gained on looking more closely at the issue may show some quite different explanation. George's problems may be the result of a medical problem, and Julie may be covering up for an abusive partner, not self-harming. In both cases, the social worker's initial response is that there is something to consider carefully, based on knowledge and experience. 'Instinct' is important in highlighting a possible area of concern for sensitive professional exploration, using process knowledge – skilled behaviour and deliberation; personal knowledge – impressions and interpretations based on experience; as well as 'formal' propositional knowledge – theoretical knowledge (Erault 1994, cited in Rutter 2009). Hypotheses about the reason one has concern about a particular issue, or suspects that a person has shown resilience in the past in a particular area of their life, for that matter, guide the process of exploration by drawing on formal and personal knowledge. Knowledge and experience of skilled professional behaviour underpins the process.

Gordon and Cooper (2010) found that social workers appear to think on several levels at once. This involves talking and thinking about knowledge in an active and reflective way on many different levels at the same time. This knowledge they draw on may include theoretical, legislative and research knowledge.

Once a hypothesis is formulated that raises serious concern about a child, the social worker needs to take steps to find out if there is a basis for that concern or not. Concerns based on a 'feeling' or 'instinct' can be stressful for social workers because of the ethical dilemmas and feelings of powerlessness they may evoke. Concerns like these, when there are indicators that a child may be at risk but evidence is limited, are 'perplexing'. The tension between concerns and barriers to action is stressful. There may be dissonance between actions, which proceed apparently based on a partnership with parents, and the reality of unspoken suspicions. If family co-operation is absent or superficial, the 'felt problem' is even more acute.

Ixer (1999) considers Dewey's (1976) five stages of reflective practice in practical problem solving, beginning with the 'felt problem':

1   Identifying the 'felt problem': it is only possible to reflect authentically when confronted by material which is problematic, perplexing, and which presents a 'felt difficulty'.
2   Observation and refining the felt problem: experience plays a major part in this process of defining what the problem is.
3   Using imaginative thinking, a possible solution is explored. The supposition about how one might proceed is tentative and must be 'held in suspension' until such time as it is ready for realisation.
4   Reasoning is applied to the supposition about a possible solution. This is the most important stage for the success of the reflective process. Through critical reasoning, implicit knowledge that has not been brought into consciousness becomes conscious and can become part of a deliberate process of thought. Knowledge about research, theory, law, ethics, values, culture, professional practice and procedures may all come into play at this stage.
5   The last step in Dewey's five-stage process is the 'experimental corroboration' stage, when everything is put to the test through practical and mental implementation. 'This is the stage which equates with carrying out and monitoring practice intervention in social work' (Ixer 1999: 515).

Because of the need for hypotheses to be provisional and flexible and for the social worker to be open to the multiple possibilities and perspectives in any human problem:

> ... the usefulness of hypothesising does not lie in holding on to hypotheses whatever the cost. On the contrary, it means that in a dialogical view, hypothesising is essentially a process of knowing and not knowing, of holding on to and letting go of ideas and explanations, in response to the feedback from the family members. We cannot avoid having hypotheses. We operate with them all the time. But we can be vigilant, and constantly monitor the hypotheses in our inner conversation, evaluating whether they are helpful and constructive in the context of the family session.
>
> Rober 2002

Purposefulness of conversation is one of the defining properties of a professional social work conversation. While it may include casual conversation about everyday events, it circles all the time around the core task of gaining an understanding of the needs and the strengths of the service user(s).

•   What did I do to keep this conversation *purposeful*?
•   Was I sufficiently focused on the assessment task?

- Was I too task focused, giving too few opportunities for exploring the meaning of what was being discussed for the service user, for example?

Culturally, child and family social workers are encouraged to focus on risk and problem solving. At the same time, ethical principles of working in partnership and using the least coercive approach mean social workers are also pulled in the direction of construing what they see in the most favourable light for the service user. The high-risk context for child and family social work sensitises workers to risks and family problems. Pressure to close cases and manage scarce resources provides an opposite pull, in the direction of minimising risk and stressing family coping capacity. The idea of the 'rule of optimism' is a way of expressing a 'rule' that social workers, confronted with two conflicting interpretations of evidence relating to parental care, will choose the one that most favours constructing the parents as sufficiently caring and competent to look after their children. Failure to accept the possibility that a child may be at risk of harm can lead to the 'dangerous' behaviour of professionals of failing to ask sufficiently challenging questions of parents, or failing to ask children carefully enough about their experiences. Critical questions are:

- Was the balance between risk identification and exploration of problems on the one hand, and seeking information about protective factors on the other, about right?
- In my next meeting with this person/family, do I need to do more or less of either of these things?

Sheppard and Ryan (2003) describe social workers as 'rule using analysts'. 'Rules' include *application rules* about how to apply knowledge and experience – being aware of the limits of one's professional expertise, or the potential for misunderstandings in cross-cultural communication, for example; *practice rules*, that guide how social workers respond – 'rules' that people should have an opportunity to talk about things that have been traumatic for them, or intervention should be focused and brief in order to avoid dependency, for example; and *rules involving research, law and technical language*, which relate to the application in practice of research findings, not necessarily linking to particular texts or sources, and legal knowledge, and technical terms such as 'trauma', 'attachment' or 'modelling'.

Using a technical term means one accepts the theory within which it is defined, so using 'attachment' as a technical term means one accepts to some extent a specific framework of ideas about children's psychological development. An example of the last type of rule is a 'rule' that children need to spend time with one consistent person during their early years, summarised as a need for good attachment. Rules will not necessarily be invoked consciously, and may be held very tentatively. They are invoked to help make sense of a situation, and this in turn affects the way one responds to the situation. For example, whether one interprets silence as hostility, fear, hopelessness or failure to understand what is being asked is likely to affect how one responds to a silence, and that interpretation may be influenced by 'rules' about how people should respond in certain situations, and how they might be affected by social work concern about them.

The rules that are applied – often unconsciously – may have profound implications for ethical practice, as they may indicate certain courses of action and rule out others, without the practitioner necessarily having the opportunity to examine the basis on which they are making decisions on a minute-by-minute basis.

Box 3.3 Exercise: reflecting on conversations

Reflecting on the interactions that take place in an interview involves considering the *usefulness* of the conversation for the purposes of the social worker/agency, and the service user:

Did the conversation help you to achieve what you hoped to achieve during this meeting?

How did you, the social worker, and the service user between you manage the conversation? What were the key issues, and how were they negotiated?

Did it achieve something the service user found to be useful? What was this, and how do you know?

Do *you* think it was useful for the service user, or another person to whom you have a professional responsibility, such as a child or young person? How has it helped, and what did you do during the conversation to achieve this?

Were there things that could have or should have been considered more carefully: threads of conversation that were dropped too quickly; too much attention paid to a 'smokescreen' issue raised by someone else instead of keeping a focus on the key issues; questions you would have liked to have asked but did not?

How do you think the conversation was influenced by non-verbal communication and contextual factors?

What 'rules' did you rely on to help you make sense of what was being discussed in this conversation?

Has your thinking about this family/person changed in any way as a result of the session?

How can you use this reflection to develop your direct work with children and families?

Concluding comments

Social work practitioners often need to be able to make judgements rapidly. In situations such as child protection investigations, things can happen fast and there is little time for reflection. Reflection involves 'leaving' the situation mentally to reflect on it, or at least finding a degree of insulation from the pressure of 'doing'. Tacit, intuitive use is made of knowledge that is often not available for scrutiny at the time of use. Reflection is the way such processes may be made available for scrutiny. Reflection may be something one does on one's own, but it should also be a component of any supervisory relationship.

The function of reflection after action has happened (Erault's 1994 'reflection on action') is to explore what formal knowledge and which explicit and implicit – or intuitively applied – rules were accessed to inform choices taken while in the flow of a pressing process, such as a child protection investigation. Reflection should also provide a space within which to consider the way that values, rights and power affect practice. Each person's individual history is a powerful contextual factor that can influence the way a situation plays out. Reflection should include an opportunity to consider how individual experience may have helped support good practice, and whether it may have adversely affected any aspects of practice.

It is often difficult in an area of practice as complex as child and family social work to say exactly why one interview went well and another less well, or why certain interventions are more successful than others. One of the challenges of evidence-based practice in social work is that, in every situation, many factors interact to make for better or worse communication and more or less accurate problem identification. It is the same with interventions: no two are ever quite the same. Good practice transcends the application of rules rigidly, but it must be based on rational principles and ethical principles, which must be available for scrutiny if practice is to meet the requirement that it be accountable and transparent. Reflection helps practitioners and their supervisors to achieve this, by making links between actions, and through the practitioner's wide knowledge of different types of rules and knowledge and theories. It should offer five things – at least – to the practitioner that help to develop professional practice and assure practice standards:

1   Development of a theoretical base for practice that incorporates self-awareness and a strong value base as well as technical and procedural knowledge.
2   Retention of a focus on child welfare and respect for all service users, even at times when there is pressure to complete work quickly, or respond to other drivers for practice.
3   Feedback on the quality of practice, with the possibility this offers for developing appropriate professional confidence. Validation of the things that went well, as well as identifying areas for future development. Learning to think about practice – rather than 'just doing' it – is an ongoing process. Reflection is a key component in maintaining the development of competence, throughout one's career.
4   Sensitivity to the way power affects service users and ourselves in carrying out demanding work and making the delicate judgements required of a child and family social worker.
5   Consideration of the way one's professional work and personal experiences and values interact, to safeguard the well-being and integrity of oneself as a professional person, as well as the welfare of service users.

4   Assessment of parenting
Constructing meaning from detail

This chapter:

- explores what is understood, or implied, when professionals talk about parenting;
- considers the function parenting assessments play, and how they can be developed to meet the needs of those whose parenting is being assessed.

Organising principles for thinking about parenting

There are different 'organising principles' for assessment of parenting. These principles may complement each other, or appear to be in competition. They include:

- A child-centred approach, with a focus on children's needs and their wishes and feelings, and on how far parents are able to make their children's needs an organising principle for family life.
- A 'best interests' approach, in which the – professional – adult view as to what is best for the child dominates. Children's wishes and feelings may be sought and heard, but adults are likely to 'keep their hand on the microphone' and control how this information is used (Helm 2011).
- A children's rights approach, in which the focus is on the child's rights, as set out in key legislation and documents such as the United Nations Convention on the Rights of the Child and the Human Rights Act 1998.
- A screening/risk assessment approach, in which there is a focus on whether or not the child/family meet the criteria for certain types of services, including compulsory intervention. Organisational imperatives and patterns of service delivery are influential in determining the outcome of assessments.

On page 49 is a provisional definition of parenting. No definition is ever likely to be both definitive and comprehensive, since the demands of parenting change over time and vary between cultures, but the definition offered is an attempt to capture some of the essential components of parenting.

Box 4.1 What is parenting?

Providing love so a child feels valued and worthy of love, and that they are a person with rights, including the right to have their basic needs met. Bringing up children involves providing a stimulating environment in which they can develop, offering them 'scaffolding' for, but not stifling, their development (Vygotsky 1978). It involves allowing children to explore their own capacities and create meaning in their lives for themselves, as well as offering adult understandings of the world they live in. To achieve this, parents need to provide security, stability and boundaries, as well as opportunities to find out about things, so children can learn and explore with confidence and concentration. Parents need an imaginative understanding of the child's world so they can respond to the child's uniqueness and their worldview, their preferences and feelings. They must exercise judgement to prevent children from doing, or being exposed to, things that they are not developmentally ready for and protect them from harm, even when this means putting the needs of the child before the parents' needs.

Box 4.2 Exercise: reflecting on parenting

Think about your own family, in which you were a child. As a child, what did/does your family offer you that most helped you become the person you are today? What would you add to the basic definition offered above? Second, think about a family you are working with. What do they do adequately and what areas of parenting are challenging for them? Do the areas in which they achieve and do not achieve good parenting reflect the areas identified in the definition, and do they suggest any additional areas?

The object of parenting is, on a common sense level, to bring up children to independence, caring for them until they are able to live independently of their parents. However, many children continue to be dependent on others to some extent well into their adult lives, and some families stay together without an expectation that children will move away from home. Human interdependence means that 'independence' is a very relative concept. Independence has different value in different cultures, and the idea that children should grow up to be independent and move away is perhaps a Western one that has limited salience for many parents in Britain and in other countries.

An enriching learning environment isn't dependent on expensive toys: it is about offering learning opportunities through interaction with the environment, in any way that engages the child's attention. Ideas about self-confidence, individuality and self-reliance are not universal values but primarily Western ones. Other cultures value self-restraint, tolerance, frugality ...

Smidt 2006: 28

Similar considerations apply to other 'common sense' aims of good parenting – the pursuit of happiness, financial success, competitiveness and co-operation all have values placed on them that vary from place to place, culture to culture and time to time. Good parenting is a culturally contingent concept, but there are certain things that children need from their parents in all cultures, and these are things that we might reasonably regard as the essential components of parenting.

One element of parenting that is common to all cultures is a concern that children should become competent in the use of their developing skills. The things children need to become competent in include communication and the use of language, emotional competence, social skills, and the ability to regulate one's impulses and emotions. Literacy is highly desirable for those children with the capacity to acquire it, but the ability to communicate thoughts and ideas is fundamental to humans' existence as social beings. The ability to communicate is a survival skill for children from an early age: crying when hungry or in discomfort, for example. Parents' ability to establish communication with their children and nurture communication skills is increasingly recognised as a key parenting skill. Fathers, as well as mothers, have a role in children's social and behavioural development (Lamb 2010): although an obvious point, the focus of social work is often on the mother-child relationship, with fathers and male partners receiving less attention, sometimes to the detriment of making an accurate assessment of the child's family environment. When parenting is shared, the support that parents ideally offer each other is also important in the contribution it makes to the child's environment; each parent making a contribution to the child's emotional, social and physical development both directly to the child and indirectly through their support of the other parent.

Nurturing the ability to communicate in young children is vitally important because, apart from its survival value, it is through communication that children develop their innate faculty for 'making meaning'. Children quickly become actors, or 'players' in Smidt's (2006) terminology, exploring their world and experimenting with it, striving to develop a coherent and positive view of themselves and others. Parents have a responsibility to their children to provide them with an environment in which they can learn to interact with the world and communicate.

On page 51 is an 'Image of a 21st century child' based on Smidt (2006). Smidt draws on the Italian *Reggio Emilia* philosophy of young children's education, after Rinaldi (2006), in which children's learning of meaning and acquisition of competence are key ideas.

When parents offer their children a safe environment, the children are free to explore it. Children who are securely attached are identified by their exploratory attitude to the world around them, as well as their relationship to their parents (Bowlby 1954). Children of parents who are unable to provide this kind of supportive environment, including neglectful and abusive parents, also learn, but with less confidence in their secure base. The meanings they make from the events they witness or participate in may also be very different from those of children who are well cared for. Their personal maps will cover different territory, and their values and ideas about rights and wrongs may be affected by abusive or neglectful experiences. In some cases, watching and listening may be the only safe learning strategies, producing a state of apparent passivity and watchfulness. Despite this, children are often resilient and many appear to escape significant behavioural consequences of exposure to difficult situations, such as families in which there is domestic violence (Humphreys and Mullender 2000).

Box 4.3 The 21st Century Child

From birth she is engaged in building a relationship with the world and intent on experiencing it so that she develops a complex set of abilities, strategies for learning and ways of organising relationships, so she is able to make her own personal maps for her own development and orientation – social, cognitive, emotional and symbolic. She is making meaning from events from very early on and she will share her meanings through representations and language. She is a competent and active and critical child ... a player in her society. The child makes culture, values and rights and can explore a range of realities; can construct metaphors [and] make and explore paradoxes. She can invent symbols and codes and use these to help her learn to decode the conventional means of symbolisation [including] the conventional meanings of symbolisation prevalent in her culture and community. She will learn from all those around her through interaction, watching, listening, being an apprentice and a teacher.

Smidt 2006: 14–15, abridged

Consistency and meaning are closely linked, especially in the process of learning the meaning of things. One can only derive meaning from behaviour if there is some consistency. The importance of consistency in parenting is that it supports an understanding of meaningfulness – the rules of interaction – between the parent and the child, and perhaps forms the basis for more generalised understandings of meaning in the world (Stratton and Hanks 1995). The apparent meaningless of domestic violence from a child's perspective has been identified as one of the damaging aspects of witnessing it: the adults may act as if 'nothing has happened' and 'reality' may be confusing (McIntosh 2002). Assessments need to consider the emotional environment in which the child lives, and how it supports the child's developing sense of self.[1]

'Parenting' has both an active and passive meaning: 'parenting' is what parents do when they are looking after children, and it is also what children experience when they are being looked after by parents or other carers with special responsibility for their well-being and upbringing. An assessment of parenting should incorporate an understanding of how parenting works from the perspective of

- the parent giving the care; and
- the child receiving the care; and
- the professional perspective, which is informed by knowledge of child development and adult coping strategies, and steeped in the professional ethic of integrity and respect for persons.

This can be represented in diagrammatic form (see Figure 4.1 on page 52). This triangle reflects another well-known triangle which represents the dimensions of the *Framework for the Assessment of Children in Need and their Families* (DH 2000), which in turn echoes the three dimensions of parenting described by Belsky and Vondra (1989), who group factors determining the quality of parenting into 'the characteristics of the parent', 'the

the child's perspective

the
child's
welfare

the professional perspective   the parent's/carer's perspective

Figure 4.1 Perspectives on children's welfare

characteristics of the child' and 'sources of stress and support in the wider social environment'. It is suggested that, as well as taking account of the three dimensions of the Assessment Framework, assessments of parenting need to balance these other three dimensions.

There has been criticism of bias in the weight practitioners attach to the different sides of the Assessment Framework triangle. One criticism is that social workers emphasise parents' characteristics and behaviour, with a lesser emphasis on the child and their perspective (Holland 2001, 2009; McConnell *et al.* 2006; Christiansen and Anderssen 2010), or on the impact of environmental factors on the family (Jack and Gill 2003). It has also been suggested that assessment is overly dominated by professional ideas about what families should be like, and organisational imperatives such as meeting targets. Woodcock (2003) suggests that practitioners' assessments are heavily based on the social workers' assessment of the perceived personality traits of parents, but they often failed to 'think this through', to use these observations to plan interventions to change parenting behaviour. Hyslop (2009) argued that the introduction of New Zealand's standardised 'Risk Estimation System' in the late 1990s was as much about policing practice compliance as about improving accuracy in prediction of risk to children. He cites Connolly and Doolan (2007:3): '... trying to replace professional judgment with protocols, tools and guidelines ignores the fluidity of child protection practice ... Attempting to make complex matters simple by developing tools and checklists is a naïve response and more than likely to fail.' Assessment of parenting requires engagement with the logic and the narratives of family life, learned by talking to family members, as much as describing its parameters.

Evidence-based practice has been proposed as an antidote to ill-structured assessment and ineffective intervention, but has its critics, too. Nevo and Slonim-Nevo (2011) suggest that evidence-*informed* practice (EIP) is a better approach to the problem of incorporating knowledge while leaving space for dialogue with service users over what sort of intervention they would find acceptable. They offer a description of EIP:

... evidence-informed practice (EIP) should be understood as leaving ample room for the constructive and imaginative judgment and knowledge of practitioners and clients who must be in constant interaction and dialogue with one another for most interventions to succeed. In particular, we argue that research findings should not override, or take precedence over, clinical experience and clients' wishes, values and knowledge. Rather, empirical evidence is better regarded as one component in the mutual and constantly changing journey of client and practitioner.

Nevo and Slonim-Nevo 2011: 178

They follow Sen (2002) in pointing out that what one observes in any situation is dependent on one's position relative to what is being observed. In the assessment of children and families, we are never truly impartial observers, and science never provides a definitive answer as to what is right for a family or a child or young person. Assessment has to be interactive, meeting professional standards of conduct, analysis and ethics and linked to a body of relevant knowledge, while also adapting to the individual circumstances, hopes and wishes of the service user.

Engaging parents

Scott (2006) considers the way many more families are drawn into the dragnet of child protection than turn out to have child protection problems; many of whom derive little benefit, and possibly experience damage, as a result. 'We need to have the courage to ask ourselves what it is that we are currently so confident about doing in the name of protecting children, without any empirical evidence of its benefit ...' (Scott 2006:11). In attempting to address this same question concerning *what we are confident we can do*, Turnell and Essex (2006:11) seek to identify a 'mostly hidden' first voice of 'everyday caring, solution building, and compassionate action' that balances the 'dominant, professionalized, scientized second voice of assessments and interventions, policy and procedures'. One first principle of engagement has to be communicating with families using that first voice, and using it to explain and contain the things that need to be done in the 'second voice'. Rossiter (2011: see also below) has a different approach to the 'problem' of the 'dominant, scientized' voice, arguing that ethics have to come before everything else in an 'unsettled practice' of social work. Using this approach, one should approach every service user with an open mind, placing ethics before knowledge, and being careful not to impose adult – or professional – views on those of children – or service users.

Engaging parents who may be very wary of engaging with child welfare services is one thing social workers appear to do well, depending on where you look for evidence. Statistics about assaults and threats to social workers paint a concerning picture, however most assessments are completed without resort to compulsory powers, even in child protection cases. The extent to which parents co-operate with the social workers assessing them is an important aspect of all parenting assessments (Turnell and Essex 2006). While co-operation with professionals is not in itself a sign of parenting ability, or even compliance with requirements placed on them by professionals, a lack of co-operation is seen as an indicator of risk to the children of the family: refusal to co-operate with assessment and monitoring is a common trigger for the commencement of care proceedings (Masson *et al.* 2008). At the same time, it is important to be aware of the possibility that service users may subjectively have good reason for feeling that they need to conceal the extent of their difficulties. Guilt and anxiety about the things they have been unable to offer their children, for whatever reason; anxiety about the standards likely to be applied and the consequences of failing to meet those standards, and anecdotal evidence from the media and other sources, may have created a belief that it is better to avoid engagement, even in cases in which parents are not intentionally abusive or neglectful.

Co-operation, or the lack of it, may reflect parents' wishes to keep something hidden, and if it is withheld it challenges the authority of the social worker and their right to ask questions and collect information on the family, but it does not in itself mean that parents are better or worse parents. There are plenty of examples of apparently co-operative parents who were abusive, as well as examples of unco-operative parents who abused or neglected their children. Unco-operative parents who do not abuse their children seldom make headlines, and we know relatively little about them, but it is clear that co-operation with social workers is not a reliable indicator of quality of parenting. Where family problems are impacting on children, it is the parents' willingness to reflect on the impact family problems are having on the child and willingness to engage in a process of change that are important, rather than the level of engagement at a social level.

Christiansen and Anderssen (2010: 38) pose the question as to whether social workers place undue emphasis on their experience of co-operation with parents because they know less about the child's actual situation than they know about the parents' representation of the children's lives. This skewed view can lead to poorly founded optimism about the parents' standard of care, or the future of the family (Dingwall *et al.* 1983). Balancing the perspectives of children, parents and other professionals is critical, partly because it gives more rounded information but also because it allows for better analysis of that information: making meaning out of it. However, this has not always proved achievable: the dominance of parents' views and a danger that social workers will seek children's views but then be unsure what to do with this information can unbalance the process (Helm 2011).

Helm (2011) discusses another danger in family assessment, what he calls 'satisficing'. He gives the example of a social worker hearing a child anxiously asking where her absent father is, and assuming that she is missing him, when the alternative, and better explanation was that she was afraid of him and wanted to know he was not about to reappear. The acceptance of a 'good enough' explanation without testing it is 'satisficing' – taking the first, perhaps intuitive, explanation without applying rigorous thought to it and exploring alternatives. The reflective practitioner will consider various explanations for what they have seen and heard, and be aware that the explanations that come most readily to mind may not be the correct ones. Our prior experience – personal and professional – primes us to identify patterns and apply them to new situations. This may be helpful, drawing on practice wisdom to understand what we are looking at, but if assumptions are not subject to thoughtful analysis and checking out with the family, they can mislead us.

Uncertainty and applying rules

Social workers are 'street-level bureaucrats' (Lipsky 1980): expected to make decisions in situations of uncertainty and ambiguity that have far-reaching consequences for those who are the subject of those judgements. They are expected to realise goals that are both broad and idealistic but they have to achieve this with limited resources at their disposal and based on information that is often ambiguous or incomplete (Christiansen and Anderssen 2010). Evans (2011) notes that social workers' status and self-identification as professionals means that their use of discretion may take account of managerial imperatives more than Lipsky suggests: '... "professional social work" itself is a portmanteau term' (Evans 2011: 386) which contains many variations on themes including applying rules, using discretion and using ethical principles to reach decisions. However, in the absence of concrete information that indicates that authoritative action is mandated, use of statutory powers may be delayed until further information makes the need for them unambiguous. This is the dilemma social workers face, often characterised as 'damned if you do, damned if you don't': it flows from the inevitable reality that family assessment in cases of risk involves managing a high level of uncertainty when levels of care provided hover around the uncertain threshold for compulsory action, and information itself is often partial and unreliable. This means there is always scope for an alternative analysis to be presented 'after the fact' if things go wrong. Many – non-child protection – family assessments are not carried out under such pressured situations, but some uncertainty often remains. Accepting this uncertainty is an important step in managing it.

Munro (2011: 17–18) says:

> This links to the second major driver of change: trying to manage the uncertainty inherent in the work. Child protection work is intrinsically difficult because uncertainty occurs in two main stages of work. First, abuse and neglect often occur (although not exclusively) in the privacy of the family home so they are not readily identified ... This means that when a child is suffering or likely to suffer abuse or neglect in the home, it can be concealed ... the signs and symptoms are often ambiguous and a benign explanation is possible.
>
> The second stage at which uncertainty arises is when making predictions about children's future safety. The big problem for society (and consequently for professionals) is establishing a realistic expectation of professionals' ability to predict the future and manage risk of harm to children and young people ...
>
> It is important to be aware how much hindsight distorts our judgment about the predictability of an adverse outcome. Once we know that the outcome was tragic, we look backwards from it and it seems clear which assessments or actions were critical in leading to that outcome.

This *hindsight bias* cannot be avoided but, during the course of an assessment, one can reflect on the information available, the sense that is to be made of it, and why a particular explanation or understanding appears to be the best fit. While this cannot 'proof' judgements against the bias that comes later on from knowing the end of the story, it can provide some protection against selecting explanations that are not, on closer analysis, a good fit with all that is known about a family. Use of supervision and recording key points in discussions about cases may help to counteract 'post hoc' views that the explanation chosen was incompatible with known facts.

Given the lack of clarity over exactly what the thresholds are for being a child in need, or initiating care proceedings, this is not surprising (Dickens 2007). 'High-stakes' risk-screening decisions have to be made under conditions of uncertainty, while '... pressures to improve performance [*to avoid critical incidents, manage demand, and avoid hurting innocent families*] place conflicting demands on all stakeholders within the child protection system' sell 2006). Rossiter (2011) discusses an ethics of 'unsettled practice', challenging dea of practice in which the social worker has already considered which theoretical pectives and possible interventions she will bring to a meeting with a service user. The worker's view of the client is already shaped by these preparations before the meeting, and reflection in which the social worker draws on her own experience may confound the problem further. Rossiter argues that the individuality of the service user, their unique 'face', is threatened by these 'totalising' professional practices, and the professional 'story' they help to construct. Instead it is suggested that there should be openness to 'fluid possibilities', and ethics rather than facts and theories should direct practice. Parton and O'Byrne (2000: 33) argue that social workers are distinct in their willingness to:

> ... forsake the formality of their roles, and to work with ordinary people in their natural settings, using the informality of their methods as a means of negotiating solutions to problems rather than imposing them. Imposed, formal solutions are the last resort in social work, whereas they are the norm in other settings.

'The script is not the play' (Hyslop 2009), in the sense that one may prescribe the way that social work ought to be done, and provide standard tools and formats, but the relationship between the worker and client continues to be critical for the success of any intervention. The 'script' does not really determine what happens in each encounter with real people. Relationships continue to be at the heart of assessment practice in child and family social work, however important standard tests, processes and procedures may be. Parton (2008 cited in Hyslop 2009) describes social work as a 'qualitative exercise in possibility' – an opportunity to explore how the script may be developed to support individuals in making positive choices about their future.

Thresholds for compulsory intervention

The tendency to intervene authoritatively in response to a 'trigger event' – a serious event that differs from the mainstream of events in the life of the family/child – has been noted by both Christiansen and Anderssen (2010) and in the UK by Dickens (2007). Dickens argues that in neglect cases in particular there is: '... a substantial body of research that shows the long-term damage caused by chronic neglect to children's physical, intellectual, emotional, social and behavioural development' (Dickens 2007: 78). Despite our knowledge that neglect is damaging to children, even without the 'decisive incidents' that often trigger legal intervention, the focus of social work and legal practice remains very much on incidents: 'dramatic manifestations' that act as 'catapults' that take a neglect case into the legal arena. Identifying the point at which parenting is too poor to be acceptable is highly problematic. Munro (2010) suggests that social work's concern with 'thresholds' is problematic in working with children and families. It creates a focus on deficits and degrees of severity rather than a concern to assess according to need and provide services, as was intended after the 'refocusing' of local authority services following the publication of *Messages From Research* (DH 1995) and the introduction of the *Framework for Assessment* (DH 2000). This is not surprising when demand for resources outstrips supply, but it has created an ingrained culture of division: division between the eligible and ineligible which has echoes of the earlier Poor Law approach to welfare, and division between service users and providers of services, where the former may see service providers as unhelpful gate-keepers rather than sources of support.

Thresholds: an integral part of assessment practice or a problem in practice?

Thresholds are crossing points from one space into another. In social work, the idea of thresholds has become commonplace, particularly in relation to children in need and children on the edge of care proceedings. The question often asked is: does this child meet the threshold criteria for services – do they fit the definition of a 'child in need' under s17 of the Children Act 1989 – or do they meet the definition of a child suffering or at risk of significant harm in s31 of the same Act?

Thresholds are problematic. There are two reasons for this: they suggest a dichotomy between those who should have services – with or without parental desire for them – and those who receive nothing, and they are not applied consistently between areas or across time. There is a gradient of need, and indeed a gradient in level of service provision, but thresholds create a disjunction between those who cross the threshold and those who do not. There is evidence that thresholds exclude many children and parents who would benefit from services (Sheppard 2009), and many children are the subject of multiple referrals before eventually receiving a service. Mannion and Renwick (2008) found that those children who were referred to children's services in New Zealand but were not seen as qualifying for services included many who presented in the case notes with multiple issues of suspected neglect, emotional abuse and behaviour/relationship difficulties. The care and protection issues for this group of excluded children are hard to substantiate and treat (Drake and Jonson-Reid 2007). The obstacles to identifying need can lead to repeated presentations to care and protection agencies:

> The research into these issues indicates that children who suffer neglect and emotion-al abuse are particularly vulnerable to flying beneath the radar of formal intervention by child protection agencies. Because these forms of maltreatment tend to be difficult for child welfare agents to identify and substantiate, children in these circumstances may spend extended periods of their developmental years unnoticed yet exposed to an extremely detrimental environment, which provides poor life experiences and cumulatively leads to poor life outcomes.
>
> Mannion and Renwick 2008

High levels of demand for services almost inevitably lead to the threshold becoming a mechanism for *excluding* applicants for services, rather than identifying children who would benefit from services. This is possible because it is difficult to specify what the threshold should look like in detail and there is considerable scope for discretion. Operating statutory children's social work services relies upon the ability of social workers to assess parenting accurately and fairly: the *Framework for Assessment* (DH 2000) is an attempt to make assessments of parenting more comprehensive, balanced and standard in format, thereby increasing fairness, consistency and transparency, but variations in the way it is used mean that there are limits to this – and perhaps this discretion and variability has both positive and negative aspects. It allows for a positive use of professional discretion.

Dalgleish (2003) argues that it is futile to continue to debate the issue of the threshold between 'risk' and 'need' if practice diverges once practitioners apply their own context-influenced individual interpretations of the threshold criteria. When practitioners are using the same scale for assessment, but are operating at different thresholds for intervention, the problem is one of varying thresholds, even though the scale being used may be identical. Districts, teams and individual practitioners have '... experiences and history [which] have led them to have different thresholds' (Dalgleish 2003: 94). The issue for professional practice seems to be identifying the reason the practice varies in individual cases: is it because of varying levels of need and family circumstances, or for reasons of procedural expediency, agency gatekeeping, or some other reason?

The introduction of the Sure Start programme, the Children Act 2004, and the setting up of Children's Centres, were signs of a recent political will to promote social integration and prevent intergenerational transmission of poverty (Broadhurst *et al.* 2007). Whatever the social and economic value of large-scale early intervention projects such as Sure Start, one effect of this tendency towards more comprehensive support for parenting has been an increase in family assessment. Sure Start in particular has led to an increase in investigative child protection through increased Section 47 referrals and increased numbers of children with child protection status, in addition to an increase in assessments carried out within the projects themselves (Broadhurst 2007).

Dickens (2006) discusses the ambiguity inherent in the legal and practice framework. The definition of neglect,[2] for example, raises questions about what sort of event might raise professional alarm and trigger compulsory intervention: neglect in one dimension of care may not be paralleled by neglect in another, for example. Social workers are placed under strain to defend their practice while working in partnership with parents, and finding an interpretation that appears fair, and just, and defensible while keeping the child the focus of concern.

> The same omissions may affect some children – for example, those with disabilities – more seriously, more quickly, than others. Equally, some children seem to be remarkably resilient in the face of adversity. The uncomfortable implication is that apparently identical parental behaviour can have very different consequences for different families. Such dilemmas help to keep cases at the 'least overtly coercive' end of the spectrum ... but even so, concern in some reaches such levels that care proceedings are considered necessary to safeguard the child's welfare.
>
> Dickens 2006: 81

Parents may have strengths that support the child's well-being, but specific areas of risk to a child in their family may still be high. For example, maternal warmth and affection are strengths, but may not be effective protection against being harmed by domestic violence, for example. In assessing parenting where risk is an issue, there are four distinct areas that need to be considered:

- family strengths and resources;
- areas of difficulty with parental care;
- risks to the child;
- protective factors.

Social workers' relative slowness to take authoritative action on the basis of their own assessments, as opposed to 'critical incident' intervention in family life, is perhaps in part the effect of a lack of confidence in the weight of those assessments. This appears to be particularly problematic in neglect cases:

> Society and social workers accept the need to remove severely battered or sexually abused children from their natural families for good. However, society finds it harder to accept that there is a far larger number of children who suffer significant harm from neglectful parenting to their detriment and to the future detriment of society.
>
> Hoghughi 1998: 295

Cases tend to move into a phase of compulsory intervention only when a 'trigger' offers itself, rather than on the basis of critical assessment of the situation (Christiansen and Anderssen, 2010: 39), especially in neglect cases. Durrant (2006) provides evidence that, properly resourced and embedded in a wider programme of social change, policies such as the attempt to 'refocus' on prevention can be effective. She cites the example of Sweden, after policy changes including a ban on physical punishment was introduced:

> Sweden has seen a dramatic shift in child welfare measures taken over the past two decades. In 1982, the most common child welfare measure involved placing children in out-of-home care. But by 1995, out-of-home care had declined by 26%, by then constituting the least common child protection measure. It is likely that this shift reflects the greater emphasis that Sweden has placed on prevention and parent support over the past 20 years and the substantially lower likelihood of parents striking their children in moments of conflict.
>
> Durrant 2006

Assessments of parenting are inevitably shaped by the twenty-first century preoccupation in Britain, as in much of the Anglophone world, with risk assessment and thresholds for services and compulsory intervention. This represents one of the main functions of assessment in terms of social policy; the other main function being the delivery of targeted preventative services. Retaining a balance between the two is a challenge for policy and practice, at the levels of government, agencies and individual practitioners. If services are to achieve the goal of intervening earlier to prevent problems getting worse and becoming harder to fix, somehow the balance needs to be struck in such a way that those at highest risk receive a service before things become desperate, which means high-quality early assessment has to be an intrinsic part of the social work role.

Setting the context for assessment of parenting

'Constructing meaning from detail' is the sub-title of this chapter: at this point it is timely to consider what is looked for in an assessment by different 'stakeholders', including parents, children, social work employers, courts, and others. Different stakeholders will be looking for different things from the completed assessment. Social workers need to be clear what or whom it is for, its intended – provisional – scope, and what it is hoped it will achieve. This may help to guide what information is to be collected, and how it is to be collected.

Kellett and Apps (2009) identify a range of formal and informal methods for collecting information in assessments of parenting, set out below. These are not specific to social work assessments, but reflect the ways a range of professionals may set about collecting information, and the particular value of information from particular settings.

When the assessment is beginning there may be disagreement about its purpose, which may be explicit or not, and it may not initially be clear that the social worker and the family have different ideas about the purpose of the assessment. This can cause frustration, disappointment or suspicion. It is important that the aim of the family assessment

---

Box 4.4 Collecting information

How information is collected	*What information is collected*
Discussion(s) with parent	Physical, mental and emotional health of parents; family background and history; wider/extended family; self-defined issues and concerns; own parenting background; employment and social deprivation; family and community resources available; previous support
Consulting other professionals (either pre- or post-meeting)	Previous contact with services; previous support received; number/type of referrals; previous assessments/observations/reports; ordering additional assessments to be made
Observations of home and physical environment	Basic care; risk and safety factors; other family members present; levels of stimulation; family routines; hygiene and cleanliness; housing and family resources available; substance misuse; interactions between parents and other family members
Observations of child	Health and social development; emotional and behavioural development; interaction with practitioner and other adults
Observations of parent(s)	Engagement with practitioner; attitude towards child; attitude towards identified problems; motivation to change; how parents talk about their child; interactions between parents and other family members
Observations of parent and child	Relationship between parent and child; verbal and non-verbal interaction; how parents talk to their child; emotional warmth and demonstrable affection; guidance and boundaries

Kellett and Apps, 2009

is clear, to the people who are its subject as well as to other professionals. Resolving disagreement is a key aspect of the social work role from the start of an assessment, and it may grow in importance as the assessment progresses. When care proceedings are being considered, it is a formal requirement that issues are set out and possible ways of resolving difficulties explored (Public Law Outline 2010).

Christiansen and Anderssen (2010) suggest some different reasons for disagreement between parents and professionals. These include:

- parents' lack of understanding of the situation for the child;
- differences in understanding the issues at stake;
- fear of the differential in power between parents and local authority services.

It has been suggested that social workers tend to downplay dissent with parents and '... emphasise experiences of co-operation with the parents because this is what they know, while to a far lesser degree they know the child's actual situation ...' (Christiansen and Anderssen 2010: 38). Much of the information social workers have about the welfare of children, especially younger ones, comes through the parents, reducing the scope for disagreement to things they have witnessed: seen or heard or sensed for themselves. Even when the evidence is there, confirmation bias means that it can be hard for social workers to move from a collaborative to a confrontational mode of operating. Confrontation with parents in assessment may be seen as going against the spirit of partnership, or risking future access to the child. However, access without effective and honest engagement with parents leaves the child, the worker and the agency at risk in different ways. Failing to express felt concerns is as contrary to the spirit of partnership and openness as failing to acknowledge observed strengths. The reasons given for avoiding confrontation need to be examined carefully: do they stand up to scrutiny as being in the best interests of the child?

Resolution of disagreement – or attempting it – involves exploring with parents what their beliefs are about their own parenting and what good parenting really is, and identifying areas of difference between their views and those of professionals involved with the family. Parents may dispute the need for an assessment, or believe themselves entitled to services that they have been refused. Part of the process of dispute resolution may involve explaining the social work and agency role, and why the assessment is taking place. One outcome of the process may be clarity about what the disagreement is about, and why it cannot in the end be resolved to the satisfaction of the parents. Parents may struggle with the question 'why now?' if problems have been going on a long time, especially if they have been refused help in the past.

Complex ideas may be involved and 'bundles' of ideas may need to be separated out. In a complex thought such as: 'I love my children and do my best for them, therefore they are all right', it may be possible to value the first two assertions – that the parent loves his children and does his best for them – while maintaining a position that the children are in need of assessment and of services to support the parent as well as the children. This process may be helpful in clarifying areas of difference but also identify areas of agreement that may form the foundation for further work. This may call for work to be done in all or any of Christiansen and Anderssen's (2010: 38) potential areas of difficulty:

- What is the parent's understanding of the child's situation?
- Why is the child's welfare an issue for professionals, and 'why now'?
- What is the social worker trying to do, and what rights do the parent and the agency/ worker have in this situation?

Clarifying areas of disagreement is potentially useful for the additional reason that it offers an opening for exploring parents' values and principles for bringing up children; including questions about what they believe to be 'good enough' parenting, and what they believe to be really good parenting. Exploring the reason that parents and professionals disagree about expectations of themselves as parents, or expectations they may have of their children may offer useful information about the way parents construct the task of parenting. 'Good enough parenting' as an abstract concept is difficult to define for professionals and academics, but in each family parents will have ideas about what parenting *should be like* for their own child, whether or not they are able to meet those expectations themselves without additional support. It also offers an opportunity to explore the contribution made to parents' style of parenting by their personal background, including their own history and cultural context.

The assessment process may be seen as a series of stages or levels, overlapping and possibly recursive, looping back to refine and develop ideas introduced at an earlier stage:

- The 'empirical' component: gathering information about the child, their family and their social, cultural and economic environment in the present and relevant life history.
- The 'aspirational' component: finding out about the views, wishes and feelings of the child and relevant family members.
- The 'dispute resolution' component: identifying areas of disagreement between professionals and family members, and using this as the basis of further discussion to understand the basis of the disagreement and find a way forwards.
- The 'transformational' component: considering what changes are desirable from an agency/professional point of view, who in the family wants things to change, and what needs to be done to remove barriers and make it possible. Sometimes these changes may involve use of legal powers: they will not always be by agreement.

An assessment of risk is shared between all four aspects of an assessment: the known facts about the risk to the child; the child's and other relevant people's wishes and feelings; the level of agreement and co-operation from the family, and the likelihood that change will happen within a reasonable timescale for the child. These factors then need to be considered together to make sense of the whole picture.

Going beyond 'good enough parenting'

The phrase 'good enough parenting' is commonly used in assessment of parenting. It has been argued that it has had the unfortunate effect of focusing the minds of some of those carrying out parenting assessments on the lowest tolerable level of parenting, a 'lowest common denominator' approach to parenting assessment (Edwards 1995).

Responsibility for the phrase 'good enough mother' is attributed to Donald Winnicott to describe mothers with enough parenting skills to care for their children and meet their needs but who are not, and should not be expected to be, 'perfect'. Their mistakes could even be a source of strength, as when children see parents tackling errors they begin to locate themselves in a world where everything is by nature imperfect, and strategies are needed to deal with the necessary 'imperfection' of the world. The phrase was adopted by others such as Hoghughi and Speight (1998) who defined it thus:

Box 4.5 'Good enough' parenting

We can define good enough parenting as a process that adequately meets the child's needs, according to prevailing cultural standards which can change from generation to generation. Of course all children need physical care, nutrition, and protection. Over and above these basics, the child's emotional needs can be regarded under the following three headings:

1   love, care, and commitment;
2   consistent limit setting;
3   the facilitation of development.

It is vital to realise that the long-term provision of all three aspects of parenting is essential to ensure that the child grows up into an emotionally secure, fully developed, and competent adult. See: http://adc.bmj.com/content/78/4/293.full

---

Parenting is partly culturally determined (Hoghughi 1998). Any practice, culturally sanctioned or not, that can be demonstrated to have negative effects on children's health and development is likely to be judged unacceptable but, as ever, there is scope for argument; the common practice among the wealthy of sending very young children away to boarding school is sometimes cited as an example of behaviour that might be seen as abusive were it not for the fact that it is an established practice of a socially powerful group. And 'negative effects' are also culturally defined.

Korbin (1994, cited in Azar and Cote 2002) suggests that culture is relevant to 'risky' parenting in three different ways: first, there are cultural practices that are viewed as abusive or neglectful by other cultures but not by the family's own culture; second, there is parenting that departs from the family's own cultural norms and accepted parenting practices; and last, there is harm that is societally induced which is beyond the control of individual parents. Parenting assessments need to distinguish in what way 'culture' is relevant to child care in a nuanced way, avoiding attributing parenting behaviour – positive or negative – to 'cultural practices'. Smidt (2006: 14) argues that: 'Currently in the UK there are many projects designed to "teach" parents how to "parent". This clearly based on some image of the good parent and this, by definition, is a monocultural, oversimplified and western model.'

Kellett and Apps (2009) researched professional views of good enough parenting: from family support workers, teachers, paediatricians, and health visitors. Their sample identified the following features of good enough parenting:

• meeting the child's health and developmental needs, including providing basic care, and providing love and affection;

- putting children's needs first;
- providing routine and consistent care; and
- parental acknowledgement of and engagement with support services.

In contrast, the use of 'good enough parenting' is in danger of being adapted to fit the needs of a threshold- and risk-dominated service, in which 'strengths' are balanced against 'risks' to see which has the greater 'weight'. This is arguably a very low standard for parenting: what Kellett and Apps (2009) call a 'bottom line' approach – in which any situation in which a child is not being harmed, or not being harmed very much, may be seen as 'good enough'. There are also dangers in balancing *strengths* against *risks*, which is arguably like balancing apples against pears; they are unlike qualities and do not 'cancel each other out'. If any of the core components of parenting are missing, the presence of some other 'strength' may make little difference to the level of harm caused.

The *Framework for Assessment* (DH 2000) gives no indication as to how the various factors on the assessment triangle should be weighted (see Jack and Gill 2003), and social workers often have difficulty in integrating the discrete areas of knowledge it generates into a coherent analytical statement about the child's well-being and the parenting they are receiving. Woodcock summarises a parenting capacity assessment as follows:

> The assessment of parenting will not simply involve appraising the development of the child to assess how well the parenting task is carried out, but also the way other determining factors of the ecological parenting model influence the parental capacity to carry out that task. Sometimes the parenting will be worse, sometimes it will be better. Under the Framework [for Assessing Children in Need and their Families], the emphasis will be on 'judgement' and to facilitate this social workers will need to have an understanding of how the different factors fit within a framework, rather than existing as individual attributes of 'vulnerability'. It is this careful analysis of interacting factors that is considered to provide an insight as to the effects upon children in families.
>
> Woodcock 2003: 101

The South Australian approach to parenting assessment is similar in some ways to the DH (2000) approach, with explicit prior emphasis on *parenting capacity*: '... only when parenting capacity is either found to be adequate or plans are developed to address its shortcomings do the dimensions of parenting as listed in the Framework have relevance and use in planning parenting interventions' (Donald and Jureidini 2004: 7).

For referrals involving allegations of harm, the first step is to establish the carer's level of acceptance that the harm has occurred, and the degree of responsibility taken for it (Donald and Jureidini 2004: 14). The detail of parenting assessments is seen as crucial for children because it is not the type or severity of abuse that predicts the future well-being or safety of an abused child, but *the level of disturbance in parenting*.

Parenting assessments need to go beyond describing the characteristics and patterns of parental functioning in childrearing and other roles, to provide some possible explanations for problematic parenting and suggest interventions that might be effective with the family to improve child outcomes and child safety. They need to identify things that could make things go worse for the child – warning signs – as well as potential sources of

---

Box 4.6 The South Australian approach to parenting assessment

1   How well could these parents perform the tasks required of them given optimal circumstances?

   • How able is the parent to create and sustain intimate relationships with their child such that the needs of the child can be empathically recognised and met?
   • How aware is the parent of potential or actual effects of adverse relationship stresses on their child, especially family violence?
   • How able is the parent to avoid dangerous impulsiveness and to take responsibility for their behaviour?

2   How difficult is this child to parent?

   • Some developmental phases are more demanding on parents and some children are more difficult than others.

3   What is the level, nature and context of the socio-environmental structural support in which parenting is occurring?

   • This includes knowledge about practical parenting skills as well as external factors such as the availability of family, community, professional and statutory supports.

   http://www.community.nsw.gov.au/docswr/_assets/main/documents/
   research_parenting_capacity.pdf

---

strength and factors that might help things to get better, and have an insight into what it is like to live as a child as a member of the family.

Time and relationships in social work

Assessment needs to be able to go beyond the 'surface static' notion of parenting (Woodcock 2003) and explore the problem through time and in analytic depth. It must consider whether abuse or neglect is a continuous 'steady state', episodic, or a one-off event, and what may make it improve or get worse. Woodcock (2003) expands the 'surface-static' notion of parenting as having a number of elements:

•   practitioners' 'surface' responses did not address psychological factors underlying parenting problems, even where they had identified such factors;
•   they tended to rely on exhorting the client to change, rather than using responses informed by psychological observations;
•   when change did not occur, practitioners often perceived that this was due to some 'resistance' by the client, rather than a result of the continuation of the same factors that created the behaviour in the first place.

The converse of this last is the point that when parents *do* change their behaviour in response to encouragement to do so, it is essential to acknowledge their own agency in creating a new pattern of behaviour.

Time and relationships are both important in assessments in a number of ways. Parenting is an interactive process (Reder and Lucey 1995). Parents bring to it their own issues: their own history of being cared for, and the impact that their life experiences have had on them since they became independent adults: 'The poorer the quality of people's relationship history and social environment, the less robust will be their psychological make up and ability to deal with other people, social situations and emotional demand' (Howe 1997: 175).

Working relationships based on Carl Rogers' qualities of genuineness, warmth and empathy have been presented as the 'gold standard' for social work relationships for almost half a century, but the modern context of time-limited assessment and a heavy emphasis on risk assessment in children's services means that these ideals may be hard to realise in a pressured organisation. Relationship building, to the extent that this involves establishing a working relationship for the purpose of collaboration in completing the assessment, is a key aspect of assessment practice (Ruch 2005).

Trevithick (2003: 167) discusses the importance of relationships as the platform for work with service users:

> Part of this task is to find out what is going on and how – if at all – past events may be being replayed in the here-and-now. Relational difficulties abound within social work largely due to the impact of childhood experiences.

Assessments will not always be able to explore these intensely personal issues during the brief assessment period, but adult difficulties in relationships are a recurrent theme in social work. Their significance should at least be noted in order to understand the child's situation, and for consideration in any future work with the family.

Understanding adult attachment patterns is important: adults' ability to care for others is affected by their later, as well as their early, history. While early experience is significant in shaping development, the idea that development is rigidly 'staged' has been replaced by a more subtle appreciation of the impact of experience over time. There may be sensitive periods for the development of certain abilities or personal qualities, but experiences that fall outside this period may still be highly significant for later development.

The worker–service user relationship may be used to help service users to identify what goes wrong in other relationships, but this is only possible through spending time exploring with parents how their relationship histories have unfolded and how the quality of their relationships with others impact on the quality of their lives and that of their children.

> It is impossible to ignore the misery that results from failed relationships. The suffering caused when people feel abandoned, unwanted, uncared for, isolated can be unbearable for many human beings. It can leave people feeling de-energised, depleted, lacking in motivation, and without a sense of hope and optimism about their lives and future ... On the other hand the pleasure and joy caused by positive relationships can be immensely uplifting, re-energising, and lead to profound feelings of connection, hope and possibility.
>
> Trevithick 2003: 168

The relationship between social worker and service user may be brief, and the 'relationship' in one sense a superficial one, yet the quality of the engagement may make even a brief working relationship highly significant. Service users' personal histories often include trauma, loss and the experience of 'failure' – in school, employment, or relationships – according to social norms, although on a closer view they often represent a story of resilience, ingenuity and survival in overcoming significant odds (Trevithick 2003; Ghate and Hazel 2002). As Smidt put it: 'Parents [in poverty] often struggle to know how to deal with the problems they face. Often these parents are characterised as inadequate or uncaring, when, in reality, they are merely overwhelmed by what life has dealt them' (Smidt 2006: 11).

Flexibility and order

Parents need to be able to combine two qualities that are somewhat in tension with each other: flexibility and order. Parents need to be able to respond flexibly to the changing demands of parenting, and to be able to provide children with the security of a sense of order too. Children need to learn to be able to regulate their own feelings, with the security of knowing that they are safe with their carer. The parent's ability to 'read' the mind of their child appears important in this process, too. Fonagy suggests that an individual's capacity to *mentalise* is central to their ability to regulate affect (Fonagy *et al.* 2002). Painful feelings in the caregiver or the child are rendered manageable because the caregiver understands painful feelings as mental states, rather than concrete reality. This allows the caregiver to remain both emotionally engaged with the distress their child expresses sometimes, and sufficiently in control to be able to contain the infant's distress and make it tolerable, and ultimately manageable by the child him or herself. In this way, a parent's own resilience, based on their capacity to 'mentalise', enables them to offer their child a sense of security and order.

At the other extreme, parents who are unable to manage their own emotions and find them alarming are unlikely to be able to help their young children to manage their fears, and may frighten their children as well as themselves with their own uncontrolled emotions. Assessments of parenting may, depending on the presenting issues, need to examine the caregivers' ability to manage and regulate their own emotions while they are responsible for the care of their child. This may require specialist assessment if, for example, the future of the child within the birth family is at issue. In less severe cases, in which parents may themselves have a history of trauma, bereavement, abuse or neglect, exploring with them how they manage any overwhelming feelings of sadness or anger, for example, may help identify a need for counselling support that may in turn help the parent to manage the parenting role with more consistency and confidence. Smidt (2006) expressed concern about parents in poverty being viewed as 'inadequate' parents because they are overwhelmed: one danger is that of being overwhelmed by practical difficulties and lack of – attractive – choices, but being overwhelmed by feelings associated with the problems of being in poverty as well as other stresses may make parenting difficult too.

Messages From Research (DH 1995) stressed the importance of parenting that is consistent, warm, and gives children positive messages about themselves. Positive parent–child interaction supports the development of a positive self-concept on the part of the child: their *internal working model* reflects their intrinsic worth and value (Bowlby 1954). Patterns of interaction or transactions between the parent and the child become translated into a representation of how the world works, and how they fit in to it: this is the 'internal working model'. This, in attachment theory, forms the basis for the development of a range of beliefs and behaviours that may continue into the child's adult life, affecting their adult attachments and their interaction with their own children (Bretherton 2006). Defences developed in childhood can, it is argued, interfere with consistently sensitive responding to parents' own child's needs. Patterns of behaviour that are not consistent are difficult ones from which the child can construct little meaning: about who one is oneself, what kind of people one's parents are – and therefore what other people may be like – and how the world 'works'. Patterns of family interaction are not fixed, but fluid and emergent, a product of the interaction between the family members and their wider social environment, and therefore open to change. Van IJzendoorn (1992) argues that there is no necessary and direct link between parents' early attachment experiences and their parenting behaviour. New experiences can change the way we relate to others: '... a good friend, spouse, or therapist can provide a "secure base" for exploring and working through adverse childhood experiences. In addition, parenting behavior is influenced by the social context. A supporting social network might moderate the effects of otherwise unfavorable circumstances ... '. Assessing capacity to change is one of the most challenging parts of an assessment (Munro 2011).

Putting it all together

Critical practice in assessing parenting involves considering what has been found out about the child and his or her family, and considering from the perspective of the child what their experience is of living in the family; considering where the child's best interests lie; considering what the child has a right to that they do not have and may need or want; and considering what risks there are to the child as well as the protective factors in place. The *International Definition of Social Work*[3] reinforces the importance of human rights, empowerment and well-being. Assessment approaches need to have the potential to support problem solving and empowerment, and the development of mutual respect. The distinctive contribution of social work is to explore linkages between people, and between people and their environment, including their social and organisational context. Understanding motivation, social behaviour, vulnerability and resilience are important aspects of the assessment, but they are not distinct areas to be completed in a compartmentalised assessment: they are integral to the whole. Figure 4.2 attempts to pull together some of the themes from the literature that suggest ways of differentiating between 'surface' and 'depth' and 'stasis' versus 'dynamic under-standing' in parenting assessments.

Questions to consider when drawing an assessment to a conclusion include reflecting on the family's motivation, problem solving skills, hopefulness – do the family believe things can get better? Are things getting better, or worse, or remaining the same for the child? What makes a difference – positive or negative – to the way things are now, and what do you think holds them in a steady state if they do not seem to be changing?

Viewed in this way, assessment is not purely, or even primarily, a descriptive activity but an inquiring and analytical one.

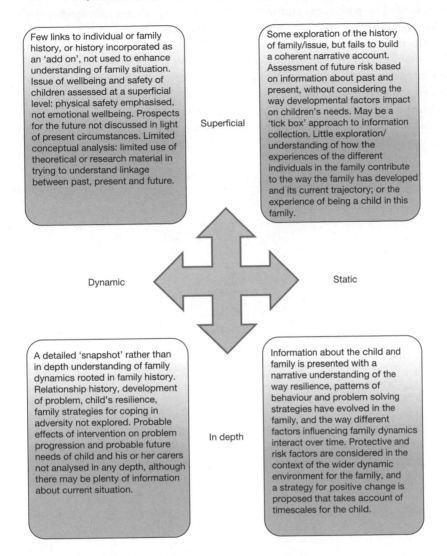

Superficial and depth, static and dynamic approaches to assessment

Few links to individual or family history, or history incorporated as an 'add on', not used to enhance understanding of family situation. Issue of wellbeing and safety of children assessed at a superficial level: physical safety emphasised, not emotional wellbeing. Prospects for the future not discussed in light of present circumstances. Limited conceptual analysis: limited use of theoretical or research material in trying to understand linkage between past, present and future.

Superficial

Some exploration of the history of family/issue, but fails to build a coherent narrative account. Assessment of future risk based on information about past and present, without considering the way developmental factors impact on children's needs. May be a 'tick box' approach to information collection. Little exploration/ understanding of how the experiences of the different individuals in the family contribute to the way the family has developed and its current trajectory; or the experience of being a child in this family.

Dynamic

Static

A detailed 'snapshot' rather than in depth understanding of family dynamics rooted in family history. Relationship history, development of problem, child's resilience, family strategies for coping in adversity not explored. Probable effects of intervention on problem progression and probable future needs of child and his or her carers not analysed in any depth, although there may be plenty of information about current situation.

In depth

Information about the child and family is presented with a narrative understanding of the way resilience, patterns of behaviour and problem solving strategies have evolved in the family, and the way different factors influencing family dynamics interact over time. Protective and risk factors are considered in the context of the wider dynamic environment for the family, and a strategy for positive change is proposed that takes account of timescales for the child.

Figure 4.2 Superficiality and depth, static and dynamic approaches to assessment

Concluding comments

This chapter has explored the enormous complexity of the task of assessing parenting, and summarised some key ideas from the literature that may provide material for reflecting on one's own practice and how it might develop with growing experience in child and family social work. The way we think about parenting is partly determined by the theories we choose to describe it: dyadic or multi-dimensional; children as passive recipients of care or active agents/'players'; based on European models of childrearing, or open to global ideas; through the subtle and nuanced ways of thinking that break down some of the categories to combine these elements in different ways. It is inevitably affected by our own experience of being parented or parenting, and immersion in the experience of engaging with other people's families throughout a period of professional development.

A good assessment, it is suggested, involves using professional knowledge, personal and professional experience, and empathy and insight gained over the time spent talking with people, including children. It approaches each situation as new, with a firm base in ethics and awareness of the uniqueness of each situation. It looks for solutions and seeks ways of working with the family's strengths, but with a clear focus on the child's right to a standard of care that will enable them to attain their potential in the future, making the most of the opportunities life affords them.

5 Narrative and understanding the family's world

Questions and stories in working with children and families

This chapter:

- explores the importance of narrative in working with service users;
- considers some of the ways in which social workers use their unique focus on understanding personal experience through contextualised narratives and 'use of self' to identify the support needs of children and young people and their parents;
- discusses the importance of communication skills in constructing, or co-constructing, narratives to explain difficulties and seek ways of addressing them.

Introduction

If an interview is 'an exercise in verbal skills' (Rutter and Taylor 2002: 43), social workers need skills that are specifically verbal skills, as much as they need skills and knowledge in other areas. The question as to what makes social work a specific discipline has not yet had a definitive answer. *The International Definition of Social Work* (IASSW/IFSW 2000) provides a broad-brush conceptual basis for thinking about social work:

> The social work profession promotes social change, problem solving in human relationships and the empowerment and liberation of people to enhance well-being. Utilising theories of human behaviour and social systems, social work intervenes at the points where people interact with their environments. Principles of human rights and social justice are fundamental to social work.

The Commentary to the definition notes that social work takes many forms, and that practice is diverse, varying from one social, cultural, historical, political and economic context to another. It identifies the 'holistic' focus of social work as a unifying factor, but it is arguable that a stronger unifying theme is the relationship-based nature of the work.

All social work involves having conversations. There are different kinds of conversations – formal interviews, family meetings, discussions during conferences, therapeutic or counselling conversations, chats over a cup of coffee – all of these are part of the bedrock of professional social work activity. If social work has a defining characteristic, it is perhaps the intensely conversational aspect of the work. Conversations are the main means by which information is obtained, understanding is gained, agreements are made, processes of change are negotiated and monitored, and support and validation are offered. What is done in 'doing' social work is largely having purposeful conversations. This is why the idea of 'use of self' is so important: the social worker's most important professional tool is herself or himself; one's distinctive voice expresses that self.

For the service user, their voice is also one of the most important things they bring to the relationship. The importance of 'being heard' and 'being listened to' recurs again and again in studies that speak of service users' experiences of being users of social work services.

If the conversations that social workers have with service users are so special and so important in making social work what it distinctively is and offers, it is surprising that there is so little known about the ways in which social workers use conversation in their everyday work. One might well ask what special verbal skills social workers develop in holding conversations with service users, and how social work conversations differ from other conversations. Other professions also use conversation as a core skill – counsellors, therapists, advocates, general practitioners, and many different kinds of 'advice workers'.

Conversations in social work are concerned with building a picture that is contextualised: as the *International Definition* states, its focus is 'holistic'. The problems that people have are understood in light of the 'multiple, complex transactions between people and their environments' (IASSW/IFSW 2000: Commentary). The way in which social work sets about solving problems with, or for, service users is intimately tied up with developing a narrative with service users that explains what the problem is, how it arose, what it means to the service user and to other people who are important in their life; explores past attempts at solving the problem; and, in turn, suggests ways in which a solution might be imagined and possible ways of attaining it. Conversations are the medium through which powerful narratives may be constructed, conveying to the worker a deeper understanding of the service user's perspective, and suggesting ways of bringing about change. By a 'deeper understanding', what is meant is that the experiences of the other person are understood in relation to their personal history and cultural context, their meaning for that person, and sensitivity as to why particular aspects of a person's life have such significance that they can continue to have effects that reverberate and affect other aspects of their lives on into the present. Significant events that have happened to the other person are understood – somewhat – from their perspective, including aspects of their emotional significance and their impact on the way they understand themselves and the world.[1]

It is accepted that many problems cannot be 'solved' through talking, or even through talking and action within the limits of what is possible. Poverty, illness and discrimination cannot be changed through conversation, although new ways of coping with them and mitigating their effects may emerge through conversation. However people who use social work services do solve their problems with support: things improve, cases are closed and many people do not need further support after this point. The construction of a narrative

– or narratives – within which the meaning(s) of a person's problem can be expressed and explored and solutions considered is a critical aspect of the social work role.

Munro (2011: 163) quotes with approval Ferguson (2011), who states:

> The extent to which social workers are able to *delve into the depths* to protect children and *explore the deeper reaches and inner lives* of service users – the degree to which they feel able to get up and walk across the room to directly engage with, touch, and be active with the child or follow through on seeing kitchens and bedrooms – is directly related to how secure and contained they feel in separating from the office/car. They can only really take risks if they feel they will be emotionally held and supported on returning to the office that their feelings and struggles will be listened to. *Workers' state of mind and the quality of attention they can give to children is directly related to the quality of support, care and attention they themselves receive from supervision, managers and peers.* (emphasis added)

The image of reaching into depths and inner lives is a powerful one, conveying the exploratory and sometimes risky nature of the work. The risk, in this case, is primarily the risk associated with exploring previously hidden issues that may raise painful memories and feelings, for service users and for practitioners. Emotional support for social workers, stressed by Ferguson, is a crucial component in providing a service that is emotionally responsive to the needs of service users, responding to need within a holistic and narrative frame.

Narratives, the self and social work

Social work has been described as taking a 'narrative turn' (Riessman and Quinney 2005; Rutten *et al.* 2010). Narrative study is about human interaction in relationships, the 'daily stuff of social work' (Riessman and Quinney 2005: 392).

How is 'narrative' defined? Not *all* speech or text is narrative and, although stories are narratives, storytelling is only one of a number of forms of narrative (Riessman and Quinney 2005). Reports, arguments and question-and–answer conversations may also be or contain narratives, but storytelling typically involves longer turns at talking than is customary. For the purposes of this discussion, a narrative will be taken to include any sequence of statements that describes an event or set of events to present a meaningful account for a particular audience. This could be a social worker, or therapist, or other person. It may be an unbroken narrative account, or elicited with prompting or through conversation, but the key features are the wish to communicate a particular, personally meaningful account of events. Information is ordered. It may be ordered temporally, running forwards or backwards through time, or thematically, around particular issues.

> The act of telling can serve many purposes – to remember, argue, justify, persuade, engage, entertain, and even mislead an audience... The persuasive function of narrative is especially relevant for social work. Some clients narrate their experience in ways that engage and convince, while other tellings can leave the audience skeptical, inviting counter-narratives.
>
> Riessman and Quinney 2005: 395

Stories 'draw us into the world of the other'; they offer specific information rather than general statements, evidenced and illustrated by specific events in time. Stories also provide a particular interpretation or frame for the events described. Many of the stories that are of concern to social workers deal with difficult material, are emotionally loaded and are capable of more than one 'explanation'.

> Narratives are event-centered and historically particular, located in a particular time and place. Stories concern action, more specifically human action, and particularly social interaction. Stories have plots. They have a beginning, middle and end, so that while they unfold in time, the order is more than mere sequence but reveals a 'sense of the whole'. Stories show how human actors do things in the world, how their actions shape events and instigate responses in other actors, changing the world (and often the actors themselves) in some way. Stories also reveal the way events and other actors act upon someone, shaping her possibilities, the way she views herself and her world. Whether hinted at or baldly stated, stories explore the complex motives that drive individuals to act in some ways rather than others and they also reveal the constraints of environment, of body, of social contexts that delimit a person's possibilities for action.
>
> Mattingley and Lawlor 2000:7

Riessman and Quinney (2005: 393) suggest some questions that we may ask when we act as professional listeners of stories:

- For whom was the story constructed?
- How was the story made?
- For what purpose was the story constructed?
- What cultural resources does the story draw on?
- What is taken for granted in the telling of the story?
- What does the story accomplish?
- Are there gaps and inconsistencies that might suggest counter-narratives?

Narrative understanding evaluates every part of a narrative, having regard for the *sequence* and *consequence* of the narrative. Sequence means the way the material is organised: is it in time order, is it chaotic, or orderly? Consequence relates to the meaningfulness of the material for its particular audience: is it meaningful? Stories are often told in a way that gives them a unity and coherence that exceeds what really happened in practice (Cronon 1992). The narrator chooses how to construct the narrative, adapting it for the particular audience and, at the same time, creating themselves within the narrative. The audience for the story is an important element in its creation.

Stories, then, are about far more than sequences of events. They add detail such as motivation, and explanation for the way things happened, why they happened in one way and not another. Different causal explanations may be considered, some more dependent on the choices made by the person telling the story, others emphasising lack of choice and environmental factors. Some make more explicit reference than others to the idea of the 'self' as an active agent.

Narratives – stories, and the questions that help us formulate those stories for ourselves or for others – are key in creating a sense of self continuously existing through time. The 'self' is important in social work conversations because these conversations are, in part at least, about understanding the 'self' of the other, and because the social worker has as their primary tool for discovering the 'story' of the other their skill in having a conversation. This is essentially a way of using social, cognitive and intuitive aspects of one's 'self'.

The idea of the 'self' is complex, made up of different ways of thinking about the self or personhood. The nineteenth century psychologist William James categorised the different aspects of the self. His first category was the *physical* or *material* self, which incorporates the body, the way we dress, also our home and property and our family, 'bone of our bone and flesh of our flesh'. James clearly appreciated the phenomenon we now know as social exclusion, its material and psychological components and its devastating impact on sense of self:

> ... a part of our depression at the loss of possessions is due to our feeling that we must now go without certain goods that we expected the possessions to bring in their train, yet in every case there remains, over and above this, a sense of the shrinkage of our personality, a partial conversion of ourselves to nothingness, which is a psychological phenomenon by itself. We are all at once assimilated to the tramps and poor devils whom we so despise, and at the same time removed farther than ever away from the happy sons of earth who lord it over land and sea and men in the full-blown lustihood that wealth and power can give, and before whom, stiffen ourselves as we will by appealing to anti-snobbish first principles, we cannot escape an emotion, open or sneaking, of respect and dread.
>
> James 1890: 295

The *social self* was recognised by James as having as many facets as we have different social groups to whom we relate, and this is a natural aspect of the different roles others need us to fulfil: friend, parent, manager, etc. This may be harmonious or discordant 'splitting'; discordant when we need to keep a part of ourselves hidden because we are ashamed of it or think others will think it shameful. Our abilities and choices in adhering to social rules affect our social self: 'The code of honor of fashionable society has throughout history been full of permissions as well as of vetoes, the only reason for following either of which is that so we best serve one of our social selves' (James 1890: 296).

The *spiritual self* is a person's inner or subjective being, including things like our prized willpower, ability to argue and make fine distinctions, as well as our moral constructs and our conscience. James introduces the 'momentous and in some respects ... rather mysterious' idea of reflection when discussing the spiritual self. '[O]ur considering the spiritual self at all is a reflective process, is the result of our abandoning the outward-looking point of view, and of our having become able to think of subjectivity as such, *to think ourselves as thinkers*' (James 1890: 297, original italics).

James was very interested in the relationship between the body and the 'self'. In seeking to understand what we are that is more than the sum of our body parts, he considered how what we think is accompanied by physical sensations. His idea about the 'self of selves', innermost self, or ego, is that it is the most vividly felt part of the self, and it is also embodied thought:

> ... the acts of attending, assenting, negating, making an effort, are felt as movements of something in the head ... In attending to either an idea or a sensation belonging to a particular sense-sphere, the movement is the adjustment of the sense-organ, felt as it

occurs. I cannot think in visual terms, for example, without feeling a fluctuating play of pressures, convergences, divergences, and accommodations in my eyeballs. ... My brain appears to me as if all shot across with lines of direction, of which I have become conscious as my attention has shifted from one sense-organ to another, in passing to successive outer things, or in following trains of varying sense-ideas.

James 1890: 305

James captures the idea that thought can have powerful physical correlates, so talking about past events can 'take one back' there in a way that has a physical reality to it. In exploring people's narratives of self, we are engaging with them while they are engaging with the physical memories of what has happened to them: happy, sad or traumatic, we are asking them to re-live aspects of the past so that we may understand it better. This may be especially demanding for service users whose very idea of self may have been threatened by the difficulties they have encountered, including social responses to stigmatised aspects of the self such as disability, addiction and mental illness. A century later, Ferguson (2009) discusses 'embodied telling' and 'embodied listening'. These terms refer to the ability of the social worker to relate to their physical environment, to be able to use this experience in describing the experience of a visit to a family, for example, and the ability to listen to and use this 'sense data' to understand a child's world.

Gallagher (2000) discusses the way the concept of the self has become more complex since James's era, to include other ideas of the self, such as ecological, interpersonal, extended, private, embodied, and cognitive aspects of self. The idea of the narrative self has developed since James's discussion, too. The sense of the self as existing through time is sustained by narratives. The *extended self* is essentially a useful fiction, based on narratives that we create, which in their turn create an extended sense of self. This narrative self extends through time, into our history of past events and into an imagined future (Gallagher 2000: 16).

Language is essential for the creation of a narrative or autobiographical self. It gives us the opportunity to create narratives about ourselves, but at the same time it is an inescapable fate. We have little choice but to create stories: '... for the most part we don't spin them [*the stories*]; they spin us' (Dennett 1991: 418 cited in Gallagher 2000: 19). In creating stories to describe what we do and who we are, we create scripts that we follow, sometimes to our gain, and sometimes to our detriment.

> ... with language we begin to make our experience relatively coherent over extended time periods. We use words to tell stories, and in these stories we create what we call our selves. We extend our biological boundaries to encompass a life of meaningful experience ... we cannot prevent ourselves from 'inventing' our selves. We are hard-wired to become language users, and once we are caught up in the web of language and begin spinning our own stories, we are not totally in control of the product.
>
> Gallagher 2000: 19

Gallagher (2000, after Dennett 1991) presents in graphic form two different models of the way narratives may link together to form an integrated sense of self (Figure 5.1). It arguably represents a linguistically based development of James's ideas about splitting, and harmonious and discordant representations of the social self. The different narratives and stories, discordant or harmonious, are linked to form an entity we call the 'self'.

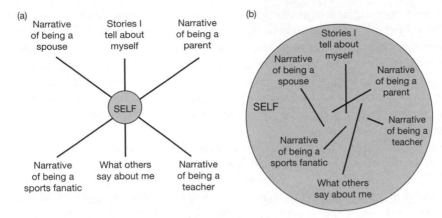

Source: Adapted from Gallagher (2000)

Figure 5.1 Linking narratives to form an integrated sense of self

In the first model, all the different narratives meet up, but in the second model, a more distributed, decentred, extended self is created, in which the various narratives meet but co-exist in more complex and fluid ways. In both, the stories that people tell about themselves and the stories that are told about them meet, but they vary in the emphasis they place on the importance of the stories coming together to form a single central 'self'. Gallagher (2000: 20) argues that the second model allows us to see the self as:

> ... the sum total of its narratives, and includes within itself all of the equivocations, contradictions, struggles and hidden messages that find expression in personal life ... this extended self is decentered, distributed and multiplex. At a psychological level, this view allows for conflict, moral indecision and self-deception.

The integration of our various life-stories into a coherent – or fairly coherent – whole is subject to cultural influences; the 'meta-stories' that shape the development of our auto-biographical stories (McKeough and Malcolm 2011).

The value of narratives for social work

Some studies have found that case management systems decrease the professional content of service user–social worker interactions and reduce participation in planning processes, but other studies suggest they can also increase participation and increase profession-alism in assessment. The truth is perhaps that, whether structures and systems support or interfere with spending time with service users, some practitioners will always find a way to do it, and some agencies or supervisors will always find ways of supporting it. The central importance of talking with service users is indisputable. Service users place a high value on reliability, dependability, the giving of useful accurate information, and empathy (Tregeagle and Mason 2008). The quality of interaction, including the quality of conversa-tion, is clearly very important to service users.

Empathy is an important aspect of the skill of maintaining a conversation, especially about sensitive subjects. It is a *relational* concept. The practitioner brings their own feelings and experiences into play, and uses them in relation to the other person, creating vulnerability for themselves by doing so. The power relationships between service users and practitioners matter in a conversation, people vary in their inclination to understand others and in their accuracy of understanding: '... the powerful and powerless ... tend to differ in their motivation to take the other's role and in the accuracy of their interpersonal understandings' (Forte 1998: 27).

There is less motivation to understand another's point of view, or to access one's own feelings and make oneself vulnerable through having empathy for their position, from the standpoint of the more powerful partner in a conversation. Stories may be truncated and stripped of their content, including content relating to gender, ethnicity, disability and other aspects of the story that may be cumbersome and not address directly the task set for the more powerful professional listener. Such narratives may be adequate for the completion of forms but are unlikely to serve the other functions – discussed below – that exploring narratives in conversation can have for the service user.

The importance of narratives has been explored in nursing in relation to life-threatening incidents in critical care. Williams (2009) argues that patients who experience incidents that disturb their existing self-concept, for example experiences that challenge their concept of themselves as strong, coping people, often have difficulties in constructing a coherent narrative to describe their experiences. Events that cause psychological trauma may impact on self-concept; in turn, the absence of a coherent narrative to describe and explain the past, including the trauma, is a risk factor for psychological recovery from trauma. Conversely, patients who can construct coherent narratives of their experience are likely to have begun to recover, so the extent of coherence in narrative is an indicator of the extent to which patients who have experienced trauma have made a recovery from it.

Stories from personal experience are like other types of story in that they are actively assembled and reassembled: they are not an exact representation of the past (Habermas and Paha 2001). They are not just memories to be passively retrieved. Stories or narratives may be constructed or co-constructed with support from a social worker who is skilled in asking questions that prompt re-evaluation of the story, working towards a coherent version of events that is consistent with cultural expectations – for example, expectations about patient or victim behaviour. This may be an important part of the recovery process. Social workers having skilled conversations with service users about their stories are not only gaining an understanding of the deeper currents of another person's reality, they are also helping to organise their autobiographical self, create coherence and (co-)construct a narrative that may help recovery from trauma and identify ways of moving on in the future.

The ability to use narratives to deal with difficult situations, such as conflict situations, appears to be associated with coping better with conflict (Harris and Walton 2009). Narrative ability may be helpful in organising our response to difficult events in the past, and in making adaptive, morally and interpersonally more developed responses while difficult things are happening to them. Narrative ability may be more useful than its obvious role in describing and ordering information, including information about the self.

One feature of many narrative accounts is the attribution of relatively unproblematised characteristics to people in the narrative; a person may be ascribed a character that is 'good' or 'bad', trustworthy or untrustworthy, etc. While narratives may help service users to order and explain their experiences, when social workers create narratives to order and explain events such as an injury, or the quality of childcare, they need to guard against resorting to these kind of 'false opposites' or false dichotomies – when two things are presented as mutually exclusive opposites, although they may not be true opposites and there maybe many shades of possibility in between.

Three reasons for asking people to tell their stories

Social workers need to work from a position of respectful uncertainty, while '...paying attention to the internal features of accounts' (Taylor and White 2000: 53; Taylor and White 2006). Listening respectfully to narrative accounts is a way of discovering more about depth and detail in personal perspectives on events. The following points from Mattingley and Lawlor (2000) expand our ideas about the complexity of even those narratives that may appear relatively 'simple'. Listening to narratives means:

- asking people to 'relive' moments or episodes in their past to give them an opening to the 'rich emotional landscape of powerful experiences';
- offering the social worker an opportunity to learn about those experiences;
- understanding lives as 'storytelling and storymaking enterprises'.

Mattingley and Lawlor 2000: 4

Narrative 'recreates experience through the eyes of the experienced, and brings with it the richness of personal and social history' (Kirsh 1996: 58). The interaction between stories and culture is a powerful one. Stories are a way of illuminating a culture as well as a personal history: if the two are entwined, one cannot do one without also doing the other. '[W]hen practitioners and family members interact, their values, assumptions and perceptions about the interaction are shaped by their membership in these cultures' (Mattingley and Lawlor 2000: 7). There is potential for misunderstandings when an interviewer and a person being interviewed come from different cultures. Narrative accounts add depth and detail, illuminating the world of the person being interviewed; encouraging people to tell their stories reduces the chance that they will be misunderstood because the listener has access to the depth and detail needed to help them make sense of what they are being told. The person telling the story has control over what they say and how they say it:

- **Detail:** the teller decides what goes in the story.
- **Length:** the teller decides how long it needs to be and when it ends.
- **Organisation:** the teller organises the account around his or her own sense of the meaning of the story. The way the story is told is part of the meaning-making of storytelling.

Telling the story may have direct and indirect benefits for those who tell the story. They may find the telling therapeutic, and derive a sense of self and voice from telling their story; trauma, illness and interventions by professionals can all undermine the sense of having a 'voice' and telling the story may help to redress this. The storytelling may be directly beneficial to them. They may be offered more appropriate and effective help if they are offered space to tell their story rather than only being able to speak by answering generic, if relevant, questions – as happens when a standard assessment process is used. An indirect benefit is that other future service users with similar stories may be helped more effectively through the greater understanding that the practitioner gains through the experience of listening to the story.

> Stories may offer a prime avenue for healing itself where healing is defined, in part, by a recovery of self. Serious illness or disability may wound the person – robbing the individual of their sense of self – as much as it harms or impairs a body.
>
> Mattingley and Lawlor 2000: 5

Narratives, autobiographical reasoning, and working with children and young people

Habermas and Paha (2001) suggest that children begin to learn how to tell a story from life experience at between two and six years of age, but the ability to create a coherent narrative about one's life develops more slowly. It is only in adolescence that *autobiographical reasoning* becomes fully developed:

> A sense of identity is constructed in the process of creating a temporally, thematically, and causally coherent narrative that fits with one's cultural conceptions. Autobiographical reasoning, then, is the self-reflective process of creating interpretive links between life's events, which allows adolescents to interpret and evaluate experiences and, in turn, make meaning of their lives.
>
> McKeough and Malcolm 2011

McKeough and Malcolm argue that stories help us understand the world, and they also help us to understand our own actions, desires and wishes, and the intentions and motivations of other people. Narratives, in this view, have a dual function for the developing individual: understanding of the world, and understanding of the self. Cultural, personal and familial histories are all engaged in the process of creating stories that sustain our identities.

Life story work is an activity carried out by social workers – and often by social work students – as a task that has relatively low priority in many busy social work teams. For some children who are in care or who have been adopted, the story provided by the agency that planned their early care and arranged a permanent home for them – if permanence was achieved – takes the place that family stories, photo albums and other records of a shared life that began before the child was born take for children who grow up in their birth families. The case of Gaskin, who sought access to his complete social work records from the time he was in local authority care was based on the premise that for him, those records were the only record of 'family life' that he had, and took the place for him that parental memories have for children who do not grow up in care (*Gaskin v. UK* (1989) 12 EHRR 36). Life stories are generally seen as an important artefact: something that is created and given to the child prior to permanent placement, for example. A narrative sensitivity to children's developing identity suggests that the value of the physical story-book is far greater than the sum of the facts it contains. Its main value is its potential to be used, discussed and mulled over later on, and used as a source as children grow into adolescence and start to create their own autobiographical identity.

By middle childhood/early adolescence children begin to explore the multiple possibilities of role, motivation and intention in their stories, reflecting a need to integrate or explain discontinuities or tensions in their own personal histories:

> A bifocal structure emerges around fourteen years of age ... with the inclusion of competing traits or intentions that create a socio-psychological dialectic and cause a struggle within the character. To illustrate, a character might be torn between wanting to be a cool person but also wanting to be a responsible person.
>
> McKeough and Malcolm 2011: 62

Narratives do not exist in a social vacuum: we tell them to ourselves and to other people, as well, and our personal narratives are 'entangled' in the narratives of other people (Gallagher 2000: 20). Adolescents seeking to build an integrated sense of self need to be able to engage with the multiple and often conflicting narratives they encounter and carry out the complex task of reflecting on them and interpreting them and their relevance for themselves. Through this process a more integrated view of who they are and what their 'self' is emerges. The stories they have told themselves and rehearsed help them to attain the capacity to '... analyze a story's message, apply it to life, abstract truths that also apply to others' lives, and ultimately generalize what might be' (McKeough and Malcolm 2011: 64).

Younger children create different kinds of stories: ideas about temporal progression are not rigidly applied, and work with them around constructing narratives should not be tied to a temporally rigid progression from more distant to nearer past, as with older children and adults (Habermas and Paha 2001). Younger children may find it harder to put events in date order as their time schemas are not yet highly developed. They also tend to report fewer internal 'feeling states', and are less likely to reflect on the motivations of

---

Box 5.1 An adolescent 'theory of meaning-making'

It is this de-emphasis of plot and emphasis on the character's psychology that we see in adolescents' autobiographical reasoning; their focus is more on interpreting events rather than merely recounting them. This allows them to present a more integrated and cohesive account of the event, themselves, and their belief system, as well as to develop a more comprehensive theory of personal meaning-making. Thus, as they develop, adolescents increasingly engage in self-reflection and create integrated storied accounts that situate events in their lives in a historical past, which allows them to understand the present and anticipate the future. In so doing, they create accounts of self that are temporally, thematically, and causally coherent, which support their development of a narrative identity.

McKeough and Malcolm 2011: 69

others than older children and young people. The relevance of this when interviewing younger children being asked to describe abuse or neglect for evidential purposes is clear: expectations of storytelling – in the sense of giving a narrative account of something that has really happened – should be linked to a developmental understanding of the way children think when they create narratives, and those listening to those stories should bear developmental factors in mind when assessing their significance as evidence of the past.

Problematising, reflection and the (co-)creation of narratives

A qualitative research interview has been described as 'a conversation with a purpose'. A social worker talking with a service user is also having a purposeful, skilled conversation. Considering the similarities and differences between the two types of conversation helps highlight some of the important features of social work conversations.

Both types of conversation are intended to collect information, reflect on it, analyse it, draw conclusions from it, and often to synthesise it with information from other people – other interviewees, family members, etc. In both situations, it is important that the person carrying out the interview sets aside, as far as possible, their own preconceptions about what might be said or intended by the person with whom they are speaking. The participants to the conversation are likely to have come from very different cultural contexts. This is simply a statistical likelihood: age, gender, race, education, place of birth and upbringing, class, income, religion ... there are so many dimensions on which the participants to the conversation may differ that it is reasonable to start by assuming that most conversations are in some sense 'cross-cultural'. The participants need to find ways of communicating across cultural differences, and often communicating about them, if there is to be 'deep' understanding of the other's narrative. Interviewers in both situations have to find some way of managing the 'multi-modal' nature of communication. When we have a conversation with someone, we are constantly picking up non-verbal cues and responding to tones of voice, observing how the other person is responding to what we say and do during the conversation. The things that people consider key in a narrative may be signalled, by phrases such as, 'I haven't said this before ...' 'I remember clearly that ...' 'This is hard to put into words ...'. Other markers that are sometimes used to signal that something significant is being described are the elaboration of details such as specific time when something happened, relating specific pieces of dialogue, or 'setting the stage' with fine detail. The cue may be non-verbal, such as a pause before speaking. Verbal communication has a very high status, and forms the basis of most reporting in social work records, but when we are having a conversation with somebody, non-verbal aspects of the conversation and things like tone of voice and pacing of speech are perhaps as important to its outcome. Our ability to respond to non-verbal cues and things left unsaid is perhaps as important as our responses to what is said.

There are some very significant differences between research interviews and social work interviews. Research interviews generally have a specific research question to address; a topic or theme to explore. They do not have as a goal changing the attitudes, values, behaviour, mood or future plans of the other person. Social workers are engaged in gathering information, reflecting on it, analysing it and drawing relevant and useful conclusions from it, like research, but unlike research the conversation is also a possible opportunity to change the way the person thinks and feels and what they know: it is a means of acting to change the world directly. Offering positive regard, empathy, reflective comments and advice are all part of a process of seeking to influence the other person: the researcher has no aim to change their participants, and may have gone to some lengths to design the research to avoid doing so.

In many social work conversations, a primary aim is finding out more about the service user's circumstances, wants and needs. Assessment is a major focus of social work activity, in child and family social work as in work with adult service users. The use of assessment protocols such as the *Framework for Assessment* (DH 2000) means that questions may be asked according to a predetermined format, with scope for supplementary questions to clarify particular points. Some workers have a more conversational style than others, and skilled workers may be able to carry out an assessment using a framework such as this without the fact that they are following a formula being particularly intrusive, or appearing to dominate the conversation. Despite this, it necessarily provides a logic for asking certain types of questions, and the effect of this is inevitably to direct attention away from other types of questions that are not included in the framework.

The process of co-constructing and (re-)constructing meaning

The creation of meaning is a joint process, mediated by conversations during which there is a co-production of meaning. The interaction is always 'the joint accomplishment of both participants' (Suoninen and Jokinen 2005: 474). However, Suoninen and Jokinen argue that the creation of meaning in social workers' conversations with service users is not an 'innocent' activity. The service user's experiences and understandings about their life experiences are discussed and interpreted through a subtle process. Meaning is created, but this subtle process knowingly pushes the creation of meaning in certain directions. Knowledge is produced and identities are created as social workers persuade service users to 'reconstruct' their stories in subtle ways.

This process of reconstruction is arguably a particularly marked feature of many social work conversations, as opposed to conversations in other professional roles, because social workers are often engaged in trying to make sense of confused information, chaotic situations, and situations in which there are a number of possible interpretations or accounts.

Box 5.2 Exercise: think about the *Framework for Assessment* (because it is so widely used and likely to be familiar to most readers)

How do, or did, you use it? (For example, go through it item by item; have a general conversation and check at the end if everything has been covered; pick out the items that seem most relevant to the situation and focus on those, etc.)

Did you find that it provides all the prompts you need to gain a good understanding of a family's situation when carrying out an assessment?

What are the areas that you most commonly found you needed to ask additional questions about that were not covered in the Assessment Framework?

It may be unclear – and very important to establish – which account has the most 'objective truth'. There are often practical or moral reasons for preferring some interpretations over others. The idea of social work as a *moral* activity as well as a practical or clinical one is relevant here. It makes a difference how reality is described in moral terms: who is a victim, who is a 'perpetrator', who is a 'good' parent, and who is deserving of support and the investment of resources. It makes a difference because the construction of an account that defines some actors as deserving or undeserving, or dangerous or benign, for example, shapes the way that they will be responded to by service providers. May Chahal and Kwong Har (2010) analyse reflection as a combination of being aware how meaning has been arrived at, and what alternative meanings might have been constructed from the account rendered. Listening to and responding to narratives is a major part of this process.

Suoninen and Jokinen identify four strategies by which the (re)construction of meaning is managed by social workers:

- persuasive questions;
- persuasive responses;
- asking for explanations;
- encouraging questions.

Of these four strategies, the first and third are mediated by the social worker asking questions. These questions – persuasive questions and ones that press service users to explain themselves – are not 'innocent'. By saying they are not 'innocent' questions, Suoninen and Jokinen mean that they suggest certain answers. They draw attention to certain things that are deemed to require an explanation.

Persuasive questions are perhaps the most recognisable of the 'subtle' persuasive techniques. If telling people they need to think differently or do things differently is unlikely to achieve much positive change, an alternative strategy is to ask questions that contain 'hints' as to the type of answer that is expected. In this way, service users can be guided towards a reappraisal of their construction of 'reality', and therefore a reconsideration of what actions they might take in response. A fictitious example below concerns Julie, a parent, and her two-year-old son George:

SW: How are you getting on with the 'Stay and Play' sessions?
JULIE: Well, it's all young mums there, and I don't really talk to them much.
SW: Yes, but how are the sessions going?
JULIE: Fine, but I'm about ten years older than most of them.
SW: Hmm. How about George, does he enjoy them?
JULIE: Yes, but he is always fine with other kids; I mean, he's around other kids all the time anyway.
SW: But is it helpful, you know, with you feeling so fed up of being in the flat, and George getting bored too?

The social worker clearly indicates that she is looking for some other answers than the ones Julie is giving her. She shows no interest in Julie's attempts to talk about her feelings, about being a relatively 'old' parent, nor her feeling of isolation when she goes to the sessions. The repetition of questions shows that the answers being given are not the ones looked for. Julie is being invited to think about ways in which the sessions are positive, how she is 'getting on', not about how she is *not* getting on. 'You know' is a device to encourage and suggest that Julie does know what she should be saying – she has the answers, and needs to search for the right way to give them. It might be an invitation to Julie to rethink her account and adapt it to fit the more upbeat account being sought. Julie is invited to comment – positively – on George's experience. Julie agrees, but sticks with her interpretation – the sessions are not really useful – by qualifying her agreement: '... he is always fine with other kids anyway'. Non-innocent questions give cues and directions that may be counterproductive for hearing the service user's views.

Persuasive responses by the social worker give the service user the clue that their explanation has not been accepted or taken at face value. They are aimed at persuading the other person to change their original answer; 'changing their reasoning' to fit with the social worker's reasoning. Persuasive responses may be neutral responses such as, 'Oh, really?', or, in Suoninen and Jokinen's example, just 'Huh'. The 'Hmm' in the conversation above suggests the social worker is having to think about how she manages her side of the conversation: it is not going as planned and she is having to consider what to do about it. This could signal to Julie, if she picks up the signal, that something is not going as intended and that her answers are not satisfactory. Persuasive responses are typically passive; a refusal to engage with the account given by the service user, or an invitation to them to look again for an explanation or account that does engage the social worker's attention and interest. How successful they are as a strategy for persuading the service user is presumably affected by the service user's interest in engaging with the social worker. Such passive responding may not persuade service users who do not wish to engage, who are not 'compliant'. It may be very important for service users that the social worker is persuaded of the validity of their construction of events, others will be far less concerned with persuasion.

This brings us to Suoninen and Jokinen's third persuasive strategy of *asking for explanations*. We make choices in conversations about which things need explanation, and which things are so obvious that they need no explanation. If a parent leaves a violent relationship, this may be seen by most social workers as needing no explanation, there being a 'cultural' belief in social work that this is responsible parental behaviour. On the other hand, not leaving requires explanation, and is therefore defined a suitable subject for questions. James-Hanman (2011) discusses the way our own preconceptions lead us to seek to answer certain types of questions. She uses the example of domestic violence and the question, 'Why does she stay?' to explore the value-loaded nature of many questions. This echoes Suoninen and Jokinen's idea of the non-innocent question. James-Hanman seeks to highlight the unintended consequences of asking questions based on preconceptions that have not been reflected on, nor the value-laden assumptions that underlie them considered. She argues that the question: 'Why does she stay?' is loaded with preconceptions and assumptions about how women in violent relationships 'should' behave.

James-Hanman (2011) lists the assumptions she has identified packed into the four words of the question: about the possibility for the woman of escaping violence, her responsibility for escaping violence, that staying is passive, and a value judgement that the consequences of leaving are preferable for her and her family than staying put. This example highlights the power questions have to conceal as much as they reveal. The value base and assumptions underlying the question are only revealed through

---

Box 5.3 Why does she stay?

'Why does she stay?' *That is the wrong question* to ask about domestic violence and is based on several false assumptions. First, it assumes that leaving ends the violence. It doesn't. It is at the point of separation that most women are killed; many more are assaulted, raped and harassed for weeks, months or years.

It also assumes victims are responsible for stopping the abuse. Why do we even care whether she stays or goes? Her behaviour is not the problem.

Also implicit is that women are somehow 'putting up with it' and leaving is the only option. In fact, abused women try a variety of strategies. Some issue threats, of leaving or involving the police, some physically fight back, others try to reason or modify their behaviour. To label these efforts as 'putting up with it' is insulting and inaccurate.

The question also ignores what happens when she seeks help. Many service providers expect that women should behave like 'proper victims'. ... It means crying in court if you want to secure a conviction and avoid being seen as vindictive.'

James-Hanman 2011 (emphasis added)

---

reflection, which reveals the extent to which it is not really an 'innocent' question. Social workers are also under pressure to produce explanations; indeed Pithouse (1987: cited in May Chahal and Kwong Har 2010) suggests that the way social workers 'tell' the case can be, and perhaps often is, used as a proxy measure for assessing the competence of social workers in practice.

Suoninen and Jokinen's fourth persuasive strategy is the use of *encouraging questions*. As a conversation progresses, the social worker is influencing the way the conversation is managed. This is a two-way process: the service user is also seeking to influence the way their story is told, and how it is interpreted. However, the asking of questions to direct the conversation is a technique that is probably used far more by social workers than by service users.

Rutter and Taylor (2002: 36) suggest that a potential problem with breaching the usual conventions of conversation by repeating questions 'persuasively' may mean that disconfirmatory evidence may be lost. The other person, faced with a 'persuasive' repeated question may assume that their first answer was incorrect or unsatisfactory and try another one. On the other hand, giving up too quickly and accepting an answer that is superficial or unlikely to be true also risks missing data. Questions that are intended to persuade the person to look at the 'facts' a certain way risk gaining a distorted view of what has happened because the style of questioning may be too persuasive.

Some approaches explicitly focus on the way questions shape this meaning-making process and encourage the service user to 'rethink' their problems. Motivational interviewing is one such. Using this perspective, the conversation is not primarily an occasion for the social worker to find out about the service user, but an occasion for the service user to find out more about themselves: what they really want, and what they might be able to do to achieve desirable goals. The conversation itself is an important part of the intervention.

Power, stories and conversations

Power affects how we listen. A key factor in how we listen to narratives may be the power we feel ourselves to have relative to the storyteller. Forte (1998) suggest that it affects how far we are prepared to 'take on the role' of the narrator when we listen to their story. Power affects *role-taking*, where role-taking is somewhat similar to empathising:

Box 5.4 ... the key elements *of role taking* are:

1   a perceptual, cognitive, affective, and imaginative process;
2   used to anticipate, understand, interpret, infer the covert and private feelings, cognitions, and intentions of another person or group of persons;
3   in order to coordinate one's overt conduct, behaviour, or actions with that other.

Forte 1998: 29

Social workers have power in their dealings with service users. While they do not have all the power, they do have structural power. Forte (1998) argues that while social and institutional interpretations of worth affect the distribution of power, advantage and attention on the larger scale, they also affect everyday interaction and communication processes at the 'micro' level. How much power we believe we have influences how we listen. Having power means that the motivation to be empathic, to take on the role of another person, is weaker than for those who are in less powerful positions, who may be very motivated to pick up on verbal and non-verbal cues to help them to·be aware of the thought processes of the powerful.[2]

Forte also notes that the distribution of power is complex and multi-dimensional: social role occupied, age, gender, ethnicity and other factors interact to affect the balance of power within any dyad and it can change with context, subject discussed, etc. It is not always clear in advance which factors will be most salient in determining the power balance in any encounter. What Forte highlights is that, where there is a power differential, the more powerful listener may be tempted – consciously or unconsciously – to pay less attention and be less inclined to engage the role-taking aspects of listening that involve the imagination, private and emotional processes – those aspects of role-taking that can make the listener feel more vulnerable.

Power allows social workers to have conversations that breach the usual rules of conversation, avoiding subjecting oneself to scrutiny and maintaining the focus on the service user's narrative. This involves 'breaches' of the ordinary conventions of conversation in certain key ways. May Chahal and Kwong Har (2010) identify certain 'non-ordinary' features of social work conversations:

- The topic may be explicitly defined, rather than occurring 'naturally'.
- The parties to the conversation accept that the conversation may follow patterns that

are not 'ordinary' – for example, discussing what they should talk about, or being 'probed' on their answers.

- The range of topics is restricted with an occupational focus on the service user, and on 'matters of the heart' – what people feel.
- The social worker is socially authorised to identify the topic of the conversation, direct the service user to explore personal areas of experience, and ask probing questions, or persistently interrogate in a way that is not permissible in 'ordinary' conversation
- There is no expectation of reciprocity – that the social worker will submit herself to the same type of questioning – though this may happen, possibly in an attempt to challenge unilateral authority, or to establish a 'rapport of equals'.

Concluding comments

Service users' opportunities to tell their story are shaped by the power that social workers hold, and the forms in which those stories are told and listened to are shaped by a web of cultural and other contextual factors. This is a process that happens all the time, whether it is consciously part of practice or not. What is suggested here is that the use that service users make of narratives is something that is important: reflection on when, how and to whom stories are told. The narratives themselves are important, and worthy of reflection in themselves. The response of the listener is another aspect of story-telling that is important: the person hearing a story has been a part of the process of its creation. The roles taken by social workers in conversations highlighted by Suoninen and Jokinen (2005) and May Chahal and Kwong Har (2010) suggest that there is plenty of scope for social workers to consider how they do or do not facilitate service users' narration of their stories, and appreciate the value of those stories (Mattingley and Lawlor 2000). Social workers also may reflect on how their own vulnerability is both engaged as a positive way to understand the story through role-taking, and what support they may need in taking a more narrative approach to social work with people who have often experienced, and may be currently experiencing, traumatic events.

- Give people time to tell their stories.
- Narratives that illuminate the other person's experience and understanding of their life take time, but help to make sense of 'factual' information.
- Narratives offer the possibility of insight into the world of the other person: insight that helps to develop the depth of analysis that can underpin a plan for work with the family.
- Listening to and taking note of narrative accounts from service users may help to make interventions congruent with the needs and wishes people identify for themselves, reducing resistance and supporting engagement.
- Listening to people's accounts of traumatic things that have happened to them may help them to organise their thoughts and move towards recovery, but it also takes a toll on the person listening, who may be made vulnerable themselves.
- The social worker should have access to supportive supervision to help them process the painful things they may have listened to, which may have personal resonance for them.

6   Social work and poverty

A complex relationship

This chapter:

- considers the implications of poverty for social work practice with children and families, including the Child Poverty Act 2010;
- addresses the idea of poverty and the problem of defining it;
- outlines the policy framework for working with families who are resource-poor;
- explores some practice implications of poverty when social workers work with children and families in need.

Introduction: what is poverty?

> The experience of poverty in childhood is clearly damaging and it permeates every facet of children's lives ... Yet evidence from children and young people also shows how active and resourceful they can be. They are not passive victims of poverty but rather mediate, negotiate and seek to control the experience of deprivation where and when they can. However, these strategies of survival – working, moderating needs, covering up, protecting their parents and making do – are often hidden and can be highly detrimental to children's well-being'.
>
> Ridge 2009: 91–92

Recent statistics (DWP/DfE 2011:14) show that in the UK:

- 2.8 million children (22 per cent) were in relative income poverty in 2008/09;
- 2.2 million children (17 per cent) suffered from both low income and material deprivation in 2008/09;
- 1.6 million children (12 per cent) were in absolute poverty in 2008/09;
- about 2 per cent of children lived in persistent low income – that is, in relative poverty for three out of four years – between 2005 and 2008.

Poverty is a contested term: it may be defined in different ways, all of which are somewhat problematic. The dramatic gap in average income between those who live in the richer 'developed' countries and people living in many of the poorest countries makes an absolute definition of poverty that applies in all countries difficult: the cost of living and the resources necessary for life vary from country to country, an obvious example being the cost of heating in cold countries. Another problem with defining poverty using a dividing line is that:

> ... we may be selecting a line where experiences of those just on either side of that line are actually quite similar. ... Even so, the statistical approaches adopted do try to make such a division, and attempt to select points where there are groups on either side of the line, which are similar within themselves and different from the other group in terms of their deprivation.
>
> MacKay 2008: 44

Strier and Binyamin (2010) describe three broad categories of theories for explaining poverty: *individual theories*, which locate the responsibility for poverty on the individual who, through lack of will or lack of ability, fails to participate productively in the market economy; *cultural/behavioural theories*, which locate the responsibility for poverty on shared values, norms and behaviours that are inconsistent with economic productiveness; and *structural explanations*, which account for poverty in terms of multi-level oppression. From a structural theoretical perspective, poverty is linked to the cycle of market fluctuations and market-related factors such as low wages, low unemployment benefits, unemployment, etc. There are also structural barriers to escaping poverty including poor education, poor health services and low access to credit, among other things.

These different theoretical perspectives suggest different policy approaches to the problem of poverty: attempting to change the attitudes and skills of poor individuals – 'individual' theories; challenging the 'culture of poverty' through changing social norms and values; and lastly through changing the economic and political structures that affect the kind of life choices poorer people can make and maximising their ability to be socially mobile while protecting the income of those who are unable to earn enough for themselves.

Poverty is not a straightforward concept. The title of this chapter reflects both the complexity of the idea of poverty in a post-industrial and global context, and the complexity of the relationship between social work and poverty, given the high proportion of its clients who are poor. Poverty may be defined in different ways, bringing different numbers of people into the definition depending upon its reference points.

The UN Definition of Poverty is set out below. It highlights the wide-ranging effects of poverty, which go beyond their immediate physical consequences, such as hunger and untreated illness.

> Fundamentally, poverty is a denial of choices and opportunities, a violation of human dignity. It means lack of basic capacity to participate effectively in society. It means not having enough to feed and clothe a family, not having a school or clinic to go to, not having the land on which to grow one's food or a job to earn one's living, not having access to credit. It means insecurity, powerlessness and exclusion of individuals, households and communities. It means susceptibility to violence, and it often implies living on marginal or fragile environments, without access to clean water or sanitation.
>
> *UN Statement on Poverty*, UN 1998

Currently, the 'international poverty line' is set by the World Bank at US$1.25 a day, although as noted this may be contested as a 'convenience figure' that does not apply equally in all countries. Absolute poverty is the level at which there are only enough resources available to individuals to provide the absolute minimum for subsistence, and there may even be a lack of some of those resources. It is 'a condition characterised by severe deprivation of basic human needs, including food, safe drinking water, sanitation facilities, health, shelter, education and information. It depends not only on income but also on access to services' (Gordon 2005). Some of those resources are generally linked to income, such as food, but others are a reflection of the level of services provided in the region in which people live. This includes resources such as state-provided education and healthcare.

Relative poverty is a measure of poverty that includes not only items needed for survival, but also items needed because they are essential for participation in social customs – such as celebrating Christmas or other religious festivals; and obligations and activities – such as visiting relatives, or having friends in for a meal occasionally (Gordon *et al.* 2000; Gordon 2005; Joseph Rowntree Foundation n.d.). Townsend's classic 1979 definition of poverty states that individuals and families are in relative poverty: 'if they lack the resources to obtain the types of diet, participate in the activities and have the living conditions and amenities which are customary, or at least widely encouraged or approved in the societies to which they belong' (Townsend 1979: 31). It is typically defined as 50–60 per cent of national median income (Unicef 2000).

The current measure of relative poverty in the UK is household income of less than 60 per cent of equivalent median income before housing costs (HM Treasury 2008; Dyson 2008). The median net household income in Britain is £21,000, and 60 per cent of that is £12,700 a year, or £244 a week. After deducting housing costs, that means £206 a week for a family, or £29 a day, as the boundary between relative poverty and the non-poor (Dorling 2010).

Poverty and social work have a long association: social work came into existence largely as a response to problems associated with poverty, first in religious organisations, then in non-religious ones (Weiss and Welbourne 2008). Although social work in Britain does not have an official remit to work with poverty, and only minimal direct roles, powers or responsibilities in relation to the relief of poverty, a high proportion of those who are referred to social workers are poor, and working with poverty is, whether fully acknowledged or not, de facto a central part of the social work role.

Children's views of poverty, and some views from parents

The most comprehensive source of information about children's views of what poverty means to them is in Ridge (2009): the following section owes much to this study. Ridge's review highlights the need to complement our qualitative and statistical knowledge about poverty with an understanding of the subjective experience of poverty. Children are arguably some of the people most severely affected by poverty, as it impacts on their future life chances but they have little power to 'change the odds' in their favour. Children experience poverty in different interacting dimensions, set out in the box on pages 92–3.

Ridge's research review shows that children are not just 'passive victims'. They used various strategies to cope themselves and to help their families to cope, including earning

Box 6.1 Children's experience of poverty

- **Economic deprivation:** children were anxious about the adequacy of income coming in to their households and were afraid there would not be enough money for them and for their family's needs.
- **Material deprivation:** children lacked important childhood possessions, like toys, bicycles and games, and they also expressed concerns about being short of essentials and everyday items, like food, towels, bedding and clothing.
- **Social deprivation:** poverty restricted children's chances to make and sustain friendships, and reduced their opportunities for shared social activities due to the costs of attending social events, inadequate and expensive transport provision and the expense of hosting social occasions within their own homes.
- **School deprivation:** children experienced restricted opportunities at school, largely through an inability to pay for resources such as study guides and exam materials, and restricted social opportunities through an inability to pay for school trips and other social activities. Inability to pay for compulsory items, such as uniforms, could also lead to conflict with teachers and disciplinary action.
- **Visible signs of poverty and difference:** a lack of the same material goods and clothes as their peers, and an inability to take part in the same social and leisure activities meant that children experienced bullying and were fearful of stigma and social isolation.
- **Family pressures:** children showed keen insight into the challenges and demands that poverty generated for their parents and anxiety about inadequate household income, household debt and their parents' well-being and working conditions. They also often tried to moderate their own needs in response to their parents' financial difficulties.
- **Tensions with parents:** conflicts sometimes arose with parents who were under severe financial pressure, or who sometimes had to work long hours or rely on childcare that children did not enjoy.
- **Additional responsibilities:** children in low-income working families were often taking on additional responsibilities in the home, including housework and caring responsibilities, or engaged in paid work themselves to ease financial pressures at home and to gain access to their own money.
- **Poor quality housing:** this affected children's health and well-being, and meant that children had difficulties in sleeping, studying or playing at home.
- **Homelessness:** children experienced considerable anxiety about the quality of their temporary accommodation including a lack of privacy and no space for play. This affected their health, their school lives and their social participation.
- **Poor neighbourhoods:** deprived neighbourhoods created particular problems for children who described them as insecure and sometimes dangerous. They experienced a lack of safe space for play and a dearth of local and low-cost leisure facilities.

- **Living in rural areas:** meant that disadvantaged children lacke
  tunities for shared play, were reliant on inadequate and costly r
  and were unable to meet the high costs of participation. This
  dren often felt confined within their local environments.

  Ridge 200.

money themselves so they do not have to ask parents for it, and to supplement the family's income. They also contribute to the running of the home through helping with house-work, childcare and other 'in kind' contributions, '... playing an important role in medi-ating and managing the experience of poverty within families' (Ridge 2009: 31). They also sometimes conceal their own needs to reduce financial pressure on parents, as parents conceal theirs in order to retain money for their children's needs. Children of low-income parents expressed concerns about the impact poverty and its correlates such as living in damp, unhygienic, overcrowded housing had on their well-being, including their health, education, sleep and opportunities for play.

Another aspect of poverty is that, when it was not a long-term condition, it often came into children's lives accompanying some other stressful event in the family: loss of a job, family breakup, illness, etc. 'Poverty brings uncertainty and insecurity to children's lives, sapping self-esteem and confidence and undermining children's everyday lives and their faith in future well-being" (Ridge 2009: 29).

Parents also talked about the psychological effects poverty had on them. Ridge (2009: 62) notes:

> ... heavy demands that poverty imposes on people's capacity to cope with everyday economic and social pressures and manage family life under severe financial restric-tions. ... A key dimension emerging from these accounts is about choice; there is a fundamental lack of choice that is a central experience of poverty.

Parents may feel trapped: 'I don't look forward because there's nothing to look forward to. We can't afford anything to change' (Parent quoted in Sharma and Hirsch 2007: 16).

Parents often go without things to try to meet their children's needs. They have to balance different kinds of expenditure: necessities, socially important expenses such as birthday gifts and celebrations, meeting daily needs versus saving for future expenses, and trying to avoid debt. Extra needs that suddenly appear can lead to severe financial difficulties, and using the expensive credit available can lead to further financial difficul-ties. Employment may reduce family poverty, but may also be poorly paid and unpredict-able, sometimes with hours that are incompatible with the usual childcare arrangements. Childcare costs may be expensive. Long hours spent by parents in low-paid work places other demands on the family, including on the children, who may have to find ways of managing with parents being physically present much less, even when the children are not at school or nursery, than before the parent started work (Ridge 2009). Social exclusion is a constant issue:

Today, despite a doubling and redoubling of national incomes in most nations since 1950, a significant percentage of their children are still living in families so materially poor that normal health and growth are at risk. And as the tables show, a far larger proportion remain in the twilight world of relative poverty; their physical needs may be minimally catered for, but they are painfully excluded from the activities and advantages that are considered normal by their peers.

Unicef 2000: 3

The pattern of poverty in Britain

In 2000, Gordon *et al.* highlighted the declining standard of living for Britain's poorest at the end of the twentieth century. The people most likely to be in poverty included women, children, large families, and young people: the poverty rate for lone parents with one or two children was particularly high at over 60 per cent. Poverty is therefore not unusual or atypical in Britain, especially for children.

In 1983 14% of households lacked three or more necessities because they could not afford them. That proportion had increased to 21% in 1990 and to over 24% by 1999. (Items defined as necessities are those that more than 50% of the population believes 'all adults should be able to afford and which they should not have to do without'.) By the end of 1999 a quarter (26%) of the British population were living in poverty, measured in terms of low income and multiple deprivation of necessities.

Roughly 9.5 million people in Britain today cannot afford adequate housing conditions. About 8 million cannot afford one or more essential household goods. Almost 7.5 million people are too poor to engage in common social activities considered necessary by the majority of the population. About 2 million British children go without at least two things they need. About 6.5 million adults go without essential clothing. Around 4 million are not properly fed by today's standards. Over 10.5 million suffer from financial insecurity. One in six people (17%) considered themselves and their families to be living in 'absolute poverty' as defined by the United Nations.

Gordon *et al.* 2000

The UK has one of the highest child poverty rates in the industrialised world, and one of the highest rates of relative child poverty in Europe (Dorling 2010). In 1990, a table of relative poverty in various countries of the world gave the bottom four places to the United Kingdom, Italy, the United States, and Mexico (Unicef 2000). In a later table of material deprivation in rich countries, the bottom four places are occupied by the UK, Ireland, Hungary, and Poland.

Comparison across a larger group of European countries looking at children at risk of poverty over a more recent period shows British children occupying a more central place in the table, while the proportion of children at risk of poverty remains at levels comparable to the previous table, which used a measure of 50 per cent of national median earnings as the threshold for poverty.

This suggests that while children in the United Kingdom may be at high risk of poverty, they are not alone among the children of the relatively affluent Eurozone in being at high risk of poverty and the disadvantages it confers. After six years of decline, the level of child

Table 6.1 Historic child poverty figures in six European countries

	European Community Household Panel		EU Survey of Income and Living Conditions	
	1997	2001	2005	2007
Belgium	14	12	18	17
Denmark	6	7	12	10
Finland	5	9	10	11
Netherlands	13	17	15	14
Sweden	7	7	9	12
UK	27	23	22	23

Percentage of children living in poverty in six European countries, EU Survey of Income and Living Conditions 1997–2007, Child Poverty Unit 2009: 20.

Permission to reproduce kindly granted by CPU.

Table 6.2 Children at risk of poverty[1] in 15 European countries from 2006 to 2009

	2006	2007	2008	2009
Ireland	22.5	19.2	18.0	18.8
Greece	22.6	23.3	23.0	23.7
Spain	24.5	24.3	24.4	23.7
France	13.9	15.3	16.5	17.3
Italy	24.5	25.6	24.7	24.4
Hungary	24.8	18.8	19.7	20.6
Netherlands	13.5	14.0	12.9	15.4
Austria	14.7	14.8	14.9	13.4
Poland	26.3	24.2	22.4	23.0
Portugal	23.7	20.9	22.8	22.9
Finland	9.9	10.9	12.0	12.1
Sweden	15.0	12.0	12.9	13.1
United Kingdom	23.8	23.0	24.0	20.8
Norway	9.3	11.0	9.6	11.5
Slovenia	11.5	11.3	11.6	11.2

Source: Adapted from "At-risk-of poverty rate by detailed age group", Eurostat SILC[2] © European Union, 1995–2011

Note

1 The 'risk-of-poverty' threshold is defined for the purposes of these statistics as having an equivalised disposable income below 60 per cent of the national median equivalised disposable income (after social transfers). It is therefore a relative, not absolute, threshold; it varies between countries with the national median income. It therefore reflects patterns of income as well as the proportion of children in the lowest income group.

2 My thanks are due to Steven Munn of the Child Poverty Unit, Sheffield, for drawing my attention to these more up-to-date and inclusive figures.

poverty started to rise again in 2009 (Brewer *et al.* 2009). In the UK, the full impact of recession and financial crises in Europe is as yet unknown, but one possibility is that more children will live in households in which no-one is in work (Brewer *et al.* 2009; Hirsch 2009).

Poverty carries pervasive social costs for children as much as for adults. Horgan (2007: 57) found that:

> ... for children growing up in poverty, life itself is a struggle and their keen awareness and worries about non-educational issues – like clothes for non-uniform days, the walk to and from school, vandalism and so on – mean they have less energy to focus on their education. By contrast, better-off children can take life for granted and can concentrate on using education as a way to get on in the world without worrying about material things.

The intractability of the problem of child poverty in affluent countries is not restricted to the UK, or to Europe. In the USA the 2010 Child Well-Being Index (CWI) shows that: '[t]he percentage of children living below the poverty line is expected to peak at 21 percent in 2010, the highest rate of child poverty in 20 years' (Land 2010). Even countries with low levels of child poverty, such as Denmark and Finland, have had difficulty sustaining this over recent years, while the UK, with its relatively high level of 27 per cent of children living in poverty in 1997, has managed to reduce that level to just below one quarter of children. It remains to be seen whether that small gain can be retained, built upon, or will be lost in the economic downturn and political move towards the centre right that has affected most countries of western Europe over the past two or three years.

Poverty as an issue of gender and ethnicity

Employment is seen by governments as a major plank in a strategy for tackling child poverty, but on its own it does not guarantee an escape from poverty. About 55 per cent of children currently in poverty are living in working families (DWP/DfE 2011). It can be difficult to distinguish between the effect that the causes of poverty have on children and families, and the effect of poverty itself. Possible causes include wider environmental factors, such as living in an area where there are more jobseekers than jobs; and inter- and intra-personal factors such as parental work skills and life skills, attitudes, social and practical abilities, and the effect of any medical or health conditions. Children are affected when parents, especially lone parents, who are usually women, are disadvantaged in the job market:

> Clearly, the economic climate and local labour market conditions are important determinants of employment opportunities, as are factors such as transport and childcare. Personal constraints can also hinder many parents from entering, staying and progressing in work. For example:
>
> - Low skills reduce the probability of getting or progressing in work;
> - Poor physical or mental health and disability can seriously limit opportunities for parents to enter and remain in the workforce;

- Caring responsibilities can make balancing work and family life difficult;
- Family breakdown and crisis can make searching for work very difficult and also increase the risk of dropping out of the labour market.

Child Poverty Unit 2009: para 27

While poverty is not restricted to any ethnic groups and both men and women experience poverty, some groups are more at risk of experiencing poverty than others. Ethnic minority citizens are generally at higher risk of poverty than white citizens; however, the causes of poverty differ between groups, so it is not possible to identify one cause that applies to all ethnic minority groups.

Platt (2009) notes that ethnic minorities make up 12 per cent of the population and 15 per cent of children, but 25 per cent of children who are in poverty. Over half of children from Pakistani and Bangladeshi families are living in poverty: two and a half times the average. Some factors that affect the general population affect ethnic minorities differentially: single parenthood, large families and families in which no adult is in employment, for example. Platt concludes that, in addition to the effect of these various risk factors on the chance of a family being in poverty, there is a 'poverty penalty' for ethnic minority families (Platt 2009: 4). They are more likely to be in poverty than white families even when relevant family characteristics are held constant. This applied to all the main ethnic minority groups.

The 'poverty penalty' refers to 'unexplained' differences in poverty risks, not differences recognisably attributable to discrimination, '...[n]evertheless, it is likely that discrimination may contribute indirectly to ethnic poverty penalties through impacting on pay, household level labour market probabilities and so on' (Platt 2009: 56).

As well as considering the risk of being poor at any given time, Platt discusses other dimensions of poverty: the risk of *entering* poverty, and whether poverty is long term or recurrent, as opposed to a short-term condition, or the chances of *leaving* poverty behind. She found that: 'risks of entering poverty having not been in poverty around two years earlier, were significantly greater for Indian, Pakistani, Bangladeshi and mixed ethnicity families with young children than for white majority children,' and that: 'Poverty persistence and risks of poverty entry vary across groups, suggesting that, for children from some groups, particularly Pakistani and Bangladeshi children, poverty is relatively long-term or recurrent, with the majority of children from these groups living on the margins of poverty' (Platt 2009: 8 and 5). This echoes Sharma and Hirsch's (2009) finding that poverty causes a loss of hope and belief in the future: for some families, poverty appears to be harder to avoid and harder to escape. Platt (2009: 3) argues that ethnicity should be central to the child poverty agenda, but so far it has not been researched nor has detailed analysis and understanding been actively pursued. She argues that there is clear evidence that the differences in rate of poverty across different ethnic groups cannot be attributed wholly to their family characteristics – such as family composition. Greater risks of poverty apply to children from minority groups than to similar children from the white majority.

Given the number of children living in poverty in families headed by a lone – usually female – parent, child poverty is also a gender issue. Children brought up in households headed by a single female parent may face higher levels of financial strain. Although many lone female parents manage very well, the views of children and parents discussed above reflect the stresses that poverty places on parents and children. Lone parents have to take sole responsibility for managing on an inadequate income and for taking steps to lift the family out of poverty, if they have the opportunity to do so. Being a parent with sole responsibility for childcare means that the tension between investing one's time in working to generate income, and spending time with one's children may feel much sharper than for parents who share childcare. If the financial gains for the family are not great, the advantages to the children may not be immediately obvious.

Measures to take children out of poverty involve taking parents out of poverty; many of these will be single female parents. Social measures and financial policies, including tax measures as well as income support, need to be planned with the effect they will have on parents, women, and children considered carefully.

> ... a key consideration remains startlingly absent [from the March 2010 Budget]: the impact these different approaches would have on the economic status and contribution of women. We know that failure to consider how policies impact differently on women's and men's incomes and wealth is likely to worsen women's economic inequality, a key part of the wider income gap which all political parties acknowledge needs narrowing for the good of us all.

> Pickett *et al.* 2010

This argues for serious consideration to be given to the differential impact of fiscal policies on women, in order to avoid taking steps that will further disadvantage them.

Poverty as a challenge to parental coping mechanisms

Although few would disagree that poverty is bad for children, damaging to their life chances and their health and well-being, it is not easy to say exactly what effect poverty has on children because its effects are so variable and strongly mediated by parental strategies for coping with poverty. While money alone is not the key to bringing up children successfully, family income has a significant effect on the kinds of choices that parents can make in bringing up their children. Poverty often impacts on parental mental and physical well-being and this, in turn, affects their ability to parent.

Poverty is a risk factor for children as a group: children who grow up in poverty and in households where no adult is in work are much less likely to obtain 'good' school qualifications. Only 36 per cent of children eligible for free school meals achieve five A–C GCSEs compared with 63 per cent of other children (DCSF 2007). The complex association between poverty and child neglect and abuse is discussed further below. The most obvious effects of poverty on many children are on their health and physical development. For some, educational progress is affected, and for others the main impact is on their social development. The extent to which poverty affects children depends on the ability of their parents to protect them from its damaging effects. Some parents make considerable sacrifices to do so, as the testimony of children and parents discussed above demonstrates, although the impact of living in a poor neighbourhood with few resources will inevitably impact on the whole family in some way. Other parents may be overwhelmed by their circumstances or the scale of the challenge, hampered by the effect of poverty or other stresses on their own coping mechanisms.

State intervention in family life under specific circumstances is generally seen as desirable: there is little support for the view that the state should not intervene in cases of child abuse, for example. However, there is scope for considerable debate about how and where the lines should be drawn: what justifies compulsory state intervention, and what justifies the provision of services by agreement with the family? 'The key question is not *whether* the state should intrude into family life, but *how* and *when*.'[1] The definition of significant harm in s31 of the Children Act 1989 appears to set a clear threshold for compulsion in family and child support, resting on the idea that parents should provide a 'reasonable' level of care to their children. However, poverty challenges social workers and courts to interpret the definition in a way that is fair to parents – who may feel they are doing all they reasonably can under difficult circumstances – and to children – whose health and development may be being avoidably impaired, but the poverty affecting the whole family may be a significant factor impinging on their development. This can make it difficult to determine whether a child in a poor family, 'bumping along the bottom,' is neglected by parents who are not coping well, or a victim of the high level of economic and social inequality in Britain. Sympathy for parents and concern for children can appear to pull in different directions. When a child is being ill-treated through physical, sexual or emotional abuse, there is a often clearer moral mandate for compulsory intervention, although even in such cases the abuser is often a 'victim' themselves: of poor parenting, poverty, illness, abuse, etc. Neglect is arguably more challenging in terms of moral judgement, since neglected children often live in families in which poverty is impacting in similar ways on the well-being of all members of the family. The differential in life expectancy of rich and poor reflects the way that poverty has a continuing detrimental developmental effect across the lifespan:

> The health of people in England has improved markedly over the last 150 years. In 1841 life expectancy at birth for men was 40.2 years and for women 42.2. By 1948 it was 66.4 and 71.2 years respectively. In 2000 the figures were 75.6 and 80.3. However, despite these huge improvements, there are marked differences in the health of different groups. Such health inequalities show themselves in many ways. The most notable English statistics relate to the life expectancy of different social groups; the higher an individual's social group, the longer he or she is likely to live. There are striking differences between rich and poor areas. In 2006 a girl born in Kensington and Chelsea has a life expectancy of 87.8 years, more than ten years higher than Glasgow City, the area in the UK with the lowest figure (77.1 years).
>
> HCHC 2009: 9

Life expectancy is one way of measuring health inequalities: expected length of life without health problems is another. Women in the most deprived wards in the UK on average succumb to poor health 13.6 years earlier than their counterparts in the least deprived wards (HCHC 2009: 16). The situation for men is little better. There are also wide differences in health by ethnic group, not all of which are explained by income. However, the most notable feature of the graph reproduced below is perhaps the extent to which Pakistani and Bangladeshi adults, the poorest groups in Britain by ethnicity, suffer limiting long-term illness. Poverty, development across the lifespan, social exclusion and health appear closely interconnected, although the precise mechanisms by which this operates are still not fully understood. Diet, lifestyle and psychological well-being are all likely to be highly influential.

Poverty has a negative impact on adults as well as children in poor families, but for child and family social workers the primary focus has to be on the well-being and development of children, recognising that supporting parents to be the primary providers of adequate care is likely to be the best option for all children. Recognising the challenges faced by parents is an essential component in assessing parenting capacity: carrying out assessment along the 'environmental' dimension of the Assessment Framework is the formal mechanism for achieving this (DH 2000). This information needs then to be integrated with material from assessment on the other two dimensions of the assessment triangle. This involves considering how poverty affects parenting capacity: how 'reasonable' is the quality of parenting under the circumstances experienced by the family?

A parent may be offering the best care they can, and it may be reasonable under the difficult circumstances in which she is parenting, but still the level of care the child is receiving may not be reasonable enough – measured objectively – to sustain a reasonable level of health and development. The recurrence of the word 'reasonable' reflects the discretion the social worker has to make judgements:

1   about the parent's efforts to overcome structural and environmental difficulties, such as poor housing and a lack of employment locally, in order to promote her child's welfare; and

2   about whether or not the health and development of the child is 'reasonable' in all the circumstances.

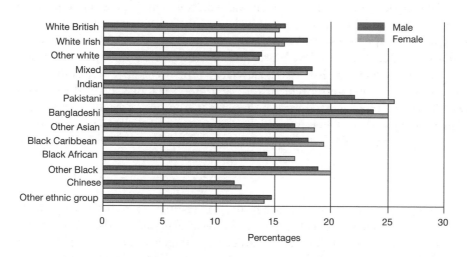

Source: Office for National Statistics licensed under the Open Government Licence v.1.0. http://www.publications.parliament.uk/pa/cm200809/cmselect/cmhealth/286/28605.htm

Figure 6.1 Age-standardised limiting long-term illness: by ethnic group and sex

Neglect and abuse have to be identified on a case-by-case basis using a range of criteria: these differ with regard to how easily they may be viewed as 'objective' criteria. They are also interpreted differently by different professionals (Regehr *et al.* 2010). There is arguably a significant element of *moral* judgement in the way these criteria are defined and applied in practice: this fills in some of the gaps in formal definitions as part of the reserve of largely implicit knowledge derived from experience of professional problem-solving known as 'practice wisdom'. There are choices to be made in every assessment about how far different factors are foregrounded in the analysis at the end: the struggle faced by parents, or the impairment of the life chances of the child – who may have speech delay, educational difficulties, health and dental problems or social difficulties, all of which might be remediable under more propitious circumstances.

If, as it appears, it is sometimes difficult to tell how far childhood adversity is a result of poverty rather than poor parenting, then the boundary between neglect and circumstances causing hardship is less clear than might at first appear. When there is an issue of child neglect in the context of poverty, it is suggested that whether a family is identified as needing 'elective' services or compulsory intervention depends on six factors – there may be more, but this sets out the main dimensions:

- the nature and extent of the challenges faced by the family;
- the resources they have at their disposal to meet those challenges;
- professional judgement about the effectiveness and appropriateness with which they use those resources;
- professional judgement about the attitude of the parents to the child;
- the impact on the child of the lack of resources available to them, including material resources and parental time and positive attention;
- evidence of any developmental impairment in the child.

Parents who use coping mechanisms that are not socially sanctioned and that may have a negative impact on children, such as drugs or alcohol, are likely to 'fail' the test because of professional judgement that resources are being used inappropriately, the child's welfare is not being prioritised, and their children may receive little positive or reliably consistent positive attention. A parent who spends money on expensive trainers instead of school uniform presents a more challenging test: from the parent's perspective this may represent a sacrifice to provide a child with something which helps them be socially included with their peers (see Gillies 2005, discussed on page 102). Different weightings placed on school attendance and social participation underpin different possible interpretations of the parent's behaviour as either irresponsible, or sensitively caring.

It not suggested that poverty should be used to excuse and ignore poor parenting. Assessments need to include an understanding of the reasons why people act as they do, and seek the subjective rationality that may sometimes lie in choices that may appear irresponsible or irrational. Understanding the impact of poverty on what parents do, including the lack of choices open to them in many cases, is part of the process of understanding the problems parents face and the help that may be needed (Sharma and Hirsch 2007; Ridge 2009).

Poverty and coping behaviour

Coping behaviour is a way of dealing with stressful and demanding events and situations. Lazarus and Folkman (1984) defined coping as the 'cognitive and behavioural efforts used to manage a stressful situation and to manage the negative emotions that result from the stressful situation'. Coping is what people do to manage stressful events or situations in their lives, and includes any attempt or effort to manage stress, regardless of whether or not it solves the presenting problem. Context is an important determinant of whether or not a coping strategy will work. Stress that stimulates successful coping can enhance life, while stress that is overwhelming is damaging, so attempting to cope in contexts in which nothing much is likely to be helpful may in itself be unhelpful, making passivity arguably a rational 'coping strategy', although it is unlikely to ameliorate the situation. In some situations, simply avoiding making things worse may be the best that can be hoped for – echoing the comments made by a parent in Ridge's (2009) study about 'not looking forward'. The negative emotions resulting from unsuccessful attempts to cope may be difficult to manage (see Lazararus and Folkman's definition, above).

Coping behaviour can also form the basis of a virtuous cycle, whereby the fact of coping builds resilience for the future: '... when families have ample coping strategies, it provides for a stronger, more functional family unit' (Paster *et al.* 2009: 1338). Paster *et al.* researched the coping strategies of parents with disabled and non-disabled children. They found that stress that leads to *unsuccessful* attempts at coping damages families' ability to function. Lack of financial resources limits the range of coping strategies open to people even as it places additional demands on them. Family functioning may be affected by the stress placed on parents by their own inability to successfully 'problem solve' their family's difficulties.

Gillies (2005) discusses the way low-income parents, especially mothers, may be seen as being in poverty through individual failure, rather than because they are victims of the inequality of society. Gillies argues that the current emphasis on family support represents a 'top-down' projection of middle class values and standards on to families, supporting conformity while it promotes access to parenting resources. Adaptive coping responses by parents to address their specific and difficult circumstances may be misinterpreted as poor parenting. For example, providing computer games may be seen as demonstrating a lack of commitment to education and 'improving' activities, although to the parent it may be a way of offering interesting activities in the home when life outside is fraught with dangers: virtual reality may be safer.

This construction of parents living in poverty as 'poor parents' provides a rationale for increased state intervention in the lives of poor families; parents are responsible for a 'cycle of deprivation', which needs to be 'broken'. The idea of a 'cycle of deprivation' goes back to the Conservative government of the 1970s, when 'breaking the cycle' was a policy aim (Joseph 1975), and has continued to exert influence over policy planning ever since. While the intergenerational transmission of poverty, also conceptualised less oppressively as low social mobility, is a problem the UK needs to address at the policy level, care needs to be taken, when assessing individual parents, to attempt to understand the interplay between poverty, coping strategies and the exercise of choice, as well as the limitations imposed by environmental factors and any opportunities available.

The way in which problems are defined and constructed affects the kinds of solutions identified as desirable. If people experiencing poverty experience their problems as primarily linked to lack of income, but social workers define their problems as primarily about motivation, parenting skills, or other explanations for family difficulties, there is an evident lack of agreement about the kinds of approaches that are likely to be of use in solving the problem. The truth may lie closer to one explanation than the other, and probably often have elements of both. In this scenario, both types of difficulty need to be acknowledged to facilitate engagement with service providers.

Congruence and co-operation

Cleaver and Freeman (1995) developed the idea of the 'operational perspective': professionals describe events in particular ways to serve a particular function, such as the role of the account of events in child protection processes. If the operational perspective distorts the family's account of the problem, congruence is unlikely, unless there is tacit agreement to gloss over difficulties that no-one wishes to acknowledge: a very dangerous situation in child protection practice.

Platt (2007: 326) defines congruence as '... the consistency between a social worker's understanding of a family's circumstances and that of the parents or children'. Co-operation is associated with congruence: without a shared understanding of the problem, co-operation is likely to be lower, and where there is co-operation, compliance is likely to be superficial. Platt (2007) defines co-operation as the extent to which the social worker perceives family members to be working with services in a constructive and compliant manner – families would presumably use a different definition. Levels of congruence were found to be highest in cases where concerns are acute rather than chronic, and where concerns are about supporting families rather than child protection concerns. In other words, it is easier to reach agreement when the cause of the difficulty is recent and the problem is of sudden onset, and when adequacy of parenting is not identified as part of the problem by the social worker.

Farmer and Owen (1995) stress the importance of agreement being reached in child abuse cases, and discuss three dimensions to agreement:

- agreement about *commission*: whether or not abuse is substantiated;
- agreement about *culpability*: about who caused the abuse;
- agreement about *risk*: about whether the child remains at risk.

The level of agreement, about the problem and its causation, between worker and parent in the early stages of an investigation affects their continuing working relationship. Achieving congruence is important, but only if it can be achieved while maintaining a clear focus on the child, their needs, and any risk to the child (Platt 2007).

The precipitating factor for care proceedings is often the withdrawal of co-operation by a parent (Masson *et al.* 2008), although Dickens (2007) found that non-co-operation can also prevent care proceedings starting because it hampers the collection of evidence. Either way, loss of co-operation is unlikely to be beneficial for children. This does not mean that one should agree with the parents' account regardless of the evidence, but it does mean taking a respectful position with relation to the parents' understanding of the situation and acknowledging their perspective – including any understanding they have of the reason they have experienced difficulties in caring for their children, if such an acknowledgment is made. Identifying areas of congruence may be helpful. Platt (2007) describes congruence further:

- congruence over *what the problem is*;
- congruence over *what is needed to address the problem effectively* – including services that might be offered and taken up.

Co-operation also has different elements to it; various indicators that there is a 'working relationship' between the parents and the social worker. Booth *et al.* (2006: 1000) define co-operation as having three characteristics:

- acknowledgement of the seriousness of the worker's concerns;
- willingness to co-operate in addressing these concerns;
- commitment to change.

Platt's (2007) research suggests that social workers may sometimes believe that a good working relationship with a parent in itself confers some level of safety on their child. Failure to develop a reasonably trusting relationship with a parent may foreclose any opportunity to address the family's problems in partnership, but placing too high a priority on building a relationship with parents can undermine the focus on the welfare of the child. A good working relationship with parents may not be a reliable indicator that parents are likely to improve their childcare, but lack of agreement about the nature of any problems the family may have, and what should be done about them, makes for a poor prognosis for intervention. Parents and workers may see the significance of resources for the family's difficulties very differently.

Platt (2007) found almost no instances of complete lack of congruence between parents and workers where the issue was about children in need. This is different from the high levels of incongruence found by Cleaver and Freeman (1995) and Farmer and Owen (1995) in child protection cases, but even in Platt's study there was only one instance of 'complete' congruence. In the remaining cases, congruence was partial or apparent – congruence perceived by the parent while the worker had a wider agenda that was not shared by the parent. This suggests that apparent compliance may work in two directions: social workers as well as parents may give the appearance of holding more congruent views than they do in reality.

Platt (2007) depicts graphically how congruence, co-operation and good working relationships can support each other, but may also be represented as independent dimensions. Parent–worker relationships may be mapped against these two axes.

Conceptual gaps and practice wisdom

Strier and Binyamin (2010) critique the existing approach to anti-oppressive practice, arguing that there is a gap between the existing literature, which focuses on teaching anti-oppressive practice, and the way in which organisations and structures actually support such practices. They argue there is a mismatch between social work ethics, which value

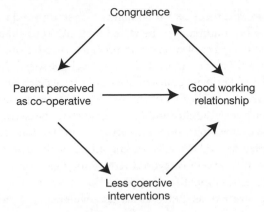

Source:Adapted from Platt (2007)

Figure 6.2 The interrelationship between congruence and co-operation

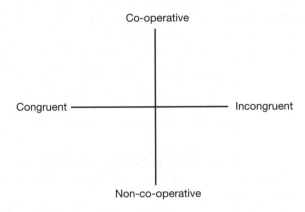

Source: Adapted from Platt (2007)

Figure 6.3 Assessment of co-operation and congruence

individuals, self-determination and respect for persons, and the ethos of the organisations in which many social workers are employed.

Strier and Binyamin (2010) note that various studies have found that those who use social services find them dehumanising, oppressive and bureaucratic; services have become increasingly focused on regulatory activities and reducing dependence on 'welfare' (Welbourne 2010), leading to the development of 'uncertainty, confusion and loss of understanding of role and purpose' in social work services (Carey 2008: 91, cited in Strier and Binyamin 2009: 4). Structures and organisations are designed to engage with service users in a way that emphasises individual responsibility. Problems are often defined in terms of deficiencies in parenting skills, even when a major component of the problem is a family resources issue. Different 'players' in the process of supporting a family may understand the issues differently, too, according to the ethos of their own organisation.

An example of the possible effects of this focus on individual responsibility and poverty comes from Broadhurst *et al.* (2007), who comment on the raised rates of s47 (child protection) referrals in areas in which the first wave of Sure Start projects were set up. These areas were specifically chosen because they were areas with high levels of social deprivation and poverty. Broadhurst *et al.* (2007) express concern about constructing the rise in s47 inquiries in these Sure Start areas as an indicator of the success of the early intervention/prevention approach to children's social inclusion. They argue that claims made by the National Evaluation of Sure Start team that an *increase* in child protection referrals and registrations are indicative of effective early intervention contradict the claim made for the Sure Start programme that early intervention would reduce the need for later and more coercive intervention by the state in family life. It appears that it has increased the rate of coercive intervention in the poorest areas, but there is also evidence that children in some Sure Start areas – which vary widely in their effectiveness – have received benefits in terms of health and developmental outcomes. The projects with the best integration with health services appear to have been the most effective in this regard (HCHC 2009). The economic evaluation of Sure Start programmes concluded that modest economic benefits to children had already been seen in Sure Start areas, but the full economic benefits would not be measurable for some time to come.

Box 6.2 Key messages from the National Evaluation of Sure Start Programmes: An Economic Perspective (National Evaluation of Sure Start Team 2011)

- On average, Sure Start local programmes (SSLPs) cost around £1,300 per eligible child per year at 2009/10 prices (or £4,860 per eligible child over the period from birth to the age of four).
- The economic benefits of early childhood interventions can be high, but they typically do not emerge until at least fifteen years after the intervention begins.
- By the time children reached the age of five, SSLPs had already delivered economic benefits of between £279 and £557 per eligible child. These benefits relate to the fact that parents living in SSLP areas moved into paid work more quickly than parents in comparison areas.
- There are several other small scale positive outcomes of SSLPs as measured at the age of five years, which have the potential to generate economic benefits in the future. These outcomes are:
  - less harsh discipline in the home;
  - lower rates of family chaos;
  - a richer home learning environment.
- There was also one potential source of negative economic impact: mothers living in SSLP areas reported higher rates of depression. Maternal depression s associated with children developing behavioural problems and with lower hool attainment.

The foregoing suggests that integrated services can have a positive impact for ch at risk of poor outcomes, partly through increasing access to universal service, as health services. In doing so, they may 'sweep up' more families whose children are suffering significant harm related to abuse and neglect, occurring in the context of a life in poverty. Referral through the medium of child protection referrals may or may not have been appropriate in individual cases, but s47 does not necessarily always equate to 'coercive' intervention beyond the assessment itself. If families are engaged to accept help, and the help that is offered seems to the family to have value: tailored to support them and address felt need, the level of coercion for the parents may be subjectively very low. If service providers have little to offer that the family want, the level of coercion may remain high. The quality of dialogue about the causes of, and possible remedies for, childcare problems, and the quality and relevance of service provision locally available, will be factors – though not the only determinants – in shaping how compulsory services are in practice.

Is there an association between poverty, and child abuse and neglect?

There is an association between social work interventions with children and families and poverty: the majority of users of child and family social work services are living in low-income families. However, the nature of the relationship between these two factors is not known: it is possible that people on low incomes are subject to higher levels of scrutiny and professionals are therefore more likely to detect and refer child protection concerns in low-income families. The evidence from the first wave of Sure Start centres – discussed on page 106 – supports the idea that higher levels of 'policing' of the childcare practices of low-income families may be partly responsible for identifying larger numbers of children at risk of harm. This describes a reporting bias towards poorer families. It is also possible that the range of psychological and social pressures that accompany financial and social stress make it harder to be a parent. Some parents with histories of personal difficulty may be vulnerable to both poverty and problems with parenting. Possibly all three factors operate to some extent to contribute to a situation in which children living in poor environments and in families on low incomes make up a disproportionately large number of children on social work caseloads. Set against this is the large number of families living in poverty who provide good parenting, against the odds: it is emphatically stated here that poverty does not, of itself, make for worse parenting.

Statistics from child protection intervention data show a higher rate of all types of abuse in children of parents living in poor environments. Key points from a recent Dyson (2008) study on poverty and child maltreatment are set out below:

- A number of prevalence and incidence studies have highlighted the link between poverty and child maltreatment, especially neglect, emotional and physical abuse.
- While research shows an association between neglect and poverty, it does not mean that poverty causes neglect or abuse. The majority of families living in poverty do not maltreat their children and parent effectively.
- There are no large-scale studies that specifically examine the nature of the relationship between poverty and child maltreatment in the UK, but the most common

explanation centres on the stress factors associated with poverty and social deprivation, which are further compounded if drug misuse and mental health issues come into play.

Dyson 2008: 1

The same report also states that:

Children who experience both poverty and maltreatment are doubly disadvantaged because the experience of maltreatment may in turn further undermine life chances in the long term. While there is a vast amount of research on poverty and the link to maltreatment, there is a dearth of research in the UK exploring the nature of the relationship between the two.

Dyson 2008: 2

The double jeopardy of abuse or neglect linked with poverty is a situation that appears to be particularly high risk for children, both for their long-term outcomes and for their safety in the short term. It appears from the various high-profile inquiries into child abuse, and others that are less well known, that abuse in the context of poverty gives legitimate cause for concern about child safety, especially when it is compounded by other difficulties such as drug or alcohol problems, mental health difficulties, domestic violence. These appear to be predisposing factors for the relatively rare examples of very serious abuse and neglect (Brandon *et al.* 2008a; Rose and Barnes 2008). However, evidence also supports the idea that less serious, but still significant, neglect and physical and emotional abuse is linked to income:

... about one-third of all respondents ... agreed with the statement that 'there were always a lot of worries about shortage of money' in their families when they were children, but this proportion rose to 65 per cent among those who had experienced serious physical abuse or serious neglect, and 71 per cent of those who had experienced emotional maltreatment.

Dyson 2008: 15

There was also an association between young adults' economic status and a history of abuse: compared with respondents in professional jobs, those working in semi-skilled or unskilled jobs were three times more likely to have suffered serious physical abuse, and ten times more likely to have experienced a serious absence of care in childhood.

Bifulco and Moran (1998) found that women from poor childhood homes were twice as likely to have suffered abuse or neglect than those from homes that were not poor (77 per cent versus 38 per cent), and when more than one form of abuse had been experienced, the association between abuse and poverty was even stronger. Forty-five per cent of the women they talked to who came from poor childhood homes experienced more than one form of abuse compared with 15 per cent of those who had not experienced poverty. The association between abuse, and poverty appears to be stronger when abuse is a more serious problem, at least in terms of the range of kinds of abuse experienced by children. However, single types of abuse occur relatively rarely: most abuse occurs as part of a spectrum of types of abuse, and combinations of abuse are commonly observed where abuse occurs at all.

The interactions between poverty and child abuse are complex. It seems likely that most abuse goes unreported. Sneddon *et al.* (2010) found no association between women's socio-economic status and a history of maltreatment, except for physical abuse. Occupational status was not linked with a history of emotional or sexual abuse, or emotional or physical neglect. Simply knowing whether abuse did or did not take place is also only part of the story:

> Unpicking the shared variance between different subtypes of maltreatment is complex and challenging. Many other variables influence the impact on the child such as frequency, intensity and duration of abuse, as well as the relationship with the perpetrator and how the victim perceives the abuse.
>
> Sneddon *et al.* 2010: 42

We have seen that there is good evidence that poverty and child abuse are associated in some way, although how we should understand that connection is still not entirely known. There are different possibilities:

- Poverty itself impairs parenting capacity, given the challenges poor parents face in terms of daily survival and the limited resources available to them.
- The reason some parents are in poverty is because they themselves have had difficult early lives which have placed them in a 'cycle of deprivation': their early deprivation has made it harder for them to acquire or use essential parenting skills.
- Some parents have made lifestyle choices, including using drugs or alcohol, which prevent them from escaping poverty, or actively place them in poverty and additionally impact on their ability to parent their children.

In summary, there is an association between poverty and child abuse, but it is a complex one. Only some kinds of abuse may be more likely in poor families, although it may be more easily detected in poorer families skewing the picture. There may also be an association with severity or chronicity of abuse, but research has yet to answer these questions satisfactorily.

The Child Poverty Act 2010

In 2008 the then Labour government published its '2020 vision' for ending child poverty in the UK, '... a UK where children grow up free from deprivation and disadvantage, and birth and social background do not hold people back from achieving their potential' (HM Treasury 2008: 15). The 'vision' covered a range of measures to combat child poverty, including encouraging people into employment, revision of the system of income support, and professional intervention to address some of the cultural and behavioural effects of poverty on families:

> ... the child must be at the centre of a joined up approach to services, with professionals and front line workers playing a key role ... families should be supported by both universal and targeted services that are non-stigmatising and provide families with the support to break cycles of poverty and raise aspirations ... preventative services

[should] ensure that families get the support they need before they reach crisis point ... [and it should be] culturally acceptable to ask for help and for professionals to challenge behaviour.

HM Treasury 2008: 14

There is a potentially strong role for social work here as part of preventative services providing 'home-based intervention in which both support and challenge are an integral part of the approach to families on low incomes' (HM Treasury 2008: 15).

The Child Poverty Act 2010 contains a commitment to eradicate child poverty by 2020, and attempts to bind future governments to pursue this aim, by ensuring that, '... sustained action must be taken to tackle child poverty by this, and future, governments, by the devolved administrations, and by local government and their partners' (Department for Education 2011). The Secretary of State has to account for progress towards what are described as 'challenging targets', or any lack of progress. It applies to England, Scotland and Northern Ireland; Wales has already begun making its own arrangements to address child poverty (the Children and Families (Wales) Measure) and so is not included in the 2010 Act. Child poverty strategies prepared by all the Devolved Administrations must be considered in future UK child poverty strategies.

The key elements of the 2020 plan are, in summary:

- more parents to be encouraged to join the workforce as a route out of poverty;
- revision of the system of Income Support with a view to reducing further the number of children in poverty;
- preventative services targeting families in poverty, to be non-stigmatising but challenging when needed.

The Act sets a number of targets. Section 1 sets out the '2010 target': the number of children living in 'relative low income' families (see below) in the financial year beginning 1 April 2010 should be 1.7 million children or fewer. The Secretary of State must report to Parliament by June 2012 on whether or not this target has been met; and if it has not, why it has not.

This section of the Act also sets a benchmark for future progress, against which future levels of relative low income and progress against the 2020 targets may be measured: a 'snapshot' against which the combined impact of the broader range of government and other policies and other factors, including global economic factors, may be measured. This is designed to provide an 'accountability framework' and a focus and motivation for future change.

The Act sets out a further four child poverty targets to be met by 2020:

- Relative low income: by 2010, less than 10 per cent of children will live in relatively low-income families;
- Combined low income and material deprivation: by 2020, no more than 5 per cent of children will live in such households;
- Absolute low income: no more than 5 per cent of children in this group by 2020;
- Persistent poverty: no target set yet.

This makes measurement complex, but is designed capture the many facets of child poverty: it is a complex phenomenon. The *relative low-income group* comprises households with net income that is less than 60 per cent of median net household income. (The EU defines relative poverty as 50 per cent of median income or less.)

The *low-income and material deprivation group* includes children living in households whose net income is less than 70 per cent of median household income and in 'material deprivation', which has yet to be defined in regulations to accompany the Act. The aim is to capture some wider aspect of children's living standards to include, for example, the availability of money for heating, or family celebrations. A family with higher income but high necessary expenditure related to, for example, disability, might be included (House of Lords 2009: 14, 42, 45).

The *absolute low-income group* includes households with income that is less than 60 per cent of an adjusted amount linked to changes in the value of money, to measure poverty against a measure that is held constant over time. This is important in times of recession or growth, when median incomes may change significantly.

Persistent poverty is defined as being in a household that falls within one of the first three groups for three out of four consecutive years: there is no target for this as yet.

The Secretary of State must develop a UK strategy to address child poverty, and consider which groups of children in the United Kingdom appear to be disproportionately affected by socio-economic disadvantage, and consider the likely impact of each measure on children within each of those groups (Child Poverty Act 2010 Section 9). The national Child Poverty Strategy must be reviewed and updated every three years until 2020. In addition, the Government must provide Parliament with an annual report on progress.

The Act creates a Child Poverty Commission, and places a duty on the Secretary of State to lay before Parliament a UK strategy for addressing child poverty, in accordance with the targets in the Act. The advice given to the Government by the Commission must be published.

Since the '2020 vision' was published, a new government has been elected in Britain, and a review of poverty in Britain has been commissioned, chaired by Labour MP Frank Field. Field has stated his intention of choosing a different way of defining poverty, moving away from the 'relative poverty' definition that links it to 50 per cent – for EU statistics – or 60 per cent of median income – the UK 'relative low income' definition – to introduce some other measure, unknown at the time of writing. Field is on record as saying that he intends the new measure will be '… a more meaningful goal in terms of income, and to link it to the non-monetary factors that are crucial to the successful nurturing of children' (Field 2010a).

This recognises that poverty has more wide-reaching effects than can be measured by looking at patterns of family spending alone, but the decision to look for another definition of poverty that differs from that used in the European Union and the 2010 Act would make both European comparisons and comparisons over time problematic. The first measure, relative low income, was chosen to be consistent with European measures and allow international comparisons: 'Measures of relative low income are widely used in industrial nations, and this is the most widely watched indicator in the European Union' (House of Lords 2009: 14). From this, one can see that while poverty is clearly a political issue, even the definition used to identify its presence and levels in society is a highly political issue.

It is true that the impact of poverty on children is moderated by numerous factors. Children of poor but capable parents, who are highly committed to their children, appear to be shielded from the worst effects of poverty, because many parents will go without themselves rather than let their children be undernourished, and parents are often creative in the use of limited resources. Extended family and friends may also buffer the worst effects of poverty on children. Children of parents on low incomes who spend unwisely, perhaps incurring onerous debts or servicing expensive addictions, have much poorer prospects in terms of their material circumstances. This does not, however, seem to make it any less important to know how many parents are having to use ingenuity or call on family and friends to cope with the material demands of parenting, nor how many children are affected by that daily struggle to provide, whether managed well or badly.

The Child Poverty Strategy 2011

In April 2011 the UK government published the document *A New Approach to Child Poverty: Tackling the causes of disadvantage and transforming families' lives*. Within it is the first governmental Child Poverty Strategy (DWP/DfE 2011). The foreword, by Ian Duncan-Smith, sets the tone. This strategy is based on the belief that, '[p]overty is about more than income, it is about a lack of opportunity, aspiration and stability' and the remedy for this problem is primarily to be through paid employment, 'First, we must ensure that families can work themselves out of poverty – if they do the right thing we will make sure the system makes work pay' (DWP/DfE 2011: foreword).

Only the most severely disabled parents are not expected to work. They should be supported to live 'with dignity'. The Foreword continues:

> We recognise that some families face complex barriers to work, many of which cause intergenerational disadvantage. To address the root causes of poverty we will deliver early and effective interventions through the Work Programme targeted at vulnerable groups. All families should benefit, where possible, from the opportunities of employment. ... Our proposed design should enable most families with children who have a parent in full time employment to have an income that lifts them out of poverty. The same should apply for lone parents who work at least 24 hours per week or more.

> DWP/DfE 2011: 3

Local authorities are to receive a pot of funding, the Early Intervention Grant, that will not be ring-fenced and is to be used to address persistent child poverty in local communities. The advantage of such a scheme is that it offers local authorities flexibility to explore local need and consider what they can do to help the most vulnerable children, young people and the most disadvantaged families in their area (DWP/DfE 2011: 36). The intention is that a 'joined up approach' will be used, so social workers could potentially have new opportunities to intervene with the most vulnerable children and their families in their area. There is no specific mention of social work. Community Budgets will act as pooled funding to develop 'innovative, integrated solutions to difficult problems'.

The disadvantages of this approach appear twofold: first, funding which is not ring-fenced may be used to support other urgent needs, and second, the fragmented approach which will inevitably follow from lack of clear guidance as to how the money should be spent means that a situation will arise that replicates early Sure Start projects: local diversity means that systematic and reliable study of the effects of the strategy will be almost impossible (DWP/DfE 2011: 52).

Local authorities are to lead partnership working in their area 'to reduce and mitigate the effects of child poverty through the development of child poverty needs assessments and local child poverty strategies ... [which must] strike the right balance between giving local authorities the freedom and discretion they need to get things done, whilst protecting the most vulnerable people' (DWP/DfE 2011: 56). All areas must have needs assessments and strategies in place 'to drive their priorities on addressing child poverty' (DWP/DfE 2011: 65). The range of issues the local strategies must address include 'educational failure; worklessness; family breakdown; severe debt; and health issues, such as alcohol and drug addiction' (DWP/DfE 2011: 63).

The current pattern of consumption of benefits in kind – that is, not money or subsidies – by income is set out in graphical format in Field (2010b: 80):

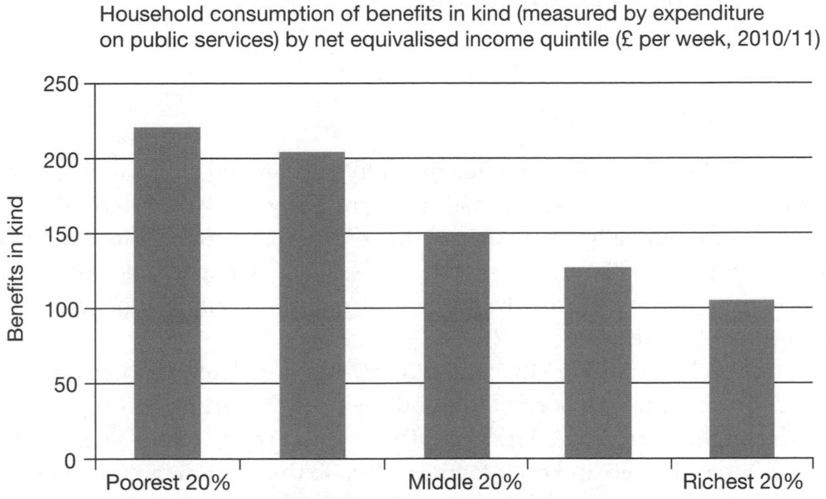

Household consumption of benefits in kind (measured by expenditure on public services) by net equivalised income quintile (£ per week, 2010/11)

Source: Annex B of the October Spending Review. Permission to reproduce kindly granted by Frank Field MP

Note: The analysis covers around two thirds of resource DEL expenditure consisting of many of the services delivered by The Department of Health; The Department for Education; The Department for Work and Pensions; The Department for Communities and Local Government; The Department for Business, Innovation and Skills; The Department for Transport; The Department for Energy and Climate Change; Local Government; The Ministry of Justice; and The Department for Culture, Media and Sport. It excludes the Devolved Administrations.

Figure 6.4 Household consumption of benefits in kind

What this demonstrates is that benefits in kind are an important contribution to the welfare of children in every kind of family: the richest 20 per cent of families consume half the level consumed by the poorest 20 per cent. They are, appropriately, used more heavily by the poorest families, but all children benefit from public services in kind. Given this, the existence of 'stigmatising' services seems unnecessary.

> Reflecting an increasing professionalization of childrearing practices, recent policy documents have emphasized the need for all parents to have access to support, advice and guidance. Implicit in this approach is the notion that 'socially excluded' parents in particular are isolated from the information and assistance that enables effective parenting.
>
> Gillies 2005: 70

Sure Start was an attempt to de-stigmatise or 'normalise' service use, so we should perhaps not be quick to criticise 'middle class colonisation' of targeted services, as long as this does not make them less accessible to families with the lowest incomes (Sheppard *et al.* 2008). If the Child Poverty Strategy is successful, we should see both targeted and universal services developed further to address the causes of poverty, while it has been promised that an overhauled benefits system will help more parents to move out of poverty through what promises to be further development of the 'welfare to work' approach which started with the New Deal programmes of the late 1990s onwards (Daguerre and Taylor-Gooby 2004).

Conclusion: poverty and social work

Parents bringing up children in poor environments often have limited access to informal support and make only limited use of semi-formal and formal services, although those that do use formal services are generally satisfied with the service they receive. Most parents bringing up children in poverty manage against the odds, showing remarkable optimism against a background of substantial disadvantage, and managing family finances well despite very low incomes (Ghate and Hazel 2002).

On the other hand, children who are living in poverty are more likely than other children to be 'in need' because the lack of resources and the pressure this places on parents, who may have vulnerabilities of their own. The effects of poverty are easily overlooked in assessments of children in need and their families, despite the prominence of environmental factors in the 'assessment triangle' (Jack and Gill 2003). The third, 'forgotten', side of the triangle (Jack and Gill 2003) adds detail and depth to the issues explored under the Parenting Capacity dimension. While abuse and neglect are established matters of concern for child and family social workers, poverty can become the 'wallpaper' that is clearly visible but seldom considered.

The *Framework for Assessment* (DH 2000) requires social workers to consider the effect of interaction between the different factors that influence the quality of parenting and childhood experience along all three dimensions of the Assessment Framework. Poverty, its effects, and sometimes its causes, are vulnerability factors for many of the children who come in contact with social workers. A recent Serious Case Review report (Cantrill 2009) concluded: 'There is no evidence that a generic assessment was undertaken that looked at the fact that the children as well as experiencing physical and emotional abuse were also living in poverty.' It is arguably an unspoken norm in social work that responsible parents are expected to take steps to protect their children from the effects of poverty through careful use of scarce resources. They are expected to show economic resourcefulness and restraint, a test parents with more money at their disposal do not have to pass. Assessments and interventions need to take account of all relevant aspects of children's experience and, if they are living in poverty, their economic circumstances are likely to be highly relevant in understanding the care they receive, their environment, their development, their well-being and their life chances.

The Child Poverty Act 2010 is highly relevant for social work. It attempts to address the material difficulties experienced by so many children who are social work service users by requiring local authorities to put strategies in place to address those difficulties. Social workers should be key contributors to exploring patterns of poverty, developing strategies to address poverty and its effects, and implementing and evaluating the effectiveness of those strategies. Whether social work becomes a key player or not depends on the profession's ability to establish itself as having professional expertise in this area. Given its role working at the interface between families and their environments, and its concern for social change and problem solving (IASSW/IFSW 2000), this is an opportunity to be pursued with purpose.

Part 2

Social work and the management of risk, and support for colleagues

7 Risk in child and family social work, part 1

The idea of risk and uncertainty in social work

... risk is the necessary accompaniment of the transformation of a society of pawns, directed at the whim of the gods, into a society of actors managing their own destiny.

Rothstein *et al.* 2006

This chapter:

- considers what is meant by the idea of 'risk' in the context of child and family social work;
- looks at how social workers might approach thinking about risk during the assessment process;
- discusses how experienced practitioners may use reflective judgement to enhance their practice in assessing risk.

Introduction: risk assessment and 'changing the odds' for vulnerable children and young people

Risk assessment is closely tied to a belief that we can 'change the odds' in risky situations. An assessment of risk is generally carried out to ascertain what the level of risk is in relation to a particular risk factor, so that something can be done – assuming the level of risk identified warrants action. It implies an active approach to risk: risks are not things to be accepted passively, but things that can be manipulated, managed and sometimes avoided altogether. It is useful to assess risk if we believe we can do something about it once we have assessed it. We can seek to change the odds of an adverse event happening by taking steps to try to prevent the event happening in the first place, or, if this is not possible, by putting measures in place to limit damage if it does happen.

Different ways of thinking about risk assessment: actuarial and clinical risk assessment

Munro (2008) discusses the difference between actuarial and clinical risk assessment. She suggests that actuarial risk assessment, based on instruments that rely on research into the factors most commonly found to accompany child abuse, has limited value in predicting which children are at risk of abuse, partly because of the large number of false positives they are likely to generate. A false positive in this context is an instance of a family being identified as abusive when they are not, in fact, abusive. Limitations of actuarial assessments may be a matter of the level of development of actuarial assessments currently available: in future, better-validated actuarial assessments may have greater predictive value. At present most risk assessment relies primarily upon clinical judgement.

> Overall, actuarial instruments seem to have great potential for assisting professionals in making assessments of risk by providing a formal means of computing the best available evidence on risk factors. However, they require very extensive testing before they can be relied upon. They also play only a small part in the overall management of a case, providing a judgement about the probability of harm at a particular point in time.
>
> Munro 2008: 71

Different levels of risk are seen as acceptable for different types of risk. Certain activities and situations have defined risks attached to them but people find them and the associated level of risk acceptable. Hill walking is one such. There is a 'trade-off' between the level of risk and the consequences if the adverse event happens. Farmer (1981) argued that high probability adverse events are acceptable to people if the adverse consequences are small, as in the case of hill walking. The greater the negative consequences, the less likely the risk will be considered acceptable, described by the 'Farmer Curve' plotting severity against public tolerance. We tolerate the risk of a nuclear accident in a nuclear power station because we believe the probability of such an accident happening to be very low, although the consequences would be very severe. The 'Farmer Curve' defines acceptable risks. In child protection, this means that the more severe the likely consequences of an 'adverse event', such as a parent seriously harming a child, the less likely we are to tolerate even a very low probability of it happening. This may explain why neglect has been seen as 'neglected' (NSPCC 2007): although the cumulative effect of long-term physical and emotional neglect on a child may be very severe, the effect of each isolated incident of neglect may be hard to identify against a background of barely adequate care the rest of the time. Risk is not just about objective probabilities; it is also about our own subjective feeling that something is 'safe enough', or not. Neglected children may be less likely to trigger a 'risk management' response from those who see them, especially if they do so regularly.

Theories about how risk may be assessed may not correspond to what social workers actually do in practice, however. Nevo and Slonim-Nevo (2011) discuss evidence-based practice (EBP) and evidence-informed practice (EIP). They quote Jenson's (2007) definition of EBP as '... a process that requires practitioners to identify, evaluate, and apply evidence pertaining to a client's problem to subsequent practice decisions' (Jenson 2007: 571). Horwath (2006) explores the importance of the 'missing' psychological domain in professionals' decision making. Personal, professional and organisational factors are all potential sources of influences in deciding what is 'high risk', as is the practitioner's own value base and intuition. She states: '... assessment practice is as much a practice-moral activity as a technical-rational one. In other words, it is both a head and a heart activity' (Horwath 2006: 1285). Factors affecting practitioner's judgements about neglect include:

- the practitioner's own perception of what comprises neglect;
- the extent to which 'gut feelings' influence their judgement;
- their interpretation of their role and the views of their colleagues and team manager;
- their perception of social work services; and
- their own personal feelings such as guilt, fear, over-empathy and anxiety about the response of the community.

As a result, assessment tools such as the *Framework for the Assessment of Children in Need and their Families* (DH 2000) can only go so far towards making child protection practice 'safe', because professional judgements involve:

- interpretive use of knowledge;
- practical wisdom; and
- a sense of purpose, appropriateness and feasibility.

Horwath 2006; Erault 1994

How do people think about risk, and why do we sometimes get it wrong?

Slovic *et al.* (2002) suggest that science indicates that that there are two fundamental ways in which human beings comprehend risk. One of them is *analytic thinking*, which is relatively slow, effortful, and requires conscious control. Analytic thinking about risk is essentially a risk factor approach: it uses formal logic, calculations of probability and assessment against known risk factors. The other way in which we comprehend risk is *experiential*: drawing on images and associations that are linked to feelings and moods. It is 'natural' and instinctive, and used much more commonly to make everyday judgements about whether or not to do something we perceive as risky. Slovic *et al.* (2002) argue that it is a mistake to view this type of response to risk as irrational: we need both types of reasoning to respond effectively to risk. Both rational and experiential risk assessment has something useful to tell us. We need 'feeling' responses as well as 'cold' rationality: rational decision making involves both kinds of response because, without feeling and emotion, we may be less well equipped to analyse the risks we are weighing. The emotional response helps us to engage with the risk and seek ways of dealing with it but, if there is too much emotion, it may impede the slow, effortful process of analytic risk analysis. Rational and emotional responses complement each other.

Reason (2000) considered the reasons people make errors. Errors are most likely to be noticed when they have serious consequences: reviews of Serious Case Reviews are examples of cases in which any errors identified are likely to be causally linked to the death of or serious injury to a child. By contrast, a culture of examining 'near misses' looks at cases in which errors may have been made but where other factors prevent the harm from happening. Reliability is a 'dynamic non-event': when timely human adjustments prevent errors happening, the avoidance of error attracts little attention.

Reason (2000: 768) describes the problem of human error as being capable of being viewed in two ways: the *person approach* and the *system approach*.

Reason argues that one of the reasons the 'person' approach is common is that finding an individual to blame is psychologically satisfying. It also has the advantage of concentrating

---

Box 7.1 Ways of viewing human error

- *The person approach*: focuses on the errors of individuals, blaming them for forgetfulness, inattention, or moral weakness. It focuses on errors and violations of procedure. Errors are attributed to carelessness, fatigue, inattention, and other human failures. Responses to errors are targeted at the practitioners at the 'sharp end' – disciplinary measures, new procedures, strategies for increasing the anxiety of practitioners about their performance, such as 'naming and shaming' those who do not meet certain performance criteria. This is a well-established way of responding to errors. It is associated with a moral analysis that holds individuals to blame for their mistakes: 'bad things happen to bad people'.

- *The system approach*: concentrates on the conditions under which individuals work and tries to build defences to avert errors or mitigate their effects. Humans are fallible and errors to be expected, even in the best organisations. Errors are consequences of human fallibility in an environmental context, rather than fallibility per se causing the errors: errors have their origins in 'upstream' systemic factors as well as in human characteristics. Workplaces and organisational processes have 'error traps' built in to them: processes that create 'traps' which make errors more likely, or less avoidable. Countermeasures are aimed at changing the conditions under which people work to reduce error traps and build in system defences. When an adverse event occurs, the important issue is not who blundered, but how and why the defences failed.

---

blame on one person, or a small number of people, leaving others free from blame. Organisations may prefer it to the more effective approach of identifying ways in which the system can change to prevent recurrence of the same mistake. 'Seeking as far as possible to uncouple a person's unsafe acts from any institutional responsibility is clearly in the interests of managers. It is also legally more convenient, at least in Britain' (Reason 2000: 768). The 'person' approach fails to address the system deficiencies that were the necessary context for that error being made, and offers no motivation to search for patterns of errors that might give important information about defects in the organisational system.

Reason (2000) suggests that the best people often make the worst mistakes, and this is sometimes attributable to the positions they are put in: blaming individuals is not as morally sound as it appears.

> Child protection work is not 'straightforward'. The [Laming] Report says, 'I am convinced that the answer lies in doing relatively straightforward things well'... In this I think it is right, in so far as not doing the straightforward things in child protection work can have disastrous consequences ... It is wrong in that beyond a certain point, there is nothing straightforward about most child protection work ... and here is the first of many missing links in the report. A significant factor in explaining why competent people may not manage to do the straightforward thing is that the very

unstraightforward nature of the daily task may, under certain circumstances, easily derail them from doing the blindingly obvious. Here, quite simply, we are in the area of ... the 'human factor'.

Cooper 2005: 4

Reason (2000) compared accidents in systems to events that have evaded various accident-prevention strategies at different levels in the organisation, which he compares to overlapping slices of Swiss cheese with holes in it. If there are several layers of slices, the likelihood of a serious error is low, because if the error slips through a 'hole' in one layer, there is a high probability that it will be picked up and prevented at the next layer.

Hazards, or risks, or threats, only become losses, or accidents, or serious incidents if accident-preventing mechanisms fail at every level of the organisation at once.

Reason described two types of error: *active failures* are those failures made by people in direct contact with service users, patients, or systems. They are the slips, errors and lapses of attention that are inevitable because error is a human characteristic. Usually they bring about nothing worse than a short-term vulnerability in the system's defences, only occasionally is the result disastrous. *Latent conditions for error* are part of the context for disastrous mistakes: flawed procedures, workloads that are too high, equipment inadequate for its purpose. If the latent conditions for error are addressed, the organisation becomes more reliable: better able to withstand human errors and avoid adverse events. Reason suggests that workers not worrying about 'system failure' may reduce safety, but a robust organisation has systems to make up for this:

Individuals may forget to be afraid, but the culture of a high reliability organisation provides them with both the reminders and the tools to help them remember. For

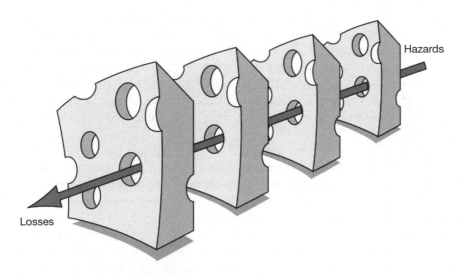

Source: Adapted from Reason (2000)

Figure 7.1 Systems of layered accident prevention

these organisations, the pursuit of safety is not so much about preventing isolated failures, either human or technical, as about making the system as robust as is practicable in the face of its human and operational hazards. High reliability organisations are not immune to adverse events, but they have learnt the knack of converting these occasional setbacks into enhanced resilience of the system.

Reason 2000: 770

Reason's model for understanding error was developed by looking at errors in medicine and the nuclear and aviation industries. Its applicability to social work has been identified (Munro 2010a; Broadhurst *et al.* 2010b). Broadhurst *et al.* (2010b) argue that high workloads generating constant anxiety, together with computer systems that add to the pressure but do not facilitate case management, create a situation of 'latent error'. Systems designed to make children safer can, it is argued, have the perverse effect of undermining the effectiveness of safeguarding processes if they are not appropriate for the task to be completed with the resources available.

Making judgements about risk: taking the wider context into account

In parenting, the day-to-day atmosphere of family life is critical. Parents probably do things that can be construed as 'abusive' at some level on a frequent basis, but much of this has little lasting effect on children because any potential negative effects are buffered by their mainly positive experience of being parented. While a dismissive comment by a tired parent to a child may be the same kind of comment an emotionally abusive parent might make, within the context of secure and loving parenting the risk of harm to the child is negligible. The important issue is whether the parent's behaviour is likely to cause significant harm to the child. The characteristics of the child, the behaviour of the parent and the wider parenting context all affect the answer.

Risk management in social work is about mitigation as well as prevention. Some children will already have experienced harm before they meet a social worker and, for them, any risk assessment will need to consider how that harm may impact on their present and future welfare, and what steps might be taken to reduce it. Risk assessments are not carried out just to assess the level of risk, but to inform the process of 'changing the odds' for the child from a prognosis that is poor to one in which the child is supported to become more healthy, more successful, more happy, more integrated into society and more resilient (DCSF 2011).

Risk assessments are inevitably based on *theory*. They are about cause and effect: we have views about what is likely to cause harm to a child, and what will help them to grow into happy, integrated members of society. Risk assessments are also closely tied up with social expectations of appropriate parental behaviour. They are also therefore based on *values*. Recent years have seen an increasing emphasis on the importance of *evidence*: evidence about situations that are high risk for children, such as studies of Serious Case Reviews, and from evidence-based practice (Ofsted 2008, 2009, 2010, 2011, and see below). The assessment of risk indicates we wish to take control of risk – to 'manage our own destiny', as Rothstein suggests in the quotation at the beginning of the chapter. Theory, values and evidence – which support or challenge our theories – are the tools we use in trying to manage our own destiny and, in child and family social work, to 'manage the destiny' of vulnerable children. This is why the collection of evidence is only the first step in carrying out a risk assessment.

For most social workers, working with children, young people and their families at an experienced practitioner level, assessment of risk is probably an integral part of their professional role. All social workers need to be aware of potential risks to children and young people, whatever setting they work in, and to be able to respond confidently and competently to safeguard them when appropriate. In other chapters of this book we explore some of the specific settings and knowledge that social workers may use in making risk assessments. In this chapter, we consider some underpinning ideas about risk and focus on it as a subject for reflection in its own right.

Risk is about coping in an uncertain world: finding strategies for making sense of uncertainty, and using this as the basis for managing it, as far as possible. Risk assessments often raise questions of choice – how much risk is considered tolerable, and how that risk is to be managed. At the same time that they are assessing risk, social workers must respect people's right to make their own decisions and choices when these do not infringe the rights of others. They must respect the rights of children and young people to form their own views on what they would like to do or have done on their behalf, on the basis of accurate and age-appropriate information, and to communicate those views, and ensure their wishes and feelings are respected when decisions are being made about them. Risk assessment may be something that is done *to* people, or can be something that is done *with* them (Stanley 2007). Being responsible for carrying out a risk assessment does not imply that the sole responsibility for making decisions about risk rests with the social worker, although in child protection cases where risk is high and the person at risk is very vulnerable, the local authority may have to take some critical decisions that go against the views of parents or children. Working in partnership with parents means that, usually, the content of any risk assessment will be shared with parents and, where appropriate, with the children concerned.

Risk assessment is, itself, an inherently risky business. The assessment may be judged to have been flawed if things do not happen as was suggested was most likely, but assessments of risk are inherently probabilistic; they are not statements of certainty about the future, but statements about what is *likely* to happen. They are essentially an attempt to make predictions about the unpredictable, but this does not mean they have no value. However, it does mean that it is unrealistic, even irrational, to expect them to be 'proved right' in every case. Risk assessment should be approached in a structured, systematic and reflective way to maximise the usefulness of the knowledge that we do have, and minimise danger, arbitrariness and injustice, but risk is, as discussed elsewhere in this chapter, unavoidable.

Risk factors are useful in inverse relationship to their prevalence in the general population (Munro 2008). If a risk factor is very common in the general population, it has lower predictive value for identifying children at risk of abuse. The example Munro uses is poverty. This is strongly associated with abuse in the sense that many of those families in which abuse and neglect are identified are living in poverty, but has very low predictive power because most families living in poverty do not abuse their children. A risk factor has higher predictive value when it is uncommon in the general population and common in the abusive population. Relying on risk factors too much can lead to 'false positives' where families in which children are not abused become involved in the child protection system.

A risk assessment must first identify the different aspects of a 'risky' situation: what is it that someone – the referrer, the social worker, a parent – is worried about? What might happen? Or might be happening? Having identified what the perceived risks are, they need to be placed in the context of the family and its wider environment: information from the *Framework for Assessment* (DH 2000) and/or s47 investigation[1] provides information about the child, their family and their social context. Questions specifically about risk that should be addressed – even if the answer is not clear at this point – include:

- What does the evidence tell us about the likelihood that the adverse event(s) have happened, are happening or will happen in the future? How urgent or threatening do we feel this situation to be?
- How severe do we think the probable consequences of such adverse events might be for the child/young person, and anyone else we are concerned about who is important for the child's well-being?
- What are the aims of intervention? Are we trying to prevent something from happening, or are we looking to improve outcomes for a child in an ongoing 'risky' situation – for example, neglect?
- What can we do about the risks that have been identified? What are the available options? What resources do we have to use in this situation?
- How imminent or pressing is the risk? How much time have we got to explore options? What is the 'timescale for the child' in this situation?
- What is the likely impact on the level of risk to the child of the different courses of action open to us?
- What other – desirable and undesirable – effects might the various options have? (For example, removal of a child from the family home might reduce the level of risk to the child dramatically, but have other undesirable consequences that need to be taken into account – even though they may not prevent this from being the best available course of action).

In the following section we explore some of these ideas about the meaning of 'risk' and the way we respond to it in more detail.

What do we mean by 'risk'?

Risk is measurable in terms of the interaction between two factors: first, the likelihood that something – usually negative – may take place, and, second, the likely severity of the consequences if that something does happen. While the event that is being considered could in theory be 'good' or 'bad', riskiness is usually associated with negative outcomes.

Risk is invoked when we do not know what will happen in future but fear possible negative consequences of present or anticipated future events. Risk is therefore about *uncertainty*. We may use statistics to calculate how likely an unpredictable event is, and those calculations are a way of capturing our uncertainty.

Risk assessment is an acknowledgement of our predictive limitations. It implies that there will be failures in the prediction of likely outcomes because the concept of 'risk' itself implies that there is a limit to our ability to predict and make rational judgements on partial information. We can only make the best estimate possible with our limited knowledge and understanding: our 'bounded rationality' (Douglas and Wildavsky 1982; Simon 1957). Our ability to live with and manage uncertainty is a quality that may be seen as key to social work practice, in contrast to some other professions, such as diagnostic medicine, which aim to establish facts and certainties. Risk assessment in social work with children and families is essentially a matter of making judgements in the context of uncertainty and ambiguity (Parton 1998), and social work interventions may change family functioning and child outcomes, but we are rarely able to pinpoint exactly what aspect of the intervention brought about particular changes.

This is, in part, because the judgements that social workers are called upon to make are embedded in complex social and cultural concepts of family, parenting, child welfare, and the role of the state in bringing up and protecting children. Families, usually having rich connections with their social context, absorb influences in ways that cannot be predicted in a precise and linear way.

While families are embedded in a cultural and social context, so are social workers. What we understand to be a risk, a hazard, a threat or danger is a product of historically, socially and politically contingent 'ways of seeing' (Lupton 1999). One of the tasks social workers have to carry out is making the best possible decisions based on available evidence in the context of uncertainty and ambiguity. Despite this inevitable ambiguity in child and family social work, there is a duty on social workers carrying out risk assessments to be thorough, systematic and fair, and to make assessments that are fair and reasonable. A 'good decision' is one that is best supported by the available evidence, and informed by sound ethical and legal principles. Accepting the uncertainty and ambiguity in child and family social work does not, it is argued, mean that there is any less responsibility to choose interventions that have the best possible chance of improving outcomes for children, despite the gaps in our knowledge.

This requires a systematic, rigorous approach to gathering and analysing information, but social work also engages emotions, intuitions and values. These contrasting aspects of the social work role have been constructed as being in tension; social work as 'art' or as 'science', 'head' and 'heart' activity (England 1986). It combines both knowledge and interpersonal qualities:

> The art of practice is embedded in the capacity of the individual practitioner to form working alliances with clients, and to abstract from the generalities of accumulated knowledge to the particulars and the exigencies of a moment in time.
>
> Greybeal 2007: 519

The idea of social work as art *or* science is perhaps an example of a false dichotomy, although it is helpful in highlighting the scope and scale of diversity in the skills social workers bring to their work. Some practitioners may rely more on intuition and personal experience, while others are more interested in research and the evidence base for practice. Social work clearly has aspects of both, and a more integrated approach, valuing both aspects, is perhaps the more useful approach. Both aspects of social work with families need to be engaged in carrying out risk assessments. *The International Definition of Social Work* requires both, with its description of a broad and diverse range of roles:

[Social work] promotes social change, problem solving in human relationships and the empowerment and liberation of people to enhance well-being. Utilising theories of human behaviour and social systems, social work intervenes at the point where people interact with their environments. Principles of human rights and social justice are fundamental to social work.

IASSW/IFSW 2001

Theories, knowledge, principles of rights and of justice reflect the more scientific-rational aspects of social work, while relationships and complex interactions, not accessible to exhaustive rational analysis, reflect the more emotionally aware and intuitive aspects of the social work role. Problem solving crosses both aspects: largely imaginative in creating possibilities and communicating them to others, yet also practical in application and linked to research and evidence about what might 'work' in particular situations.

The quality of the assessment relies upon the collection of sufficient information to form the basis of a valid opinion about what is happening, or may happen, in a family, but it is the quality of integration of information and reflection on what it means for the individual child that determines whether or not it is effective in protecting a child who may be at risk, not simply how much is known. Reviews of serious cases have found that often there was quite a lot of information available about a child at risk: it just had not been put together, nor the significance of it appreciated (Brandon *et al.* 2008a; Ofsted 2010). Too often, the Assessment Framework appears to be used in a flat, non-dynamic way. This leads to the accumulation of facts but little appreciation of how to formulate the facts in the manner of a clear explanation rather than a 'dense description' (Brandon *et al.* 2008a: 63).

Box 7.2 Social work as science

Scientific, rational, formal analytical: forming and testing hypotheses; a 'head' activity

Evidence based: observation and collection of evidence a major part of the social work role

Use of knowledge of formal processes and procedural rules

Empowerment through application of human rights legislation and entitlements

---

Box 7.3 Social work as art

Imaginative compassionate understanding; a 'heart' activity

Intuitive, reflective: analysis includes reflecting on self and context

Use of interpersonal skills, especially building therapeutic professional relationships with service users

Empowerment as an objective of therapeutic interventions: related to changes in personal values and attitudes

Integration of information, interpretation and reflection in risk assessment

A recent report on 'the voice of the child' in Serious Case Reviews (Ofsted 2011) concluded that, 'agencies did not interpret their findings well enough to protect the child.' What we mean by interpretation of findings, and reflection on those findings, in connection with risk assessments, includes the following:

- All the information that has been gathered should fit together to create a coherent pattern – there should be no discordant information that suggests the explanation or story constructed to describe the family or the child's experience might be different from the version constructed so far, OR where pieces of information do not appear to 'fit the pattern', this should be recognised and reflected upon. Nothing should be left out because it is not consistent with the pattern as currently interpreted. This should include knowledge from relationship-building and imaginative understanding of the service user's experience as well as empirical evidence. Exploring inconsistencies and puzzling information is an important way of refining our understanding of how things work, including individuals and families.
- Reflection includes considering how coherent is the picture that has been constructed of the family's history and current way of life, the pattern of parental care, the experiences of the children in the family, and any explanations for any harm that may have happened. Discordant information, and the possibility that information is missing, will have been considered. Observations of relationships and responses to discussion of issues, such as children's well-being, parental responsibilities or proposals for reducing risk of harm to the children will be included, as well as information about the harm itself. The *Framework for Assessment* will be used as a tool for organising information, but such information gathering will not be seen as an end in itself. The emergent understanding or meaning-making that happens on the basis of information from all sources is the real end-point of the assessment process.
- Reflection should be informed by knowledge of research and empirical studies, law, policy and professional ethics.

France *et al.* (2010: 2) argue that: 'RFA [*risk factor analysis*] is a narrow approach that, while generating an expanding evidence base, is unable as a theoretical and empirical tool to provide an effective foundation for tackling future social problems.' One of the problems with predictions based on risk factors is that they are unable to explain the 'false positives' – those who are at risk of poor outcomes but go on to do well. Nor is it able to tell us which members of an 'at risk' group are likely to do well. The complexity of life means that children move in and out of risk groups throughout their life course: predicting risks is risky, because much of the time we know we will be wrong, especially if we rely too heavily on actuarial risk factors: statistics about large groups of people (France *et al.* 2010).

Risk, complexity and messages from Serious Case Reviews

Risks to children can be, and sometimes are, constructed as a social problem that we should be able to solve through scientific study and the investment of resources, bringing about the end of child abuse. The evidence-based practice, 'what works', approach is based on the principle that even in complex cases there are some courses of action that are more likely to succeed than others, so we can make rational choices about how to intervene with families where children are at risk of harm. In a political context in which resources are becoming increasingly scarce, choosing effective ways of using those resources is increasingly important. Resource shortages and public/political antipathy are not new challenges for social work, but expectations in terms of justifying public expenditure in social care are perhaps higher now than at any time in the past. Using information effectively to make risk assessments that make a significant contribution to protecting children is a major part of this. Serious Case Reviews are a way of learning to improve services, and a way of demonstrating that services are responsible and internally accountable, with external scrutiny increasing external accountability.

Sinclair and Bullock's (2002) study of 40 cases of serious injury or death of children rated only one as 'highly predictable' and three as 'highly preventable' – even with the benefit of hindsight. Nine of the remaining ten cases followed a history of abuse, but three quarters of the cases were classed as 'single events'. Brandon *et al.* (2008a) in their study of 161 Serious Case Reviews found that only 12 per cent of the children were on the Child Protection Register, but over half were known to children's social care.

Macdonald (2001) argued that the probability of a child death depends on a complex interplay of factors. It has long been known that children who are young, particularly under five years, or premature, or low birth weight, and 'hard to comfort' babies, and children who are seen as 'difficult to control' are at higher risk of harm than other children, but on its own this is not an indication that a child is at risk of harm from a carer: the risk attached to these circumstances is only evident when other situational and carer precipitating factors also apply (Hagell 1998). Further studies have added to our knowledge of what sorts of situations are really dangerous for children. They are, perhaps unsurprisingly, more about *constellations of factors* relating to the child, their parents, and the situation the family is in than single risk factors. It is these constellations that indicate a need for raised vigilance and concern about children (Ofsted 2010; Rose and Barnes 2008; Brandon *et al.* 2008b; Sinclair and Bullock 2002). When no single factor taken alone is seen as sufficiently worrying to raise concern about the child, there can be a lack of awareness of the need to:

- actively seek information from other sources and agencies;
- carry out the task of integration of information followed by analysis.

Apparently lower level indicators of concern that may disguise more serious issues include poor or disguised compliance with social workers and other professionals. Many perpetrators of serious crimes against their own children were perceived to have been co-operating with social workers at the time of the injury or death (Sinclair and Bullock 2002). Distinguishing between genuine compliance and feigned compliance requires a clear focus on evidence of acceptance by the parents of their responsibility.

Although the idea that serious child abuse and even deaths are wholly preventable has been authoritatively challenged (Munro 2011), what is emerging from a review of childcare social work is an emphasis on professionalism and competence in addressing those cases in which concerns are identified early enough to potentially 'change the odds' for children in the most perilous situations (HM Government 2011).

Brandon *et al.* (2008b) highlight the risks attendant on a 'preoccupation' with thresholds for services and levels of intervention. They note the importance of all staff working with children and young people being aware that intervention at any level is within the sphere of 'safeguarding' and part of a continuum that includes working with risk of harm as well as 'need'. Defining thresholds for services is a way of managing resources, but can become a means of inappropriately excluding children from protective services. Sheppard (2009) noted high levels of need for services among parents who did not meet the threshold for services, and Ofsted (2010) notes the lack of clarity about thresholds and inconsistency in applying them in children's social care.

Failure to respond to referrals and to risk has been found not to be because of a lack of concern on the part of workers, but is often a result of environmental pressure. In some cases, this has even been likened to 'paralysis':

> The findings [*of a study of Serious Case Reviews*] highlight the struggle that practitioners and managers faced in trying to deal with overwhelming workloads and cope under pressure. The additional impact of having to work with distress, volatility, hostility and violence often contributed to paralysis in the workers. To work effectively with hostility and notice potentially damaging patterns of cooperation like disguised compliance, it is arguable that practitioners need to be self-aware, flexible and sensitive to the factors underlying their own and the family's behaviour and emotions ... Besieged workers, however, may feel they have nothing left to give.
>
> Brandon *et al.* 2008b: 326–7

Entrenched problems may also trigger 'paralysis' in workers, especially in cases of entrenched long-term neglect (Brandon *et al.* 2008b: 327). Practitioners in such cases may be particularly vulnerable to becoming immobilised, and losing hope that things can change as a result of their intervention.

This book clearly cannot offer a solution to the problems of heavy workloads, but having strategies for identifying and working with resistant parents (see Chapter 9 on Working with Resistance), and demanding quality supervision that takes time to consider the worker's professional development and welfare under emotional pressure, may both help to stave off the effects of working with families where change is not sought and interventions are not welcome.

It is not possible to say with any certainty, based on cases where children have been harmed, how significant a particular family feature, characteristic or circumstance is for the safety of children because of the complex interplay of risk factors in so many of these cases. No single factor is common to all, or even most, of the cases of children who have died. It is the complex dynamics in the child's family that make the difference between high risk and relative safety (Sinclair and Bullock 2002). Rose and Barnes (2008) found that parents were often coping with a range of their own problems, including substance misuse, mental ill health, learning disabilities, or domestically volatile or violent relationships. A lack of material resources is common to many of the cases, and additional pressures, such as additional caring responsibilities, sometimes further impaired parenting capacity.

> There is a strong theme from these overviews of mothers struggling with chronic and enduring problems to do their best for their children. Some were succeeding against

all the odds when a set of pressures accumulated or unexpected incidents occurred and overturned their fragile stability.

Rose and Barnes 2008: 15

It was the combination of factors that fatally eroded their parenting capacity.

Subsequent studies of Serious Case Reviews (for example, Ofsted 2008, 2010) have confirmed earlier findings about the significance of *combinations* of contributory factors in child abuse cases: common characteristics of the families were similar to those identified in earlier reports (Ofsted 2010: 10). Brandon *et al.* (2008a) found that in one-third of cases, substance misuse, domestic violence and mental health issues were all present. These were often families with relatively low levels of engagement with children's services, but with needs that drew them to the attention of adult-oriented services, and particularly the police. 'Nearly three quarters of the children had lived with current or past domestic violence and/or parental mental ill health and/or substance misuse. The combination of these three problems can produce a toxic caregiving environment for the child' (Brandon *et al.* 2009: 43).

Rose and Barnes (2008) noted signs that social workers and other professionals working with children with disabilities may be selectively less responsive to indications that a disabled child may be being abused. They drew attention to the 'rule of optimism' as a possible explanation for the low representation of children with disabilities on Child Protection Registers, while in their study five out of 45 children had disabilities. Macdonald (2001: 11) found childhood disability was often linked with other risk factors, such as a young mother coping alone, further pregnancy, domestic violence and depression. Professionals may focus on one aspect of a child's needs, such as their complex health needs, and overlook other needs related to parental neglect or abuse (Ofsted 2010). This study also contains a caution that serious abuse can happen in families in which none of these risk factors have been identified: absence of patterns of behaviour thought to indicate high risk is not a reason for assuming a child is not at risk of abuse (Ofsted 2010: 11).

Two related factors that can affect the value of risk assessments are identified in Ofsted (2010). One is a tendency to 'start again' with each new assessment, rather than seeing the current presenting problem in light of what was already known about the family. Agencies tended to respond to each situation reactively rather then seeing it in the context of what was already known. This can lead to a culture of responding to incidents rather than carrying out a holistic risk assessment of the situation for the child or young person. This tendency to 'start again' for each incident is compounded by a tendency to re-assess families when there is a lack of trust on the part of the keyworker in an assessment that had been carried out by a colleague or previous provider of services. There may be a good reason for revisiting an assessment, but it is recommended that professionals work with the original assessment and review it when appropriate. Carrying out a full re-assessment diverts resources away from making service provision and leads to delays. Both problems are symptomatic of a failure in some cases to build on what is known, even if it is incomplete and may need revision (Ofsted 2010).

Serious Case Reviews continue to highlight the danger of the 'rule of optimism', particularly when good interactions with carers reinforce a tendency to focus on adults' strengths rather than the child's needs. The case of Caleb Ness is an illustration of a case in which parents were engaged with professionals and loved their baby, but the impact of combined stresses and risk factors led to his death at his father's hands. The Inquiry Report states that: '... we have no doubt that both his parents loved Caleb. None of the evidence we heard suggests that either ever deliberately wished to harm Caleb in any way' (O'Brien 2003).

Caleb's father had sustained a head injury that left him with psychological and physical difficulties. His mother had a long history of difficulty parenting: two older children were already in care. She also had a long history of drug use. There were warning signs that the level of risk to Caleb was increasing. Different professionals picked up various signs that the parents' problems may have progressed beyond their ability to cope with them. They included the mother's post-natal depression, and the stress on her of looking after a baby with additional healthcare needs while also supporting a dependant, demanding partner. These signs were never considered together, and their combined impact was not appreciated. Some quotes from the Inquiry Report illustrate this clearly:

Box 7.4 Quotes from the Caleb Ness Inquiry Report

'Many concerned professionals did their best for this family, but too many operated from within a narrow perspective without full appreciation of the wider picture.'
'Social workers allowed themselves to be easily reassured, largely because the couple was apparently co-operating with them. They failed to undertake a rigorous assessment of risk, and instead took at face value what they were told by [*Caleb's parents*] Shirley and Alec.'

'There was an unspoken assumption that the parents had the right to care for their baby. This dominated events to the extent that Caleb's right to a safe and secure upbringing was never the focus of decision making.'

'The diagnosis of post-natal depression in Shirley, an increase in her methadone prescription, greater confusion and depression in Alec – all should have been seen as giving rise to escalating concern for Caleb ... In fact, because the individual agencies were not working together effectively, the information was collated in a piecemeal fashion, and no single person knew all the relevant facts. No formal decision making process took place at that time, and it should have done.'

O'Brien 2003

Concluding comments

The sad case of Caleb Ness illustrates several of the points that have arisen in this chapter, and in repeated Serious Case Reviews:

- Parents who harm their children are not necessarily uncaring. Nor are they generally uncooperative: judgements about parents' attitudes and values can influence assessment of risk and leave children unprotected. Professionals can allow themselves to be reassured by factors that do not in themselves make the child any safer.
- The 'rule of optimism' may reflect the sympathies of workers assessing carers struggling to look after their children under difficult conditions. This may lead to a too-low

level of challenge of what they are told by the family. They may 'rationalise' evidence that does not fit with an optimistic view of parenting capacity and motivation.

- Combinations of factors are more powerful than single adverse circumstances or events and undermine capacity to cope. The wider perspective 360-degree view that is required for responsible decision making can only be obtained through good quality inter-agency working.
- Parents living at the edge of their ability to cope because of their own problems may find it difficult to make well-founded decisions about what is best for their children.
- In complex cases, professionals may find it difficult to identify a clear focus for intervention that *fits with their explanation* about the cause of the problem, and therefore do not address effectively either the *causes of difficulty or potential sources of harm*.

This last point is a particularly important one for the development of an effective child protection plan. Once an assessment has proposed an understanding of the cause of the problem, this should be an important component of the planning of an intervention strategy. Interventions that do not address the cause of the problem may at best offer short-term improvement, because if the cause of the problem remains unaltered, there is every reason to expect the problem to recur in the future, perhaps when professional monitoring has ceased or anxieties about the family have decreased.

8 Risk in child and family social work, part 2
Probability and different levels of prevention

This chapter:

- develops further the idea of risk as it is applied in child and family social work, with particular reference to the ideas of seriousness, outcomes of risk and prevention of harm.

Risk may be described in terms of the *probability* of an event occurring, combined with the *expected seriousness of the consequences* if the event occurs. Risk is generally associated with *negative* outcomes, and these vary in severity. It is important to consider the seriousness of the consequences that might flow from a specific event when assessing the level of risk involved: the more serious the potential consequences, the higher the level of risk. Social workers need to be able to make defensible predictive judgements that speak of both probability and severity. Section 31 of the Children Act 1989 makes the conditions for the making of a care order dependent upon establishing actual or likely harm to a child. There are two components to assessment: the likelihood of harm, and the severity of possible harm. Both are important in assessing the overall risk to the child, and demonstrating that the threshold for compulsory state intervention has been met. Judge Munby stated this clearly in the case of *Bury MBC v. D:*[1]

> ... every assessment of risk needs specifically to address both components of risk: namely the probability of the harm occurring and the likely impact if it does. In this case, the professionals had said that the probability of harm was high. The judge accepted that view, but commented that, even if the probability of harm was in fact lower than predicted, the devastating impact if it did occur meant that the risk would remain high.
>
> Eddon 2009

Even low probability events with drastic consequences may be 'high risk', and so may much more probable events with relatively smaller adverse consequences. This is particularly relevant when thinking about risk in families that neglect their children. Each individual incident or aspect of neglect may be relatively small, but if the neglectful behaviour is part of a repeated and persistent pattern of behaviour, its continuation is highly probable. Long histories of involvement and entrenched problems can overwhelm workers, who may find strategies for avoiding engagement with underlying problems (Brandon *et al.* 2008b).

In such cases the harm may also be great, even when it is less than the risk of death being discussed in the Bury case.

Box 8.1 An example of the interplay between risk and seriousness

Annie has a ten-year-old daughter Sally. Annie has a (hypothetical) rare genetic condition which Sally may have inherited, but it will not be possible to know for sure until she is 12 or 13. There is a one in four chance that Sally has acquired the condition. The consequences of the condition are largely manageable through medication, so the impact the condition will have on Sally' life is minimal, if, indeed, she has inherited it at all. The risk associated with Sally's position is therefore low although the probability that she has the condition – one in four – is relatively high. In Annie's case the consequences of having the condition have been severe because medication for the condition was not developed until she was an adult. The risk for Annie was therefore much higher when she was the age that Sally is now, although the probability of her inheriting the condition was one in four, exactly the same as her daughter's.

Risk, or the outcome of exposure to risky events, is affected by *vulnerability* and *resilience*: specific factors in individual history, circumstances and constitution that make negative outcomes more or less likely, or more or less severe, when exposed to adversity. Resilience is associated with better than expected outcomes for people who have been subject to adversity (Newman 2004). Different people respond differently to adverse conditions. Some resilience is attributable to individual factors, such as intelligence, interpersonal skills, or good early nurture, while some comes from situational factors, such as the availability of a person who shows consistent positive regard for a child. Although the probability of an adverse event happening may be the same for two people, the outcomes may be very different for them if it occurs. 'Causal pathways are seen as complex, and prediction at the individual level problematic, yet at a group level, the evidence seems strong that those children and young people with multiple risk factors are more likely to have future social problems' (France *et al.* 2010: 3, see also Farrington 2002; Hawkins *et al.* 2002).

Risk is about uncertainty, but not all uncertain situations are risky – it depends on the likely consequences. Risk assessments in social work therefore have to take account of a wide range of variables:

- the specific nature of the 'risky' situation;
- the probability of the harmful event occurring or the adverse conditions continuing;
- the severity of harm that may be caused;
- the child's resilience;
- ameliorating factors in their environment.

Such calculations can be complex, as the example below suggests:

Box 8.2 Complexity of risk calculations

Stephanie is 12. Her mother has an illness that makes her very tired and often unable to care for Stephanie as well as she would do otherwise. Her mother is her sole carer. She has three younger siblings aged eight, six and four. When her mother is well she is able to concentrate on her schoolwork and see her friends. She does well at school and has a lot of friends. When her mother is ill, she does a lot of helping around the house and looks after her younger siblings: getting them up, bathing them, and making sandwiches and other simple meals for them. At those times her schoolwork suffers and she does not see her friends outside school. For much of her life she has very little physical care from anyone else, and plenty of 'adult' responsibilities. She feels loved, cared for, and valued for the help she can give her mother. Her biggest worries are about her mother's health and the possibility that the family might be split up.

The probability that Stephanie's mother will be unwell again in the future and Stephanie be placed in the role of carer for her siblings, and possibly her mother, is high. The impact on her academic and social development may be substantial. However, there are protective factors, particularly having a valued role in a loving family, and her own abilities, including her social and intellectual skills. She is a child in need, at risk of impaired, 'suboptimal' outcomes because of the difficulty she has in prioritising the tasks appropriate to her own developmental stage: education and play/associating with her peers. There are indicators that she may be a very resilient child with ameliorating factors in her family environment, but resilience alone will not be enough to avert poorer than expected developmental outcomes without support and services, because, without support for her family, she will continue to be unable to focus on her schoolwork or have a life outside the home.

This may be contrasted with a situation in which a child is receiving little physical care because a parent is deliberately neglecting the welfare of the children; where the oldest child feels unfairly burdened with caring responsibilities for younger siblings, unvalued, and where life is unpredictable and worrying because of parental behaviour. Children in both situations are children in need, and would qualify for assessment and services. The eldest children in both situations receive similar levels of physical care, but the likely effect on the children may be hypothesised to be very different, because the contexts are so different.

Risk and prevention of harm

Risk is not a static phenomenon. Levels of risk may be constantly fluctuating. In some families where life is particularly uncertain, levels of risk may change dramatically from hour to hour, especially if the parents have severe mental illness or addiction problems.

Families in which domestic violence is a problem are another example of a situation in which the children can go from being relatively safe to very unsafe at short notice. Life may be very unpredictable. From the perspective of the worker carrying out an assessment, these situations must be regarded as high risk, if the consequences for the child of such incidents could be serious. Such situations may fall into Judge Munby's category of cases in which the consequences for the child could be 'devastating'. We cannot predict when things will next become dangerous for the children, but we know it is likely that at some point they will.

There are other situations in which the level of risk is more predictable, and children and protective parents may be supported to work with agencies to reduce the level of risk, or, to use an alternative term, avoidable harm (Wattam 1999). One dimension of any risk assessment in child and family social work arguably needs to be about what we might call the tractability of the risk: how likely is it that it will be amenable to change, and over what sort of timescale? Unpredictable risks are perhaps the most challenging on this dimension, because the fact that harmful events have not happened recently does not, on its own, indicate that they are not likely to happen in the future. One needs access to other information to know whether the risk is actually decreasing: information from an addiction support agency, mental health professionals, or reliable evidence that the abusive partner has been excluded effectively from the home.

Prevention and mitigation: risk at the proto-prevention, first and second tier of intervention

It is not possible to prevent all harm to children resulting from neglect and abuse: indeed, one could argue that very many children experience some acts that could be construed as abusive during their childhood (Radford *et al.* 2011), especially if one includes those acts that are at the more mildly abusive end of the spectrum that do not appear to cause lasting or significant harm. However, if the risk is such that the harm may affect a child's health and development, or the risk is of abusive acts that are against the law, then the state has a role to protect that child and promote their development. Children's social care providers are under a legal duty under the Children Act 1989 (s47) to assess situations in which there is risk of significant harm to a child in their area. They are also under a legal duty under s17 of the same Act to assess and provide services, as appropriate, to children at risk of impaired developmental outcomes without the provision of services. However, they are not expected to prevent risk itself: risk is an inherent aspect of life: 'A risk assessment can only identify the probability of harm, assess the impact of it on key individuals, and pose intervention strategies which may diminish the risk or reduce the harm. Assessments cannot prevent risk' (Barry 2007: 1).

Preventative interventions are sometimes classified according to the extent to which the risk has already begun to make an impact on the child and family (Hardiker *et al.* 1996). Some 'interventions' may be the result of actions taken by service users acting themselves to reduce risk to themselves and their children: 'proto-prevention' (Sheppard 2009). This may take the form of engaging others: family, friends and other sources of support in the community to address the issues they face. Universal services reduce the risk that there will be adverse events and poor outcomes for children and young people before they begin. This is *primary* or first level prevention.

Children's Centres, providing early intervention to support positive parenting skills, are an example of primary prevention. The Sure Start programmes initially targeted areas with high rates of poverty and, therefore, it is to be expected, higher than average rates of other social problems often associated with poverty and higher risks of intergenerational persistent poverty leading to social exclusion. Interventions are targeted, not on poverty per se, but on parenting capacity, on the basis that enhancing parenting skills helps parents bringing up children in economically deprived areas to achieve better outcomes for their children (NESS 2010). Although the first Sure Start Centres were in areas of high deprivation, not all those who used the Centres will have been those most in need of services (Sheppard *et al.* 2008), so the effectiveness of such initiatives can be difficult to assess. The full picture may not be available until many years have passed, although some early results are available which are mostly positive (NESS 2011). One of the issues with prevention at this level is that it is difficult to know what has influenced what when timescales are long and cause and effect is hard to establish with any certainty. There are many intervening events when the timescale for evaluation is long.

France *et al.* (2010) argue that risk reduction programmes – such as Sure Start – tend to focus on changing the child's or parent's behaviour, when the risks to children are often created by the broader social structure. They have an uneven or, at best, unproven record in terms of 'changing the odds' for the most deprived children (Taylor 2005; NESS 2010). France *et al.* (2010) argue that one of the major weaknesses of UK early intervention strategies was failure to tackle local barriers to inclusion. Focusing on families may not be enough to prevent some individuals experiencing social harm because, however hard parents try, the difficult environment for child rearing is always present (Ghate *et al.* 2008; Morris and Barnes 2008). However, such 'targeted universal' services offer the potential to intervene before problems become high risk, without the stigma associated with specialist services.

Another aspect of risk intervention is *mitigation* of harm when the feared event happens. Risk assessment can be about identifying ways of reducing harm after a potentially harmful event has happened. Services put in place to respond to harm before it becomes serious and lasting constitute *secondary* prevention. In second level prevention, families where there is an identified stress but low harm are targeted by services with a specialist remit. The fact that there is a risk of something adverse is established, although the level of risk is usually relatively low. An assessment under the Common Assessment Framework with services offered through specialised workers in universal services would be an example of secondary prevention (Children's Workforce Development Council 2011a).

When choosing factors to change to reduce risk in populations or individuals, the risk factor has to be *modifiable*: in the Sure Start example, knowledge and skills for parenting can be modified, whereas lifting families out of poverty is proving a difficult policy objective to attain. Risk factors must be identified that are both causally connected to the risk and modifiable. Below is an example from community medicine:

> Suicide risk factors within the community setting may be used to identify populations, groups, or people in populations who are at higher risk for suicide. However, population-based risk-factor modification as a public health strategy for decreasing suicide rates may not be effective if the factors chosen for modification are not causal. Furthermore, targeting of risk factors considered to be proxy measures of completed

suicide (e.g. suicidal ideation) using population-based interventions may not lead to the desired outcome (decreased rates of completed suicide).[2]

British Medical Journal 2009

It can be difficult to establish the impact and cost-effectiveness of very early intervention/prevention programmes, because they may have a big impact that is short-lived, or long latency and fail to show an effect until some time after the programme ends. However, effectiveness in secondary prevention can be observed and monitored and the intervention modified in light of feedback about what is or is not working: whether the risk to the children is increasing or decreasing, in the case of child and family social work. The *Allen Review* (Allen 2011) provides rigorously assessed evidence as to which preventive interventions can be shown to have a positive impact and have been cost-effective in reducing risks of future harm to children and young people.

Tertiary prevention happens when harm has occurred and has already had a significant impact on the individual or community. It acts to reduce the harm, ideally to restore functioning and well-being to its former level. For example, services for children and young people, and children who have been harmed by neglect and abuse need to address any ongoing needs for supportive, therapeutic or stabilising input to prevent deterioration and offset the harm already caused. Most of the work undertaken by children's social care social workers continues to be at the level of tertiary prevention, with families in which harm is already happening or where the risk of harm is high and the harm to the child may be serious. This is still the case despite over a decade of Government emphasis on the importance of early intervention (Department of Health 1995; Allen 2011) and is arguably linked to the high level of demand for third tier services.

Figure 8.1 shows how policies aimed at creating a 'seamless service', integrating social work with universal and targeted services, places social work on the high risk/high complexity right hand side of the spectrum of needs and services. However, this model is also a way of managing high levels of demand for specialist services, and there is always the risk that decisions made too early about level of need and complexity may preclude further investigation that might have revealed the extent of hidden need. Gillingham (2011) cautions against over-reliance on assessment tools by inexperienced staff, who may find them useful, providing much-needed structure while they are establishing themselves as professionals, but may inhibit the development of professional skills (see also page 144).

Parton (2011) argues that child protection social work has moved back into a position of more central importance in Government policy for children and families, despite the negative publicity after the death of Peter Connelly in Haringey in 2008. He attributes this to the work of the Social Work Task Force (Social Work Task Force 2009); the study carried out by Professor Eileen Munro (Munro 2011) is another critical component in this. One of the significant features of this process appears to be a move back towards the more focused role of *child protection* professional social workers. There are potential gains and losses for social work and for children and families in this move.

The idea of how one responds to risk, and even the nature of risk itself, undergoes change as governments change policy emphasis in relation to children at risk. Risk of harm and neglect appear to be taking a more central place in governmental concerns, and the more challenging and inclusive idea of *risk of social exclusion* has a lower profile. It is arguable

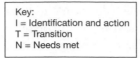

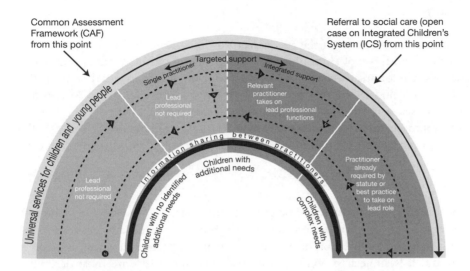

Source: Children's Workforce Development Council (2011a) *Common Assessment Framework*, available at: www.cwdcouncil.org.uk/caf. Reproduced under the terms of the Department of Education's Open Government Licence

Figure 8.1 The Common Assessment Framework

that the broader 'safeguarding' agenda; ambitious and visionary in its ambition to make Britain a fairer society, presented specific challenges for social work because of its breadth and the lack of a clearly defined role for social work within it. Parton (2011: 856) argues:

> ... in broadening the focus of what was meant by risk, there had been an elision or conflation ... of concerns about children and young people who might be at risk from a whole variety of threats, including abuse, with other concerns about children and young people who might pose a threat to others, particularly by falling into crime or anti-social behaviour. The agendas around the care and control of children and young people and those who might be either victims or villains had become in danger of being very blurred.

The containment of child protection social work within the words 'Integrated support from specialist or statutory services' in Figure 8.1 above reflects this coyness about the nature of risk, and the need for a highly specialist response to it. Children at risk of harm because of abuse are categorised together with children with severe disabilities and other children 'with complex needs'.

Social work with children and families has for some time been in the position of being part of a social project with high ideals, but limited resources with which to go beyond 'narrow' forensic child protection work and the support of children living away from home. An increased focus on the challenging risk assessment role may help re-establish social work's professional credentials, but carries other risks in terms of loss of the breadth of concern for welfare that is a central tenet of social work internationally:

> Developments in the wake of the tragic death of Baby Peter had the effect of rein-forcing the importance of child protection at the centre of safeguarding policy and practice and reinforcing the central role that social work played in this. For, while the period since the mid 1990s, particularly since the introduction of the ECM reforms, had emphasised a much broader and more positive approach to risk, the narrow forensic approach to child protection, which was so dominant in the early 1990s, had clearly been (re)confirmed as lying at the heart of current and future attempts to 'safeguard children'.
>
> Parton 2011: 872

There is the risk that social work might be pressed into a narrow, forensic role at the cost of closure of some of its potential to contribute to the broader safeguarding agenda. Social work exists largely as an expression of state commitment to protect the most vulnerable and, as a result, it is subject to policy concerns about which risks are most deserving of government attention. Levels of intervention and prevention and social work's role within these reflect social and governmental ideas about risk. Risk is therefore a politically constructed idea as well as social construct with a basis in thinking about the morality of 'good enough' care and adequate standards of living.

Socially constructing risk and the limitations of rules

Stanley (2007) notes that risk assessments are usually viewed as something created by the social worker, rather than something co-created by the family and worker together. Stanley suggests an alternative view of risk assessment as a 'tool' social workers use in exploring risk with the family to arrive at a consensus. When risk is considered as 'socially constructed' rather than an objective fact; she argues that it is better to consider the value of an exploratory, as opposed to inquisitorial, risk factor based, approach. The diffi-culty lies in cases in which consensus cannot be achieved. While risk may be socially constructed, and consensus over the outcome of assessment the ideal situation, the risks to the child may be all too real. However, this difficulty in establishing consensus in child protection cases highlights the importance of considering the extent of consensus in every risk assessment. *How far* is there consensus between worker and family over what the key issues are? Is the area of consensus about the things that have most impact on child safety, or only relatively peripheral issues or parental concerns? What are the implications of this consensus, or lack of it, for future work with the family?

Magnuson *et al.* (2011)[3] describe an emerging style they have identified in Canadian social work; a style:

> characterized by reaching for and inviting ongoing negotiation with families, with allied professionals and colleagues, and a reflexivity that is the result of the attention

focused on the professional and the need to continually defend the work and explain to others one's point of view.

This style is one they consider to be, 'prima facie, quite sophisticated, humane and ethical'. In part it is a style that has developed in response to the need to defend social work from external critique. It involves:

1   reaching for and inviting ongoing negotiation with families, allied professions and colleagues; and
2   a reflexivity that is the result of the intense attention focused on the professional and the daily need to defend and explain one's point of view.

Magnuson *et al.* (2011) argue that social work, as they observe it, is negotiation because the social worker enters conversations with families without a predetermined view as to what the outcome will be. Social workers spend most of their time in conversation: with colleagues, service users, professionals in other disciplines and many others. 'Talk is how they spend their day.' The ability to move from one conversation to another, with very diverse people and aims, and keep track of conversational threads that may run through a sequence of conversations, is a high-level skill.

Maintaining engagement and creating partnerships is one of the key functions of these conversations. Attempting to identify areas of consensus and disagreement with families may help to focus on how far working 'in partnership' is a possibility or reality. Apparent compliance may be managed by the parents through an attempt to deflect the social worker's attention on to problems over which there is agreement, but where there is little potential to improve the situation for the child. Some conversations with service users have a strong 'existential' aspect to them: exploring aspects of the relationship, often without *explicitly* doing so in words. Magnuson *et al.* (2011) describe some unspoken but powerful 'existential' questions that underlie one encounter between a social worker and a parent that are probably recognised by many child and family social workers:

Box 8.3 Magnuson *et al.*'s 'unspoken' questions

'Who are you and what can I expect from you? What are the boundaries of our relationship? How far can you or I be pushed before we push back? What are our common interests? Will I be betrayed? What are the risks to me of having a relationship with you? Can we work together on behalf of the children? Will we learn to trust each other? Will the children trust us?

The relationship between worker and service user is constructed through conversation; this is the tool through which trust is established, risks are explored, and consensus about the 'story' and the risks to the child and perhaps others is established – or not. Given the unpredictable and sometimes chaotic nature of child protection social work – the chaos deriving from the circumstances in which child and family social work operates, rather than from practice itself – Magnuson *et al.* (2011) reflect on the fact that, of necessity, child and family social workers have to be able to operate without rules, able to respond to situations and create narratives that describe them so that other professionals may see them as they do. Risk assessment is the creation of a certain type of narrative that explains to others why the worker thinks there is a risk to the child, in terms that they can understand and that are convincing. Evidence-informed practice is part of this, as is moral reasoning that reflects an informed reflective professional stance on the rights of parents and children. Parents also need to be 'convinced' that the assessment is a fair one, the narrative reflects their own experience as well as the worker's views, and that they can trust the worker enough to work with them. Magnuson *et al.* conclude that more study is needed to understand how sophisticated professionals propose and defend narratives, and how far they underpin effectiveness in promoting the well-being of children and families.

One aspect of working with families in which there are risk issues is the level of compulsion this places on the *worker*. The child's social worker is often the only person who cannot 'walk away' from the child and their parents, however difficult this may be:

> To almost everyone else, work with the client is subject to the discretion of the professional ... All can decline care [except the social worker]. This is true even in extreme situations, including those when a worker has removed a child from a dangerous home late at night. Several professionals have stories of staying up all night taking care of little children in the office, because there was no shelter and no foster parent willing to take the children. To get help, workers frequently have to rely on their wits and persuasive abilities.
>
> Magnuson *et al.* 2011

Social workers find different ways of coping with this pressure to 'be there' for families and provide some kind of answer for employers as to what is happening in those families. Gillingham (2011) reports that reliance on assessment frameworks provides a sense of structure to some new workers, but inhibits the development of professional judgment and engagement with the complexity of people's lives. Magnuson *et al.*'s (2011) research suggests it is expertise in the unstructured – in the sense of absence of formal prescription about how to do it – skills of use of conversation and the creation of narratives that are key in assessing and working with risk.

Creating narratives through discussion with service users and other professionals, managers, etc. involves social workers talking about their own beliefs and attitudes. This can make them vulnerable, too. Stanford (2011) argues that doing risk assessments places social workers' identities and sense of self under pressure. Carrying out risk assessments offers challenges to identities and cultural beliefs, norms and practices. The workers' identity may be placed at risk as a result of these pressures. Horwath considers the role of various influences on the way professionals make sense of complex information: '... reflecting on how knowledge about a case is constructed and interpreted in light of a practitioner's personal, professional and organisational situation' (Horwath 2006: 1286). The practice-moral aspects of assessment – or making a judgement – about risk and harm involve recognition that '... individuals do not fit neatly into boxes and that personal and professional values and beliefs influence judgements' (Horwath 2006: 1286). However there is a level of personal exposure in risk assessment as a result of this. The conversations and narratives that social workers create have

---

Box 8.4 Advocacy and control - contrasting approaches to risk assessment

Social workers who advocated for and protected their clients, and maintained a focus on clients, as opposed to their own 'at risk' identities:

- contemplated personal and professional morals, ethics and values;
- reconsidered the reality and degree of risk for clients and themselves;
- believed in the possibility of change for clients; and
- reflected upon theoretical and practice frameworks.

Conversely, social workers who adopted a stance of controlling and dismissing their clients and who thereby focused more upon their own, as opposed to their clients', 'at risk' identities:

- did not (re)consider the reality and degree of risk;
- did not consider change was possible for clients;
- did not consider theoretical frameworks;
- emphasized their organisational and personal contexts.

After Stanford 2011

---

relevance for service users, but may also have implications for the worker and their own sense of self. Stanford offers a binary description of the ways social workers approach the issue of risk: linked to whether the primary focus of the workers' concern is their own or their clients' 'threatened identities'. However it is suggested here that it is likely that many workers combine elements of both approaches in different situations and at different points in time.

This suggests that reflection on the impact that risk assessment work has on individual workers is important to maintain social workers' openness to the possibilities in any situation in which children may be at risk. Supervision needs to address the impact of risk assessment on workers' identity: cultural, ethnic and gender issues especially.

Talking about risk is to 'speak it into existence'. It can then be consciously analysed and made subject to critical thinking (Søndergaard 2002). Talking about it brings it into focus, and also creates a responsibility to respond to it: a moral imperative to 'do something' about it. However, service users themselves may reject some of the labels that are applied to them: they may not see themselves as 'victims', 'perpetrators', 'at risk', ' vulnerable', or even as 'survivors'.

Signs of Safety

This brief section does not attempt to explain the whole of this approach. Further reading is required to appreciate the approach and do justice to it (see for example Turnell 2010 for a detailed overview). However, it is discussed here as an alternative to the traditional risk factor based model of assessment that will be most familiar to many readers. The *Signs of Safety* approach aims, like the *Framework for Assessment* in Britain, to take a developmental approach, with an emphasis on openness with the family about risk, and the participation of the family in identifying information that is particularly important for the assessment:

Box 8.5   The Signs of Safety approach to risk

- is simultaneously forensic in exploring harm and danger while at the same time eliciting and inquiring into strengths and safety;
- brings forward clearly articulated professional knowledge while also equally eliciting and drawing upon family knowledge and wisdom;
- is designed to always undertake the risk assessment process with the full involvement of all stakeholders, both professional and family; from the judge to the child, from the child protection worker to the parents and grandparents;
- is naturally holistic (some assessment frameworks trumpet their holistic credentials but often do so by slavishly and obsessively gathering vast amounts of information about every aspect of a family and child's life that then swamps the assessment process and everyone involved with too much information) since it brings everyone (both professional and family member) to the assessment table.

Turnell 2010: 21

It takes the developmental idea further by explicitly asking workers to explore interacting influences on child development, positive and negative. Understanding the way things change for the family and the child over time is an essential component of this. The Signs of Safety (Turnell 2010) approach encourages practitioners to consider especially how *resources* affect risk in families, and consider any lack of 'fit' between the family's resources and their needs. Risks are therefore analysed through different levels of contributing factors, intra- as well as extra-familial, the wider society and the child's immediate family environment.

Howe (1996) discussed 'surface and depth' in social work practice. Strategies for engaging with the complexities of lives, understanding and interpreting them in their dynamic depth, were, he argued, in danger of being relegated to a place of secondary importance. Understanding sequences of events and their interaction requires a more complex and creative approach to information gathering, analysis and intervention than one that is 'surface' and 'static'. It acknowledges the practical and moral complexity of most 'real world' problems faced by child and family social workers. It also involves taking time to ask questions about what has been happening as well as what is happening now, and conversational skills associated with advanced practice rather than use of assessment tools alone, however useful those tools may be for specific purposes. France *et al.* (2010) emphasise the human skills required to do preventive childcare risk assessment work: the warmth, humour, tenacity and other personal and interpersonal skills. These are aspects of the 'art' of social work that are hard to quantify and are, perhaps for that reason, given relatively little emphasis in studies of effectiveness and outcomes; but undertaking the kind of assessment envisaged in the Signs of Safety approach is impossible without developing the skills of having a meaningful conversation about risk and risk factors with child and adult service users.

Risk reduction and risk to organisations

A final reflection on risk addresses its implications for organisations employing social workers. Risk is a two-edged sword in the sense that if risk to individuals is realised as harm, this also has an impact on organisations attempting to manage the risk. As a result, through a process of 'risk colonisation', the idea of risk and its management increasingly define what regulators do as well as what practitioners and service providers are expected to do:

> Risk has become embedded in regulation in two distinct ways. First, there has been a quantitative expansion across policy domains of the regulation of both traditional and novel risks to members of society and their environment, which we term societal risks ... Second, there has been a qualitative shift towards the management of institutional risks. By institutional risks, we mean risks to organizations (state or non-state) regulating and managing societal risks, and/or risks to the legitimacy of their associated rules and methods. Increasingly, the language and methods of risk analysis are being used to manage threats to both regulator and regulated organizations such as delivery failure, budget overruns, liabilities, and loss of reputation. In other words, there has been a growing emphasis on the risks of risk management.
>
> Rothstein *et al.* 2006: 95

Social care providers are increasingly regulated with the aim of reducing risks to the public, but '... constrained resources, competing priorities, cognitive uncertainties, bounded rationalities, conflicting interests, ungovernable actors, and unintended consequences' make this a challenging agenda (Rothstein *et al.* 2006: 96). Regulators of public services have limited capacity to control societal risks, but have to manage the risk to the organisations delivering services anyway. Failure to do so threatens the legitimacy of the organisation to manage risk, as has happened in local authorities in which there have been high profile child deaths. Exposure to risk creates problems for service organisations; '... such problems can be aggravated if central government acts to reduce its own business risks in resolving policy uncertainties by delegating resolution of those uncertainties to enforcement authorities' (Rothstein 2002: 2; Hood and Miller 2009).

The dismissal of staff at various levels of organisations that have encountered such difficulties can be seen as a way to limit damage to organisational credibility.[4] This may be seen as a less than satisfactory way to enhance the credibility of organisations that work to reduce and manage risk to vulnerable citizens, since it tends to focus the public gaze on allegations of incompetence rather than competence. It is to be hoped that the more systemic approach to understanding and responding to risk accepted by the Government following the Munro Review will help identify positive ways of responding to situations in which risk progressed to serious harm, while retaining the essential principle that there must be clear lines of responsibility and accountability in child protection social work.

Concluding comments

Risk assessments bring a range of processes into play: the technical-rational processes of structured information-gathering, consulting an evidence base – itself based on selection of evidence according to principles that are shaped by the researcher's interests and prior knowledge and beliefs; developmental theories; and local policies and procedures. Risk assessment tools are similarly based upon assumptions about what constitutes riskiness (Garland 1997). There is inevitably uncertainty at practitioner level about the elements involved in assessments of risk: the weight to be placed on the evidence base; the flexibility allowed in the use of assessment tools and the scope practitioners have for discretion and use of judgement. This is an inevitable result of the diversity and complexity of risk, and a reflection of the role of professional judgement.

This chapter explored how ideas about levels of risk, which are a starting point for a more nuanced consideration of the way actual level of risk in any situation is assessed through conversations, are co-created by workers and service users, and draw on and sometimes challenge workers' own identities. Attempting to reduce risk is itself a risk enterprise, for organisations as well as workers. Finding ways of working more closely with families is self-evidently a desirable aim, as long as it can be done without child safety being undermined by false compliance. Perhaps the most important challenges now for further work in developing practice in working with risk in child protection are:

- the development of techniques for reducing families' resistance to risk assessment through the use of skilled conversations and approaches to assessment that value the family's experience;
- the development of expertise in differentiating between interventions that are reducing risk to children in individual cases, keeping them safe enough, and those that are ineffective or undermined by the family, leaving children unprotected.

9   Working with resistance

The challenge of working with involuntary service users

This chapter:

- raises awareness of the importance of having skills for working with non-compliant or aggressive involuntary service users;
- considers possible organisational and individual social worker responses to aggression by parents and carers.

The definition of an 'involuntary' service user used in this text is someone who does not wish to be the recipient of services, or who is not averse to receiving services but does not want the ones they are being offered. Watson (2006) describes a 'traditional' definition of resistance in counselling as being about reduction of self-disclosure because it makes the service user uncomfortable or anxious. It is also seen as 'inappropriate or unproductive activity on the part of the client' (Watson 2006: 5), but he notes that this does not take account of the different sources of resistance. This may originate with, or be enhanced by, the client/service user themself, or the person working with the service user, or their social environment. In some cases, services are being grudgingly accepted or tolerated because the service user thinks things will be worse for them if they do not co-operate; in other cases, they are given little choice because legal measures are used or threatened to make them comply. In such cases, compliance may be genuine, if reluctant, or be apparent rather than real, and more like disguised non-compliance. In this chapter, most of what is being considered relates to working in cases defined as child protection cases – for example, s47 inquiries, child care proceedings – and cases in which safeguarding concerns are present although the case may not currently be defined as a 'child protection' case.

Non-compliance and non-engagement may be very obvious, showing itself when service users are never there when one calls, or never answer the door. It may show itself through the use of aggressive and intimidating behaviour to limit access to the family. But it may be much less obvious, concealed behind apparent co-operation and compliance, even eager compliance, friendliness and willingness to discuss problems and issues.

Brandon *et al.* describe the families involved in the Serious Case Reviews they studied:

> Three quarters of the 40 families did not co-operate with services. Patterns of hostility and lack of compliance included: deliberate deception, disguised compliance and 'telling workers what they want to hear', selective engagement, and sporadic, passive or desultory compliance. Reluctant parental co-operation and multiple moves meant that many children went off the radar of professionals. However, good parental engagement can sometimes mask risks of harm to the child.
>
> Brandon *et al.* 2009: 3

One serious Case Review noted the father had moved the family 67 times in order to maintain his secretive abuse within the family (Cantrill 2009).

When concern about a child's safety or welfare is the trigger for involvement with a family, it is likely that parents' first responses will include anxiety and defensiveness. It is a reasonable starting point for work with involuntary service users to expect that they will be anxious about the intentions of the social worker and worried about the possible outcome of any assessment. The more problematic the parenting, the more the parent may feel they need to hide the truth by any means at their disposal. This is not irrational, nor does it mean necessarily that they do not want things to get better for their children. It is, however, an obstacle that may need to be overcome at the start of the majority of child protection interventions.

The task of the social worker is to find a way of engaging the parent(s) or carer(s): addressing their concerns while retaining a primary focus on child welfare. The parent's intentions towards their child, their view of their own capacity to parent, and their willingness to reflect on their parenting capacity with a view to improving it, all potentially influence their level of engagement. These are all aspects of the assessment itself, so assessing the degree to which parents are willing to engage with social workers is necessarily a key part of the assessment itself. Another relevant factor is their belief as to what social workers do, and how good they are at doing it. Parents are likely to have been bombarded by negative stereotypes of social workers in the press, so, as with the initial anxiety they are likely to feel when they become involved in safeguarding processes, this cannot be dismissed as irrational. It may need to be addressed openly, with reassurances that removal of children is a last option sought only in a minority of cases, and with legal safeguards in the shape of court processes.

Engagement with parents provides four key things that are needed to be an effective safeguarding social worker:

- agreement by the family that the social worker has a *legitimate aim* in working with the family, the focus of the work being on the welfare of the child;
- agreement that the social worker has a *mandate to practice* with the family – is a qualified professional in a legitimate professional role;
- the family is prepared to share information about their family that is truthful, relevant and includes key information;
- trust in the worker's integrity and judgement, so that the worker and the family can begin to explore possible options for improving parental care, if this is needed, based on openness and co-operation.

Some of these may be achieved while others are not. Some parents may agree that the social worker has a legitimate aim and is a suitably qualified and experienced person to carry out child protection work, but not trust them, nor share information that they know will reflect badly on them as parents. Fear of loss of face, lack of motivation to change, lack of commitment to the child, fear of loss of the child, and psychological factors such as feelings of helplessness and depression may all influence capacity to engage with social workers. Learning difficulties may be a factor in non-engagement if workers have not taken the time necessary to explain things and repeat information if needed, or find user-friendly ways of explaining why they are there (McGaw *et al.* 1998; McGaw 2005; DH/ DfES 2007; Cleaver and Nicholson, 2008; SCLD 2009).

Parents may appear to engage with social workers, but this may be a strategy to reduce professional concerns. Apparent compliance by parents is common in families who seriously harm children, (Brandon *et al.* 2009). The ability to engage with parents and children and work with genuine co-operation needs to be balanced by awareness that compliance may in some cases be feigned, or be genuine but limited to selected areas the parent wants to discuss while other important areas are kept 'off limits'.

If one works from the premise that most parents want to be 'good' parents, and seeing children flourish is a source of pleasure for most parents, then an important task for the social worker is to persuade parents that positive change is an achievable goal, and working to improve their parenting would bring benefits for them as well as their children. This is ideally the rationale underpinning intervention, rather than the requirement that parents meet social work agency expectations, since it is much more likely to bring about lasting change than a change which is undertaken to 'get the social workers off our backs', which may lead to short term change but no more. Unless the parents see some reason to carry on parenting in a different way, it is likely they will revert to doing what they did before. There should be some benefit for the parent as well as the child, be this in terms of self-respect, pride in their children, improved parent–child relationships, decreased hostility in the household, or some other reason for finding the new way of parenting 'better' than the way they were parenting before.

To explain: 'Do this, or we shall have to consider removing your children,' is often said to give an honest evaluation of the situation for the family, and such tough messages have to be given. However, if this is not accompanied by exploration of positive reasons for changing the way parents care for their children, there is little positive incentive to engage. This may lead to *apparent* compliance, when the parent appears to be doing what is expected of them without any real commitment to the process of change, or is concealing the fact that they are not actually complying at all. If what is being sought is lasting change, the parents need to be engaged in developing the strategy for change and want the same outcome – better parenting – for themselves and their child. Part of the challenge may be to explore what the parents think of as 'good parenting' and begin the process of reflecting with them on what this means.

Mandell (2008) defines 'use of self' as including the use of communication skills, insight, self-awareness, values and beliefs, biases, attitudes, openness, genuineness, warmth and non-judgemental attitudes. Dewane (2006) adds personality, relational dynamics and self-disclosure, among other things. These attributes are the building materials for a number of activities that are essential for successful engagement with service users, including:

- conveying empathy and respect;
- building rapport and trust;
- setting and maintaining boundaries;
- establishing confidentiality;
- modelling constructive social behaviour (Mandell 2008: 237).

Mandell (2008) notes that social workers closely associate the attributes associated with use of self with personal integrity, especially when there is tension between their own values and instincts and the dictates of the professional code of ethics. Critical reflection is an important part of this process, linking ethics, values, beliefs, and perception of the way one fills the professional role. Critical reflection about parenting may be used with families, as well as being a private activity or something done in supervision. Families may learn through modelling of reflective thinking how to begin to think differently about their own parenting. Changing the way people think about what they do is part of creating change that will last longer than the time taken to become a 'closed case'. Mandell argues further that a commitment to critical reflection on the part of social workers should be supported by the agencies that employ them, and this has the potential to: '... contribute to systemic changes that put care before power in the way that child welfare operates' (Mandell 2008: 245).

Parents who are angry because they are innocent and feel unjustly accused, and parents who are angry and defensive having injured their child, may be difficult to distinguish: Dale *et al.* found that:

> Authentic responses of parents who have been mistakenly accused of child abuse (e.g. anger, challenging and lack of cooperation) are largely indistinguishable from defensive behaviour of parents who vigorously, yet untruthfully, deny being responsible for serious abuse. How to distinguish between the two? The signs that are presented by these very different scenarios can appear to be superficially similar. This is a key area where professional presumptions and prejudices can lead to significant errors of judgement.
>
> Dale *et al.* 2002: 55

However, resistant parents are not always angry: they may present as co-operative. Below is a suggested set of areas to consider when reflecting on whether co-operation is genuine or not. It is not intended that this should be viewed as an exhaustive list, nor a substitute for the exercise of judgement in individual cases.

More overt resistance: parents who are threatening or aggressive

In some cases resistance is not disguised by apparent compliance, but is very apparent. In some cases it takes the more extreme form of threatening behaviour and aggression, or even violence. Information about frequency is patchy, but there is some evidence that it is not uncommon. In Angus, Scotland, 279 social workers reported they had been assaulted over a two-year period 2008–2010. The Labour spokesman for justice is reported as saying that these figures are 'extremely concerning', and indicated that 'it was vital that the council ensure social work staff are protected and not sent into situations where they are at threat' (Strachan 2010). While all councils should take steps to ensure social workers are not sent into situations in which they are at risk, evidence suggests that this is

---

Box 9.1 Warning signs when thinking about whether parental cooperation is genuine

- The parents limit the range of areas they are prepared to discuss and they are not prepared to discuss in any detail issues that challenge a view of them as 'good enough' parents.
- The parents are very keen to keep the focus of work on issues that are of concern to them, such as housing, benefits, their own health, the demands placed on them by agencies, childcare, etc. and far less keen to discuss child welfare issues.
- The parents frequently give explanations or accounts that cannot be checked, and do so more consistently when the questions are about 'difficult' issues.
- There is information from other sources that contradicts information given by parents, and attempts to explore these differences are seldom productive nor lead to any clear understanding of the reason for the discrepancy.
- Significant areas of information are missing and difficult to fill in satisfactorily, for example, how a child spends their time when not at school in a case of neglect.
- Agreements that parents will do certain things – take a child to a clinic, clear up the kitchen, etc. – are often not kept, or the only agreements that are kept are the less significant ones from the point of view of the welfare of the children.
- Things never seem to change very much, despite apparent commitment to improve parenting or the family environment.

---

still a common occurrence. Assaults against social care workers account for 19 per cent of all injuries involving assault in all employment sectors, despite the fact they represent only 5 per cent of the workforce. On average, three social care workers are assaulted every day (Lombard 2010a). This estimate, including social care workers who are not social workers, is taken from statistics that only include injuries leading to absence from work for three days or more, so they probably significantly underestimate the problem.

While the risk of being assaulted, threatened or verbally abused is becoming smaller for workers in most occupations in the UK (HSE 2011), it is increasing for social workers and social care professionals (HSE 2009). The culture of blame of social workers perpetrated by the media may be a factor in this, but increasingly limited public resources, increased expectations in respect of social workers' caseloads, and practice increasingly driven by performance indicators are other factors that may be creating higher tensions between service users and social workers.

Sixty-five per cent of social workers working in local government in 2008 had encountered verbal abuse, 26 per cent physical threat, 9 per cent violence, and 31 per cent bullying in the past two years (Unison 2008b). Many local authorities have little centrally held information about the level of dangerous incidents other than those leading to injury, and there is not a prevailing culture of learning from 'near misses', when workers manage to leave a situation which feels dangerous without physical harm (Unison 2009). Given the scale of the problem, it is advisable for all employers who expect employees to go into situations that may trigger threatening behaviour to consider running training on managing aggressive behaviour. This chapter is not a substitute for such training, with opportunities for role-play and to consider local factors in the management of risk. Urban areas present different issues to large areas with more widely distributed populations, for example. Rather it considers some theoretical and policy issues that underpin working in an environment in which there is often an element of fear and threat felt by both workers and service users, often despite the best efforts of social workers to create positive working relationships.

Knocking on the door in child protection cases

Child protection work involves offering a 'service' to service users who may not define themselves as such, and may not wish to be users of social work services. Sometimes it involves engaging people who do not object to being service users, and may already be users of targeted services through choice. Sometimes parents who are the subject of a child protection investigation have previously approached children's social care for support and not received a service because they did not meet 'threshold' criteria at that point, only to find themselves the subject of compulsory assessment and investigation. It is, above all, stressful for parents.

As well as being stressful for parents, investigation in child protection cases can be stressful for social workers. It is the part of the work that probably places the most pressure on the ability to identify relevant information quickly, accurately and comprehensively. The family home is another world, critically different from the meeting spaces and clinics of the professional office environment. It is an environment in which any sense of professional power and being in control of the process may be placed under intense pressure by parents who are hostile, aggressive or controlling. The social worker may feel powerless. Within the family home, the parents have the right to determine who enters and who is excluded unless there is a warrant or other legal provision overriding this.

Having gained entry to the family home, physically moving, stepping over the boundary into someone else's home, someone else's space, into 'another world' (Ferguson 2009: 475) social workers may feel threatened: not only with violence, but also with expulsion from the home, exclusion from future visits, and possibly being seen by their employer as having 'failed to engage' the family. Ferguson (2009) describes the 'stage management' and manipulation of the child protection worker that may be going on during a home visit when the adults' resistance is channelled into avoiding social work scrutiny, diverting attention from things that would reveal the true condition of the children.

At the same time, the family members, or some of them, may be intent on concealment.

> [H]aving to knock on a door and tell a complete stranger that they are under suspicion of maltreating their children is deeply, personally and professionally challenging for even the most experienced workers.
>
> Ferguson 2009: 427 after Turnell and Edwards 1999

First steps in a child protection investigation, before meeting the family, include a strategy meeting to plan the investigation. Strategy meetings are an opportunity to seek information from other agencies about factors that may indicate the level of risk to the social worker before they leave the office, especially if there are indicators that the family may react in an angry and threatening way. An assessment of risk should be carried out before the worker leaves, if there are indications that the visit might carry risk for the worker, and visiting should be planned taking into account agency policies relevant to worker safety, such as any policy on lone working. Support and backup should be planned in case the worker needs to call for support or advice, and any agency policy relating to working with hostile or aggressive individuals should be considered.

Three different perspectives: an advisory model from the US, the European Directive approach, and the Newham Protocol for addressing violence and aggression in the workplace

The United States Department of Labor (2004) *Guidelines for Preventing Workplace Violence for Health and Social Care and Social Service Workers* provides advice for employers and employees on workplace safety. A key aspect of this advice is the reminder that all employers have a general duty under US law to provide a workplace free from 'recognized hazards likely to cause death or serious harm'. In the US in 2000, 48 per cent of all non-fatal injuries from occupational assaults involved healthcare or social service workers; the majority of them healthcare workers, but with social service workers following fairly close behind. The risk factors they identify include the practice of solo working with people who may be frustrated by long delays in treatment etc., and '[l]ack of staff training in recognizing and managing escalating hostile and assaultive behavior'. Poorly lit parking areas place staff in situations in which they are vulnerable. Service user factors, aspects of normal working practices, failure of managerial planning and elements in the physical working environment are all highlighted in this excerpt from the list of risk factors. The US recommendations have a number of elements:

- Management should demonstrate concern for employee health and safety with a 'zero tolerance' policy that shows equal commitment to the safety of workers and service users; there should be clear and accountable allocation of responsibility for worker safety, and a comprehensive system of counselling and debriefing after violent incidents. Everyone, including front line workers, needs to understand their responsibilities in terms of reporting incidents and responding to them and organising/taking part in training around recognising and responding to escalating agitation, aggression and criminal intent.
- Worksite analysis should be used to identify specific areas of high risk or hazards. Analysis of workplace security can identify trends and patterns: characteristics of assailants, victims, 'risky' jobs and locations and effectiveness of risk reduction strategies already in place.
- 'Engineering' the workplace: considering the arrangement of furniture, exits, locking devices, alarms, mobile phones, CCTV, lighting, security of external doors and windows, and transport. Also considering service user comfort in waiting areas, provision of sensitive and timely information to people waiting, and decreasing delays in waiting time. Signing in and out systems to keep track of staff movement and follow up if people do not report back when expected, 'buddying' and use of designated contact people.

- Providing follow-up services for workers who have suffered violence or intimidation. These may include counselling for trauma, fear and self-blame, also critical-incident debriefing, to help reduce after-effects of exposure to violence.
- Employees should receive regular training on managing aggressive behaviour and avoiding violence, also guidance on supporting colleagues who have experienced violence.
- Lastly, there should be regular evaluation of the worker safety programme.

UK law is less detailed but UK employers have a general duty under s2 of the Health and Safety at Work Act 1974 to ensure, *so far as is reasonably practicable*, the health, safety and welfare of their employees at work. The regulations that accompany the 1974 Act are largely focused on suitability of premises, rather than risk from other people, and do not include the type of proactive hazard identification and risk management indicated in the US guidance. However, UK employers have a 'duty of care' to their workers:

> If the mutual trust and confidence between employer and employee is broken – for example, through harassment and violence at work – then an employee can resign and claim 'constructive dismissal' on the grounds of breach of contract. ... Workers who are assaulted, threatened or abused at work also have legal remedies available to them under civil law. These can result in damages against the employer or individuals, the most common remedy for which is a personal injury claim.
>
> ACAS 2010: 8

New guidance based on European collaboration over setting standards in the workplace, *Preventing Workplace Harassment and Violence* (ACAS 2010), covers a range of situations in which intimidating behaviour might occur. It states that harassment and violence can:

- be physical, psychological, and/or sexual;
- be one-off incidents or more systematic patterns of behaviour;
- be amongst colleagues, between superiors and subordinates or by third parties such as clients, customers, patients, pupils, etc.;
- range from minor cases of disrespect to more serious acts, including criminal offences, which require the intervention of public authorities.

The definition of harassment and violence is broad, but the protection the Directive makes for workers is arguably weak. Employers must provide for the health, safety and welfare of their workforce, but only as far as is 'reasonably practicable'. They have to assess risks to their workers, including risk of reasonably foreseeable violence, and develop a plan to prevent or control risk; consult with the workforce when carrying out risk assessments and when acting on them; and ensure employees are aware of their violence and harassment policy. This includes awareness of the *worker's* responsibilities in relation to it.

Employers should provide '... a clear statement to staff and service users that harassment and violence will not be tolerated ... together with information on how to report harassment and violence [*and*] be clear what constitutes unacceptable behaviour on the part of managers/other workers as well as service users or members of the public and a statement of their overall approach to preventing and dealing with harassment and violence, including any training they provide (ACAS 2010: 7). The European Directive booklet signposts a range of useful documents, including other guidance and relevant legislation.

Independently of the European Directive, and more focused on social work problems with aggressive service users, the London Borough of Newham developed a protocol for working with violent and aggressive families. This followed a Serious Case Review in their area (London Borough of Newham 2008). The Newham Protocol highlights some of the possible consequences for children of aggression directed at social workers:

- parents using the same qualities and behaviour they may be using to intimidate children – aggression, physically threatening behaviour – against adults, thereby placing children beyond the reach of welfare services;
- insufficiently rigorous investigation of concerns about children's welfare;
- withdrawal of services to the family, leaving children at risk.

The consequences for children of intimidation of social workers by parents are highlighted:

Box 9.2 Excerpt from the Newham Protocol

- As part of professional practice, there will be occasions when individuals come into contact with behaviour that may cause them to feel threatened or intimidated. There is evidence from a Serious Case Review in Newham that aggressive behaviour from parents and carers can seriously impact on the way that professionals interact with these families. In practice this may mean that practitioners avoid conflict with parents by avoiding difficult discussions or even by avoiding contact with the family altogether. This can mean that the protection needs of the children in the family may be overlooked.
- Where service users are seen as frightening by professionals, this can have a serious impact on the work done with the service user. In some cases this may result in a withdrawal of services. Where a family has children, withdrawal of services means a reduction in the monitoring of these children.
- It is important to realise that where a parent or carer is perceived as dangerous to professionals, there is a strong possibility that they are also dangerous to their children. If professionals are scared and intimidated by a person it is very likely that children in that person's care may be at risk.

London Borough of Newham Protocol 2008

Some of the possible consequences noted in the Newham Protocol could result from aggression that has not been responded to adequately by the agency. Social workers have a responsibility to ensure that their practice remains at an acceptable standard to safeguard children despite threats, and their employers have a responsibility to them, and to the children involved, to support them adequately in dealing with aggression. It cannot be acceptable to withdraw services or reduce protection of children at risk because of the very parental behaviour patterns that place the children at risk. To do so would send children the message that their parents are so powerful in their aggression that other adults cannot help them: they are beyond help.

If parental behaviour cannot be managed safely by one person, it is the responsibility of the worker and the agency and their partner agencies to ensure that children continue to receive a service. Multi-agency planning processes may be necessary, and the Protocol considers this:

Box 9.3 Where the parent or carer of a child with a Child Protection Plan is judged to be violent and aggressive:

- Information about the risk presented by the family should be shared with other professionals in the core group.
- Individual agency workers should discuss with their supervisors how best to work with the family and monitor the safety and well-being of the children.
- There should be careful discussion with the chair of the Child Protection Conference as to whether the parent/carer should be excluded from the Child Protection conference.
- The Child Protection Plan should acknowledge the risk to workers presented by the family and include this in the risk assessment for the children.
- Where there are continuing serious concerns about the safety of workers or of children within the family, the case should be referred [to] ... the LSCB for consideration and recommendations.

London Borough of Newham Protocol 2008

Inter-agency working at all levels of the relevant organisations, from front line worker to senior management, is indicated, with information shared – proportionate to the level and nature of the concerns – in order to facilitate safe working with the family. The expertise and organisational knowledge and authority of managers, Independent Reviewing Officers, colleagues in other agencies and Local Safeguarding Children Board members may all need to be invoked, depending on the extent of the threat to the welfare of the child, and the level of threat to the worker.

Supervision and the avoidance of 'pitfalls'

Reflective practice includes considering one's own responses to situations that are intimidating, frightening and aggressive, and how they were managed. 'Critical incidents' in which a threatening situation was negotiated are opportunities to consider how to manage aggression if it happens again. Any worker who feels intimidated by a service user should raise this issue in supervision. The reasons one may feel intimidated range from overt verbal and physical threat to more subtle use of physical presence or sexual innuendo. The positions people occupy in a room or their posture can convey a message that is threatening

– standing or sitting too close, standing in front of the door, maintaining a fixed gaze or trying to 'lock' eye contact – without any verbal threat being made. The use of terms that imply over-familiarity or comments on the worker's personal appearance – positive or negative comments – may carry a message that the worker is seen as lacking authority, and not respected. Animals can be used as a source of threat, especially dogs. What is perceived may be a feeling of discomfort, when the use of authority is made difficult by the feelings created in the worker. The perceptions and mental responses that cause this feeling may be hard to describe or document: 'gut feelings' about the intentions of another person.

A personal view is that continuing with an interview when feeling unsafe is unlikely to be productive, even if the threat does not materialise. If the person who is being threatening is aware of the effect they are having, the interview will tend to reinforce the idea that the worker is relatively powerless. If the threat cannot be defused rapidly, for example by acknowledging the anger and/or distress of the person who is being threatening and inviting them to explain how they see the situation, or explaining why one has come to see them in as non-threatening a way as possible, then ending the interview as swiftly and coherently as possible is probably the best option. Factors that can reduce judgement, self-control and inhibitions, such as drugs, alcohol or mental ill-health, are reasons to take threats particularly seriously, as is a history of violence towards other people. The next step is to consider with a manager how best to proceed after leaving. Joint visiting is probably the most common and easily organised way of dealing with visiting families where workers feel unsafe, but agencies vary in their willingness to use resources in this way. Court orders or a police presence are other strategies.

Social workers who have had the experience of an aggressive interview should be able to use supervision as a space in which they can discuss their feeling of being unsafe, and consider what the basis of those concerns is – evidence that it is not safe to visit that household alone; the level of threat this may convey; and what might be done to make contact with the family safer and less intimidating for the worker. Supervisors should be open to discussion of safety issues, and be vigilant when staff show reluctance to visit alone or express anxiety about visiting certain families. Social workers may be reluctant to appear over-anxious, or think that feeling intimidated some of the time is a normal part of doing child protection work to be tolerated, or believe that their fears will not be taken seriously. None of these are good reasons for not taking feelings of being unsafe seriously and discussing them with a supervisor. The feelings of being unsafe may be an indicator that the agency needs to think further about the care and safety of children in the family.

Feeling unsafe may prevent a worker from intervening effectively with the family on behalf of the child, and lack of formal systems to support them may be part of the reason such organisational neglect of children can happen. Broadhurst *et al.* give as one of the new pitfalls for workers and their managers in child protection that: 'There is insufficient support/supervision to enable practitioners to work effectively with service users who are unco-operative, ambivalent, confrontational, avoidant or aggressive' (Broadhurst *et al.* 2010c: 7).

Threats may be about physical harm, but can take the form of threats to complain about the worker or making allegations of unprofessional conduct. Workers may feel anxious about their ability to defend themselves against any of these threats. The fact that so much social work takes place in places like service users' homes and without another professional present can make social workers feel vulnerable, as in the case of Kyra Ishaq

(Birmingham Safeguarding Children Board 2010). Joint visiting may be important not only for the physical safety of the worker who is threatened, but also to protect their professional status.

Ferguson (2009) describes the 'intangible' nature of some families' communication about what is and is not 'permissible': 'Unconscious communication occurs when the message "don't move" and "don't ask to see, listen to, walk with or touch the child" is projected into the worker by abusive and/or fearful carers' (Ferguson 2009: 475).

Such unconscious communication can have an inhibiting and partly immobilising effect. Reflective practitioners can use the visit that led to these feelings as a 'critical incident' and analyse how this feeling arose, what perceptions it was based on, and what effect it had on the worker's behaviour. One outcome may be ideas for strategies to prevent the assessment or family support being undermined by intimidating behaviour, while keeping the worker safe. Another may be ideas for agency provision needed to support staff in exposed roles.

Involuntary service users are more likely to be accessed by going to where they are, to assess their home environment, and to ensure that they are seen. Asking questions that challenge the family's view of itself, or disturb the 'front' it has constructed to face the outside world carries risks. The reality is that social workers have to leave relatively safe spaces such as the office – although risk in the office should not be overlooked – and go into environments they do not control in order to find out about children's lives, and employers and social workers need to be mindful of the risk aspect of the work.

Working with and around resistance

Where there is an aggressive and hostile response from a member, or members, of the family to the social worker, it places the worker in a situation in which they may be all too well able to appreciate the feelings of powerlessness and fear that certain individuals are able to generate in others. This may help them in making an assessment of the situation in which any children or other vulnerable people in the household are living. The negative aspect of this is that it is deeply uncomfortable, may be dangerous, and may trigger feelings of anxiety, which interfere with the ability to carry out an assessment. Very often, it may act as an impediment to detailed assessment and decision making. This may be because the social worker is physically prevented from gaining access to information. They may be unable to gain physical access to areas of a house, for example, or speak freely with children or adults who could tell them what life is like in the family but are afraid to do so. Stress may also interfere with the ability to process information. Ferguson (2008) notes:

> Encounters in child protection are full of fateful moments that require professionals to have the skill, courage and personal resources to ask the really hard questions. Whether they do so is directly related to the quality of the support available to them in their organisations, where they need space to think, process their feelings and gain insight into their experiences.

One member of a family may be the primary source of resistance and opposition. Not all members of the family may feel the same way about the social worker and their role, although some may be happy for the aggressive person to speak for them. Others may be afraid to challenge that person even if they do not agree with them or approve of their behaviour. Dominant personalities within the family may mean that only the most hostile voices are heard. Some members may be resistant while others are open to outside help. A high proportion of child protection cases are ones in which domestic violence is an issue. It may take time and work to identify how the different family members position themselves in relation to social workers, as well as each other.

Service users' expectations as to what they can expect from a social worker confronted with aggression will vary, too. In the box below is an extract from a conversation between a social work researcher and a service user who succeeded in leaving a controlling and sexually abusive relationship with her father. The service user is appreciative of the bravery shown by the social worker, who stood, perhaps literally, in front of the service user to confront her abuser.

Box 9.4 What do service users living in aggressive families think 'good' social work is?

TRISH: What [did] you find helpful that social workers have done?

SUSAN: Someone to sit down with you, to discuss your problems ... that you know deep down in your heart, they will help you.

TRISH: And how would you know that, what would be the difference? How would a social worker be different doing that than just listening?

SUSAN: Showing it, showing it [by] their reaction ... They get up and do it. They don't just sit down and write it all down ... When you need their help, they're there ... Well, if you've a man ... that hurts you in any way, you're terrified of them ... you know how bad they are when they want to be. When someone brave enough goes up and faces them, and you're right behind them, you feel great. A good strong social worker goes up and doesn't care ... Yeah, that would be the way. I know a few women that had social workers in the past that wouldn't go near their homes ...

TRISH: OK. And what effect did that [*social workers avoiding visiting*] have then on those women?

SUSAN: It sends them back down, back down ... it doesn't build their confidence up.

Walsh 2006: 47

Box 9.5 Questions for reflection

Do you think Susan's social worker was brave and a good social worker, or was she irresponsible if she put herself at risk? Or both? How do you balance the tension between pressure to enter a dangerous and potentially violent household, and the responsibility to take reasonable steps to keep oneself safe?

Walsh (2006: 49) argues that a therapeutic approach to change with resistant service users involves being clear from the outset about the difference between *agency goals* and *client goals*: the things the agency says need to change, and the things the service user would like to change. This involves 'accepting and starting from a point of belief in a client's resources and skills' so the service user's ability to identify valid goals is respected. The goals that are selected for work must be consistent with agency goals. Walsh argues that attempting to impose change is less likely to be successful than supporting change that is identified as desirable by the service user, so this is less likely to trigger or maintain resistance. The level of commitment to change is likely to be higher if the change is also seen as desirable by the service user, so the durability of change is also likely to be higher.

Walsh refers to de Shazer's (1992) concept of different levels of commitment to change to assist in facilitating rather than imposing change. In complex situations, where families have multiple issues and difficulties that may encompass intra-personal difficulties and challenges, it may be difficult for social workers to know where to begin. Faced with complex interacting difficulties and initially resistant service users, the temptation may be to fall back on the formula of standard patterns of service provision rather than responding creatively to each individual situation. Walsh's discussion highlights the fact that 'resistance' is a catch-all phrase that may oversimplify a complex issue.

Some service users may appear resistant because they believe that what is being offered to them is other than what is actually on offer. Explanation of the assessment process and discussing the agency's/nationally accepted philosophy that the preferred outcome of social work involvement is supporting the child in the family rather than removing children may defuse some anger and fear. Woodcock (2003) identifies the often poor match between social workers' understanding of the aetiology of parenting difficulties, often based on developmental theories and systemic perspectives of how families work, and the strategies employed by social workers attempting to grapple with these difficulties on behalf of the children, which are often prescriptive and limited by the resources on offer. Standardised responses from a limited menu of service possibilities – provision of family support workers, parenting education, increased monitoring of home circumstances – may be offered in the absence of time or felt expertise to tackle complex issues. Resistance may be based on the mismatch between the problem and the solution being offered, which may be perceived by the family as lack of care or attention to the detail of their lives. Standard assessment tools, insensitively applied, may exacerbate the situation.

Family/parenting problems may be understood conceptually by social workers in complex terms, including hypothesising about parents' psychological well-being, addiction problems, and relative powerlessness in the context of controlling relationships, poverty and a poor social environment for parenting. Parental understandings of their difficulties are likely to be based on narrative accounts of their experiences over a period of time; these chronological accounts, unlike those of the social workers, are not necessarily linked to formal theories about the way the world works. They will probably incorporate plenty of *informal* theories about the way their environment and society has influenced their life. The reflective response is to consider the plan for provision against the problems felt to be real and pressing by the family, and ensure that the family's agenda is considered as well as the agency one in seeking to improve the circumstances of the child.

A degree of worker helplessness may mirror service user helplessness when faced with the enormity of the project necessary to achieve change in some cases. This is where Walsh and de Shazer's recommendation that the social worker identifies areas for change 'starting where the client is' is relevant. It involves an open exploration of the service user's view of their current situation to identify which areas are ones which the service user themselves is dissatisfied with and would like to change, and which areas of their lives are open to change, while maintaining a position that certain goals have to be part of the plan for change, particularly those concerned with increasing child safety and well-being. This echoes practice in many Family Group Conferences, in which the family is invited to develop a plan for protecting the child, but the arbiter as to whether or not the plan is robust has to be the local authority with safeguarding responsibilities (Family Rights Group 2007).

Such a course of action may commit the worker and service user to a longer journey than that involved in a standard assessment. It may involve identifying aspects of the service user's life that maintain the status quo and the barriers to change, as well as looking for opportunities for change and ways in which it may be maintained. Questions about *maintenance of behaviour* become key. Instead of formulating a childcare problem in terms of *what is wrong and what needs to change*, the focus is on, *why are things like this and not otherwise? And how can they begin to get better?* The social worker's task is to identify the things the service user wants to change – that will remove or reduce the threat to their child's well-being – and support them in identifying ways of making this possible. This is not incompatible with explaining the risks if change does not happen, nor keeping a reasonable time frame for the child in mind and on the agenda.

If one starts from the premise that most people do not really want to harm their children, it is likely that there will be goals that most service users can 'sign up to' which are compatible with the aims of the agency. The challenge is to find ones that are realistic and achievable within the timescale for the child, and to monitor progress fairly and openly.

There are some caveats to trying to work with resistance in this way:

- The family agenda may be determined by the member who has the most influence within the family. This is unlikely to be a child, and it may not be the person who does most of the caring for the children in the family. It may be someone who is not present at the meetings: some male partners may exercise a great deal of influence over what happens in the family, but rarely be available for meetings, either because of work or because of a reluctance to become involved. The under-representation of men and reliance on female parents is an identified problem in social work. It is important to consider who is setting the agenda in the family, and whether everyone in the family is prepared to commit to the same agenda for change.
- The family may agree to an agenda for change that addresses their own concerns – for example, housing issues – but progress on other areas of concern may be blocked. The family may use lack of progress in intractable areas – such as resolving housing issues – as a focus for sessions, or even a justification, perhaps unspoken, for not looking at other issues.

Assessing risk: a checklist of things to consider

First, it is noted that checklists are never complete: they cannot be fully comprehensive. Second, while we may have ideas about some of the factors that place workers at higher risk, this does not mean that people in other situations should be considered safe.

Broadhurst et al. (2010c) suggest a 'risk checklist' for social workers. It covers practical arrangements for visiting, timing and venue of visits, and issues of communication within the worker's network. A reasonable assessment of level of risk depends on the accuracy and completeness of information available. When there is concern that a service user may present a risk to workers, it is important that there is appropriate sharing of information between professionals.

In addition to the items on Broadhurst et al.'s risk checklist, there are other questions that might be asked when planning to meet the family of a child when there have been concerns over threatening or intimidating behaviour:

- Might it be possible to meet one of the parents/adults in the household safely if the other is not present? If so, what would be the ethical implications and safety implications for other people in the family?
- Are there particular risk factors for aggression, such as a history of mental illness or drug or alcohol abuse that might affect self-control?
- Is there evidence that the aggressive adult has been a victim of abuse themselves, and if so, how is this victimisation relevant to the current situation? May this make them more likely to be stressed and anxious, and perhaps aggressive, when discussing abuse?
- Is there evidence of use of threatening behaviour or violence against other people, including other professionals working with the family, or assaults on other people

---

Box 9.6 Risk checklist for workers

- Why am I undertaking this visit at the end of the day when it is dark and everyone else has gone home? (Risky visits should be undertaken in daylight whenever possible)
- Should this visit be made jointly with a colleague, other professional – for example, health visitor or police – or manager?
- Is my car likely to be targeted or followed? If yes, it may be better to go by taxi and have that taxi wait outside the house while I complete the visit.
- Do I have a mobile phone with me or some other means of summoning help – for example, a personal alarm?
- Could this particular visit be arranged at a neutral venue? How might I then organise to see the family at home under safer conditions?
- Are my colleagues/line managers aware of where I am going and when I should be back? Do they know I may be particularly vulnerable/at risk during this visit?
- Are there clear procedures for what should be done if a professional does not return or report back within the agreed time from a home visit?
- Does my manager know my mobile phone number and network, my car registration number, and my home address and phone number?
- Do my family members know how to contact someone from work if I do not come home when expected?

Broadhurst et al. 2010c: 28

that may have led to a caution or criminal charge being brought, or evidence of domestic violence?

- What are the implications of this aggression for working with the wider family?
- If you have already been the target of intimidation from a member of this family, what were you doing/saying at the time the threat began? Were there any particular triggers for aggression in the conversation that you can identify? Former children in care may feel prejudged because of their history of growing up in care, for example, and people not familiar with the system of child protection in the UK, such as asylum seekers, may believe that a social worker has the power to remove children at will, and thought the threat of removal was immediate. Or was the threat apparently a direct response to the fact that their parenting was being assessed?
- What was your response to the aggression/threat? Did it appear to help the situation? Or make it worse? What else might be helpful if such a situation occurs in future?
- Were you able to leave the room/home/building without obstruction when you ended the meeting? How can you keep your exit as clear as possible?
- Did the intimidation appear deliberate and premeditated, or impulsive? Both carry risks. The fact that it has happened once is itself a reason for thinking it is likely to happen again.
- Were comments made that were aimed at one worker personally, such as racist comments, which suggests they may be at particular risk?
- Is the service user aware that they were experienced as being intimidating, and that there may be consequences flowing from this?

Some service users may request a change of worker in the hope that the new worker will be more sympathetic to them. *Working Together* (DCSF 2010) states:

Box 9.7 Request for a change of worker

5.161   Occasions may arise where relationships between parents, or other family members, are not productive in terms of working to safeguard and promote the welfare of their children. In such instances, agencies should respond sympathetically to a request for a change of worker, provided that such a change can be identified as being in the interests of the child who is the focus of concern.

While the idea of handing over a challenging family to a new worker may sometimes be attractive, the important issues in deciding whether or not to agree to the change are the probable impact on safeguarding, and the probable impact on worker safety. If the family might work better with a new worker, this is a good reason for change but does not necessarily reflect badly on the first worker. The new person may be able to start with a clearer set of shared assumptions about the problem and possible ways of moving forwards, building on the work done by the first worker.

If the request is made in the context of intimidating or aggressive behaviour by family members towards the first worker, it is important that the change of worker is not used as a way of disqualifying the first worker's assessment – provided the assessment itself appears sound and based on adequate evidence. If the request appears to be part of an attempt to avoid engagement, the agency should consider how to maintain consistency of approach to the child's needs and follow-up of plans that are already agreed. The family may be exercising a legitimate right in requesting a change of worker, but this should not be a means to disqualify workers who have behaved in a professional manner in their dealings with them.

The case of Kyra Ishaq illustrates the potential that parents can have to intimidate professionals from finding out about the welfare of their children: '... the power dynamics lay with the parents and not with the rights, welfare and protection of the children' (Birmingham Safeguarding Children Board 2010: 73). The powerlessness of service users relative to professionals is often noted, but power is a complex concept. People hold different kinds of power in relation to each other. The social worker in a child protection case holds considerable 'statutory' power, but this does not make the service user 'power-less' in all respects. They may control the flow of information about the family, restrict access to the child, and use their influence within the family to prevent the social worker from making an accurately informed assessment. Other family members may be intimidated too; they may be more vulnerable to reprisals and more immobilised by fear than the social worker.

If a social worker is unable to gain the depth of information needed to understand how a child is being cared for, they need to consider:

- Am I able to talk to the child without feeling that someone is making sure I only hear from them what the adults in the family want me to hear?
- Am I able to see the child's bedroom when I ask to do so, or can I only see it by arrangement, or not at all?
- Are other professionals – health visitor, education professionals, etc. – able to gain access to the family home and see the child, or are they being kept at arm's length too?[1]
- How urgent might the situation be? Gaps in information may suggest concealment of evidence and indicate the child may be at risk of significant harm. If this is the case, and information suggesting the child is not at immediate risk cannot be obtained, the grounds for an application for an Emergency Protection Order, Child Assessment Order, or police protection may be met.

A contrasting situation is when some service users make their homes accessible and are very willing to talk about themselves and their family, but this does not make the child any safer because the engagement, real or apparent, does not lead to any change in their parenting behaviour. The issues that matter for the welfare of the children are not addressed, or not addressed effectively. The history of child protection tells us that home visiting is not a guarantee that children will be protected. Stevens and Cox (2007) argue there is an implicit assumption that a child protection plan and home visiting will make a child safer.

The visits should create a space for the practitioner to monitor and work with the family. The intended outcome of this intervention should be that the child remains safe. It is argued that this represents an implicit linear understanding that this activity will protect the child (i.e. intervention should equal protection).

Stevens and Cox 2007: 1325

These authors challenge the idea of risk assessment as a process in which the various risk factors can be 'added up' to achieve an estimate of the overall level of risk.

Research into abuse-related child deaths and serious injuries suggests that risks are not additive: more risk factors may place a child at higher risk, but it is not possible to say that a child with two risk factors identified is at twice as much risk as one with only one identified risk factor. It is the interaction between risks and protective factors at any given time that makes the difference to the safety of the child. One additional risk factor, such as the illness of a supportive grandparent, may enormously increase the risk to a child, but only because of the presence of certain other risk factors, such as maternal mental ill-health. Families make adjustments all the time to adapt to cope with adversity, but when the family is unable to adapt to cope with one more thing, children in the family may suddenly be at very increased risk: '... the concern here is that procedures and standards based on linear models have the potential to produce an element of false security, especially when one considers how stressful and demanding it is to be charged with protecting children' (Stevens and Cox 2007: 1326).

Access to the home and the child may provide some reassurance that the child is well, but home visits in themselves give children little protection and may lull agencies into thinking that things are improving in families when they are not. Unless there is reason to be confident that parents are working openly with the worker, home visits may have little value. It is the quality of information that matters: and the worker's alertness to small signs that things are genuinely improving – since improvement is rarely dramatic and obvious – or small discrepancies and signs that indicate that things are not quite as they are being described. It is this alertness to small signs of compliance and co-operation, or resistance and concealment, which makes a crucial difference between effective and ineffective safeguarding.

The social worker may accept the constraints placed on them by the family as a compromise in order to succeed in continuing to monitor the child, albeit less effectively than the child's situation may merit. Compromised monitoring may be seen as better than no monitoring at all – but this calculation, which seems on the face of it to make sense, may conceal the fact that no effective monitoring is going on. The absence of effective monitoring is not seen because the appearance of doing so conceals it.

Why might a social worker accept the compromised monitoring permitted by an apparently fairly compliant but manipulative or intimidating parent?

- The injunction to work in partnership with parents is a potent factor in many social work texts and guidance, and may be applied beyond its reasonable limits. The often-quoted principle that, for most children, the family is the best place to be brought up is also very potent and may deter thinking about use of legal powers, for example.
- Working in child protection is challenging: those who undertake this work expect it to be difficult. Rather than saying, 'This is not working', there may be a feeling

that however difficult the situation, the worker owes it to the child/themself/their employer to keep trying to create a positive working relationship with the parent.

- There may be a genuine belief that the compromised monitoring is keeping the child safe enough, and safer than they would be without it. If a child protection plan specifies visiting with a certain frequency, a worker may see this as important but have lost sight of the object of the plan, which of course is not 'visiting' per se but securing the sustainable welfare of the child.

Why might people use threats and intimidation against social workers?

Families who resist involvement are not necessarily abusive towards their children: there may be many reasons for resisting social work involvement. These include fear, or a prior history of involvement with social workers that was not positive for the family, or stereotypical beliefs about the kinds of actions social workers may take. Neither apparent co-operation nor resistance are reliable indicators that a child is safe or at risk, but resistance creates the greater difficulty for social workers because of the limits it potentially places on social work observation of children's welfare.

Parents who are involved in child protection processes are 'involuntary' service users, in receipt of services because there is a perceived problem in their capacity to care for another person, which they may or may not recognise themselves; or because they possibly pose a threat to the well-being of their child.

Involuntary service users are particularly likely to present difficulties in terms of hostility and aggression, for the simple reason that neither they nor the social worker can simply walk away. The responsibility that the State has towards certain vulnerable people means that services cannot generally be withdrawn, and the potential for conflict comes from the 'compulsory' nature of the contact between worker and service user. There is a further threat to the service user because contact with professionals holds dangers for them: serious ones that may restrict their liberty, in the case of people with mental health problems; and removal of their children in child protection investigations. It is not reasonable to suppose that parents are able to make accurate judgements as to how likely it is that their children will be removed from their care: media portrayals of social workers are alarmist, and the criteria for holding child protection conferences, developing child protection plans and removing children from parental care are not perhaps consistently applied, and not well understood even by other professionals working with children (Brandon *et al.* 2008b)

One obvious reason why some parents are resistant to involvement, or use intimidation to avoid contact, is that they have heard that social workers take children away for no good reason. They believe what they have read in the papers, which leads them to think that social workers do not have the ability to make good judgements about which children need to be removed from parental care and which parents should be supported in caring for their children. They may have had negative experience of involvement with professionals in the past, perhaps exacerbated by their own negative attitude. If their child is the subject of a child protection investigation they are possibly aware that there are aspects of their parenting that fall below a socially desirable standard, even if they are not neglectful or abusive parents. Anxiety over the possible outcome of any inquiries may be a powerful factor in causing aggression. Aggression and intimidation are sometimes effective strategies for dealing with certain types of problems, and the parents may have had experience of using it to good effect – from their perspective – in the past. They may see the aggression as a way of keeping social workers at a distance and controlling their interaction with them, in order to conceal abuse, or as a way of defending their family from what they see as threatening intrusion by 'the authorities'.

Working with parents who are hostile and aggressive may risk pushing a social worker towards a polarised view of the family, identifying with the dangerous situation the child appears to be in and responding to the sense of danger and threat in the family home. On the other hand, aggression makes it difficult to challenge parents, who may use it as a tactic to conceal abuse and neglect. Both responses to aggression are problematic, because parents may believe they have valid reasons to be angry even when they are not abusive or neglectful parents, and compliance with controlling behaviour by parents renders the worker ineffective to protect children who are at risk of harm. Where families have established a pattern of dealing with problems by responding with anger, the social worker needs to find a way of working with the family without putting themselves at risk. Minuchin argued that family violence was often linked to powerlessness, and interventions need to be aware of the way power is held and used by different family members, and of the way others see their own professional power; or lack of it, depending on context. 'When we try to intervene [*in cases of family violence*] by controlling the parents or with concern for the child alone, we can only produce a continuation of the pattern' Minuchin (1974).

Concluding comments

Threats and intimidation may be based on a real intention to harm, or as a 'bluff' to deter further intervention. However, some people who are angry and upset may appear intimidating when they are agitated or angry, without intending to intimidate or appear threatening to others. Ascertaining what motivates the aggression: fear and defensiveness, or aggression and deliberate threat, may be impossible at the time of the threat. If the person who is being aggressive does not respond quickly to attempts to reassure them or offers to discuss things more calmly, the self-protective strategy of leaving the situation is sensible. It is what happens next that matters. If there are children who may be at risk in the care of the aggressive person, it is not an option to leave them unsupported because of parental aggression. Having left the situation, the social worker needs to consider how to proceed. This should involve discussion with their line manager, and possibly with other agencies, including the police if there are child safety concerns. The decision as to what happens next should be taken rapidly, and include consideration for the worker, the children involved, and any other family members who may be vulnerable. The aggressive adult may calm down and apologise, but the fact that they have been aggressive should be factored in to planning the next and any subsequent contact with them.

People who use intimidation in an attempt to solve the 'problem' of concern about their parenting may be relying on a habitual way of responding to threats. The threat response may be the result of fear and feelings of powerlessness based on other experiences of trying to argue their case to those 'in authority'. On the other hand, threatening behaviour may be part of an established pattern of behaviour.

Social workers are vulnerable to assault and intimidation, partly because of the work they do, and also because of the relative privacy of many of the situations within which they work. The emphasis on confidentiality for service users may contribute to a sense that what happens in meetings between social workers and their clients is 'private', despite the official function of these occasions. An increasing emphasis has fallen on the processes of social work from an organisational point of view: how information is recorded, how quickly tasks are completed, and other organisational outcomes. The relative invisibility of social work home visiting to the 'organisational gaze' renders it less amenable to audit processes. It also places social workers at high risk of developing idiosyncratic practices, including taking unacceptable personal risks.

10 Drugs and alcohol and child and family social work

This chapter:

- identifies key themes in current research relating to working with parents who use illicit drugs or alcohol;
- links research to best practice with families in which an adult carer is misusing drugs or alcohol.

Defining the problem

This chapter is not intended as a complete guide to working with families where drugs or alcohol are a problem. Specialist training can provide specific information about the effects of different drugs. It can also enhance skills in working with drug-abusing adults, and collaborating with other professionals involved with substance misusers. The aim of this chapter is to present an overview of research-based knowledge about intervening in families with children where alcohol or other drugs are a problem.

The use of drugs is widespread: the legal drug, alcohol, is widely consumed, and a large proportion of the population has tried illegal drugs at some time in their lives. The use of drugs, legal or illegal, is not necessarily problematic and does not inevitably impair parenting. We do not know how many parents manage to raise children successfully despite misusing drugs or alcohol, but there are indications that children can be resilient and parents can be resourceful in balancing parenting and their own drug-related needs. The support of wider family can make a positive difference to children's lives, but often at a considerable cost to relatives, often grandparents, who may make substantial sacrifices to support their children and grandchildren through a period of parental drug or alcohol misuse.

The presence of drug or alcohol misuse together with other complicating factors such as depression, domestic violence or homelessness is more concerning, since the probability of successfully managing a substance misuse problem together with other personal stresses and the demands of parenting appears to be lower than managing without such complicating factors. The social isolation and membership of selective networks associated with substance misuse also affects quality and type of social support available.

It is often the combination of problems that gives cause for concern:

> While substance misuse can impair parenting capacity, harm is not inevitable and rarely exists as a consequence of substance misuse in isolation. Poverty, social exclusion, poor housing, a stressful environment, family tension and conflict and a lack of psychosocial resources etc. collectively heighten the risk of harm.
>
> Manning *et al.* 2009: 377

Difficulties range from dependency – physical and psychological addiction – with short- and long-term social and physical ill effects, to binge drinking, when physical addiction is not present but consumption is periodically high with negative consequences for the binge drinker. Consequences may be social or physical: interference with the ability to do one's job or meet family responsibilities; drink-driving and arrests or accidents associated with drink-driving; other accidents associated with drinking; alcohol-related criminal offences; alcohol-related medical problems; and relationship problems caused by alcohol use. 'Problem drinking' is used here to encompass the range of patterns of alcohol use that have significant negative physical and social consequences for the drinker, or their family. In this context, quantity of alcohol consumed is less significant than the social consequences of drinking.

While children can show resilience and few negative effects of growing up with a parent who misuses drugs or alcohol, once children have come to the attention of children's social care and there is an issue with drugs or alcohol in their immediate family, there are also grounds for concern about the impact the problem may be having on other family members, especially children (Copello *et al.* 2005). It has been argued that the presumption that parents will usually or often be able to cope with both addiction and bringing up children runs counter to research findings (Barnard 2007). The threshold for coming to the attention of children's social care may be high when there are strong motives for concealing difficulties: '... children affected by parental substance misuse can be hard to reach. It is sometimes only recognised when the harm becomes so serious that child protection and/or statutory care agencies become involved' (Scottish Government 2006).

The profile of many problem drinkers and drug-takers is frequently complicated by experience of past or present trauma, such as that caused by victimisation. Substance-abusing women, in particular, may have complex histories that can have an impact on their parenting, sometimes with disastrous effect. Parents who misuse substances may need support with a range of problems if their parenting is to be successfully maintained. The not unreasonable belief that they should seek to become drug- or alcohol-free in the interests of their children may be correct in theory, but in practice often involves exposing the substance misuser to the need to find alternative strategies for addressing a range of other difficult issues that the drugs or alcohol have been used to mask.

The extent of the problem – alcohol

The UK Government definition of a 'binge drinker' is someone who drinks more than six units of alcohol on a single occasion (women) or eight units (men). This is twice the recommended daily maximum of two to three units a day for women and three to four units a day for men. Manning *et al.* (2009) set out to identify profiles where the risk of harm to children could be increased by patterns of parental substance misuse, based on data from five UK national household surveys. They point out that this definition of a 'binge drinker' does not mean that any parent who binges is a risk to children, although they may be so. Equally, it does not imply that a parent who drinks less than this does not present a substance-related parenting risk. There are additional terms that describe more chronic problematic alcohol intake: *hazardous drinking* – when alcohol consumption increases the risk of harmful consequences for the drinker or for other people; *harmful drinking* – when alcohol intake has consequences for physical or mental health; and *dependent drinking* (Manning *et al.* 2009).

Manning *et al.* (2009) found about 81 per cent of the adult population were current drinkers, about 7 per cent were at least mildly dependent on alcohol and about 17 per cent had engaged in binge drinking during the past week. Around one third of people who engaged in binge drinking had a child in their household, and about a quarter to a third of all children under 16 lived with at least one adult who 'binge drank' according to Manning *et al.*'s definition. Around 4 per cent of children were living with only one parent who was binge drinking. Twice as many children (8 per cent) lived with two adults, typically parents, who were both binge drinkers (National Treatment Agency 2009). A similar number (8 per cent) lived with an adult with a mental health problem, and about 2 per cent of children were living with a binge drinker who also had a mental health problem.

The extent of the problem – drugs

About 4 per cent of children under 16 live with an adult who used drugs in the past month, and about 1 per cent live with someone who used a Class A drug – cocaine, hallucinogens, ecstasy and opiates – in the past month.[1] Over 4 per cent of children are thought to be living with a problem drinker with a mental health problem, and 1 per cent with a problem drinker with a concurrent mental health problem who also used drugs (Manning *et al.* 2009). On the basis of data indicating that there were approximately 330,000 problem drug users in England, about a third of whom may be parents, the 2008 drug strategy for England aimed to prioritise treatment for cases of drug and alcohol addiction affecting children. This is probably an underestimate of the size of the problem (HM Government 2008; Manning *et al.* 2009). The 2010 drug strategy continues the approach of the 2008 strategy with a similar commitment to supporting families affected by drugs or alcohol: 'We will establish a whole-life approach to preventing and reducing the demand for drugs that will ... break inter-generational paths to dependency by supporting vulnerable families' (HM Government 2010: 9).

The policy basis for implementing this is to be through multi-agency co-ordination of local services:

> We know that tailored and co-ordinated support packages around the needs of the whole family can be effective, with savings estimated at £49,000 per family per year ... significant funds have been shifted from the centre to the local level enabling local partners to work together ... In addition, Community Budgets will be established for

16 local areas from April 2011. These will pool funding from a range of Departments, enabling local areas to deliver better outcomes for these families. The government intends to roll out Community Budgets nationally from 2013/14.

HM Government 2010

Many areas already have protocols setting out how local agencies should work together to respond to safeguarding concerns and treatment needs; a 'model' protocol is being developed by the National Treatment Agency. Drug and alcohol services should be represented on all local Safeguarding Children Boards. Clinical advice from the National Treatment Agency (Strang 2011) is that treatment should:

- incorporate wider social interventions as well as medication to support recovery outcomes;
- include considered provision of medications including opiate substitution treatment (OST) to gain maximum benefit;
- guard against incorrect provision or unnecessary drift into long-term maintenance on substitute prescriptions.[2]

Some responsibilities of Children's Social Care in relation to parents who misuse substances and their children

- Routinely record information about substance misuse by parents on children's case records and any other relevant internal data collection system.
- Ideally there should be a professional with experience of substance misuse mistreatment to act as a single point of contact for children, family and drug and alcohol professionals.
- Parents should be given advice about local treatment services and the option of a referral there discussed with them.
- All statutory meetings and some non-statutory meetings in respect of children and parents' case reviews should invite somebody from the other relevant services, adult or child, to attend, and adult substance misuse professionals involved with the family should receive copies of minutes of significant meetings about children of the family.
- Intervention with families should be informed by an understanding of substance misuse and its impact on children, possibly involving the expertise of services for young carers.
- Local authorities should provide training in substance misuse for professionals working with families. There should be central planning that takes account of the needs of children in families where parents misuse drugs or alcohol.

DCSF 2009: 14

A dramatically higher proportion of children known to social services are likely to be living with a drug- or alcohol-dependent parent than those in the general population.

Forrester and Harwin (2008) found that almost a third of all cases referred for long-term allocation in four London boroughs involved concern about parental substance misuse, and similar results have been found in other areas (Hayden 2004; Fraser *et al.* 2009).

Problem substance misuse and parenting

In this chapter, 'problem' use is defined as using any drug to the extent that it has an impact on health, or capacity to hold down a job, or relationships with friends and family, or otherwise on the person's ability to function in society. In the context of social work with children and families, it is the relationship between drug or alcohol misuse and parenting capacity that is of particular concern. Drug and alcohol use is problematic for an increasing number of adults. The increase in alcohol-related illness and deaths for both men and women is rising steeply in the UK, in contrast to the situation in most Western European countries. It is also estimated that within the 20–24 year old age range, nearly 10 per cent of women and 20 per cent of men may be problem users of illegal drugs (Velleman and Templeton 2007).

In considering whether consumption of drugs or alcohol constitutes a problem, there are various aspects of the issue to consider. Not all drug users or problem drinkers harm their children (Manning *et al.* 2008: 377). Assessment for children in families where an adult is dependent on drink or drugs needs to be carried out with regard for all the dimensions of

---

Box 10.1 Velleman and Templeton's (2007) dimensions of family life often disrupted by alcohol or drug misuse

Rituals: the ways families celebrate religious or family occasions, such as Christmas or birthdays;

Roles: as one family member develops a substance problem, others take over their roles, for example, finances, disciplining, shopping and cleaning;

Routines: when behaviour becomes unpredictable it creates difficulties for the family in planning or committing to routines;

Communication: alcohol and drugs have a major effect on communication between family members;

Social life: families may become increasingly socially isolated owing to the difficulty of explaining that a family member has a drug or alcohol problem, or due to the social embarrassment or unpredictability associated with drinking and drugs;

Finances: a family's finances can be hugely affected by reduction in income – for example, owing to job loss – and spending of such income as is obtained on alcohol or drugs instead of more vital items;

Relationships and interactions: for example, both the misuser and their partner may become much more neglectful of other family members; aggression and violence are much more likely: more than 80 per cent of cases of violence between spouses are alcohol-related and 20–30 per cent of child misuse cases involve parents who are heavy drinkers [similar findings for problem drug users].

the *Framework for Assessment* (DH 2000), and specifically to consider the effect substance misuse has on relationships within the family, and the way it affects parenting roles and the achievement of basic family tasks. Dimensions of the 'third side' of the triangle – the dimension of the Framework that addresses environmental factors impacting on a child's development and well-being (see Jack and Gill 2003) – are important since children are likely to need support from a wider group of people than parents alone, especially if they live with a single substance-abusing parent.

Parents may function very differently at different times, so the assessment needs to aim to cover parenting at its best and at its worst, to gain a rounded picture of children's experiences within the family. Information about any strategies the adults in the family have for coping with unpredictable levels of competence on the part of the substance misuser is important for understanding how children are safeguarded at times of high risk of misuse or neglect. Understanding the way parenting roles are shared within the family is important, as children may need to take on more roles when parents' capacity to fill them is impaired. This may include taking inappropriate responsibility for themselves – getting themselves up for school, for example; caring for younger siblings, including babies; or caring for the parents themselves when they are incapable of doing so. Parenting may be distributed between a number of people, and vary in ways that are not predictable.

While practical arrangements for childcare are important, patterns of emotional care are arguably of equal importance for the future well-being of children from babyhood onwards. Unpredictable behaviour entails unpredictable emotional availability and responsiveness of parents to children. The withdrawal of maternal emotional responsiveness, even in the very short term, is a known cause of distress to young children (Allen 2011). The impact on young children, whose attachment patterns are still at a relatively early stage of development, gives cause for particular concern. When carrying out an assessment of a family with a substance-misusing parent, gaining a picture of the parents' ability to provide *consistency* across all the dimensions of the assessment framework is important, as well as having a picture of the 'highs' and lows' of parenting.

Assessment needs to explicitly address the extent to which parenting is affected by substance misuse, and the likely effect of any deficit in parenting on the child. *Pattern* and *context* are highly significant when seeking to identify the extent of risk to the children. This includes the risk of long-term harm to development – emotional, educational, physical, psychological/self-esteem, sexual, moral and social – through growing up in a family whose 'organising principle' is parental substance dependency, as well as the risk of harm through specific incidents. Incidents of harm may be caused by parental lack of self-control and aggression directed at the child or at others, or by neglect and lack of awareness or concern about the risks to children from environmental hazards – including drugs, medication stored in the home, traffic, needles, heat sources, etc. – and from other people – risk of sexual misuse, for example. Parental misuse of drugs/alcohol may be associated with the exposure of children to witnessing violence directed at another person, or exposure to criminal activities.

Humphreys *et al.* (2005: 1304) note a tendency for service users to become 'pigeon holed' as belonging to one category of service user, for example, as having drug or alcohol problems or experiencing domestic violence, and receive services for that issue but are seldom in receipt of support for the full range of problems they face: '... [i]n the process of referral and help-seeking, one or the other issue becomes lost'. Similarly, assessment needs to be sensitive to the full range of interrelated difficulties that may affect children in families where drugs or alcohol are being misused, and avoid focusing on one problem alone. To do so may create a more manageable focus of work with the adults, but lead to an underestimate of the level of risk to the children. The parent may have an invest-ment in focusing on a problem that they feel less ashamed about, or more able to address with support, but this may not be the problem that is having the greatest impact on the children. Compliance can therefore be genuine, but limited in scope and ultimately serve to conceal the lack of engagement relating to other issues. It may also lead to an underestimate of the difficulty of getting help. Refuges for women who are victims of violence may exclude women with drug problems, and being addicted to illegal drugs may make seeking help from the police for victimisation by a partner more difficult. Violent partners may also make seeking help for addiction impossible, even when the woman is motivated to do so. Many homeless shelters exclude substance users, as do temporary hostels and 'B&B' hotels, so that children may be at risk of being accommodated by the local authority due to homelessness; although substance misuse may be the root cause of inability to find accommodation. Maintaining an open mind about the way issues interact is important during the assessment, and also calls for analytical skills in piecing together an understanding of the way the different forces affecting a child act in concert to protect or place them at risk.

Children in families affected by drugs or alcohol may have begun to develop their own coping strategies, which may be more or less effective in keeping them safe. Their wishes and feelings will be important in planning support for the family. This is particularly important for older children who may feel they have taken on responsibilities to keep the family together by caring for other family members, seeking help, or hiding the extent of the family's problems. All family members are likely to have become accustomed to

---

Box 10.2 General issues to consider during assessment of families include:

- *Who* is adversely affected by this behaviour – drug/alcohol dependency or prob-lematic consumption, for example bingeing?
- *How* are they affected?
- *How much* are they affected?
- *What* is it about the person's behaviour when they take drugs or drink that is problematic?
- What steps do family members take to *minimise impact* on the children, and what evidence is there that these strategies are successful?
- Is it a problem some of the time or all of the time: is there a particular *pattern* to the consumption or times when it is particularly risky?
- What interacting factors *add to the vulnerability* of the affected children, and what factors offer some protection from harm?
- *How resilient* do the children appear to be in this situation, and what concrete evidence is there for this?

maintaining secrecy about their lives (Kroll and Taylor 2002). Establishing trust may take time. Workers need to reflect on what they may mean to the child: how far do they offer the promise of things getting better, and in what ways may they also appear to be a threat to the vulnerable status quo in the family? What might help to make them trustworthy from the point of view of a child in this particular family?

The focus in this work is not primarily on the behaviour of the adults involved – although this is obviously key – but on the effect the adults' behaviour has, or risks having in future, on the children and young people for whom they have responsibility. Younger children are relatively passive participants in the parents' lifestyle. As they get older they are likely to become increasingly active in making their own choices about how to cope with the parent's problem. These choices may add to their safety, or expose them to higher levels of risk.

A problem that can start before birth, and continue into adulthood

Maternal drug or alcohol misuse can affect children from conception onwards. Alcohol and drugs such as amphetamines, barbiturates, cocaine and opiates can all pass through the placenta to affect unborn children, who become passively addicted. After birth, they may suffer from the after-effects of exposure to these substances, known as neonatal abstinence syndrome. Before birth, the foetus may grow more slowly, including slower growth of head circumference, and there is evidence that later problems with behaviour, respiration, attention and cognitive functions, among other things, may all be traced back to exposure to drugs while in the uterus.

The nature and extent of problems is difficult to predict prior to birth, as there is wide variability in individual responses. Newborn babies may need to be given small quantities of the drug used by the mother and weaned off it gradually. A longer stay in hospital may be required, with implications for mother–baby bonding. Breast-feeding may be inadvisable too. Symptoms of neonatal abstinence syndrome include high levels of crying, irritability and being hard to comfort; sleep problems; poor feeding and slow weight gain; diarrhoea, vomiting and tremors. The symptoms usually start within a few days of birth and may last a few days, or continue for months. The effects of antenatal exposure to drugs or alcohol can make babies more demanding to care for, which can be especially problematic if their main carer is abusing drugs or alcohol.

> Prenatal drug use has been associated with potentially deleterious and even long-term effects on exposed children. However, estimating the full extent of the consequences of maternal drug misuse is difficult for many reasons. Multiple individual, family, and environmental factors –such as, nutritional status, extent of prenatal care, neglect or misuse, socioeconomic conditions, and many other variables – make it difficult to determine the direct impact of prenatal drug use on the child.
>
> NIDA 2009

After birth, the negative effects of parental substance misuse may continue. The direct effects of substance misuse on parenting capacity may be compounded by material deprivation if most household income is spent on drugs. Parental involvement in illegal activities, including purchasing drugs and engaging in illegal or otherwise risky activities to

---

Box 10.3 Hidden Harm: Next Steps sets out guidance for best practice with unborn children of substance abusing mothers in Scotland

- *identifying* as early as possible in pregnancy the possible spectrum of risk to, and needs of, both mother and baby, and alerting services before the birth;
- *developing* effective care plans and regular and realistic review of the plans;
- *offering* a range of multi-agency/multi-professional approaches to care, that are non-judgemental; and
- *ensuring* that no pregnant woman, misusing substances, arrives at a maternity unit to give birth without her situation being known and without support being available for her and her child.

Scottish Government 2006

---

finance the purchase of drugs may impact on children. Parental criminalisation may mean that children are deprived of a parent when the parent is imprisoned. The social stigma of being a member of a household identified as a drug user's or problem drinker's household may cause social problems for children, possibly compounded by the social impact of being neglected, itself a possible cause of isolation from peers. Older children may struggle to develop an identity for themselves that is not adversely affected by the family's relationship with drugs or alcohol.

There may be serious consequences for the emotional welfare of children of substance misusers. Nearly half the children of problem drinkers sometimes feel that parents do not love them (Velleman and Templeton 2007). Emotional as well as physical abuse of children by a substance misusing parent is not uncommon (Kroll 2004; Laybourn *et al.* 1996). The need to prioritise a supply of drugs, which is an almost inevitable effect of addiction, leads some parents with substance abuse problems to take chances with their children's welfare (Barnard and McKeganey 2004).

Many factors can ameliorate or accentuate the difficulties experienced by children living with drug-using parents. Drug or alcohol use may not be a 'freestanding' problem, but a symptom of some other difficulty of the parent's, such as a mental health problem, domestic violence, or the continuing effect of unresolved childhood abuse. To add to the risk factors impinging on children of drug users, polysubstance misuse is 'increasingly the norm' (HM Government 2010). Whether or not there is support for the parent in relation to the other problems they may be experiencing may be a factor in determining how capable that parent is to care for their children. However, too much emphasis on the needs of the parents can undermine a focus on the child's needs, as happened in the case of Caleb Ness (O'Brien 2003). The dangers of over-emphasis on the parents' needs has been noted in a number of Serious Case Reviews (Ofsted 2010).

Manning *et al.* (2009) argue that it is not just the absolute quantity of drugs or alcohol consumed but also the pattern of use that affects the way substance misuse affects parenting. Different patterns of use present different challenges. 'Binge' use by parents who are otherwise caring and capable parents presents different problems from chaotic

Box 10.4 Risk factors related to parental drug and alcohol use

- 'Bingeing' leading to loss of physical capacity to care for children in periods of extreme intoxication.
- Chaotic and unpredictable lifestyle.
- Poverty because household money goes on drugs, alcohol, etc.
- Emotional neglect when parents' ability to respond to children's emotional needs is impaired by intoxication or being 'hungover' or experiencing withdrawal symptoms, also unpredictable and inconsistent emotional responding to children.
- Emotional abuse if parents' feelings of worthlessness, poor self-control, anger and physical discomfort cause them to vent this on their children.
- Physical neglect, which may be linked to poverty, or impaired capacity to perceive or respond to children's physical needs, or lack of motivation to do so. Effects may include hunger and poor nutrition – for example, a diet largely of sweets, or lack of routines – for example, irregular bedtime, poor hygiene, inadequate bedding or clothing.
- Physical abuse linked to lack of parental self-control during intoxication/withdrawal, or as a result of parental failure to protect from abuse by others.
- Injury or death through accidents associated with low levels of supervision by parents, low levels of safety awareness, needles and other drug paraphernalia left lying around, or medication, for example methadone.
- Vulnerability to sexual abuse because of poor assessment of risk and inadequate supervision by parents.
- Loss of a parent through parental accidental overdose, interpersonal violence, suicide, imprisonment – and the worry that this may happen.
- Educational neglect: poor school attendance and poor support for educational activities.
- Social exclusion related to poor physical condition of household and of children, social stigma of addiction.
- Social isolation from peers.
- Disrupted relationships with wider family, for example, grandparents, aunts and uncles.
- Poor or ambivalent attachment of children to parent who misuses drugs/alcohol linked to unpredictable behaviour and emotional lability of parent. Hospitalisation of child for treatment of neonatal withdrawal symptoms may also affect mother–baby relationship.
- Exposure to criminal activities, witnessing interpersonal violence.
- Disrupted lifestyle, determined by parental needs not children's needs.
- 'Parentification' of children: children may be pressed into roles caring for parents or younger siblings.
- Distorted communication within the family – the 'elephant in the room'.

long-term use. Children of different ages have different care needs, which interact with parents' pattern of use. The problem with labelling parents as 'drug addicts' or 'alcoholics' and seeing this as the primary or only problem is that the substance misuse may be a symptom of something else. Resources for drug treatment are rarely accompanied by other specialist services such as psychotherapy, specialist counselling, or anti-poverty measures. People whose lives include a long history of ill-treatment and who have become substance addicted in the course of such ill-treatment by others, may not perceive their own situation as remarkable, and may need support to develop the self-worth needed to begin to address their addiction problems and their other difficulties.

Adverse experiences in childhood, including exposure to parental substance misuse, may be associated with a higher risk of heavy drinking or drug use in later life, contributing to an intergenerational 'cycle of addiction'. However, many people have difficulties with substance misuse without such a problematic family background, and many children of drug- or alcohol-dependent parents do not become drug or alcohol dependent themselves. As with other hypothetical 'cycles', exposure to adversity in childhood is a risk factor for adult difficulties, but the causal relationship between exposure and adult outcomes is not a simple or straightforward one. Many interacting factors come into play, including the resilience of the children/adults involved and the availability of support at critical times.

Growing up with an addicted parent increases the risk of a wide range of adverse experiences for children. As well as risks to the child directly, there are also risks to their

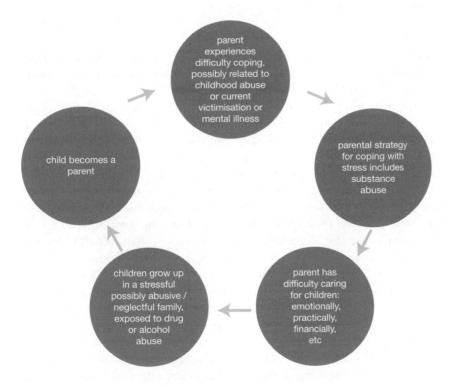

Figure 10.1 The idea of a 'cycle of addiction', or the possible interaction between adversity and addiction

network and family, including a higher risk of parental separation or divorce. Frequent moves may disrupt friendships, or relationships may suddenly end. Substance misusers are at higher risk of contemplating suicide, and deliberate or accidental overdosing may be a threat of which children become aware. A number of very vulnerable children live in households where alcohol or substance misuse is associated with violence. In Scotland, Manning *et al.* (2009) estimated that 2.5 per cent of children live in households where there is alcohol-related violence; the figure for substance-misuse related violence is 1.2 per cent. They further estimated that about half of the children in these households have witnessed drug- or alcohol-related acts of violence. Of an estimated 334,000 children living with a dependent drug user in 2003, 107,000 children lived with a parent who had taken a drug overdose.

Growing up in a household where children experience adverse events increases the risk they will become substance dependent, especially if they have seen substance misuse modelled as a way of coping in adversity. Young people are more vulnerable than adults to the onset of both addiction problems and mental health problems, and a difficulty in one area may make for vulnerability in another:

> Those experiencing mental ill-health have a higher risk of substance misuse. The majority of mental illness starts before adulthood. Other behavioural problems, including substance misuse also start more often during this period. For young people, emotional and behavioural disorders are associated with an increased risk of experimentation, misuse and dependence.
>
> HM Government 2010: 7

Another factor may be that children of addicted parents have lower self-esteem than children whose parents are not addicted (Godsall *et al.* 2004). Less competent, less conventional parenting may affect children's self-esteem, and lower self-esteem on the part of the children may contribute to their vulnerability to abusing drugs or alcohol when they get older. Interventions that promote the self-esteem of children of addicted parents may help to promote resilience and decrease the possibility that the cycle will be repeated in the next generation, even when parental behaviour is resistant to change (Brook *et al.* 2007).

Intervention early in the child's life was more likely to have a positive outcome. Forrester and Harwin (2006) found that children removed from substance-abusing parents did better than those who remained at home, even though it seems probable that the children who were removed from their parents came from the most difficult family situations. A valuable resource for identifying approaches to working with children and families that have been shown to have a positive impact in rigorous evaluation of effectiveness is the *Allen Review* of early intervention strategies (Allen 2011). Early intervention can mean intervening to promote the well-being of young children, and also means intervening early in the development of a problem affecting a child or young person. While the Allen Review does not recommend any approaches specifically aimed at families in which substance misuse is a problem, it is a valuable resource when considering what type of approach might be effective with a particular family. It is worth making the point again that substance misuse often occurs in combination with other problems, and assessments need to aim to explore the range of problems, even if it is unlikely that one intervention can target all of them at once.

Being a parent may provide the motivation the substance misuser needs to enter treatment and complete it, or to cut back on drug use, or to stop using altogether. Fraser *et al.* (2009) found that 13 out of 18 families interviewed cited a wish to improve relationships with their children as an important factor in deciding to moderate substance misuse. The aim may be to improve their care of their children, or to enable them to resume care of them, or just to have a better relationship with them while they live with someone else. The barriers are substantial, but desire to recover their relationship with their children may be a spur to entering '... the frightening road to recovery, where they confronted the consequences of their past failures. They did so because of their children' (Hardesty and Black 1999, cited in Rhodes *et al.* 2010: 1490). Parents who are unable to do this may still care *about* their children, even when their ability to care *for* them is compromised (Bancroft *et al.* 2004, cited in Fraser *et al.* 2009).

Interventions that alcohol- and drug-related research suggests may be helpful for children: resilience and stress

Velleman and colleagues (Velleman and Templeton 2003; Velleman *et al.* 2008) consider the effects on children of living with drug or alcohol dependent parents in terms of:

- the *stress* it causes;
- the *strain* of living with addiction,
- the *coping mechanisms* required to manage it, and their effectiveness, and
- the *support needs* of children and young people in families where addiction is an issue.

The *Stress-Strain-Coping-Support* (SSCS) model is based on international research that suggests there is a '... core set of experiences, common across the world, experienced by family members of those with alcohol or drug problems' (Velleman *et al.* 2008: 387). Children and young people attempt to find ways of coping with these stressful experiences. Adaptive coping strategies foster resilience. The key to *resilience* in childhood is linked to the development of psychological *strategies for coping* with adversity.

Resilience is demonstrated or manifested in the *responses* of a person – child or young person – to the adversities they face. It is not a static trait, but the product of interaction between the person – with their biological and genetic characteristics – and their social environment. Whether a child is able to show resilience or not is, therefore, to some extent conditional on the opportunities available to them. It is not to be confused with *protective factors*, which are features of the person's environment, not qualities of the child. Being resilient in the present increases the probability that someone will show resilience in the future, but it may vary over time, increasing or decreasing as circumstances change (Velleman and Templeton 2007: 81-2). It can therefore be nurtured, but cannot be taken for granted, assuming that a resilient child will continue to cope.

Resilience is mediated through *psychological coping strategies*. Workers need to consider the range of strategies used by any individual child or young person in coping with the stressful situation in which they are living, the effectiveness of these strategies, and their probable longer term effect on the young person's social development and chances of future social inclusion and self-fulfilment. Some strategies provide the basis for resilient behaviour that enables children to escape adverse parenting relatively unscathed, while others that are useful in short term may be harmful in the longer term (Velleman and Templeton 2007).

One example of a strategy that may be very useful in the short term but harmful in the longer term is social withdrawal. This may promote safety in the short term in a chaotic or abusive family, but may have damaging long-term effects if it leads to social isolation and negative introspection in adolescence. Another strategy that may have long-term negative effects is 'escaping' to join another social group. Some adolescents may seek to escape a difficult home life by becoming closely involved with a peer group, possibly putting themselves at risk of becoming involved in antisocial activities.

Young people who are most likely do well in difficult circumstances include those who feel able to take control of their lives, set their own goals and work towards them, taking advantage of such opportunities – including educational opportunities – that come their way. These findings in relation to children and young people whose parents misuse drugs or alcohol mirror research into the factors that foster success in young people in care (Jackson *et al.* 2005). Support is important to enable children and young people to take more control over their lives, but support is not enough on its own to create resilience: it is the interaction between the young person and their environment which makes the difference between being a survivor or a casualty of parental substance misuse (Velleman and Templeton 2007, 2008). Engaging the young person's motivation and confidence appears to be a key component in fostering resilience in children and young people facing a range of challenges, and may be as important in terms of long-term benefits as the provision of the support that needs to accompany it. However, a resilient child may still be at risk of harm and even death: resilience is, as noted, a quality of the interaction between a child and their environment, and a very hazardous or neglectful environment may still be beyond the coping skills of the child. There are moral reasons and legal safeguards for not relying on children's resilience to keep them safe and well, even though fostering resilience is likely to be an asset for the child when care falls below optimal levels.

Gender of significant adults in the child's life

Substance abusing parents who are responsible for children's day-to-day care are more often women than men, and are often lone parents (Forrester and Harwin 2006). Tracy and Johnson (2007) review the literature relating to women with substance misuse problems, and note the association between substance misuse and depression, anxiety and post-traumatic stress. When substance misuse and mental illness occur together, women are more likely to have a history of physical and sexual misuse as well as victimisation and homelessness in adulthood. Women with substance misuse problems include some extremely vulnerable, multiply victimised women. The majority of families headed by a lone substance-abusing parent are female-headed families, which can make children's access to a non-substance-abusing carer difficult (Forrester and Harwin 2006).

Men are also important in children's lives, and attention needs to be paid in assessment as to which men feature in children's lives, and what roles they play. They may be present as resident fathers in the family, and may have a positive or negative influence on the well-being of the family and the children. They may have an important influence on child welfare even though they are not living in the same household as the child, again, influencing things for the child for better or worse: as a supportive other parent, or as someone

Box 10.5 Factors promoting resilience

- A stable, preferably non-addicted parent figure, ideally present consistently from early childhood.
- Someone the child/young person can talk to, and a supportive wider social network.
- Feeling loved and cared for, even in the context of family disruption.
- Family cohesion and harmony.
- Opportunities – for activities, achievements, positive life planning.

Coping strategies, in order of frequency used by children and young people

- *Social support*: the most frequently used and most effective strategy for coping with alcohol problems in the family. Spending time with other people who are not causing the child stress: family, other grown-ups and friends. Ideally on a regular basis and with a consistent person or group.
- *Wishful thinking*: the next most frequent strategy used by children, but not very effective except perhaps as an 'escape' in the short term.
- *Problem solving*: the most useful strategy after seeking social support. Highly linked to indicators of resilience. Seeking ways to actively cope, including engaging other adults to help.
- *Emotional regulation*: could be either shouting and screaming, or trying to calm oneself down. Ranked by children as moderately effective.
- *Distraction*: trying to think about something else, watching TV, playing a game. This was considered by children to be a fairly effective coping strategy, after seeking social support and problem solving.
- *Social withdrawal*: this was ranked quite low for usefulness, and although it may remove the child from danger in the short term, if pursued as a longer term coping strategy, it may place the child or young person at risk of other negative outcomes, as discussed above.
- *Cognitive restructuring*: trying to see the problem more positively, or blaming someone else for the problem, not taking blame on oneself.
- *Resignation*: doing nothing, believing nothing can be done.
- *Self-criticism*: blaming oneself, thinking one might have contributed to the problem. The last three strategies were ranked by the young people as the least effective, although accurate attribution of responsibility has been found to be important in other situations in which children have been victimized, such as sexual misuse.

Indicators of resilience

- Deliberate planning by the child for their future life.
- Positive self-esteem.
- High sense of self-efficacy and feeling in control of one's life.
- Good problem solving skills.
- Good social skills.
- Previous experience of resilience and success.
- Values that support positive use of skills and abilities.

after Velleman and Templeton 2008

who threatens the family's security. They may be unrelated men who are the mother's partner: long-term and stable, or new and a somewhat unknown influence. They may be relatively invisible to child welfare services, unless efforts are made to find out about them. They may wish to be more visible and engaged – as Peter Connelly's father reportedly did – or less visible – as was the case with his mother's partner (London Borough of Haringey 2009). Understanding a child's world involves finding out about the men who are involved in the child's life, as well as the women. Bias in social care processes and established ways of thinking that exert a subtle continuing influence on practice need to be interrogated to avoid a narrow focus on one parent or one gender.

Children living with a substance-abusing lone parent whose other parent is not a substance misuser may have feelings that are hard to reconcile about *both* their parents. The parent with whom they live cares for them, but the care they receive may not be adequate; the other parent may appear capable of providing better care but does not, for whatever reason, protect them from harm or neglect. This may be inexplicable to the child (Kroll 2004: 135).

Velleman and Templeton (2008) explored children's views of both mothers and fathers who drink. Children were more likely to argue or fight with their mother when she was drinking than with their father; more likely to threaten their mother that they would run away if she did not stop drinking; more likely to feel responsible and guilty if the drinker was their mother; more likely to feel blamed for their mother's drinking than their father's; and more likely to take on household chores usually done by their mother than by their father. They were also twice as likely to be upset, cry and worry when the drinker was their mother. Children appear more likely to take responsibility for drinking and its practical and emotional consequences when the parent who drinks is their mother. The gender of parent who was drinking made little difference to the likelihood that children would feel alone, scared, angry or frustrated because of parental drinking, but lone female parents may place their children at higher risk of the stresses and strains that oblige children to try out the coping strategies discussed above.

Box 10.6 Exercise: promoting resilience

Look at the list of factors that promote resilience, coping strategies and indicators of resilience on page 185.

Consider the ideas of *self-esteem, self-efficacy* and *feeling 'in control'*.

In what ways do you think being the child of a problem drinker may affect self-esteem, self-efficacy and feeling able to control one's life?

How do you think resilience-promoting factors – family and social factors – and coping strategies – children's ways of trying to cope with parental drinking – can reduce the threat to children's sense of self-esteem, self-efficacy and feeling of being 'in control'?

What messages for practice can you draw from this exercise? Think of six specific things that one might do in working with the family of a lone parent who is a problem drinker with children aged five and 13 to try to promote the children's resilience.

The 'elephant in the room' and the problem of talking about drug and alcohol problems in the family

Where there are concerns that a child has suffered, or is at risk of suffering, significant harm, the question arises as to how the views of the child can be obtained. Children of drug and alcohol misusers are often aware from an early age that they need to be careful what they say to people inside and outside the family, having grown up in an atmosphere of secrecy and denial. Certain things may be seen but not discussed, taking on the puzzling character of an unmentioned 'elephant in the room' (Kroll and Taylor 2002).

Children who are very young are highly dependent and vulnerable, and also often unable to describe what has happened to them. This makes the skill of the social worker in establishing effective communication with parents particularly important. Parents may not be open or honest, and assessments need to take account of the uncertainty this brings to the assessment process. A distinction needs to be drawn between those things that one can be confident are true, the things that may be true but cannot be verified, and things that have not been confirmed and may not be true, or appear to be untrue. Certainty may be elusive, but this does not prevent attempts to evaluate the confidence that can be placed in what has been said (Munro 2011).

Kroll (2004: 132) describes the culture of 'denial, distortion and secrecy' often associated with substance misuse which cuts users off from their communities and families, isolates children from potential sources of support, and makes children feel 'shut out' of the lives of adults, including their parents. They may feel obliged to keep their parents' secrets while also wanting people to try harder to find out what is happening to them and their family.

Barnard (2005) reflects on the precedence taken by drugs, and the 'myopic focus' on them of drug-addicted women. At the same time, social workers need to avoid a similar myopic focus on the issue of substance misuse and retain the ability to look at all the available evidence about strengths and weaknesses in parenting capacity. They also need to look more widely at risks and resilience: children's responses to parental substance misuse may continue to cause them difficulty, even if the parent stops abusing drugs or alcohol. Children may need support in their own right, and reducing intake of drugs or alcohol may raise other issues for which the user needs support.

Children learn to avoid or not respond to problematic things that happen to the adults around them. Intoxication, withdrawal symptoms, unpredictable mood or behaviour, unexplained adult injuries, unreliability and breaking promises for unconvincing reasons are possible examples. Things may happen that are not understandable without an understanding of substance misuse, yet no explanation is offered. The illusion of normalcy may be fragile at times, for the benefit of the adults' self-esteem as much as for the children (Rhodes *et al.* 2010). Children may realise that there is a problem, and that things are different in other families, but be unable to name the problem or discuss it with anyone. They learn it is something that cannot be talked about, or only talked about to people that the child feels they can trust (Kroll and Taylor 2002). Children find having good social support and someone to talk to enormously valuable; having someone to talk to is probably the most valuable strategy for coping with parental addiction. Nevertheless, research indicates that most young people find it difficult to cope in families with drug and alcohol problems and many feel that they have little support in coping (Velleman *et al.* 2008). This does not mean that children and young people will find it easy to trust professionals who offer support. They may feel responsible for parents and their siblings, placing them in a dilemma with conflicting loyalties. At the same time, as they begin to understand that drugs are dangerous, they may become anxious about the future if no help is given to the family (Barnard and Barlow 2003).

Specific questions that practitioners should seek to answer when carrying out an assessment under the *Framework for Assessment* (DH 2000) in cases of parental substance misuse

- What is the quality of relationships within the child's wider family, and how do drugs/ alcohol impact on family relationships?
- What is the pattern of caring within the family: who in addition to the parents does what caring, for whom, and how and when do they do it?
- Is there a family routine that privileges children's needs?
- What is the pattern of use of drugs or alcohol by the parents?
- What is the parents' level of awareness and responsibility in relation to drug-related risks, including risks associated with the presence of drug paraphernalia, drugs and prescription drugs, such as methadone, in the household?
- Are children likely to be exposed to violence or criminal behaviour linked to drug or alcohol consumption?
- What arrangements, if any, are made by the parents or others – for example, other relatives – to keep the children safe while parents are intoxicated?
- How well is the family integrated into a network of support that is not primarily drug- or alcohol-related? Or are they socially isolated?
- Do the children have access to support from adults that they feel they can talk to, who listen to them, and whom they see regularly and trust?
- What is the level of the parents' a) commitment and b) capacity to ensure that their consumption of drugs or alcohol does not impact negatively on their children? What evidence is there of this?
- What are the views of the children on their quality of life and the quality of their care by their parents?
- What is needed to keep them safe, and what would promote their resilience?
- In view of all the above, and information from the three domains of the *Framework for Assessment*, what is the actual or likely impact of parental substance misuse on children's emotional, physical, educational, sexual and moral development?

The barriers to achieving such a detailed assessment of the impact of drugs or alcohol on children's lives are – at least – threefold:

- Fear of repercussions if problems associated with drug taking or alcohol dependency are discussed honestly: fear that the parents will lose the care of their children, and the threat of possible criminal sanctions for taking illegal drugs.
- The level of stigma associated with drug taking and alcohol dependence is a disincentive to discussing it.

- A culture of denial and minimisation may mean that the habit of ordering thought and speech to deny the reality of what is happening is a deeply ingrained habit, or has become automatic.

Substance misuse and the extended family

Extended families can be a source of much-needed support for families with a substance-abusing member, but substance misuse may lead to strained relationships within the family (Barnard 2003). Parents' substance misuse may be linked to childhood difficulties, indicating that family relationships have been problematic for a long time. While assumptions about the cyclical nature of addiction may be simplistic, addiction can impact on family relationships across generations. Parents whose own parents step in to support their grandchildren may struggle with mixed feelings of relief, gratitude, resentment and humiliation as the grandparents take on the role of family 'rescuer'. Issues of who is to blame for the state of the family may be a potent trigger for conflict.

Grandparents – or other relatives – may resent the consequences for themselves of becoming a carer, even as they act to protect their children and grandchildren from harm. The consequences of becoming involved may include: the psychological stress of worrying about children's and grandchildren's safety and welfare; loss of leisure; the physical demands of childcare 'second time around'; the drain on financial resources; and the strain on relationships within the wider family – who may have different views on the best way of managing the situation. Their age, health, financial and family circumstances are all relevant to the ease or difficulty with which they can offer help. The attitude of the substance-abusing child/parent to being helped by their parents is also important. The undermining of their role as parents may be difficult for them to accept, although this may be outweighed by relief that someone else is taking over the burden of childcare.

Grandchildren who have become used to life in a family without clear rules and routines may not adapt quickly to life in a differently ordered household, although others may adapt quickly to a more ordered and safe environment. Impaired attachments and atypical expectations about family life may make them challenging to care for. Grandparents and other relatives who take on the parental role may need substantial support (Kroll 2007). Households with no other children in the family may struggle most (Farmer and Moyers 2005). Kin carers struggle more to cope than unrelated foster carers, often with fewer resources and backup but, despite this, the rate of breakdown of placements appears to be similar. More than half the kin carers in one study had to cope with hostility and aggression from parents or other relatives. Alliances between parents and carers against the social workers, or within the extended family against the carers, were sometimes issues too (Farmer and Moyers 2005).

Empathy, interviewing, engaging and reflecting

Barnard (2005) discusses the importance of workers who are dealing with substance-abusing parents retaining their sense of compassion and empathy for those they are working with. They are experiencing severe social problems including long-standing difficulties and challenges often going back to childhood (Forrester and Harwin 2006). Compassion and empathy are important to promote successful engagement, especially when sensitive subjects are being discussed. The absence of compassion or empathy is likely to trigger resistance, which may take the form of denial of the problem, or minimisation of its consequences (Forrester *et al.* 2007; Forrester *et al.* 2008).

Reflective ability is also important for parents. Barriers to reflection for substance-abusing parents may include a preoccupation with their own needs, and difficulty focusing on uncomfortable aspects of their own performance as parents. Reflective function involves being able to consider the possible thoughts, motivations and feelings of other people and link these to one's own behaviour, feelings and thoughts (Slade 2005). It requires a capacity for *mentalisation*: a concept developed by Fonagy and colleagues over a number of years to describe the reflexive understanding of one's own and others' mental states.[3] Drug and alcohol users may be in denial over the impact of their addiction problem on others, especially their children, impacting on their ability to perceive and make sense of others' emotional experience. Their ability to *make meaning* out of interaction with their children and others is an important part of managing their role as a parent:

> The process of making meaning of internal states serves crucial intrapersonal functions; it provides the means to discover and give voice to vital aspects of subjective experience, and allows for deep and broad self-knowledge. This process, whereby internal experience, feelings, and intentions are mentalized, leads to the development of structures crucial to self and affect regulation.
>
> Slade 2005: 2

Parents who are less able to reflect on their own behaviour, or the experiences of their children, and how the two may relate to one another, are less well equipped for the demands of parenting than someone who has more highly developed reflective capacity. Low ability to enter the world of their children, due to addiction or other reasons, may raise concerns about the parent's responsiveness to their children's needs. Substance abusing parents' accounts of their parenting may be very subjective (Barnard and McKeganey 2004; Barnard 2005) and it is probable that their accounts of other aspects of their lives may also be subjective, possibly distorted by guilt, denial and wishful thinking. A parent who is very wrapped up in their own needs and has difficulty in discussing their children's thoughts or feelings, or presents an unrealistic picture of how their children may feel in difficult circumstances, may give grounds for concern about their ability to put their children's needs before their own interests.

Reflective questions may also attempt to explore parents' understanding of themselves: how they respond to pressures or positive experiences, for example. Social workers may use reflective questioning to explore parents' capacity to understand their children's experience, and their own part in shaping it. Barnard and Barlow (2003) found that once they were in recovery, formerly drug dependent parents were able to recognise and discuss their earlier denial. This suggests that addicted parents do not lack the capacity for empathy and mentalisation during periods of drug or alcohol misuse, but it is suppressed – possibly to protect parents' self-esteem and view of themselves as 'good enough parents' – during an episode of drug dependence. Limited ability to consider the impact of their substance abuse on their children would be an indication that the parent is in denial about the impact their problem has on their children.

Reflective function is a measure of the way people attribute meaning to their own and other people's actions, and make sense of the world (Fonagy *et al.* 1998). Parental reflective functioning relates to the capacity to hold the child's mental state in mind and relate it to other things that are going on, including one's own state of mind. It consists of:

- awareness of the nature of mental states;
- an explicit effort to tease out mental states underlying behaviour;
- recognition of the developmental significance of mental states;
- recognition of mental states in relation to the person one is talking with.

Fonagy et al. 1998; Slade 2005

This capacity to process interpersonal experience and make sense of each other enables us to understand that our own and others' behaviour:

> is linked in meaningful, predictable ways to underlying, likely unobservable, chang-ing and dynamic feelings and intentions. The more that human beings are able to envision mental states in the self or other ... the more likely they are to engage in productive, intimate, and sustaining relationships, to feel connected to others at a subjective level, but also to feel autonomous and of separate minds.

Slade 2005: 271

Questions about parents' perceptions of their children's thoughts and feelings may reveal how much they are in touch with their children's experience, giving an insight into how far they are able to prioritise their children's needs. If they are unable to think about or discuss their children's needs in an organised way, this is a poor indicator that they will be able to perceive and respond to those needs. However, without a degree of trust between service user and interviewer, it is difficult to distinguish between resistance to engagement, on the one hand, and denial and lack of capacity on the other. Parents who misuse drugs or alcohol may feel shame about what they do: about having a substance misuse problem, and about some of the things they do in order to accommodate addic-tion. The problems that may compound drug and alcohol problems, such as victimisation, involvement in criminal behaviour, mental distress and child neglect, are also problems that are highly stigmatised, potentially adding to feelings of shame (Taylor *et al.* 2008). The feeling that they will be blamed for their problems may make people defensive, sensitised to perceived criticism, and likely to respond very negatively to it. Aggressive responses may be linked to fear of what may happen as a result of social work intervention, the user's low self-esteem, and the poor view they think others are likely to hold of them.

Moral judgements about parents' lifestyle and childcare can interfere with social workers' ability to maintain 'pluralistic compassion' for both parents and children (Barnard 2005). Fook *et al.* (2000) use the term 'critical acceptance' to describe a mental and moral approach in which people are expected to take responsibility for their actions, but the process of reviewing those actions is concerned with change, not blame. Change is pursued through reflective analysis in an environment characterised by respect, accept-ance and a non-judgemental approach. The aim of reflective analysis is to unsettle assump-tions, especially about power, in order to explore possible ways of bringing about change (Fook 2007). While the aim of intervention with parents is to bring about change in their behaviour, this always has to be balanced against the timescale for the child, whose developmental needs become more, not less, pressing during a period of neglect.

In practice, with parents with substance dependency problems, there is no possibility of not holding them *responsible* for their parenting, while they have the care of their children or responsibility for their well-being, but *blaming* them for what has happened is unlikely to promote change. It is likely to be counter-productive: increasing shame, denial and avoidance. An attitude that is respectful and non-judgemental but firmly committed to the desirability and necessity for change offers a more productive starting point for analysis of the problems the parent is experiencing (Etherington 2007). If there is a possibility that a care, or other court order may be sought, this needs to be made clear. There is a risk this may be heard as a threat by parents, but the alternative, not explaining the parameters for engagement, would not be open or honest and therefore would be contrary to social work values. This is not the same as using a care order application as a threat, since it is one of a number of possibilities and the parents have the power to make changes, or not, to determine the outcome. It is likely that the distinction may seem rather fine to parents who are struggling to cope, however.

The vulnerability of children in many drug- or alcohol-abusing households means that workers' concerns are appropriately directed at safeguarding children. Many of these are especially vulnerable because they are very young. Hospitals are major sources of referrals since they see mothers during pregnancy and babies showing signs of withdrawal symptoms. Substance addiction professionals are likely to become involved with these families, although they are rarely the source of referrals to children's social care. When alcohol misuse was the reason for allocation of a social worker – often with older children aged between two and 13 years – substance misuse professionals were less likely to be involved with the family (Forrester and Harwin 2006).

Women with a dual disorder – substance misuse and mental ill-health – have been found to have very small social networks. Many members of their network were rated by them as 'supportive', but not supportive of their efforts to address substance misuse (Tracy and Johnson 2007). Children, however, are an exception, in that research shows that these members of substance misusers' networks do not want their parents to take drugs or alcohol, and often provide support for their parents' attempts to address their substance misuse. They also offer their parents social support, even at young ages (Kroll 2004; Tracy and Martin 2007; Fraser *et al.* 2009).

Practitioners need to distinguish between *sources of support* and *sources of support for sobriety and recovery*. They also need to be aware that while the focus is on parents supporting their children, in practice quite a lot of support may be flowing in the opposite direction in families in which parents have a severe addiction problem. Tracy and Martin (2007) suggest that when women stop using drugs or alcohol, they may also need to find a new social network to support them, and to avoid re-victimisation: in itself a significant challenge. Children may need support to give up acting as carers when parents cease to misuse substances and start to cope better. Empowering parents to become effective parents changes the balance of power in families in ways that may require considerable adjustment by other family members – who may have become used to high levels of independence and self-reliance as well as offering support.

Difficult and challenging questions need to be asked of parents when there are concerns about drug- or alcohol-related child misuse or neglect, however uncomfortable the parents find it. Answers often need to be probed where inconsistencies appear or answers seem improbable. Parental discomfort and anxiety may make the interview stressful for the social worker conducting the interview. When parents respond defensively or aggressively, this cannot be a reason for abandoning inquiry into the welfare of the children. Workers may reflect on possible reasons other than a preference for the 'status quo' that may make it difficult for parents to discuss addiction and its related problems, and use this reflection in thinking how to work with the family and plan subsequent interviews. Supervision should be an important part of this process of seeking support and developing skills in safeguarding children in families in which adults misuse drugs or alcohol.

Barnard (2007) takes the view that parents who are drug users can only bring up children without causing negative effects on the children when their drug habit is stringently controlled. Parents who use drugs have often told researchers that their addictions are likely to put children at risk of harm: of emotional neglect, if not other harm (Rhodes *et al.* 2010). On the one hand, commitment to being a 'good enough' parent and controlling drug use to minimise its impact on children may give resilient children the opportunity to develop without harm, but the risks of relapse into poorly controlled drug use, self-deception and damage to children is a risk in all families in which a parent is addicted, especially if there is no non-addicted adult taking a parental role in the family. Assessment needs to capture the subtle interaction between protective factors and risks, and have an opinion on the volatility or stability of arrangements made for children's care. Intervention needs to take account of the multi-dimensional nature of the problem, involving other agencies as appropriate, with the worker having access to supervision to help keep the needs of parents and children in perspective in line with agency responsibilities to both service users and staff.

Avoiding resistant responses and working towards engagement: good practice in interviewing in cases where parents misuse drugs or alcohol

- Use a mixture of open and closed questions, with frequent open questions to encourage parents to give their account in their own words. This may make the interview take longer – for example, issues to be covered in completing an assessment under the *Framework for Assessment* (DH 2000) – but may also make it more informative. *Normalising comments* may help to open up discussion, by giving reassurance that the experiences that are being discussed are not unique – the parent being assessed is not the only one who has had such experiences, and others have similar problems. It also speaks to the legitimacy of the worker – reinforcing their experience and expertise in working with people who have problems with substance abuse while also being a parent. (Questions such as: 'Sometimes we find when this happens, certain other things happen, is that how it is for you?') The normalisation of the event can be a powerful opening to disclosure.
- Avoid posing too many 'either/or' type questions, since you may have not considered all the possibilities. The binary choice you offer could be a 'false dichotomy', closing down the possibility of exploring the meaning of a more open question and offering a more nuanced answer.
- Use reflection as an *interview technique* to create prompts to explore in more depth the meaning of things the parents or children have said. This may be *simple* reflection,

reflecting back understanding of what the other person has just said. It may be *complex*, for example, identifying a theme that runs through the conversation, or identifying an apparent contradiction between two points of view apparently held simultaneously. Reflections are not questions, but invitations to expand on what has been said, or correct impressions given. They may stimulate *reflective discussion* from the other person.

- Reflective discussion may help explore parents' *reflective functioning*. This is exploration of their capacity to reflect on their relationships with other people: children, other professionals, their partner, their parents, and important others. Explore their understanding of other people's thoughts, motivations and feelings and children's needs.

Concluding comments

Hester (2011) describes the different professional groups working with people with drug and alcohol addiction problems as coming from 'different planets' conceptually. Different frames of reference are used to understand the reasons for addiction, and appraise the moral issues of responsibility for self and others, and the nature of harm. The parental duty to protect children arguably implies parental responsibility for self-care in order to be able to discharge this duty. The different 'planets' of social work, healthcare and law enforcement are often brought together to provide what needs to be an integrated service from agencies that work well together. The role of the Local Safeguarding Children Forum is important in promoting good inter-agency working practices, as Hester (2011) notes, but there are also responsibilities on workers to ensure that there is good collaboration at the level of provision for the individual family.

Research shows that parental use of drugs or alcohol – in the absence of robust alternative care arrangements – exposes children to risk of both physical and emotional harm. The more chronic or unpredictable the pattern of use, the more likely it is that parents will be unable to sustain a good level of physical and emotional care for children. The more problematic the parents find sustaining an adequate level of physical and emotional care for their children, the greater the incentive to avoid thinking about the impact of their addiction on their children. The 'elephant in the room' is something that cannot be spoken about, or thought about clearly because of the guilt this causes.

Parental resistance may be the result of fear of the consequences of discovery, as well as shame and guilt. Workers need to try to identify the barriers to co-operation, while retaining a focus on the needs of children, even when parents are reluctant to acknowledge or discuss parenting problems. The process of suppressing inconvenient information can begin even before a child is born: Söderström (2011) discusses the importance of pregnancy as a period of psychological preparation for motherhood, and how drugs can interfere with this process. Late awareness or acceptance of the pregnancy, ambivalence about becoming a mother, and guilt about the drugs already taken may be issues. If the mother decides to address her drug problem, resentment towards a partner who may continue to use drugs can put stress on the relationship with the baby's father, compounded by the loss of her usual social network. Guilt about earlier pregnancies that may have ended in difficulties may intrude. On the other hand, pregnancy can also offer the possibility of hope, a 'new beginning' for drug-using parents.

While a new baby may propose a reason to start a new life, a child who has lived for some years with addicted parents may have been exposed to chaotic parenting and emotional or physical neglect: patterns may have become established that are very difficult to break and the motivation to consider a 'new start' may be weak. The risk of losing a child may provide motivation, but Pajulo *et al.* (2006) suggest that parental bonding and drugs and alcohol are both sources of intense pleasure: the one can 'hijack' the other. The effect may be that the strength of the parents' attachment to drugs interferes with the parents' ability to bond with their babies and support their secure attachment to them. They suggest that a focus on nurturing parent–child attachment in treatment of addicted mothers is as important as a focus on drug treatment.

Parental use of drugs and alcohol follows a wide range of patterns: the negative effects of use of alcohol or drugs may be offset by responsible arrangements for care of the children, especially when parental use is intermittent. The critical factors are arguably not the level of consumption, but the pattern of consumption, its behavioural, social and economic consequences, and the impact this has on the children.

11   In care and going home

Working with parents towards reunification

This chapter:

- explores some of the main dimensions of reunification practice, and its legal and ethical underpinnings;
- considers some of the key research findings in relation to children returning home after a period in care.

Introduction

Concern about permanency has its roots in concern about the psychological well-being of children in care: 'Children need to know that life has predictability and continuity; they need the reliability of knowing where they will be growing up' (Maluccio and Fein 1986: 3).

Based on this premise, disruption to children's family life in the interests of protecting them needs to be balanced by planning processes that provide reassurance and address the instability and insecurity created by state intervention. This involves assessing their psychological and other needs, and addressing the needs of the parents to assess their potential for resuming care of their children. Reunification practice is a complex issue and this chapter aims to explore some of its main dimensions.

One of the most important considerations when thinking about reunification is giving thought to the reasons why the children first came into care. If the family needed support at the time the child entered care but either refused help or it was not available, then returning the child without addressing those support needs is likely to be prejudicial to the welfare of the child rather than helpful. The parents' support needs may also have changed over time, and this needs careful assessment. The support needs of the *child* may have changed during the time they have been in care, too, especially when children have been in care for a long period. Lastly, the separation between parents and child will have particular and specific implications for parents and children: how has a period of living apart affected their relationship?

Roger Morgan, Children's Rights Director for England, carried out a consultation with children in care to find out what they thought about the relationship between family support and coming into care. Nearly half the children consulted believed they would not

---

Box 11.1 Planning a return to parents'/family care – main areas to consider

- Have the problems that led to the child/young person coming into care been addressed, and have they changed over time? (Children's difficulties/parental difficulties/environmental factors leading to episode in care)
- What are the support needs of the child/young person likely to be if they return home?
- What support are the parents – or other family carers – likely to need to help them resume responsible care of the child/young person and safeguard their well-being?
- What are the main challenges that the child/young person and their family face in making a return home a success?

---

have needed to come into care if their families had received more support, but over a third said that, even with additional support for them and their families, they would still have needed to come into care (Morgan 2011b). For this last group of children, returning home could be highly problematic unless it can be shown that things have improved substantially in terms of the whole environment the parents are able to offer the children, and that parent/child relationships currently provide a healthy basis for resuming life within the family. This means assessing that the quality of contact between the child and their family will be important for the robustness of any plans to return children home.

Almost half the children included in Morgan's consultation thought that more support from the social worker, through home visits, for example, could have helped keep the children out of care (Morgan 2011b). This shows that many children and young people value the impact that regular visits by a social worker can have on their well-being while living with their families. Social workers need to reflect on the way their work is valued by children and young people, and consider how children and young people may see their input separately from the views expressed by their parents. Parental resistance does not imply that children are reluctant to see the social worker working with their family. Sometimes parents would also have welcomed more input, too (Sheppard 2008). Keeping in mind the importance of the child as the primary focus of concern means the social worker always considering the child's view of the services being offered, be it under s47, s17, s31 or s20 of the Children Act 1989.

Morgan (2011b) found that about half of all children in care thought more support would have been needed to keep them safe and well at home; presumably this is often needed at the point of return home if it is to be successful. Nearly half of the children in care thought they still needed to be in care, and less than one in five of the children thought they could currently go home to their parents. This suggests social workers' judgements about the ability of parents to provide adequate care for children is often consistent with the views of the children and young people themselves, but many children in care do not think they still need to be there.

This research also suggests that any optimism about the potential of a period in care alone to bring about improvement of parenting capacity would be misplaced. Children had concerns about parents' continuing incapacity to look after them, about pressure to return home when it was not what they wanted, and about the level of support that would be available to them when they returned home. Parenting capacity does not necessarily improve when parents have a break from parenting, indeed there is little reason to suppose that it would unless the difficulties relate to transient stresses or problems that are self-limiting – although children also saw respite care as a useful way of relieving pressure. An important finding in this research is how much importance children attach to direct social work input.[1] This should encourage social workers in the current project to review the focus of child and family social work and support professional refocusing on skilled direct work with children and families (Munro 2011).

Time to go home?

Time is always an issue in social work. There is never enough of it, and in many settings social workers' performance is partly measured against their ability to work to demanding timescales. These timescales are justified on the basis that they promote the welfare of service users, for whom 'waiting' is problematic, but the reverse of this is that pressure to complete tasks to time can, in a system under pressure, create a *lack* of time to spend with individual service users. Time is especially important for children, as their development continues regardless of their circumstances, but is also profoundly influenced by the circumstances in which they find themselves; circumstances over which they themselves often have very little control. It was perhaps the problem of delay in finding 'permanent' solutions to the care needs of young children in care that first focused social work's attention on the significance of time, and the 'ticking clock'. In the 1970s Rowe and Lambert found that 75 per cent of children in care had been there for more than two years; the majority of these were expected to stay there until they were 18 (Rowe and Lambert 1973). Although the situation in terms of the flow of children in and out of care is different now, the issue of purposeful planning for looked after children has increased in importance.

Recently the trend has been for more children who come into care to stay longer. Although the number entering care in Britain has decreased over the years, the increase in the time they stay in care means that the number of children who are looked after by local authorities has been increasing. There are approximately 64,500 children in care in England, an increase of 7 per cent since 2006. Children in care on care orders tend to remain in the care system the longest, longer than those who are accommodated with parental consent. Children on care orders make up about two thirds of the 'care population', contributing to the slowing of the rate of 'exit' from care. The proportion accommodated rather than in care on care orders has, however, been increasing over recent years, and currently stands at 33 per cent of children in care. The way a child comes into care and the age at which they enter the care system affect their probable length of stay, as well as the destination when they leave care: return home, return to other family members, adoption, etc. Timing of entry to care relative to the onset of family problems is also an issue. Thoburn states that:

> ... despite the intention of the legislation, policy in England veers towards the 'permanence' model brought over from the United States in the 1970s. High thresholds for entry into care are accompanied by attempts to ensure that those who do enter leave

as soon as possible through return to their parents or relatives or through adoption. These high thresholds, without the necessary investment in high quality services to vulnerable families at home or after reunification, have resulted in some children entering care too late when it is harder to turn things around for them.

Thoburn 2008: 15

About 70 per cent of children in care are in placements with foster families. The age range from which most children are fostered – about 40 per cent of the total – is 10–15 years (Harker 2011). Older children in care are those for whom permanency options are likely to be either a return to parents/other family or long-term foster care. Cost is an unavoidably significant factor in planning for looked after children: the average annual cost of looking after a child in care is in excess of £37,500 (Harker 2011), so supporting a return home with services makes sound economic sense, as long as the return is realistically likely to be a success for the child and family.

The majority of looked after children eventually return home (Sinclair *et al.* 2007). More than half of all children who enter the care system return home to their birth parents or other family members, and about 40 per cent return home to a birth parent within a year of entering care (Thoburn 2009). About a third of all looked after children are long-stay children in care. The longer a child is in care, the lower the probability they will return home. In Northern Ireland it was found that children whose case was open for less than a year were four times more likely to be returned to birth parents within a year than those whose case had been open between one and two years, and 25 times more likely than those whose case had been open three to four years (McSherry *et al.* 2010).

The reasons children enter care affect the chances of their returning home. Farmer and Parker (1991) distinguished between the 'disaffected' and the 'protected': children whose care needs rest on their need for protection from their parents. Some parental problems are more amenable to change than others. Children whose parents abuse alcohol have a lower probability of being able to return home than children of parents who do not, for example (McSherry *et al.* 2010). The family's attitude to the child entering care is significant, too: whether the child was accommodated at the parents' request, or removed compulsorily, or accommodated with parental reluctance, possibly under threat of care proceedings. Long-standing parental problems, including housing problems and poverty; having a single parent as a carer prior to coming into care, and coming into care under compulsion are contra-indicators for an early return home (Thoburn 2009). When considering the prospects for reunification with the birth family during the early stages of a child's time in care, it is important to consider what parental changes are needed, and the type of support the parent may need to achieve that change. A realistic timescale based on the child's developmental needs is important, as well as a strategy for ascertaining whether or not progress is being made towards the goal of reunification. This will be confirmed through the process of formal reviews of the child's care plan, so preparation for care plan reviews needs to include considering ways in which other agencies can contribute to an assessment of parental progress with certain types of problem, such as substance abuse.

The factors that support or hinder a return home may include the problems displayed by the child or young person: behavioural problems, for example. For some families, change may be needed in the behaviour of both the young person and the family. The parents' behaviour may have been a causal, amplifying or maintaining factor in the child's behaviour, so a change in the child's behaviour while they are in care may not be enough to be confident that a return home will work. Parental and child motivation to change may be a factor: parents who have identified a young person as 'the problem' in the family may have low motivation to consider their own responsibility and capacity to improve family functioning. Specialist intervention may be required to help them prepare for the young person's return.

Thoburn's (2009) research review also suggests that the attitude of foster carers to the parents and the child appear to affect the child's chances of returning home, too: whether they support contact and return to parents, or conversely, would like to have long-term care of the child, and therefore have low motivation to promote a return home. This would seem to have implications for the management of 'twin track' planning, since placing children with foster carers who would like to have long-term care of a child themselves may have a significant impact on the likelihood that reunification with parents works out.

Processes regulating children's time in care in the UK are more coercive than in some other countries, primarily because in the UK – as in the US and Canada – if 'permanence' cannot be achieved within the relatively short period of six to 12 months through return home to the birth family, there is an expectation that some other route to permanency will be explored. This places pressure on parents to resolve what may be long-standing problems if they are to regain the care of their children, for which they may need significant support (Thoburn 2009). Thoburn's comment, quoted on pp. 198–9, about the high threshold for entry into care is relevant here: if children only enter care when problems have become entrenched, tight timescales for resolving those problems set parents a challenging task. However, more relaxed timescales risk leaving children languishing while parents make repeated attempts to sort out their difficulties.

Permanency planning is a very carefully managed aspect of the care system, through processes for the review of children's cases – Looked After Child Reviews. This system is used for planning the return to birth families or long-term foster care but there is often little certainty as to how the relationship with the child's family is going to be supported once a child has returned home, especially if they have been accommodated under s20 and responsibility for their care passes back to the parents at the point of return home. Children on care orders may have a period of 'statutory' oversight when they return home before the care order is discharged.

Support for looked after children who return to their birth families has often been poor, and many children re-enter the care system at some point (Wulczyn 2004; Farmer *et al.* 2008). Seeing the care system as a 'last resort' may not be helpful for children if it leads to poorly planned, crisis-driven entry to care. Thinking about care as a desirable strategy for supporting a child and their family would give a very different message to families about the rationale for, and value of, care but, for this to be generally the case, a change in threshold criteria for entry to care and policies for supporting the return home are needed. However, at a local level, individual practitioners can consider the value that being in care can give to children, often recognised by the children themselves (Morgan 2011b), and use the care planning process to focus on making positive changes in children's families, except in those relatively few cases in which a return home has been ruled out.

Children's rights while in care, and the United Nations Convention on the Rights of the Child

An underpinning principle of childcare law in the UK and in European legislation is that children are best brought up by their family, unless this is not a reasonable or safe option for them. The starting point for thinking about the future of a child who enters the care system therefore needs to be: 'What needs to happen to enable this child to return to live with their family?' When this is not likely to be an achievable goal other permanency options need to be considered. Some children who enter care later in childhood may return to their parents as adolescents. For these children, time spent in care needs to have supported the maintenance of relationships with their family, even if an early return home was not possible on entry to care.

Not only do the parents have rights in respect of their children, children also have rights in respect of their parents: a right to 'belong' to their parents and to the society into which they were born, and to know and be cared for by their parents, at least 'as far as possible'. This 'belongingness' is formalised through the markers of registered name and nationality as well as the right to be cared for by the parents.

Box 11.2 Article 7 (1) UN Convention on the Rights of the Child

The child shall be registered immediately after birth and shall have the right from birth to a name, the right to acquire a nationality and, as far as possible, the right to know and be cared for by his or her parents.

Children in care and their parents have legal protection for their right to private and family life under Article 8 of the European Convention on Human Rights (ECHR) and Article 8 of the Human Rights Act 1998, just as when children are living at home. The UN Convention on the Rights of the Child (UNCRC 1989)[2] protects parents' rights to exercise their parental responsibility in relation to their children, and the right of children to maintain a relationship with their parents. This extends beyond the parents to the extended family:

Box 11.3 Article 5 UNCRC

States Parties shall respect the responsibilities, rights and duties of parents or, where applicable, the members of the extended family or community as provided for by local custom, legal guardians or other persons legally responsible for the child, to provide, in a manner consistent with the evolving capacities of the child, appropriate direction and guidance in the exercise by the child of the rights recognized in the present Convention.

Many children in care do not see as much of their birth families as they would like, especially their fathers (Timms and Thoburn 2006). Various factors may intervene to interfere with contact: motivation on the part of the parents, carers and social worker, parental behaviour and risk factors, distance, and other factors such as parental illness are all part of the complex web of issues that may affect frequency of contact. The importance of contact for the children concerned may be immense (Thoburn 2008), but on the other hand, it does not have a straightforward relationship with reunification. Children in care feel that children and young people should have more recognition of their right to influence the contact they have with their family (Morgan 2011b). They do not want contact with birth families imposed on them: they suggest that the choice should be theirs, not the prerogative of parents (Morgan 2011b). This view of contact as the right of the child rather than the parents is complex, as parents also have family rights. Factors to take into account when balancing parents' and children's wishes in relation to contact include the age of the child and the history of parental behaviour towards the child, but, at the end of the day, both have rights to 'family life', and the suspension of parental contact with children in care without a court order is only lawful for brief periods.

For accommodated children, denying reasonable requests for contact is not lawful. This places the social worker in the position of having to negotiate arrangements that parents and children find acceptable, unless they are prepared to go to court to enforce them. Considering the purpose of contact is important, as contact for its own sake can be a 'road to nowhere': frequency of contact with infants does not produce better rates of return home (Humphreys and Kiraly 2011), and it is possible that the quality of contact, and support for development of parenting ability through contact, is as important as frequency when planning for return home from care.

Arguably, most s20 accommodation has as its starting point that the child is going home in the fairly near future. There are exceptions: asylum-seeking children who have no one with parental responsibility in a position to offer them care, for example. If parental responsibility is needed by the local authority to manage family contact, maintain security of the placement, or engage in meaningful planning for the child's future, a care order will generally be the more appropriate course of action whenever the 'threshold criteria' relating to unreasonably poor parental care and significant harm or uncontrolled behaviour are also met (s31 of the Children Act 1989). Initial discussions about the purpose and likely duration of accommodation under s20 are important because they should form the basis of later planning. Trust and openness are especially important at this stage, because the point of entry to care is the first step in a process that will, in many cases, lead to the child's eventual discharge from care through a return to the care of their parents.

Children have a right to expect that their relationships with family members will be protected and promoted while they are in care. Contact has to be enough to maintain 'personal relationships; it has to include *direct* contact, and to be regular unless 'contrary to the child's interests'. If contact is not regular or frequent enough for the child to maintain a parent–child relationship then the local authority is in breach of the child's UNCRC rights, unless it can be shown that this is contrary to the child's interests. If an older child does not wish to exercise his or her right to contact and the parent does, it follows that it would have be shown that contact was not in the interest of the child. Parents' rights are not negated when a child says they do not want to see a parent: children's wishes and feelings do not automatically override those of parents. Adults are generally more effective

Box 11.4 Article 9 UNCRC, sections 1 and 3

1   States Parties shall ensure that a child shall not be separated from his or her parents against their will, except when competent authorities subject to judicial review determine, in accordance with applicable law and procedures, that such separation is necessary for the best interests of the child. Such determination may be necessary in a particular case such as one involving abuse or neglect of the child by the parents, or one where the parents are living separately and a decision must be made as to the child's place of residence.

3   States Parties shall respect the right of the child who is separated from one or both parents to maintain personal relations and direct contact with both parents on a regular basis, except if it is contrary to the child's best interests.

at getting their voices heard than children are and, for this reason, a child who does not want to see a parent may find that their wishes and feelings are overridden, unless they can find someone to support their cause. The relevance of the discussion in this chapter so far for reunification is that there is a clear legal basis for expecting contact to be of a quality that promotes the continuance of relationships and the parental role for children in care, and this should be in place in every case in which it is not against the interests of the child to have such contact. On some occasions, however, parents and children may want different outcomes.

Interdependence and the 'ethic of care'

We need to respect children's rights, but also to see them as people whose dependency needs elicit a caring response. Holland (2009) argues that an emphasis on justice can '... underplay the relevance of the traits associated with an ethic of care' (Holland 2009: 1). A focus on rights and justice can lead to a procedural approach, in which children have those things to which they are entitled, but can miss out on things that are difficult to put in statutes and procedures (Barnes 2007). Barnes (2007) and Holland (2009) concur that rights may be pursued at the expense of pursuing other aims such as '... giving due regard to the complex emotional and practical caring (and sometimes uncaring) relationships within which the young person is situated' (Holland 2009: 2). The ethic of care draws attention to caring as both a practical activity and an ethical framework for action, it: '... emphasises interdependency in relationships and a recognition that we are all care-receivers and care-givers. In doing so it de-stigmatises and normalises care, attempting to restore it to the centre of public life' (Holland 2009: 3). Children may have had complex and interdependent roles in families in which parents have had difficulty parenting: caring for parents or siblings, for example. In order to understand the role of the family for a child and negotiate a safe return, we may also need to understand the role of the child within the family. This theme of understanding roles and experiences is echoed in discussion of empathic and emotionally intelligent social work (Gerdes *et al.* 2010; Morrison 2007). Promoting rights is not, on its own, enough to assure the well-being of children in care or to support them in achieving security and stability with their birth families. It is important to understand how the care needs of the child will be met if they return home. Caring is a dynamic, multifaceted process: assessment of the care to be given to a child on their return to the birth family might consider how its various dimensions are to be fulfilled:

- attentiveness: recognising need in others and caring about them;
- responsibility: assuming responsibility of care for others;
- responsiveness: the carer is able to put themselves in the shoes of the person being cared for;
- integrity: the ability to assess the potential dilemmas and conflicts involved in caring for another person in a given social and economic context

After Tronto 1994, cited in Holland 2009: 3

Care can involve conflict: it does not necessarily imply a harmonious relationship. The important factors are the ethical position and the caring actions of the carer, and recognition of the complexity of the task: the potential for the complex social environment to produce dilemmas and conflicts for both the cared-for and those who provide care.

Parents of children in care

The parents of children in care constitute a largely neglected group in policy, practice and research, '... in spite of the fact that these parents are often vulnerable adults who experience a profound loss and threat to their identity' (Schofield *et al.* 2011: 2). Many have complex problems linked to poverty, illness, addiction and victimisation, and parents with learning disabilities are disproportionately represented among parents of children in care (Booth *et al.* 2005). International studies have exposed the range of vulnerabilities they face in addition to the fact of separation from their children, including experience of loss and bereavement (Schofield *et al.* 2011). They are frequently subject to external threats to their well-being, as well as internal factors such as depression or disability.

Fargas *et al.* (2010) explore the impact of having a child in care on parents, mostly young mothers. The parents, who had their children back home with them, had found the time their children were in care traumatic and frustrating. Apart from the separation from their children, many of them felt 'judged' by professionals – their needs ignored, and their involvement limited through a lack of information, encouragement, or through feeling 'unwanted'. Meetings often reinforced the feeling of powerlessness. The parents who were most positive about their interaction with social workers commented on the feeling of being listened to, given time, and offered practical help. It appears that we may still have lessons to learn about involving parents and promoting the maintenance of family relationships, even for children who are destined to return home. Pressured social work teams prioritise high-risk cases, with few resources for non-urgent work, limited scope for creativity and little time to spend with service users (Broadhurst *et al.* 2007). This will inevitably impact on planning for reunification for many children in care.

Despite relative clarity about social workers' responsibilities to children in care, there is little that defines their role with parents whose children are not living with them (Schofield *et al.* 2011: 3). Parents who are looking after their children, foster parents

---

Box 11.5 Learning from research

- A focus on rights is helpful when it empowers children, families and social workers to promote and regulate family relationships while children are in care.
- A focus on the empathic capacities and caring aspects of family life is also important in assessing the readiness of a family/child for reunification.
- The care system may need to consider how it can improve its engagement with parents while children are in care so they feel involved and valued members of the child's network.
- The way in which the removal of a child from the care of the parents is handled may have long-term consequences, including for reunification.

---

and adopters, and birth parents of adopted children, all have a right to support, but birth parents of looked after children appear to be in the anomalous position of having parental responsibility – usually being the only people with parental responsibility when a child is accommodated under s20 – yet having no right to support services. Parents of children in or returning home from 'care' are under the oversight of an agency that is increasingly geared towards forensic work with children and families, and may be afraid to ask for help. Fargas *et al.* (2010) found that parents were worried about asking for help such as respite care, and fearful that they would lose their children if they were seen to 'slip up' again. At the same time, parents thought that as soon as the children were seen as being at a lower level of risk with them, all support was withdrawn. Services can appear punitive to parents:

- the focus is often on risk assessment at the point of entry to care and at the point of return, but there may be little support for change;
- when children return home, services may only be provided in a way that seems to parents like 'checking up on them'.

The significance of this is apparent when one considers that the child's best chance of returning home lies with parents co-operating with local authority expectations and improving their own state of well-being, living circumstances or any other aspect of their lives that improves their ability to parent. We know that provision is sometimes poor for children who return from care to their birth families (Fargas *et al.* 2010), but less is known about the level of provision for parents with children currently in care. Court processes frequently direct assessments that may lead to services being provided for parents, but this pressure to provide services is not present when children are accommodated.

Parents *remain* parents in a very real sense for many children in care. There is a significant minority of children for whom 'care' is a long-term option – up to a third of children stay in care for four years or more – and when placements and social workers change, parents may be the only consistent figures in a child's life (Schofield *et al.* 2007). Many parents of children in long-term care wrestle with the contradictions of being a parent and not parenting:

> ... there is no doubt that for parents of children in foster care, the continuation of a legal status as parents and of face-to-face contact (in most cases) with their children, combined with the possibility of returning to court to challenge the separation or the contact arrangements, make the process of 'resolution' and the redefining of parental identity for parents of foster children a particularly difficult and emotionally draining task.
>
> Schofield *et al.* 2011: 4

The emotional demands on parents of maintaining contact with their children may be enormous, yet rarely recognised or heeded by social workers. The stigma associated with being the parent of a child in care means that they may feel they do not have the right to grieve publicly, and suffer 'disenfranchised grief', grief mixed with feelings of guilt and anger, which may be directed against other agencies, or persons, or themselves (Doka 1989).

Parents may attempt to cope with the grief, stigma and shame in different ways, including denial of the validity of the local authority's position. This can lead to entrenched oppositional situations, in which child welfare workers find mothers 'unrepentant and unwilling' (Wells and Marcenko 2011). Recognition of the grief and guilt behind such opposition may help workers to find ways of negotiating with parents, recognising the efforts they may have made to care for their children, whatever the outcome. While shame may play a useful function in marking the boundary between acceptable and socially unacceptable behaviour, Wells and Marcenko argue that when working with mothers who have lost care of their children, an approach aimed at support rather than blame is more likely to be productive. This is especially true given the high proportion who have experienced negative significant life events, such as poverty, homelessness and victimisation: '... how others think of them and how representatives of institutions think of them are intertwined, and these negotiated views have consequences for how mothers behave and are treated' (Wells and Marcenko 2011). The approach taken by social workers at a time of trauma and vulnerability, such as removal of a child, may have profound consequences for the parent's self-esteem and for future attempts at reparative work with them.

Stigma, threatened identity and parents of children in care

Moral judgements are often made about parents who have lost the care of their children. Permanent separation of parents and children threatens parents' sense of identity as well as causing feelings of grief and guilt. It is almost too hard for some parents to think about the loss of their children at all, and some feel a 'profound sense of responsibility and worthlessness' (Schofield *et al.* 2011: 5). Some parents try to support their children's foster placements, some try to sort out problems such as drug or alcohol use but, for others, the loss of their children can lead to increased substance use. Some want revenge on social workers; others have said they would prefer to die, or for the child to die, or wish they had never been born. Some continue to fight to get their child back, but contact visits when the plan for the child is long-term care are very difficult: parents are caught between struggling to get the child back and 'giving the child up' entirely. What this highlights is the pain that is often only engaged with at a surface level by social workers, who may be coping with the grief and distress of the child and their own feelings about separating a parent and child: it may seem too painful, and the anger directed at them makes it difficult for them to engage (Schofield *et al.* 2011). This research considered cases in which reunification was not being considered. In cases in which the plan is reunification with birth parents, the risks to parental identity may be less acute but many of the same feelings of anger, guilt, grief and the wish to 'escape the pain' of dealing with the difficulties that led to the child coming into care – and the fact of the child being in care – may be present to some degree. Colton *et al.* (1997) found that service providers and service workers held an even more negative view of being in receipt of services than the parents. This has implications for the quality of work that they are able to do to address the 'spoiled identity' of parents who are struggling with issues of self-esteem after having 'lost' a child into care, whether long- or short-term.

If the parents feel this was achieved under duress, there may be feelings of betrayal. This is especially likely if the plan for a child changes from reunification to permanent care while they are away from the birth parents:

> Parents often talked of feeling that although it might have been necessary for the children to go into care at a certain point in time, they had been led to believe that they would get them back. The process of children going into care often seemed to be negotiated rather than a clearly compulsory or voluntary arrangement. But where parents' hope had remained, it was the permanent separation they struggled with and this left them moving between anger and depression.
>
> Schofield *et al.* 2007

Accommodation with parental agreement may be used in situations in which the local authority has concerns about a child but chooses not apply for a court order, either on the basis that the 'least coercive alternative' is a better way of working with a family, or because there is a some doubt about the robustness of evidence of significant harm. This has rights implications for parents, as well as raising issues of fairness, openness and local authority trustworthiness. The fact that the process is legally voluntary, rather than through legal compulsion, ignores the 'latent power' of social workers to influence people's choices by virtue of what they might do if parents do not cooperate (Sheppard 2006). Even in cases in which the plan remains reunification with parents, if parents feel they were forced into the accommodation in the first place, the basis for trust and co-operative working is compromised. On the other hand, lengthy, oppositional and expensive court proceedings do not offer a strong basis for trust and co-operation, either. The requirement in care proceedings under the Children Act 1989 that responsibility for significant harm be attributed to 'unreasonable' parenting means that working relationships with parents of children in care are frequently compromised and adversarial. Parents report feeling blamed not respected: 'boxed in' to opposition rather than collaboration (Thomson and Thorpe 2004). The most important thing for the social worker is to consider whether they need to acquire legal powers – parental responsibility – to be able to work with parents towards a return home while the child is kept safe, or alternatively eliminate the possibility of reunification. Openness about the reason for taking such decisions may avoid such feelings of betrayal later on when reunification is not possible, or, as often happens, has to be deferred for longer than parents hoped in order that they have time to demonstrate that they are able to resume care of their children.

The fact that parents have not been able to offer their children adequate care, and may have neglected or even abused them, does always not mean that they do not love them, and they may devote much of their time and energy to thinking about the child once they are in care. Professionals should seek to find the ways in which parents have acted in the best interests of their children, and ways in which they can show love and care. This is important for children, too, for whom evidence that they are loved and valued by their parents is likely to be enormously important. Hearing about the negative aspects of their care, as they are likely to do if they attend Child Protection Conferences, for example, may be distressing for what it apparently says about the value the parent places on the child. Parents whose children are in care may experience a conceptual 'gap' between their own view of themselves as essentially caring parents who did their best for their children, and professionals' views of them as parents who failed their children. There is also tension between their self-image as caring parents and their self-knowledge that they engaged in behaviour that placed their children at risk of neglect or other harm. There are ways in which this might be ameliorated:

- sharing information about the child with the parents: illness, achievements, significant events;
- enabling involvement in the child's life;
- showing respect and recognition for them as parents as well as respect for the parents as individuals. (Schofield *et al.* 2011)

Schofield *et al.* (2011) identify some barriers and enablers for social workers that underpin the quality of their practice with parents of children in (long-term) care:

- ability to manage *their own mixed feelings* about the parents' pain and loss;
- *pressure on time*: attitudes to parents affect how social workers prioritise time;
- attitudes to parents are affected by whether or not they have *empathy* for them and see them as *deserving* of their time, also whether they are *hopeful* about the parents' ability to work with them;
- pressure to *manage dissonance* when the child's placement may not be ideal, or the child may not be doing well in care after they have been 'rescued' by the social worker.

Given that many children – even those who spend several years in foster care – eventually return home or to the community they came from, it is in the interests of the children that they have a coherent account of their lives that acknowledges parental fault but also parental care, and explains why the parent's care needed to be limited for the child's well-being and safety. Working with parents to address the feelings of worthlessness and threatened identity can support them to move forwards from the low point of child removal, though recognition that they are not able to care for their child, to commitment to supporting the child's welfare while they are in care and after.

One indicator for likelihood of successful reunification – return that lasts longer than three years – is the child having been in care on a compulsory basis, and returning home initially on a care or supervision order (Sinclair *et al.* 2005). This suggests situations in which the local authority can work with parents authoritatively, where the reasons for coming into care have been established through the court process, and the local authority has a continuing responsibility for the well-being of the child after he or she returns home, may provide a better basis to work with parents than informal arrangements. It may be that the most skilled work needs to be with parents who have requested accommodation of a child, where the incentives to work with the local authority may be lower and the power and responsibilities of the local authority after the return home are much lower – although it is also arguable that the responsibility to the child as a child in need, once they have returned home, has as much moral force as the duties under a care order.

Box 11.6 Exercise: reflecting on a case

Consider a case in which you were the social worker for a child who was looked after under s20 of the 1989 Act, and was discharged home to the parents' care. What power and authority do you feel you had in that situation? How did the parents, the child and you work together to determine how this was arranged and how the child was to be cared for once back home?

What services were offered before the child returned home, and after the reunification? How far do you think they met the needs of the child and the parents?

Are there additional things that you would like to have offered that might have helped the family? Consider:

- your own professional skills and knowledge development
- your own agency's provision and the availability of services in your area
- use of processes such as Child in Care Reviews to support the reunification process.

List three things that you would like to develop through seeking further training or experience for yourself, or through use of supervision, or through promoting good practice in your agency or area.

Assessing when the time is right, and what is required to make reunification work

Two factors were identified that promoted reunification in a study of children in care in the USA:

- keeping the child's placement local;
- the provision of services directed at maintaining the relationship between children and parents (Iowa 2008).

Permanency of reunification was associated with planning that reflected a clear understanding of underlying issues impacting on parental capacity. The service plan needs to:

> ... mitigate or remedy those issues with the ownership and involvement of the parents. Achievement of these practices hinge[s] on the ability of the caseworker to visit the

child and parents frequently, to assess safety and progress toward achieving the family change needed to assure the children will be placed back home permanently. In addition, assessing conditions that indicate the right time to reunify, and planning the transition home is critical to its success. Assuring that the supports and services are in place to foster reunification is critical.

Iowa 2008

When parenting capacity needs to be developed, there should be consideration of the kinds of services the parent may need to maintain progress as well as keeping the child safe, including aftercare support, therapeutic services and respite care.

Services prior to reunification should address the needs of both parents and children, focusing on practical issues and child safety, as well as the quality of parent–child interaction and parental competencies, including communication, problem solving and anger control issues. Visits with the child while they are in foster care should be used to identify and address issues around parenting, nurturing and disciplining and boundary setting. Addressing substance abuse issues with parents before reunification takes place is important (Flood 2009). The extended families of children in care whose parents have drug problems may also have significant problems themselves (Barnard 2003), and if their support is an important part of the support plan for a child after reunification, careful consideration of their financial, practical and emotional support needs is important too.

While regular contact helps to maintain a child's attachment and sense of belonging to their birth family, the wider purpose of the contact needs to be kept under review. Parents should be supported to help them achieve their own developmental objectives that will help them in the future care of their children. Contact is generally felt to be important by practitioners, judges, families and others involved in care planning, but research into the role it plays in reunification is limited (Humphreys and Kiraly 2010). It may not be *frequency* of contact that is important in achieving reunification, but the strength of the parent-child relationship and the parent's commitment to the child (Delfabbro *et al.* 2003; Biehal 2007).

Humphreys and Kiraly (2010) conclude that high frequency visiting arrangements for younger children may cause disruption and distress for the children, without protecting the children from disrupted attachments or adding anything to the likelihood of reunification, it can be a 'road to nowhere':

> ... frequent visiting without skilled parenting support will not result in relationship building and enhance the chance of family reunification. While many other factors in the lives of mothers and fathers also need to be addressed, the lack of attention to supporting family relationships raises itself like a red flag.
>
> Humphreys and Kiraly 2010

The authors suggest that more research is needed to determine what pattern of contact will be best for individual children; the question is complex and cannot be dismissed with a 'perfunctory answer'. The quality of the relationship between parent and child prior to coming into care is a critical factor in considering frequency, duration, supervision and location of contact (Sinclair *et al.* 2005). The immediate reason the child is in care is another important factor when planning contact: whether it is in response to a short- term crisis or to address a serious and persistent problem in parenting (Biehal 2007). Age of children, length of time in care, reason for coming into care and children and parents experiencing different types of problems create a complex multivariate context for decision making.

Significant attachments developed during placement should also be taken into consideration by the social worker when planning reunification: foster families may have become very important for children in care, even after they return to birth family (Morgan 2011b).

The Iowa guidance (2008) stresses that in assessing whether or not it is safe for a child to return home, the same 'safety constructs' that were used in assessing the need to remove the child should be used to assess whether or not it is safe to go back. In other words, it is not acceptable to remove a child because of concerns about specific parental difficulties or behaviours but to return a child on the basis of a general assessment of parental capacity that does not consider these same specific issues. This echoes the finding by Woodcock (2003) that social workers seldom appeared to apply the theoretical constructs they used when analysing childcare cases in planning interventions. Agency 'insight' into the cause of problems needs to be translated into a specific and congruent course of action to address those problems. At the same time, there is a danger of 'safety level inflation', whereby the threshold for returning a child to the parents is set higher than the threshold that would be used to remove a child. This is an issue that has received little research attention, so it is not known whether children who return to the family home under court orders, for example, are only returned when the standard of care is better than the threshold used for removal and whether this explains, in part, the better outcomes noted for this group of reunified children.

Practice in the UK has some way to go in this area: 90 per cent of children who were reunified with parents were reported to have experienced abuse or neglect before coming into care, yet two fifths of children returned home without any in-depth core assessment having been carried out. Many returned to an essentially unchanged situation, and almost half suffered abuse or neglect after returning home (Biehal 2007). Accommodated children are more likely to receive poor services to support successful reunification than children on care or supervision orders (Flood 2009).

Factors to consider before implementing the return of a child to their parents (based on those in the State of Iowa practice guidance) include:

- absence of intimidation of parents by others, and the absence of threat by them to the safety of themselves or each other;
- the capacity and will to provide adequate supervision and set appropriate boundaries;
- family routines structured around children's needs, including homework, regular bedtimes, meals and school attendance;
- parents' ability to use praise and show affection and offer emotional support – strategies for bringing up children that avoid over-reliance on blame, punishment and criticism;
- parents' ability to appropriately access formal and informal support for themselves, and to offer support to each other in parenting their children.

Thomson and Thorpe (2004) advocate group work with parents as a way of addressing these feelings. One of the reported effects of group discussion was to support parents to acknowledge and begin to deal with the issues that led to the children's removal in the first place, as well as helping them to work in partnership with workers, who frequently find such relationships 'difficult' (Thomson and Thorpe 2004: 50).

Fargas *et al.* (2010) summarise some factors that contribute to the likelihood of successful return home:

- a mother who does not have drug, alcohol or mental health problems;
- the child being less than 11 years old;
- the child not having a disability;
- good quality family relationships.

They argue that it is a misconception to think that spending more time in care makes it less likely a child will go home. It is equally possible, and probably more likely, that a longer period of time in care is associated with more chronic parental difficulties and it is this that reduces the chance of a successful return home. The same parental difficulties that tend to prolong a child's time in care are also likely to contribute to further breakdown when the child returns home.

The impact of failed attempts at reunification on children is severe, greater than the effect of placement breakdown, so the stakes are very high for the children involved. Two thirds of children in a recent study of reunification had already had one or more failed attempt at 'going home' (Flood 2009). Children who remain in care for long periods often face additional barriers to reunification. Their parents' problems may be more entrenched and complex, with multiple risk factors. The children develop as time passes, sometimes acquiring new developmental challenges that need to be met by their parents, without the parents having had the opportunity to experience at first hand their child's developing personality and behaviour (Bellamy 2008: 217). The same is also true of children's developing strengths: greater maturity may have brought greater self-reliance, resilience and abilities, and the parents may find it initially difficult to accommodate the changes. Reunification is a time in which families may struggle to establish new patterns of family functioning, especially if there has been a substantial break. Reunification with parents after two years or more in care is an indicator that the child is likely to suffer difficulties in later childhood, including substance abuse, self-destructive behaviour and other behavioural problems. Possible explanations include the persistence of the parental problems that brought the children into care, including family instability, conflict and illness. Children with multiple placement moves were found to be 11 times more likely to be returned to care after reunification than children with more stable care careers (Fuller 2005 cited in Biehal 2007).

The family may not have been stable, either. There may be new children in the family, too: new step-siblings, or siblings or half-siblings born while the child was in care. Place matters to adults and children alike; to return to a different home in which a child has no prior established place may be a difficult step (Jack 2010). 'Reunifying a child is not a one-time event, it is a process involving the reintegration of the child into a family environment that may have changed significantly from the environment the child left' (Wulczyn 2004). The effect of stresses associated with reunification itself is another unknown quantity (Bellamy 2008).

Box 11.7 Summary: planning for reunification

- Are the reasons that first brought the child into care being taken into consideration in assessing feasibility of reunification with parents?
- What are the aims of contact, and how do they fit in with the overall objectives for the child and their welfare; is contact being managed and resourced to support the child and family in achieving those objectives safely?
- How is the timing of reunification being addressed in planning, and how does it fit with progress by the parents in addressing any issues or problems of their own that might impinge on their ability to parent this child?
- What kind of support is going to be needed once the child returns home? What services and resources are going to be put in place? Has a full assessment been carried out to provide essential knowledge about the level of parenting ability, stability and emotional well-being of the family?

Without children in the family for a period, parents may have become used to the absence of family responsibilities and may have to readjust to them. If there have been other children in the family, the returning child will have to re-establish themselves in a family that has been developing in their absence.

Children with disabilities: the 'reverse ladder of permanence'

Baker (2007) introduced the idea of a 'reverse ladder of permanence': children with disabilities being less likely than their non-disabled peers to achieve permanent placements such as adoption or permanent return home. When children with disabilities do achieve permanence, it is often after a longer delay: twice as many disabled children were still in care four years after entering care as non-disabled children (Cleaver 2000 cited in Baker 2007). While 20 per cent of non-disabled children in care had a plan for going home, only 3 per cent of disabled or 'borderline' disabled children had a plan for going home, and those who did go home were in care almost three times as long as non-disabled children (Baker 2007).

Social workers may be more risk-averse when making plans for children with disabilities. They are slower to return them to families they know may have difficulty coping with them. This may reflect concern about the support available for the families of children with high levels of need (Audit Commission 2003). Where there is a history of abuse or neglect, the vulnerability of a disabled young person may be a disincentive for social workers to pursue reunification. There are, therefore, possible positive and negative reasons for poor results in relation to reunification for children with disabilities: realistic concerns about the match between support needs and available services and vulnerability to re-abuse, and a lack of felt urgency to establish permanency for children with disabilities.

Social workers should reflect on the way established practice affects children with disabilities when they enter the care system. Winter (2009b) encourages social workers to think about the reasons why certain ideas and practices have dominance over others at certain times, to:

... encourage the social work profession's critical reflection about the broader 'why-is-it-being-done-this-way?' and 'how-did-we-get-to-where-we-are?' questions ... critical reflection is not an optional or a luxury extra, but instead should be an essential part of understanding the broader economic and political context, which is reshaping the role of the social worker.

Winter 2009b: 1238

Understanding why and how economic and social/organisational factors may impact on differential outcomes for different groups of children is a starting point for addressing this imbalance.

Preparation for successful return

Some of the factors that affect success of return are *parental, interactional* factors, such as harsh and punitive parenting; a lack of warmth and acceptance of the child; and failure to focus on the needs of the child. Some child factors, such as failure to respect boundaries, are also interactional problems and not simply 'child conduct' issues, since they typically involve both child and parent.

Both types of problems present challenges for social workers. Parents may be unwilling to disclose or acknowledge the difficulties they have, or may not recognise them as problems; changing behaviour to meet local authority expectations may involve giving up something which is part of a coping mechanism for the parent, such as alcohol.

It is clear that the process of preparation for a successful return home has to begin even as the arrangements are being made for the child to be removed, on that the basis of a future working relationship must be safeguarded. While parents may not agree with their child being in care, if they feel they are treated with respect from an early stage in the process, this offers a better chance of beginning the work with parents that may support a more successful return home.

Attachment is 'talked up' in local authority practice with children and families, but the theory is often applied selectively. Attachment relationships to their parents are key in the lives of most children, but children who enter the care system need to form attachments to other people. The biological relationship between mother and child may provide an ideal situation for attachment and bonding to occur, but young children may also form important attachments to their foster carers. These are seldom valued by local authorities, and perhaps not always recognised by the foster carers, but if it is true that infants have an innate need to form attachments to their primary caregivers, and the care offered by the foster carer is at least as good as that offered by the child's biological parents, there seems no reason to suppose that a child who has spent a settled period in a good foster placement will not experience significant loss and emotional distress on separation from that carer, whether it is as a result of a placement move or a return to a parent who has not been their primary carer for some time.

Timing, duration of contact, and the management of the handover should all have the same child-focused attention as the move from parental to foster care, including respect for the wishes and feelings of children about reunification, its timing, things they want to be achieved before going home, and the support they need afterwards.

Thoburn (2009: 23) summarises research on the risks associated with reunification:

Box 11.8

Child variables associated with greater risk of returning to care

- Young children taken into care because of neglect are more likely to re-enter care than children who entered care because of concerns about physical or sexual abuse.
- The child is in an older age group.
- Children with emotional and behavioural problems before and/or during care.
- Young people who abused drugs or alcohol before and/or during care.
- Young people involved in crime when in care.
- Some groups of ethnic minority children – in the UK, African Caribbean children and those of mixed Caribbean/white heritage.
- Children who have been in care for three years or more.
- The child returning home from care alone – children who return home with at least one sibling are less likely to re-enter care.
- Children who have had several placements in care.

Family variables associated with higher risk of return failure

- Child originally entered care because of parental addiction problems.
- Child originally entered care because of parental mental illness.
- Parents have poor parenting skills after the return.
- Serious parental problems – for example, intimate partner violence – not resolved when the child goes home.
- Parental hostility towards the child or ambivalence about the return home.
- The child returning to a single parent, if compounded by poverty and poor housing.
- Serious financial or housing problems.
- Lack of support from extended family or neighbours.
- Changed family composition – but only if linked with adverse consequences for the child in terms of conflictual child/ step-parent relationships.
- Conflict between siblings, especially step- and half-siblings.
- Non-compliance of parents with service plans when the child was in care and/ or after return.
- 'False compliance' with plans and/or hostility to caseworker.

Family variables associated with the return home being successful

- Parents were strongly motivated to resume care of the child.
- Parents willing to change and taking steps to do so.
- No unresolved family problems when the child returned.

Concluding comments: minimising the risks associated with reunification

Reunification is risky for children and young people. The potential for poor outcomes is higher on most dimensions than for adoption or long-term care, but it scores more highly in one dimension: it supports children to develop a more positive sense of personal history and identity. Thoburn (2009: 22) summarises the research:

> Farmer *et al.* (2008) found that of the 52 per cent of placements home that had not broken down, a third were assessed by the researchers to be of poor quality in terms of the quality of parenting and the risks to health, development and safety. They found the children who had not been the subject of care orders, as well as those who were known to have been maltreated, were at risk of neglect and poor parenting when they returned home. Brandon and Thoburn (2008) in an eight year follow up of a consecutive cohort of 105 English children suffering 'significant harm' found that more of those who remained at home throughout, and of those who had a brief stay in care and returned home and remained there, had poor outcomes (in terms of being again maltreated and being assessed as of poor well-being) than was the case for those who remained in care, or returned home briefly and were then placed in long term care.

Children and young people who return home before adequate preparatory work is done are less likely to achieve the permanent return they are seeking, and are unlikely to receive the support they and their family need once they are at home. Farmer *et al.* (2008) underline the importance of preparing the child for return home. This is perhaps particularly important for older children: adolescents who returned home with challenging behaviour patterns were more likely to return to care. When children went home because they pressed to go home, sometimes accelerating the process by precipitating placement breakdown, the prognosis was poor. Difficult child behaviours were more likely to recur than be resolved: children aged over 10 were less likely to have a successful return home (Farmer *et al.* 2008). Adults, especially parents, have to take responsibility for making the return to family work, and services need to be able to support them to do this successfully. Children returning home after a period in care may challenge their parents, testing their commitment to them. Their standard of living will have dropped, and they may be missing people they became close to in foster care (Thoburn 2009).

Some parents may be over-optimistic about their ability to rebuild relationships that may have been severely damaged by earlier parenting difficulties. McSherry *et al.* (2008) found many parents believed their children had bonded again with them straight away when they returned from care: in many cases this may be true, but parents' expectations may not be realistic. Some parents recognise that the relationship with their children needs to be rebuilt, and trust to be earned again. Unrealistic expectations on the part of parents may lead to a 'honeymoon period' followed by disappointment as old – or new – problems begin to recur. Work before the return home and during the early days of reunification should address expectations on both sides.

Some parents display considerable sensitivity to the impact of being in care on their children: Fargas *et al.* (2010: 83) quote a mother talking of the sudden severance of her son's relationship with a former foster carer: '[To] me it was breaking my son's heart and that wasn't fair. You know ... this person had been in his wee life for a while.' Other parents may feel threatened by relationships their children have built up during their time in care, and disappointed if it takes time to build their own relationship again.

Birth families differ from foster families in both their history of difficulty and in the level of support they receive when looking after children who have been in care or remain in care: birth families can be expected to have more problems, but they also receive less support (Sinclair *et al.* 2005). The problems parents experience are typically ones with chronic and relapsing patterns: substance dependency, depression and victimisation in adulthood among them. It is arguable that time-limited services aiming at bringing about lasting behavioural change through brief interventions may be very useful, but need to be supplemented by support services over a longer period (Wells and Marcenko 2011).

Post-care support is the next important item for minimising risk of breakdown. Skuse and Ward (2003) found a concerning lack of formal support for children who returned home, despite the problems experienced by the families before the children entered care. Older children experienced particular instability, often moving between various relatives, so the idea that a return home marks the achievement of stability and permanence for a child or young person may be more of an administrative fiction than a reality for many children who 'go home'. Support for such placements and the appropriateness of defining returning home as permanent were issues identified in this research. Farmer *et al.* (2008) found lower levels of breakdown of placements where parents and children had proactive, purposeful support, services such as day care were provided, and support was available from informal networks and other service providers such as schools. This often corresponded to court-directed or court-overseen processes, and tended to apply to younger children rather than adolescents. Return to the parent other than the one caring for the child at the time they entered care was more likely to succeed, with only 10 per cent of such returns breaking down within the next two years. Returning to a parent who had had a change of partner was also more likely to succeed, although Farmer and Parker (1991) suggested that a good indicator for success of return home is stability in birth family membership.

In Farmer *et al.*'s (2008) study, nine-tenths of the children had been maltreated prior to entering care, but in only a quarter of the cases had all the problems for the children and their parents been addressed prior to reunion. Almost half of reunifications had broken down in two years and a third of the children remaining at home were in situations of poor-quality care: half the children were mistreated after returning home.

The return home from care is fraught with difficulties, but variability in rates of breakdown in different areas – between 75 per cent and 32 per cent – suggests that the quality of practice can make a big difference. Rates of return can be reduced through well-planned intervention, purposeful social work with support for parents with their own problems, and behavioural support for parents and children when older children return home. Engaging with parental issues, especially drug and alcohol problems, is essential. Children may hide their feelings about their home situation once they return home: many children whose return home had been problematic confided in nobody about their feelings of sadness and anger until a research interviewer asked them specifically about their experiences (Farmer *et al.* 2008). Making time to talk to children on their own once they return home is essential for safeguarding them after they go home: reunification is a process, not an event, as Wulczyn (2004) reminds us.

12 Supporting others in their professional development

This chapter:

- considers ideas of professionalism, professional development and ways of sharing professional expertise;
- reflects on ways of promoting positive learning environments in the workplace.

For the purposes of the chapter, to avoid lengthy and repetitive descriptions of those acting as teachers or mentors or offering support with professional development of other staff, the terms 'teacher' and 'learner' are used in this chapter. It is acknowledged that these are not wholly satisfactory terms, in that the learning that is involved may be 'top down', passed from a more experienced worker to the learner, or emerge from a shared process of learning, and the 'teacher' may end up learning as much as the 'learner'. Using this shorthand to describe the person who has taken responsibility for the learning process and the one who is seeking to extend their professional knowledge does, however, make the text easier to read.

Being 'a professional': the context for professional development

Before considering ways in which experienced social workers may support other professionals in developing their professional skills, we may consider what the idea of 'being a professional' means, and the different ways in which other people may benefit from support in their learning.

The idea of being a professional is a complex one. Schön (1983) distinguishes between *technical rationality* – knowledge derived from theory and research – and *professional artistry*, which he describes a 'knowing how' based on experience and intuition. In practice, actions are generally based on a combination of knowledge and experience rather than one or the other.

There are components that relate to profession-specific knowledge and skills, other aspects relate to the value base and ethical stance expected of a professional exercising their responsibilities and meeting their duties, which links to expectations about the way a professional should conduct themselves in their private as well as their professional life:

avoiding engaging in activities that are in conflict with the ethos of the professional's work role. Some components of professionalism include:

- A commitment to an *ideal of service* to the population of service users/clients/patients: a profession as a group that uses its professional power responsibly and for the good of those it engages with.
- The ownership of a systematic body of knowledge, technical skills and procedures is a key hallmark of a profession; one may go further and say that a modern profession needs to be able to demonstrate its effectiveness, so evidence-based practice and having recourse to – or participating in generating knowledge through – systematic scientific studies of methods and outcomes is also an integral part of professional practice. The development of SCIE and the College of Social Work reflect increasing interest in and concern about this aspect of professionalisation.
- The possession of a degree of influence outside the profession: the authority to influence public policy being of particular relevance for social work.
- Autonomy in decision making, based on clinical expertise and deep knowledge of the evidence base for practice, as well as a basis in ethical practice as defined by the professional body. The control of the profession by the profession – occupational autonomy – is important, as well as individual professional autonomy, when thinking about the idea of a profession and what professionalism means.

Professionalism is widely held to imply ownership of power: some of this comes from the structural differences in circumstances of service users and social workers: some of it comes from the social worker's role as gatekeeper, holder of the keys to resources. Power is also relevant to the relationship between the more experienced worker and those who are entering the profession and learning 'the trade' of social work. The use of power may be conscious and deliberate, or it may be something that happens without the conscious knowledge of the person who exercises power; or a person doing something they would not otherwise have done because they have been influenced by another person. The professional discourse in which social work practitioners are immersed is itself a means by which powerful ideas, values and ways of seeing are transmitted from one person to another.

Professions employ strategies, language and rhetoric to define and enhance their status. These strategies are used by members of the profession and its professional bodies to present the profession to the world beyond; its public 'face' (Hoyle and John 1995). Whatever limitations this may have as a way of defining professions and differentiating them from non-professions, it serves the purpose of giving the members of professions some kind of group identity. This may include public documents such as a Code of Ethics, which functions both as a guide to practice by members of the profession and a public statement of commitment to certain values and professional aspirations. There is an expectation that professionalism involves personal commitment to a high level of ethical conduct: 'being a professional' therefore extends beyond workplace behaviour into the whole way of thinking and being. It necessitates the ability to make judgements based on both rational thought and ethical principles and values, and is therefore a personal quality as well as an occupational status. This is not to say that professionals cannot go 'off duty', but does imply that certain ways of thinking and being will be embedded in behaviour, suggesting that professionalism does not 'switch off' completely when a professional leaves their work role. Article 5.8 of the *Code of Practice for Social Workers* (GSCC 2002) states that social workers must not '[b]ehave in a way, in work or outside work, which would call into question your suitability to work in social care services'. This applies to all social care workers: it is arguable that for social workers, with their newly gained and perhaps hard-won professional status, the expectation should be higher than this negative injunction. Section 3.4.2b of the BASW *Code of Ethics* (BASW 2002) states that social workers must: '... ensure that their private conduct does not compromise the fulfilment of professional responsibilities, and ... avoid behaviour which contravenes professional principles and standards or which damages the profession's integrity ...'.

Professional development is therefore about developing and embedding a range of facets of expertise, examples of which are given below:

- **Knowledge:** research, theory, law, policy, social context for services.
- **Skills:** interpersonal skills, self-management, assessment, reflection, analysis, research, critical thinking, workload management, teamwork, ICT skills, crisis management and dealing with the unexpected, application of practice methods, dealing with complexity.
- **Values:** developing the ability to apply in practice values such as honesty and openness, respect for persons, prioritisation and service response according to need, and openness to new learning to improve services.
- **Ethics:** clarity about own and professional ethics and how they inform practice; identifying and addressing ethical dilemmas; sensitivity to ethical issues, especially when service users' interests, rights and freedoms may be affected by state intervention.

These aspects of the profession are partly for the benefit of service users, but are also aimed at increasing the prestige and power of the profession. While this may have benefits for the practitioners of the profession, the influence that professionals hold may also be used to benefit those who use the services of the professionals concerned. 'Being a professional' arguably involves 'owning' professional language – with the ways of thinking about people, issues and problems that this entails – and making a commitment to the values and ethics of the profession. From early in the twentieth century, writing on this topic by Dewey (1916), Lewin and Lewin (1948) and Kolb (1984) stressed the social aspect of reflective learning and the importance of difference of opinion in furthering learning: communication with other members of the profession is an integral part of furthering professional practice.

Erault (2005) points out that, traditionally, the prestige and specialist status that goes with being 'a professional' was linked to the professional's claim to exclusive knowledge and skill, giving them the exclusive right to identify/diagnose the client's problem. This exclusivity, as Erault discusses, has been eroded over recent decades as service users have gained increasing rights to define their difficulties and explain their own problems in their own terms. Erault (2005: 5) argues that protection for service user rights means that, where the state once acted to protect service users from unqualified practitioners, 'it now seeks to protect them from the qualified'.

Interest in professional competence is arguably a response to concern within and outside the professions generally that holding a qualification alone is not enough for a modern professional: one needs to go further and keep one's learning up to date, refine one's skills and add to one's knowledge and ability to make professional judgements. Erault's definition of professional judgement is that it is, 'wise judgement under conditions of uncertainty', in contrast with a lay view of professionals making rational evidence-based judgements – a view that has also been expressed in academic social work literature, but is currently tempered with discussion of the way research is actually used in practice, and its significance as one of a range of 'tools' practitioners draw on in making judgements (for a range of views and a perspective on the development of this idea, see for example: Macdonald 1998; Webb 2001; Beddoe 2011; Nevo and Slonim-Nevo 2011). Values, ethics, professional and personal experience, service user preference, feasibility and resource availability all affect judgements about the best course of action in any given situation. Morrison (2007) also makes the point that the exercise of judgement and decision making does not happen in an emotional vacuum: emotion is also a significant factor in professional decision making.

Seniority in the profession should arguably be based on development of professional attributes – which is one reason why it is important to be clear what those attributes are. Being able to express and explain those attributes to justify the use of authority is part of the package of 'being a professional', from which it follows that experienced and senior practitioners should have the ability to pass on knowledge to others. For less experienced professionals, 'learning on the job' is inevitable: it is not feasible to think that pre-qualification training courses can prepare practitioners with all the knowledge they will need to practise in demanding occupations, let alone in the most complex areas of work. Erault (2005) suggests that the first two or three years after qualification are those in which the greatest period of professional learning in practice occurs. A system for supporting professional development, and the role of more senior professionals in this, seems to be one attribute of social work professionalism that is currently under-developed.

At the level of qualifying in social work, it is to be expected that practitioners will be competent. This is a necessary minimum level of ability, but the aspirations for true professionalism are arguably higher than this. It has been argued that competence 'misses the point' of professionalism in professions such as social work and other people-oriented professions (Beinart *et al.* 2009) because the complex interactive processes that are the core of professional activity cannot be reduced to their component parts: the whole is more than the sum of its parts.

Competence can be clearly differentiated from experience: one may be very experienced without becoming particularly competent, and competence can be acquired at a superficial level. *Surface competence* means being able to carry out a role without critical self-awareness; without being able to ascertain why things sometimes work better at some times than at others, or reflect on how one's practice might be improved. Competence is achieved by following the rules and working to procedures, rather than through understanding the professional role and having capacity to work creatively within organisational policies and ethical guidelines to fulfil that role. A focus on accountability in state social work, in particular, has made for an increased focus on competence as a key component of social work professionalism. Accountability in an organisation with a focus on process and procedure revolves around task completion, efficiency and transparency. In contrast, the more an organisation relies upon the initiative and creativity of its professional staff, and the more scope it allows them for using professional judgement, the more individual practitioners should expect to be held accountable for *outcomes* as well as for *processes*. Competence is not to be dismissed, however. It is a:

> ... broader concept than knowledge, since it has emotional and social as well as cognitive components. Competence is based on ability in relation to the work, and is often expressed in terms of the credentials and merits of an individual ... the explicit knowledge of the novice is frequently compared to the implicit skills of the expert, where declarative knowledge is transformed into procedural knowledge.
>
> Svensson 2006: 586

The role of the person helping to develop the professionalism of another may involve considering how existing competence and knowledge may be used as the basis for the development of higher-level skilled professional judgement.

Different ways of supporting others in their professional development

There are various ways in which practitioners can support others in their professional development. These include:

- informal discussions with colleagues to share ideas and offer support, including emotional support;
- supervising other workers, providing a positive learning environment in supervision, promoting attendance at training events for other workers;
- presentations to share information, for example, with a team or group of colleagues, after carrying out a piece of research into a particular issue, attending a conference, a study visit to another country or area, or other experience that expanded the presenter's knowledge;
- disseminating the results of innovative practice; trying out an approach new to the agency and sharing the outcome;
- providing formal structured training sessions about a particular topic: traditional 'training' experiences;
- providing 'shadowing' experiences;
- co-working with less experienced practitioners;
- mentoring.

Box 12.1 Exercise: reflecting on professionalism

Consider what gives you your professional status. What do you think your professional prestige is, or should be, based on? What do you consider that you do as a social worker that is distinctive to your own profession? Within your own work setting, what is your distinctive contribution to the professional network within which you work?

In this chapter, the focus is on the last two items in the list on page 222. The discussions in this chapter are also relevant for workers supervising a social work student, but are not intended to be a substitute for specific training in student supervision, which carries particular responsibilities in terms of evaluation and monitoring of progress that are not covered here. In supporting others' professional development, we should consider what the components of professional knowledge and expertise might be.

- **Interpersonal skills** in areas such as chairing meetings, group work, managing conflict.
- **Technical knowledge**, including becoming familiar with, and competent in, negotiating practice systems, such as processes relating to investigation of child abuse, or procedures for applying to the courts for orders to protect the interests of vulnerable people, and using technology.
- **Theoretical knowledge**, such as knowledge about family systems and systemic intervention, attachment processes, or trauma and its effect on individuals, for example; information from research and knowledge of commentaries and analysis of issues central to the profession.
- **Values and ethical approaches** to social work intervention, including the ability to explore the complexities of situations in which more than one person or agency has a 'stake', and conflicts of interest between them.
- **Understanding the boundaries of legitimacy:** not just thinking what one might do in a given situation, but being aware of what is possible and situating it within moral, legal, practical, professional and organisational constraints.
- **Taking responsibility for keeping one's own practice up to date** and contributing to the enhancement of service delivery in one's area of work.

Such lists cannot be exhaustive: every reader may be able to think of aspects of their work that demand particular professional knowledge and expertise that is not on the second list, and activities that they have engaged in that do not come under the headings on the first list. They do, however, demonstrate the wide diversity of skills and knowledge, and the wide range of techniques for sharing that knowledge with other professionals.

Supporting another person in developing their professional skills also involves *use of self*. Mandell (2008) suggests that use of self involves the use of communication skills, insight, self-awareness, values and beliefs, biases, attitudes, openness, genuineness, warmth and non-judgemental attitudes. These attributes are the building materials for engaging with service users. All of them may be needed in supporting the professional development of another person. Change generally implies a degree of anxiety and uncertainty, so these skills that are used in settings with service users are also of value in the 'teaching' role:

- setting and maintaining boundaries;
- establishing confidentiality;
- conveying empathy and respect;
- building rapport and trust;
- modelling constructive social behaviour (Mandell 2008: 237).

Continuing professional development

A professional group sets entry requirements and monitors fitness for membership of the profession. In social work in the UK, this is a process that has developed significantly over the past decade, with the minimum qualification for professional membership now set at graduate level; compulsory registration for all social workers; and protection of title. Added expectations include the introduction of a period of supported continuing professional development through the Newly Qualified Social Worker (NQSW) programme and the Early Professional Development (EPD) project (CWDC 2011b). There is an expectation that social workers will maintain professional knowledge through regular and evidenced updates (TOPPS n.d.). Regular reviews of continuing professional development after initial registration is part of the process of increasing professionalisation (TOPPS n.d.). The expectation that social workers who have experience and knowledge gained through post-qualification practice should promote the learning of others may be seen as a reflection of the maturing of social work as a 'learning profession' in which experienced practitioners become a resource of specialist knowledge and expertise that may be offered to and drawn on by others.

This is a relatively new function in social work. Historically, post-qualification training tended to be centred on participation in non-assessed training courses, often arranged by employers, either directly through training officers or 'bought in' from outside experts:

> Much training delivered as in-service training has been functional rather than developmental in the wider sense of developing abilities as well as knowledge. The knowledge needed to be a professional social worker changes rapidly: the ability to learn is as or more important than the possession of knowledge that dates rapidly. New learning is essential, and being prepared to keep learning is therefore a professional responsibility.
> GSCC 2002, see also the *England National Occupational Standards for Social Work*, Point 5, 'Knowledge', TOPPS n.d.

There were two limitations to this approach: it was often unclear how much had been learned, and often it was not known how much of what was learned was used through extension of reflective, analytical practice.

Undertaking the role of supporting another professional social worker or allied professional in their development offers the opportunity to rethink the relationship between knowledge, expertise, critical practice and changing the way things are done by an individual or an organisation. One benefit of this approach is that it recognises and values the skills and knowledge of experienced practitioners. Another benefit is that it makes it *necessary* that knowledge and skills acquired during practice become the subject of reflection and analysis. Practitioners need to subject the skills and knowledge of their everyday working life to formal scrutiny. Many will have progressed to the point of having 'unconscious competence' (see box on page 225): in order to teach something, one needs to know how one does it, and be able to describe how it is done. Competence needs therefore to become *conscious*, consciously 'knowable' and explainable by the person who holds it. This requires reflection and analysis on the part of the teacher as well as the learner. The activity of teaching is a demanding one, but the benefits to the teacher may be as great as, or greater than, the benefits to the learner as new insights emerge. Becoming competent is reinforcing: and also acts as a reward because it is enjoyable, so worth pursuing as an end in itself.

Box 12.2 Maslow's four stages of competence

Unconscious incompetence: at this stage, the 'learner' does not recognise that one is unable to do something, and may feel confident that one is equipped with all the skills one needs. There is no desire to learn how to do things better, and the possibility that this is possible may not have occurred to them.

Conscious incompetence: the learner recognises that there is a deficit in their knowledge, which creates an uncomfortable feeling and may prompt rationalisations so that the need to learn new ways of thinking or working is avoided. It may prompt action to address the deficit and add new learning.

Conscious competence: the learner has begun to learn new skills, but has to concentrate on what they are doing to be able to use the new skills, like a person who has just learned to drive: it does not feel like a 'natural' activity yet.

Unconscious competence: the learner has had so much practice performing a skilled task that it is 'second nature' and can be performed easily and without much concentration or mental effort. A situational change in the demands on the learner may place them back a stage or two – as when a driver has to learn to drive a manual rather than an automatic car, for example. Other hazards are complacency, and forgetting what it is like not to have the skills one now wears so effortlessly.

One thing to note about this model is its simplicity. This is a strength: it is easy to remember and useful as a way of beginning to think about how we know what we can do and how our level of knowledge affects our performance and our ability – and motivation – to reflect on them. On the other hand, it may lead to a tendency to oversimplify. Breaking performance down into its different components may reveal that there are elements or skills that we are very good at, and others for which we have not really begun to appraise our own performance at all. Most of the tasks undertaken in social work are complex, and we may need to go beyond attaching a 'blanket' label to our skill level.

Reflective practice and preparation for the role of the teacher

One may move through all the stages of competence, from unconscious incompetence to unconscious competence, without being aware quite how this has been achieved. Use of language is an example: those who speak English as a first language generally know what the correct use of English is without necessarily knowing why we use certain forms and patterns. Someone who has a good command of English learned through formal tuition may have a much better command of the rules of English, even though they may be less 'competent' in terms of fluency or vocabulary. They may be better equipped to explain the rules of the language than someone brought up in Britain. Their conscious competence gives them an advantage in explaining how to speak English to a learner, even though they may not have the 'effortless' grasp of the first language English speaker.

Social work is complex: like language, it requires a grasp of formal rules,[1] but to practice really well one also needs to be creative and flexible in applying the rules, and able to make subtle distinctions between different options when communicating with others or choosing between multiple alternative courses of action. The specific legal and moral responsibilities that accompany the practice of social work make it important that practitioners are able to subject this process of interpreting, applying and creating one's own 'rules' to scrutiny. Those rules that are learned through professional training and practice have ethical and moral dimensions, and the skills learned or the manner of their application are not 'value free'. Dyke (2006) reminds us that there are numerous stakeholders in any professional project, and the professional owes a duty to all of them to ensure that the knowledge, values and theory they use have validity and are consistent with social expectations of professionals, particularly in relation to fairness, justice, transparency and effectiveness. Dyke follows Freire (1972) in arguing that theory is never politically neutral, and should always to be subject to review.

We judge the level of our competence against the extent to which it provides us with the ability to assist others, empower them, and support them in achieving their legitimate aims. This requires the ability to consider the impact of our actions on other people, using the 'soft skills' of emotional intelligence as well as values and ethical principles. To share that expertise with someone else may involve careful consideration as to how one has achieved competence, and what that competence consists of. To do this calls for reflection on what one does and how one does it. *Normative self-regulation* means that practitioners with an integrated sense of the operational norms and boundaries of the organisation and their profession are able to work within its constraints in a lawful and appropriate manner, without the need for an external check on their actions. They understand the task, and its parameters (Svensson 2006).

'Unconscious competence' presents a challenge to social work. If a practitioner ever reached a level of competence such that they could carry out their work without conscious mental effort, they would arguably have become 'risky' as practitioners, no longer weighing their actions or seeking to fine-tune their conversations carefully. It seems unlikely that this would happen in social work practice with children and young people and their families, because of the diversity and complexity of situations that present and the endlessly new challenges this brings. What is required is therefore a high level of flexibility in applying rules, a highly developed ethical compass, and strong reflective abilities to keep practice 'on track' in the sense of being consistent with accepted standards and up-to-date knowledge. Reflective practice is a counter-balance to a human tendency to adopt routine practices and easy solutions: the tendency to seek confirmatory evidence and dismiss disconfirmatory evidence (Munro 1999, 2008), or do the thing that appeared to work last time in a similar situation, rather than searching for the right response for the service user in every new situation.

> Reflective practice is something more than thoughtful practice. It is that form of practice which seeks to problematise many situations of professional performance so that they can become potential learning situations and so the practitioners can continue to learn, grow and develop in and through practice.
>
> Jarvis 1992

Fook (2002) argues that postmodernism opens up all areas of thought and practice to scrutiny, including our own values and the basis on which they rest, and the reason we as individuals hold them. Postmodernism does not supply a value base or moral code: in this sense it is morally neutral. Its strength, it is argued, lies in its power to open up values and morals to critical analysis. Reflexion, as opposed to reflection, happens when we reflect on ourselves, and on the influence that we exercise just by virtue of being and acting in any social context. Reflexion also happens when we consider the impact that our personal histories, our beliefs and other aspects of our selves have upon our actions and our interpretations. It also happens when we consider our own developmental trajectory, including our professional development and our own role, as well as contextual factors, in achieving it. Reflection may lead to reflexion. (See chapter 3 of Fook 2002).

In teaching, experienced practitioners may need to 'unpack' skills that they use effectively and effortlessly in order to be able to explain how they do what they do; to get to a position where they are clear that they 'know what they know' and know what more they may need to learn to achieve their aim of supporting someone else in learning from them.

Reflection may engage with the 'political' in its broadest sense. Mandell (2008) argues that reflection focused on anti-oppressive practice is concerned with the social worker's understanding of the institutions of power and their understanding of privilege and power, and his or her understanding of identity as constructed within interlocking oppressions. The object of reflection is to develop a contextual understanding of social work in which it is linked to the pursuit of justice, or at least an understanding of individual problems that relates those problems to unjust social structures. This may involve the reflector in situating themselves within complex and possibly overlapping frames of oppressor/oppressed identities (Mandell 2008: 237).

The conceptualisation of reflection which has its roots in clinical therapeutic literature, on the other hand, analyses power in therapeutic encounters and in the interactions of client and therapist, or social worker and service user, but is not open to consideration of the role of social arrangements in the genesis or maintenance of problems. Additionally, '... social work itself has typically not been problematized – that is, not critically examined – nor is there exploration of how awareness might make a difference to critical practice' (Mandell 2008: 236). Exploring how to 'do' social work may involve problematising social work itself – what are the proper aims of the agency and of social work within it? Mandell argues that neither the therapeutically derived concept of reflection, nor the anti-oppressive approach quite meets the needs of a profession in which the quality of interpersonal communication between professional and service user is a key element:

> Neither the traditional use of self literature nor the developing work on critical reflection seems to adequately capture a process of combining insight into one's personhood ... with a critical analysis of one's role as a social worker in the relations of power that create our practice.
>
> Mandell 2008: 237

Reflection may involve looking at the way we respond as individuals with unique histories: not 'throwing the baby out with the bathwater' in focusing on a variant of critical practice that excludes analysis of this 'idiosyncratic dimension of who we are' (Mandell 2008: 237).

This suggests two different applications of reflection in social work practice.

- Reflection as a way of examining the way in which power is exercised at different levels in society, including the power relations created as a result of professional/service user relationships.
- Reflection as a means of examining the effect that personal development and history has on professional responses to individual service users: the way that idiosyncrasies of birth, personality and temperament, chance, and life experience impact on our professional practice.

The solution to every practice problem or challenge subjected to critical analysis necessarily comes from a combination of knowledge about what works, the skills and resources available to the practitioner, knowledge of the range of possible and permissible courses of action, the wishes of the service user, and creative thinking – conscious or unconscious – about what might be most helpful in this situation. Analysis may enable teachers to separate out the different skills and knowledge they use, and the extent to which conscious decisions determined what they did, and how far it was the unconscious competence that comes with experience helped them to negotiate complexity and difficulty in their work. This may help them to prepare learners with the knowledge and skills they need to put new learning into practice and identify the skill sets that learners bring with them that will help them when using new learning.

When considering situations retrospectively, questions to ask include:

- What were the most important features of this event or incident?
- What went well?
- What was missed out, or might have been done better?
- What made me choose to take the actions I took?[2]

Johns connects reflective practice, self-development and self-determination as a practitioner:

> '... reflection is a good thing because it is a path towards realising desirable and effective practice in meaningful and practical ways. More than that, it is a process of self-development, of becoming the sort of practitioner you want to be.
>
> Johns 2004: 3

The aim of teaching could ultimately be to support the learner's professional development to the point where they are competent enough to be able to move away from a strictly rule-based approach to practice, but for short-term teaching this may not be a realistic aim. Creativity and flexibility are important for responding to complex new situations, but this is only safe when the practitioners' level of skill and knowledge and reflective ability give them the tools to make wise decisions in conditions of uncertainty, and to take responsibility for the quality of those decisions and actions through careful reflection on action.

Box 12.3 Example: providing support in practice

Joanne has achieved some skill in working with parents who have mental health problems. She is a trained social worker who worked as a nurse with people with mental health problems before she qualified as a social worker. She has undertaken to give Polly, a new worker in the team, some support in developing her practice with this group of service users. Joanne is aware that her success in engaging parents with mental health problems comes partly from her knowledge about mental health issues and services and her ability to stay calm and unflappable when parents are agitated or distressed. Polly has recently qualified as a social worker. She has two young children and an uncle who has a diagnosis of early onset dementia. She is not yet confident in the role of the authoritative professional making risk assessments, but she is good at engaging parents in discussion about parenting problems and she knows at first hand what it is like to be involved with mental health services. Joanne starts by listing the main law and policy provisions she thinks it would be helpful for Polly to be familiar with, prepares a summary of the main relevant research documents available on the internet and lends her a book with a useful chapter in it on parenting and mental health issues. Polly does some independent reading using these materials, and then they meet to plan a joint visit to a family. It is agreed that Polly will accompany Joanne on a visit to a family not previously known to the agency where there are child welfare concerns and mental health issues. Joanne will lead the interview and find out from the mother how she is; Polly will lead in finding out about the children's well-being. She will lead in finding out how the mother's mental health issues impact on her parenting but, if the mother appears reluctant to discuss this, she will leave the main role in the interview for Joanne. In the interview, the mother talks readily with Polly about the children, but shows a clear preference for discussing her own health concerns with Joanne. Afterwards, Polly feels that the interview did not go well, and she must have done something wrong to deter the mother from talking to her. Joanne reflects that she has highly developed skills in talking about difficult feelings with people who are stressed. She analyses what she does that helps people to feel at ease with her for the first time, and together Polly and Joanne role play some conversations. Polly learns to leave longer silences to let people think what they want to say, and to ask more open questions. Joanne feeds back to her on the aspects of the visit that went well, including her ability to draw the mother out on some of the rewards and stresses of being a parent. Joanne analyses what she does when interviewing and reflects how skillfully she manages this complex process, and considers some of its components, but reflects that her preparation of Polly could usefully have included more discussion of interviewing skills when working with people suffering from depression, before they went out on the visit.

Reflective practitioners should acquire skills in supporting learners in finding their own professional solutions to problems as opposed to following the same path already worn by the teacher:

> The best instructors are those who have made the journey for themselves, who know from experience, who guide the person to find their own way to swim well. Rather than applying rigid techniques to swim, these guides enable each individually to find their own way, a balance of challenge and support to move to greater depths.
>
> Johns 2004: 3

Problems are important opportunities in learning and teaching. They are potential assets in teaching others; opportunities for self-development, rather than obstacles to learning. Critical reflectors may seek the 'usefully problematic' even when things have gone well enough: avenues not explored; skills that were not used; questions that were not asked. To *problematise* in this context means to seek out the tensions, dilemmas and contradictions inherent in the rich information present in everyday situations as well as obviously prob-lematic situations. A degree of challenge from the person who is being taught is also to be welcomed since it is inherent in such problems that they have more than one possible solution. Again, this should be seen as an opportunity to explore possibilities rather than an unhelpful challenge to authority.

Trust and the environment for learning

Supporting another person in developing their practice can happen at a number of levels. Giving information is the least challenging, but if the objective is to help to change the way someone thinks as a practitioner, this entails a degree of trust. This needs to be two-way, with a degree of trust and respect between the teacher and the learner. Confidentiality needs to be explored. Learning involves moving people outside their 'comfort zones': teachers need to be able to recognise anxiety and respond to it supportively, but also be prepared for the fact that teaching may place demands on them that move them outside their comfort zone. They should have a right to support from their supervisor if they need a safe place to reflect on the teaching experience.

The learner needs to be able to trust the teacher, since they may need to expose their current knowledge and reflective skills to scrutiny. Mutual trust is most likely to develop when the organisational context is a supportive and enabling one. There is arguably a trickle-down effect: managerial structures that are seen as trustworthy are more likely to provide a healthy environment for sharing knowledge. Svensson (2006: 584) describes trust as:

> a rational strategy, which individuals develop in order to deal with other actors and their discretion to act. It denotes cognitive, normative or emotional expectations of one's own and others' conduct and the outcome of an interaction. ... As a mental or a personal state, trust is usually the same as an affective expectation for the environ-ment to be stable and predictable, and that one can rely on other people.

Trust is linked to three key elements: stability, predictability and reliability. The situations with which social workers work are frequently unpredictable and unstable; organisations need to support professionals by providing a reasonably stable working environment with reliable support, predictably available. The concept of *sustainable pedagogy* comes from the education literature: sustainable professional learning communities, in which learning readily occurs (White 2008).

SCIE summarises the key characteristics of a learning organisation:

Box 12.4 Key characteristics of a learning organisation

Organisational structure

Service user and carer feedback and participation are actively sought, valued and resourced, and used to influence and inform practice.

Team working, learning and making the best use of all staff skills are integral to the organisation

There is cross-organisational and collaborative working.

Organisational culture

There is a system of shared beliefs, values, goals and objectives.

The development of new ideas and methods is encouraged.

An open learning environment allows learning from mistakes and the opportunity to test out innovative practice.

Messages from research and new evidence are thought about and incorporated into practice.

Information systems

There are effective information systems, for both internal and external communication.

Policies and procedures are meaningful and understood by everybody – based on a human rights and social justice approach.

Human resource practices

There is continuous development for all staff including a clear supervision and appraisal policy.

Leadership

There is capacity for the organisation to change and develop services over and above day-to-day delivery.

Leadership at all levels embodies and models the key principles of a learning organisation.

SCIE 2005

While an individual mentor or teacher can go a long way to offset the negative effects of organisational instability, this does not address their own need for stability and support, which they may wish to discuss with their own supervisor, tutor or other person supporting them in their role as teacher.

A good basis for a trusting relationship includes setting guidelines for the aims and objectives of the learning experience; defining expectations regarding confidentiality and frequency of meeting; and making arrangements for support in case of difficulty. It allows both parties to know what the expectations are of both of them so there are no unpleasant 'surprises'. Where there is a supportive, trusted organisational context this may be easier to achieve, but in a culture of blame and uncertainty, establishing trust within the learning relationship is even more important. Links to supervisory and other managerial processes also need to be clear. If the person doing the supporting and teaching is being assessed on their ability to carry out this function, their level of anxiety about exposure to criticism may be higher than that of the learner, despite their greater experience or higher level of skill. Their experience and skills should enable them to feel valued, so they are able to be open about the knowledge they have that equips them for the role of supporting a learner in their professional development.

A model from the education literature – learning communities

Professional development may be based on traditional models of 'top-down' learning, in which more experienced staff pass on knowledge and skills through teaching sessions and mentoring, or a more collaborative model in which individuals take responsibility for nurturing 'learning communities' within which groups of professionals work together to develop improved practice. This second approach is concerned with the generation of new knowledge through co-operation rather than the transmission of established know-how from more to less experienced staff (Butler *et al.* 2004). Learning communities may produce both knowledge and skills, or enhance the context in which they are applied, leading to greater effectiveness. Professional development may be about learning how to develop and use a responsive, professional, outcome-oriented environment for practice as well as about developing new practice, or transmitting knowledge about practices to the next generation of professionals. They may be seen as an alternative to the 'top down' model of professional development in which the focus is generally on instrumental skills and knowledge.

Learning organisations have a learning culture; one that has '… a core shared assumption that the appropriate way for humans to behave is to be proactive problem solvers and learners …' (Schein 1997: 364, cited in Skinner 2005: 26). A culture must exist within the organisation in which common goals are defined, and shared norms and values shape the way those goals are pursued. At the same time, there must be sufficient openness to doing things differently to allow for creative active problem solving, and tolerance of trying things out, even though these will not always work exactly according to the aspirations people have for them.

Collaborative approaches to professional development in teaching have been described as a 'joint inquiry' approach, in which teachers consider ways of shifting practice to solve problems and try out new ways of working. Learning goals should be 'authentic', of meaningful concern to the learning community. This model allows more and less experienced professionals to learn together: there is an expectation that all participants will benefit from the process. Learning, thus constructed, is to help professionals develop a professional identity, and become active participants in their professional community (Butler *et al.* 2004). Butler *et al.* argue that their 'communities of practice' model enables practitioners to review and revise their conceptual framework in response to the way their profession is conceptualised socially. This seems particularly applicable to child and family social work, in which public expectations as to what social workers should and should not do have undergone some very public discussion over recent years:

> Rapid change and reflexivity forces people to think afresh, to reflect upon, and engage with, their social world. In late modernity people are guided less by tradition and past experience, as they are increasingly forced to reflect and make decisions amidst a whirlwind of changing information.
>
> Dyke 2006: 105

This draws attention to the fact that established professionals have reason to be reflective and open to change at all times, including when promoting the development of less experienced professionals.

Some defensiveness about one's own knowledge and skills on the part of the teacher may be unavoidable because the role exposes areas of thinking and values as well as knowledge that may be rarely opened up to scrutiny. It may be helpful to start from the premise that reflective '[p]rocesses are needed that enable people to respond to more readily available, often contradictory and constantly changing information and thereby take more knowledgeable action,' (Dyke 2006: 106). The role of the 'teacher' in the professional development enterprise is to evolve in their professional knowledge and skills as well as promoting the learning of the designated 'learner'. Schön (1987) argued that the art of the teacher is to enable the student to learn and, when the student has difficulties, it is for the teacher to examine how they can develop their abilities to assist the student. The teacher therefore needs to be able to reflect on their own performance as a teacher, and the different views the learner may bring: where does the line fall that separates values, ideals and knowledge that are core to professionalism and, as such, 'non-negotiable', and areas in which the addition of new voices and opinions may be a valuable way of shifting the teacher's practice? As long ago as 1916, Dewey argued that 'the learning of received wisdom resulted in hearsay and accumulated opinions, many of which were absurd ... people should observe for themselves, formulate their own theories and not accept the imposition of dogma as truth' (Dewey 1916, quoted in Dyke 2006). The support available to the teacher is important because it gives an opportunity to check out their own values, knowledge and beliefs and reflect on the learning experience from their perspective.

Putting learning into practice and getting feedback

Learners need an opportunity to practice their skills, so supporting others in their learning should ideally go beyond explanation and theory and offer learners a chance to put what they have learned into practice. Learning in practice has the advantage over a classroom situation that it is generally linked to the specific learning needs of the learner, and genuine practical opportunities will usually be available for learners to put what they have learned into practice and obtain feedback. Learners have been described as going through a cycle, which mirrors Maslow's four stages, discussed on page 225:

- **Pre-contemplation:** the learner is not aware of a learning need, or is in denial.
- **Contemplation:** they are aware of the need to learn, but ambivalent about change.
- **Preparation:** the learner is committed to change.
- **Action:** change through professional development is sought and attained (Milan *et al.* 2006)

Learners may start out at any of the first three stages, so part of the preparation for learning may be explaining why the learning is important and relevant for the learner and dealing with issues of resistance. In the example on page 229, Polly might have taken the view that she had no intention of working in a mental health setting and did not think it likely that she would need skills in interviewing people with mental health difficulties. Explanation of the prevalence of mental health difficulties and their co-occurrence with parenting problems among mothers with young children may be the first stage of the process of teaching and learning.

Feedback is an integral part of supporting the learner through the process of professional development. Some things to bear in mind when giving feedback are set out below:

- Feedback should be timely – generally provided soon after the learning experience.
- It should be detailed – learners tend to look for more detailed feedback than those giving the feedback think they need.
- Feedback should include both positive and challenging feedback, starting with positive feedback, and ending with a résumé of positive aspects of the learner's work.
- The person receiving feedback should have an opportunity to ensure that they have understood the feedback.
- A plan should be formulated promptly to agree the next stage to reinforce the learning and consider how it may be progressed, either by the learner on their own initiative or with others supporting them.

Part of the planning for supporting someone else in their learning should be considering how and when feedback is going to be given. How is the teacher going to ascertain whether or not their teaching has been helpful, and what further support the learner needs to progress?

In order to learn, professionals need a stimulating, challenging and supportive work environment, and clarity about the limits of their responsibility. Support, coaching, feedback and emotional support are all important for professional development. Coaching is important for developing some skills; working together on challenging tasks is a good way of learning, but there also needs to be scope within the organisation for the development of trust and a sense of personal agency.

Emotion and learning

The context for learning and acquiring a professional identity has an important emotional aspect to it. Erault *et al.* (2007) identified the importance of good relationships and an active learning culture in organisations in supporting early to mid-career learning. Consideration of the emotions and feelings that came into play during a difficult professional encounter or episode can help to identify some of the influences on actions and choices made during the situation: 'Emotions play a central role in decision making. The illusion that they can be somehow removed or put on ice whilst rational decision making is in progress is neither helpful nor possible' (Morrison 2007: 255).

Having strong feelings about a subject can make it difficult to focus on its more theoretical aspects, but that does not mean that emotion is in itself problematic for learning. Engaging with a subject as a 'whole person' involves engaging thoughts, actions and feelings, and it is commonplace that many subjects in social work engender strong feelings. They may also create feelings of helplessness or uncertainty as to what to do in the face of what can seem very considerable difficulties. Day and Leitch (2001) explore the importance of emotion in developing professional practice:

> We have two fundamentally different ways of knowing and understanding, which interact to construct our mental life. First, there is the rational mind, characterised by the logical, deductive mode of comprehension, which is careful, analytic, effective and frequently deliberate. Alongside this, however, is another system of knowing, the emotional mind, which is powerful, impulsive, intuitive, holistic and fast – and often illogical.
>
> Day and Leitch 2001: 408

This underlines the point that we have more than one way of making sense of the world, and our capacity to learn is profoundly affected by our state of feeling at the time we are learning or exposed to new experiences. Dale *et al.* (2002) note that our emotions may affect how we perceive things; a 'glass half empty' or 'glass half full' mindset may lead to different perceptions and different interpretations of the same situation, as in a situation where a child is injured but there is no adequate explanation, which has been seen as both a reason for keeping a child in hospital, or for deciding to let the child go home.

One of the starting points for reflective practice is recognition of the uncertainty inherent in any given situation. Uncertainty can be challenging and unsettling if one expects that developing professional competence means becoming more, not less, certain. Mezirow (1991) calls the experience of exposure to a situation that can lead to a substantial shift in the way things are perceived as a 'disorienting dilemma'. A subsequent period of reflection should offer a new insight or analysis – although there is no requirement that a 'definitive answer' be arrived at, given that uncertainty is inherent in complex situations such as human problems. The solution may be provisional and subject to review, but the best possible answer that can be found under the current state of understanding and knowledge. This runs counter to the human tendency to seek confirmation of one's hypotheses, and to be more open to information that tends to confirm one's views rather than challenge them. This accompanies a tendency to settle for a 'good enough' explanation rather than consider what other ways there may be of understanding the known 'facts' (Munro 1999; Ruch 2007; Dalzell and Sawyer 2007). Professionalism may therefore be seen as partly about maintaining a degree of scepticism for theories that purport to offer easy answers or universal frameworks for understanding human problems. This tolerance for uncertainty does not make teaching easier because it denies the possibility of offering simple answers, but it increases the potential richness of discussion and analysis and leaves a wider space for considering other ways of understanding human problems including, importantly, service users' own perspectives.

Morrison describes the way that aspects of personal functioning can interact with professional skills – or rather skills deficits – to create 'toxic' situations:

> ... as a mentor for managers and supervisors dealing with difficult staff management situations, it is increasingly apparent clear that the most troubling and intractable situations exist when performance difficulties occur in the context of staff who lack accurate empathy, self-awareness and self-management skills. This lack of emotional competence renders the specific performance problems, such as poor recording practice, all but unmanageable.
>
> Morrison 2007: 246

When difficulties arise that seem to be immune to resolution through reflection and critical analysis, it may be helpful to consider the part that emotional issues are playing in maintaining an unhelpful dynamic. Are there organisational issues that are having an impact on openness to professional development: the reverse of the 'sustainable learning organisation'? Is there an interpersonal dynamic that needs to be explored, possibly with support from the teacher's supervisor or other mentor?

Reflection as a tool for learning: evaluating the experience of putting it into practice

Whatever is being learned and taught, there needs to be reflection on what has been learned. This is partly because social work is not a technical-rational activity, and all knowledge and skills need to be applied in the context of appraisal of the ethics, rights and risk issues for the various people involved. Application of knowledge requires a different set of intellectual skills from those used to learn about research, policy, theory and techniques for intervention. Second, new knowledge needs to be integrated with existing knowledge. It should not exist in a 'bubble' but become part of a coherent understanding of what the role of a social worker is. Does what has been recently learned suggest that other ideas about social work might need to shift? Third, new knowledge may have personal implications for the learner. Does what has been learned challenge any personal beliefs or values, or raise questions for the learner that they may need to think and talk through in a supportive professional setting?

The first step in reflecting on an incident is to *describe* it. When teaching involves the application of new ideas in practice, a record of what was done and how it went should be made by the student; the teacher should have their own record of what they observed if they were present. Ideally, the record is made as close as possible to the event, minimising the possibility that detail will be lost through the decay of memory. The account should include not only what happened but also any thoughts or feelings experienced at the time of the incident, and any initial responses to the experience. Dale (1994: 22) proposes that '[m]istakes and setbacks are elemental features of development and learning'; if things did not go as planned, this may be seen as offering learning opportunities rather than representing failure by the learner. However, social work is strongly committed, with good reason, to the *avoidance* of mistakes, which places learners under pressure to get things right first time. Paying attention to detail at the stage of describing the event means there is greater scope for considering the possible significance of what is learned about the family/child (Dale *et al.* 2002: 56).

The next step is to *analyse* the experience critically using what Tate and Sills (2004) call a 'particular mind set'. This includes being 'kind' to oneself, not seeking to be critical in the ordinary sense of the word, but looking for opportunities for growth and self-development. Reflection may include considering all or any of the following questions:

- How did (new) knowledge/values/theory underpin my actions?
- How effective was I in achieving what I set out to/wanted to achieve?
- How did my expectations of myself and my role affect what I did?
- What influence did my emotional response to the situation have on my actions?
- What caused me to see and respond to people and events in the way I did?
- How did my expectations of myself and of others affect what I did?
- How do I feel now about what happened?
- How do I think other people experienced the event?

After Tate 2004: 3, modified by the author

These questions form the basis of a process of inquiry that should bring out the detail of what happened and relate it to the learner's skill in applying what they have learned, through a collaborative process of inquiry. While reflection can be done alone, a shared process of reflection on professional action is to be valued because it brings in the reflective skills and knowledge base of the teacher. The teacher may be able to help identify ways in which the learner has developed: reflexivity occurs when one can look back over a period of change and see how one has developed.

Social work as a creative activity

We have discussed social work as involving more than the application of rules or the use of technical knowledge, research evidence or even rational thought, although all of these are essential components of professional competence in social work. Other important aspects are creativity and imagination. The pursuit of creativity has to be tempered by strong respect for service user safety and well-being, and organisational integrity. Some aspects of creativity are set out overleaf:

Creativity and imagination allow us to imagine what it is like for other people – particularly important when working with people who have experienced trauma or are under stress – and imagine what may happen if certain things (*interventions*) happen or do not happen. Creativity is much more difficult to define and to teach than empirical aspects of social work, or even theoretical aspects that are not empirical, such as ethics and values. Creativity is central to the process of translating the 'rules' and models for practice into

---

Box 12.5 Creativity

- readiness to abandon old ways of doing things;
- the ability to come up with new ways of doing things;
- associations readily made between ideas;
- originality: newness of ideas;
- spontaneous flexibility: can come up with new ways of thinking about things even when there is no pressure to do so;
- adaptive or responsive creativity: comes up with new ways of doing things when the old ways don't work or are no longer possible.

---

good practice. Jackson talks about 'exploiting patterns of abilities', and the ability to reflect to make sense of experience:

> We need three different sorts of abilities to be successful: analytical abilities – to analyse, evaluate, judge, compare and contrast; practical abilities – to apply, utilise, implement and activate; and creative abilities – to imagine, explore, synthesise, connect, discover, invent and adapt. To these families of abilities I would add, abilities to reflect to learn from and make sense of experience. Successful people ... do not necessarily have strengths in all areas, but they find ways to exploit whatever pattern of abilities they may have in any given situation or context and align them in a way that value and meaning is created in their lives and in the communities they inhabit in any given situation or context.
>
> Jackson *et al.* 2006:2

This quotation offers a key to the challenge of developing creativity: making meaning and value through reflection on experience. Through nurturing reflective abilities, teachers and mentors can encourage the growth of creativity as practitioners learn to be more flexible and associative in making sense of experience. Creativity involves the ability to look at a problem from a different angle and find a new solution that works for the service user when they have met a dead end in the routes they have already tried, and openness to new ideas – including those that come from the service user. It also implies an ability to *think things through* – to explore the implications of different possible solutions in theory before putting the best one into practice.

Promoting this kind of professional development is far more challenging than a simple transfer of knowledge, but lays a foundation for future learning and self-development in an 'age of instability' (Barnett and Coates 2005: 8). Morrison (2007) considers *judgement* as a quality that involves inter- and intra-personal intelligence, self and 'other' awareness, and the ability to manage self and others. Both depend on making sense of a complex web of interacting factors, some inter- and some intra-personal. New ideas and creative approaches need to be used with sound judgement about what falls within acceptable limits in terms of risk to individuals and organisations, and the extent of one's own abilities, freedom of action and responsibilities as well as professional ethical conduct.

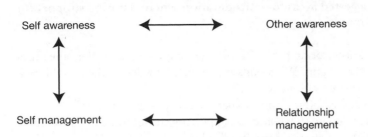

Source: Adapted from Morrison (2007: 251)

Figure 12.1 Link between awareness of self and others, and management skills

The paradox of supporting others in being creative is that it not only requires some creativity on the part of the person acting as educator or mentor; it also implies that the learner may offer – indeed is expected to offer – novel answers to questions, and new solutions to problems. These may not be the same as the solutions and answers that the teacher expected, nor may they be ones that they see as the 'best' answer, but it provides rich ground for reflection, reflexivity and exploring the ways in which the new solution differs from previous solutions, and working out which idea is the most useful – for the service user, professional, agency or society – and which has the best 'fit' with social work's ethical and moral values, which is the most practical, and so forth.

Outcomes

The focus on reflection can promote competence and independence in professional judgement based on sound ethical and knowledge-based principles. However, the objective is not 'abstract' but a specific service-user related goal: improving the service the learner offers. For this reason, it is important to define the intended end point of the 'supporting learning' process, and be clear how both parties are going to be able to evaluate the outcome of the process. An assessment of what the learner feels able to do confidently at the outset – related areas of work in which they already have competence – can provide the platform for beginning the supportive process, and for later reflection and assessment of the learning process itself. Second, the aims for what the learner will be able to do at the end of the learning process should be defined at the beginning. This may be in terms of acquisition of new knowledge, new skills, or increased confidence in using existing skills well. The developmental process may be tracked through reflective self-assessment, observation of practice, or through completion of some new work activity. The learner should have an opportunity to reflect on the learning experience and feedback to the person who took on the supportive role.

Professionals progress along a number of dimensions as they move from novice to skilled practitioner. Erault *et al.* (2007) analyse them thus:

Box 12.6 Some suggested areas for consideration when planning support for professional development

- What does the learner bring to the learning situation – what do they already do well – building on strengths? What skills and knowledge will help them in this task?
- What does the learner wish to achieve?
- What can the 'teacher' offer – time, experience, expertise, support?
- What methods are going to be used in supporting the learning of the learner?
- How is feedback to be given – 2-way feedback?
- What are the 'rules' for the process – for example, confidentiality, actions to be taken if there are specific ethical issues?
- What should happen if either the learner or teacher is unhappy with the learning experience – how are difficulties to be resolved?
- How are gains in professional development to be tracked/identified?
- How is the supportive experience to end – feedback, future development opportunities, etc.

- **Task performance:** the practitioner gains in speed and fluency of work; increasing complexity of tasks and problems are tackled; a wider range of skills is utilised; communications with a wide range of people improve, as does collaborative working.
- **Awareness and understanding:** this includes understanding relating to colleagues, service users, managers, contexts and situations and one's own organisation. Understanding of problems and risks, priorities and strategic issues and values issues are also enhanced.
- **Personal development:** gains are made in self-evaluation; self-management; handling emotions; building and sustaining relationships; disposition to see other perspectives, and disposition to work and consult with others. The ability to learn and improve one's practice and access relevant knowledge and expertise increases, as does the ability to learn from experience.
- **Academic knowledge and skills:** there is better use of evidence and argument, accessing of formal knowledge and research-based practice. Theoretical thinking develops, and the ability to 'know what you might need to know'. Knowledge and theory is used more effectively in a range of situations.
- **Role performance:** development of skills in prioritisation; a wider range of responsibilities are taken on, as is supporting other people's learning. A supervisory role may be assumed. Leadership, accountability, delegation, handling ethical issues, coping with unexpected problems and crisis management develop. Responsibility is taken for keeping up to date.
- **Teamwork:** collaboration, joint planning and problem solving develop. Also the ability to engage in and promote mutual learning, and facilitating social relations.
- **Decision making and problem solving:** knowing when to seek expert help; dealing with complexity; enhanced participation in group decision making and enhanced

problem analysis; formulating and evaluating options. Ability to manage within time-scales and take decisions under pressure develops.

• **Judgement:** concerning quality of performance, output and outcomes; priorities; value issues and levels of risk.

These categories may be used as triggers for considering what change has taken place and where progress has happened over the period of a supported learning experience.

Concluding comments – and the start of another reflective process

Clear and specific aims set out at the beginning of the learning experience, and exploration of the learner's starting levels of knowledge, skill and confidence provide a focus for support for another person's learning. Learning new things exposes people to the risk of failure as well as the possibility of mastery of new skills, and so offers both risks and potential gains. This is the case for the learner and for the teacher, both of whom expose themselves to the possibility that they will be asked to do something that stretches their abilities or knowledge. Anyone developing their skills in working with children and families will be engaging their emotions and values, as well as their mind and other senses and faculties, whether they go out and encounter new situations, or look at familiar ones from a new viewpoint. Supporting learners involves working with all of these elements. At the end of the process, these aims can provide a starting point for evaluating the experience and for the learner to feed back to the teacher. It allows the teacher to assess the quality of their own teaching and reflect on the feedback they receive from the learner, as a parallel process to the evaluation of learning by the less experienced practitioner. This process should seek to validate learning and look for ways of improving practice further.

The teacher as well as the learner both need to reflect on the experience: have they succeeded in the aims they first defined? What planned learning took place, and what additional things did they find they needed to consider as they went through the learning process? How do they know if they have learned the things they set out to learn, and how will they keep any new professional skills alive and develop them further? What might they still need to learn? How were they challenged in their knowledge, values and practice by the process? What have they learned about themselves as practitioners, teachers/mentors, and individuals? What did they do well, and what would they wish to do differently another time? What did they gain, professionally and personally, from the experience? What benefits were there from the engagement in professional development for other people, especially service users? How about the professional/organisational network within which they work? Has the experience suggested any more things they need or want to learn more about, or anything they would like to explore concerning the way their organisation supports professional development? Where do they want to go from here?

The process will, it is hoped, have given both parties to the process a sense that they have gained in competence and knowledge, which is rewarding in itself, as well as adding new skills that will be valuable in dealing with other similar challenges in the future.

Conclusion

Social work is undergoing a period of change. This is nothing new: social work has always occupied contested territory (Lorenz 2001; Dickens 2011). Earlier periods of change, or 'watersheds', include the Barclay Report of 1982 with its endorsement of community-based social work – and bracing dissenting view from Professor Robert Pinker (NISW 1982); the NHS and Community Care Act of 1990 with its establishment of social work as integral part of the new extended role for local authorities; the growth of service user and carer influence and the personalisation agenda in the 2000s (Ferguson 2007); the impact of the Laming Report following the death of Victoria Climbié (Laming 2003); and, most recently, the establishment of the Social Work Task Force and the College of Social Work and the Munro Review of child and family social work – the last three all following on the death of Peter Connelly in North London in 2007 (Department for Education 2010a, b).

This process of review and reassessment of the role of social work has necessarily had an impact on social work education and training. From its early beginnings in philanthropy, social work has moved towards a professional identity based on respect for persons, promoting individual rights while acting to restrict them sometimes in the interest of protecting others, and taking responsibility for one's own practice through critical and reflective practice (Younghusband 1978).

External pressures through policy reviews and inquiries are only part of the pressure for social work's continuing professional development. There are internal pressures too, coming from practitioner feedback and research into practice. Documented difficulties experienced by social workers in obtaining adequate supervision (McGregor 2011) and issues surrounding the role of supervision in the current economic and political environment (Noble and Irwin 2009) have, it is argued, highlighted new priorities for the profession: improving the quality of supervision and support for new and experienced workers, and increasing the capacity of social workers and managers to use reflective and analytical processes to work ethically, effectively and safely. Reflective and analytical skills are essential for working independently, as social workers routinely do, and to enable them to make the best use of supervision opportunities.

Reflective practice has a core place in ongoing professional development. Qualifying training is subject to processes of review and regulation, and there is an expectation that social workers will develop skills as independent learners before they qualify. Post-qualifying training programmes need to build on the gains made to date through the Post Qualifying Framework for Social Work (Lombard 2010b). In 2011, responsibility for post-qualifying education and training passed to the College of Social Work. All training, pre- and post-qualification, will be oriented to the Professional Capabilities Framework (PCF) developed by the Social Work Reform Board (see SWRB 2011a). The PCF also informs the supervision standards for employers (SWRB 2011b). The headlines for each capability are as follows:

- **Professionalism:** Identify and behave as a professional social worker committed to professional development.
- **Values and ethics:** Apply social work ethical principles and values to guide professional practice.
- **Diversity:** Recognise diversity and apply anti-discriminatory and anti-oppressive principles in practice.
- **Rights, justice and economic well-being:** Advance human rights and promote social justice and economic well-being.
- **Knowledge:** Apply knowledge of social sciences, law and social work practice theory.
- **Critical reflection and analysis:** Apply critical reflection and analysis to inform and provide a rationale for professional decision making.
- **Intervention and skills:** Use judgement and authority to intervene with individuals, families and communities to promote independence, provide support and prevent harm, neglect and abuse.
- **Contexts and organisations:** Engage with, inform, and adapt to changing contexts that shape practice. Operate effectively within your own organisational frameworks and contribute to the development of services and organisations. Operate effectively within multi-agency and inter-professional settings.
- **Professional leadership:** Take responsibility for the professional learning and development of others through supervision, mentoring, assessing, research, teaching, leadership and management.

These capabilities provide a new framework against which individual practitioners can think about the skills and knowledge they have already gained, the professional capabilities they can share with newer practitioners, and can evaluate their own developmental needs.

This book is an attempt to consider some key issues in developing competence in social work with children and families and to consider how critical, reflective practice and analysis can enhance practitioners' skills and confidence in the social work role. Becoming good at doing something: able to draw on one's own fund of skills, knowledge and practice experience to turn a crisis or a looming catastrophe into a manageable situation, is enormously rewarding, and perhaps the best possible reason for social workers to want to continue in practice. Starting with a situation which may feel hopeless and stuck, or chaotic and dangerous, and supporting the people in that situation through to a different one in which danger is reduced, trauma is acknowledged and may be being addressed, new opportunities have been opened up, and quality of life is improved, is the ultimate aim of intervention. These goals are often met. The extent to which problems can be solved varies, of course, but the many families that progress from needing social work support to independent coping is testimony to the success of social work intervention. Another unacknowledged sign of success – hard to quantify but nonetheless present – is the many unnamed children who avoid abuse or neglect, or further abuse and neglect, as a result of social work intervention. But this is not easy work, and it places great demands on individual social workers. The demands are on social workers' time, skill, knowledge, energy and creativity. Pressure to meet other objectives can detract from the rewards that should come from these hard-won achievements (Collins 2008).

Reflecting on practice is one way of learning to do it better, but it can also be a way of drawing confidence and reward from the work one does. Finding time for it is not a luxury. Sharing the knowledge and skill one has gained through doing the work is also a way of developing one's own practice, and exploring how far one has come.

Whatever changes there are in social work over the coming years, and it seems change is an inevitable and often beneficial process, social workers will need to be equipped to deal with innovation confidently and reflectively, taking professional satisfaction from the work that is done well, as well as learning from things that can be improved. Communicating the achievements of social work to others outside the profession is another challenge for social work over the next few years, and it is to be hoped that the appointment of a Chief Social Worker and the development of the College of Social Work will facilitate this (SWTF 2009). What will also help is having a profession that is able to identify for itself what it does well, and how it does it, and for this, reflective practice is a key skill.

There are limits to what a practitioner can learn from a book; without the opportunity to try out ideas in practice the ideas in the book have no meaning. The important things happen in the 'real world' of practice. The ideas only become meaningful when someone tries them out, maybe finding a better way of doing things as a result. This may be their own new way of doing things, developed for themself as a result of reflecting on what is in the book. If this creates a better experience for the service user, and helps the practitioner to explore their own professional skills, then the book has achieved as much as one could ever hope for it.

Notes

1 Hearing children's voices and respecting children's wishes and feelings, part 1: trust, communication and support

1 Using the term loosely to include practice that is not as thorough or analytical as it should be, and not restricting it to cases in which children came to harm.
2 The child's right to privacy comes from Article 8, the right to private and family life, in the Human Rights Act 1998, which states: 1 Everyone has the right to respect for his private and family life, his home and his correspondence, 2 There shall be no interference by a public authority with the exercise of this right except such as is in accordance with the law and is necessary in a democratic society in the interests of national security, public safety or the economic well-being of the country, for the prevention of disorder or crime, for the protection of health or morals, or for the protection of the rights and freedoms of others.
3 Article 3, Human Rights Act 1998 Prohibition of torture: 'no one shall be subjected to torture or to inhuman or degrading treatment or punishment.'
4 See DCSF 2010: 5.67: 'Exceptionally, a joint enquiry/investigation team may need to speak to a suspected child victim without the knowledge of the parent or caregiver. Relevant circumstances would include the possibility that a child would be threatened or otherwise coerced into silence, a strong likelihood that important evidence would be destroyed or that the child in question did not wish the parent to be involved at that stage and is competent to take that decision.'

2 Hearing children's voices and respecting children's wishes and feelings, part 2: the legal framework, and putting it into practice

1 *Sahin v Germany*: Chamber judgment of the ECtHR, July 8, 2003.
2 The countries that have already implemented it include Austria, Croatia, Czech Republic, France, Germany, Greece, Italy, Latvia, Macedonia, Poland, Slovenia, Turkey and the Ukraine. Several others, including Sweden, Spain, Ireland, Iceland, Finland and Portugal have signed it, but have yet to ratify and implement it.
3 The text of the European Convention on the Exercise of Children's Rights is available at: http://conventions.coe.int/Treaty/Commun/QueVoulezVous.asp?NT=160&CL=ENG
4 *Gaskin v UK* (1989) 12 EHRR 36 for the full text, and a summary of the case is available at http://en.wikipedia.org/wiki/Gaskin_v_United_Kingdom, reliability not guaranteed!

3 Reflection: theory, knowledge, identity and power in working with children and families

1 The position for third sector employers of social workers in the reform process is less clear than the implications of the proposals for the public sector.
2 Also relevant in this context is his assertion that in all creative processes there is a pre-logical phase of knowing, which he describes as 'tacit knowledge'.
3 The term 'reframing' was first used in family therapy, and is now widely associated with neuro-linguistic programming (NLP). It refers to the idea that particular types of behaviour are not

necessarily 'good' or 'bad': it depends on the context in which they occur and the 'frame' though which they are seen. Deliberately changing the frame can change one's perception of the behaviour: see Bandler and Grinder 1982.

4 Assessment of parenting: constructing meaning from detail

1 The extent to which the emotional environment of the family is important for the assessment will vary, depending on the issue referred, but in no case is it irrelevant.
2 'Neglect is the persistent failure to meet a child's basic physical and/or psychological needs, likely to result in the serious impairment of the child's health or development. It may involve a parent or carer failing to provide adequate food, shelter and clothing, failing to protect a child from physical harm or danger, or the failure to ensure access to appropriate medical care or treatment. It may also include neglect of, or unresponsiveness to, a child's basic emotional needs.'
3 'The social work profession promotes social change, problem solving in human relationships and the empowerment and liberation of people to enhance wellbeing. Utilising theories of human behaviour and social systems, social work intervenes at the points where people interact with their environments. Principles of human rights and social justice are fundamental to social work.'

5 Narrative and understanding the family's world: questions and stories in working with children and families

1 It is not suggested that this is ever a complete process, and all understanding of other people's experience is partial. However, if a representation of some aspect of the service user's reality has been discussed and agreed and led to a feeling of being understood – on the part of the service user – and the social worker is able to use this representation to draw some tentative conclusions about how to work with and support the service user, then this may reasonably be described as going beyond a superficial knowledge of the other person's experience.
2 Compare this with the extreme form of watchfulness associated with high anxiety identified in some abused children; 'frozen watchfulness'.

6 Social work and poverty: a complex relationship

1 Margaret Hodge, 2004 cited in Gillies, V. 2004 'In different worlds,' *The Guardian* December 1, 2004. (Italics added)

7 Risk in child and family social work, part 1: the idea of risk and uncertainty in social work

1 Investigation of the possibility that a child is suffering or is likely to suffer significant harm under s47 of the Children Act 1989.

8 Risk in child and family social work, part 2: probability and different levels of prevention

1 *Bury MBC v D* [2009] EWHC 446 (Fam) 4 March 2009 per Munby, J.
2 Poverty might be viewed as a 'proxy measure' for intergenerational poverty and social exclusion, and as a risk factor for parenting problems, since many parents are both poor and excellent parents, and although social mobility is low in Britain, a proportion of children born into poor families do manage to become non-poor adults.
3 At the time of writing there were no page numbers available for quotations from this advance access article.
4 No implication is intended that particular individuals were or were not culpable of breaches of reasonable expectations of professional conduct: this is a reflection on the function such dismissals serve.

9 Working with resistance: the challenge of working with involuntary service users

1   The case of Kimberly Carlile, who died in Greenwich in 1987, is another reminder of the power that a violent family member can exercise over professionals as well as children. The manner in which Kimberley was seen was 'managed' by Hall, her 'stepfather' London Borough of Greenwich (1987).

10 Drugs and alcohol and child and family social work

1   Class A/B drugs are amphetamines and methamphetamine, cannabis is a Class B drug, UK Government Drug Strategy 2010, available at: http://www.homeoffice.gov.uk/publications/alcohol-drugs/drugs/drug-strategy/drug-strategy-2010?view=Binary
2   See NTA website, www.nta.nhs.uk/news-rodt-report.aspx for updated advice.
3   See Slade (2005) for a summary of the theory.

11 In care and going home: working with parents towards reunification

1   This reflects other research: see for example the report on children's views of the Family Justice System, at the www.rights4me.org website.
2   Available at: www.unicef.org/crc

12 Supporting others in their professional development

1   In this context, 'rules' includes all the ethical principles and values, operational rules, law and regulations, theories and knowledge that a practitioner brings to their professional practice.
2   See also Tate and Sills' list of questions for reflection that expands this idea, see p. 237.

References

ACAS (2010) 'Preventing Workplace Harassment and Violence; Joint guidance implementing a European Social Partner Agreement,' available at: www.workplaceharassment.org.uk/wp-content/uploads/2009/11/HRE_100_Guidance_report.pdf

Advisory Council on the Misuse of Drugs (2003) *Hidden Harm*, London: The Home Office.

Alderson, P. (1993) *Children's Consent to Surgery*, Buckingham: Open University Press.

Alderson, P. (2000) *Young Children's Rights*, London: Jessica Kingsley Publishers.

Allen, G. (2011) *Early Intervention: The Next Steps*, London: The Cabinet Office, available at: www.dwp.gov.uk/docs/early-intervention-next-steps

Anderson, D. (2000) 'Coping strategies and burnout among veteran child protection workers', *Child Abuse and Neglect* 2000 June 24(6): 839–48

Audit Commission (2003) *Services for disabled children: a review of services for disabled children and their families*, London: Audit Commission.

Azar, S. and Cote, L. (2002) 'Socio-cultural issues in the evaluation of the needs of children in custody decision making: What do our current frameworks for evaluating parenting practices have to offer?' *International Journal of Law and Psychiatry* 25(3): 193–217.

Baker, C. (2007) 'Disabled Children's Experience of Permanency in the Looked After System', *British Journal of Social Work* 37(7): 1173–88.

Bandler, R. and Grinder J. (1982) *Reframing*, Moab, Utah: Real People Press.

Barnard, M. (2003) 'Between a rock and a hard place: the role of relatives in protecting children from the effects of parental drug problems', *Child and Family Social Work* 8(4): 291–99.

Barnard, M. (2005) 'Discomforting research: colliding moralities and looking for 'truth' in a study of parental drug problems', *Sociology of Health and Illness* 27(1): 1–19.

Barnard, M. (2007) *Drug Addiction and Families*, London: Jessica Kingsley Publishers.

Barnard, M. and Barlow, J. (2003) 'Discovering parental drug dependence: silence and disclosure', *Children and Society* 17: 45–56.

Barnard, M. and McKeganey, N. (2004) 'The impact of parental problem drug use on children', *Addiction* 99: 552–59.

Barnes, V. (2007) 'Young people's views of children's rights and advocacy services: A case for 'caring' advocacy?' *Child Abuse Review* 16: 140–152.

Barnett, R. and Coates, K. (2005) *Engaging the curriculum in higher education*, Berkshire: SRHE and Open University Press.

Barry, M. (2007) *Effective Approaches to Risk Assessment in Social Work: An International Literature Review*, Scottish Government, web only publication available at: www.scotland.gov.uk/Publications/2007/08/07090727/0

Bath and N.E. Somerset Council (2011) *Guidance for Education staff in ascertaining and recording the wishes and feelings of children*, available at: www.bathnes.gov.uk

Beddoe, L. (2011) 'Investing in the Future: Social Workers Talk about Research', *British Journal of Social Work* 41(3): 557–75.

Beinart, H., Kennedy, P. and Llewelyn, S. (2009) *Clinical Psychology in Practice*, London: Blackwells.

Bell, M. (2002) 'Promoting children's rights through the use of the relationship', *Child and Family Social Work* 7(1): 1–11.

Bellamy, J. (2008) 'Behavioral problems following reunification of children in long term foster care', *Child Youth Services Review* February 2008 30(2): 216–228.

Belsky, J. and Vondra, J. (1989) 'Lessons from child abuse: the determinants of parenting', in D. Cicchetti and V. Carlson (eds) *Child maltreatment: Theory and research on the causes and consequences of child abuse and neglect*, NY: Cambridge University Press, pp.153–202.

Beresford, P., Croft, S. and Adshead, L. (2008) 'We Don't See Her as a Social Worker: A Service User Case Study of the Importance of the Social Worker's Relationship and Humanity', *British Journal of Social Work* 38: 1388–1407.

Biehal, N. (2007) 'Reuniting Children with their Families: Reconsidering the Evidence on Timing, Contact and Outcomes', *British Journal of Social Work* 37(5): 807–23.

Bifulco, A. and Moran, P. (1998) *Wednesday's child: research into women's experience of neglect and abuse in childhood and adult depression*, London: Routledge.

Birmingham Safeguarding Children Board (2010) *Serious Case Review Under Chapter VIII 'Working Together to Safeguard Children' In respect of the Death of a Child Case Number 14*, Birmingham City Council.

Booth, T., Booth, W. and McConnell, D. (2005) 'Care Proceedings and parents with learning difficulties', *Child and Family Social Work* 10: 353–60.

Booth, T., McConnell, T. and Booth, W. (2006) 'Temporal discrimination and parents with learning difficulties in the child protection system', *British Journal of Social Work* 36(6): 997–1015.

Bowlby, J. (1954) *Child Care and the Growth of Love*, Harmonsworth: Penguin.

Brandon, M. and Thoburn, J. (2008) 'Safeguarding children in the UK: a longitudinal study of services to children suffering or likely to suffer significant harm', *Child and Family Social Work*, 13(4): 365–77.

Brandon, M., Belderson, P., Warren, C., Howe, D., Gardner, R., Dodsworth, J., and Black, J. (2008a) *Analysing Child Deaths and Serious Injury through Abuse and Neglect: What can we Learn? A Biennial Analysis of Serious Case Reviews 2003–2005*, London: Department for Children Schools and Families.

Brandon, M., Belderson, P., Warren, C., Gardner, R., Howe, D., Dodsworth, J. and Black, J. (2008b) 'The Preoccupation with Thresholds in Cases of Child Death or Serious Injury through Abuse or Neglect', *Child Abuse Review* 17: 313–330.

Brandon, M., Bailey, S., Belderson, J., Gardner, R., Sidebotham, P., Dodsworth, J., Warren, C. and Black, J. (2009) *Understanding Serious Case Reviews and their Impact: A Biennial Analysis of Serious Case Reviews 2005–07*, Research Report DCSF – RR129, London: DCSF.

Bretherton, I. (2006) 'Communication patterns, internal working models, and the intergenerational transmission of attachment relationships', *Infant Mental Health Journal* 11(3): 237–52.

Brewer, M., Browne, J., Joyce, R. and Sutherland, H. (2009) *Micro-simulating child poverty in 2010 and 2020*, London: Institute for Fiscal Studies.

British Association of Social Workers (BASW) (2002) *Code of Ethics for Social Workers*, Birmingham: BASW.

British Medical Journal (2009) 'Primary prevention: Primary physician care training', available at: http://bestpractice.bmj.com.best-practice/monograph/1016/prevention.html

Broadhurst, K. (2007) 'Parental help-seeking and the moral order. Notes for policy makers and parenting practitioners on "the first port of call" and "no one to turn to"', *Sociological Research Online*, 12(6), available at: www.socresonline.org.uk/12/6/4.html

Broadhurst, K., Mason, C. and Grover, C. (2007) 'Sure Start evaluation and the 're-authorisation' of Section 47 child protection practices', *Critical Social Policy* 27(4): 443–61.

Broadhurst, K., Hall, C., Wastell, D., White, S. and Pithouse, A. (2010a) 'Risk, Instrumentalism and the Humane Project in Social Work: Identifying the Informal Logics of Risk Management in Children's Statutory Services', *British Journal of Social Work* 40(4): 1046–64.

Broadhurst, K., Wastell, D., White, S., Hall, C., Peckover, S., Thompson, K., Pithouse, A. and Dolores, D. (2010b) 'Performing Initial Assessment: Identifying the latent conditions for error in local authority children's services', *British Journal of Social Work* 40(2): 352–70.

Broadhurst, K., White, S., Fish, S., Munro, E., Fletcher, K. and Lincoln, H. (2010c) *Ten Pitfalls and How to Avoid Them*, London: NSPCC, available at: www.nspcc.org.uk/inform/publications/downloads/tenpitfalls_wdf48122.pdf

Brook, J., Yuming Ning, Balka, E., Brook, D., Lubliner, E. and Rosenberg, G. (2007) 'Grandmother and parent influences on child self-esteem', *Pediatrics* 119(2): 444–451.

Butler, D., Lauscher, H., Jarvis-Selinger, S. and Beckingham, B. (2004) 'Collaboration and self-regulation in teachers' professional development', *Teaching and Teacher Education* 2004(5): 435–55.

Cairns, L. and Brannen, M. (2005) 'Promoting the human rights of children and young people: the 'Investing in Children' experience', *Adoption and Fostering* 29(1): 78–87.

Cameron, R. and Maginn, C. (2008) 'The Authentic Warmth Dimension of Professional Childcare', *British Journal of Social Work* 38(6): 1151–72.

Cantrill, P. (2009) *Serious Case Review in respect of Q Family*, Sheffield: Sheffield Local Safeguarding Board.

Carey, M. (2008) 'What Difference Does it make? Contrasting organisation and converging outcomes regarding the privatisation of state social work in England and Canada', *International Social Work* 51(1): 83–94.

Cecchin, G. (1987) 'Hypothesizing-circularity-neutrality Revisited: An Invitation to Curiosity', *Family Process* 26: 405–13.

Child Poverty Unit (2009) *Ending child poverty: Making it happen*, available at: www.education.gov.uk/consultations/downloadableDocs/8061-CPU-Ending%20Child%20Poverty.pdf

Children's Legal Centre (2011) *Looked After Children*, available at: www.childrenslegalcentre.comwww.childrenslegalcentre.com

Children's Rights Alliance for England (CRAE) (2010) *Human Rights Act*, available at: www.crae.org.uk/rights/hra.html

Children's Rights Information Centre (CRIC) (n.d.) *United Nations Convention on the Rights of the Child*, available at: www.crin.org/docs/resources/treaties/uncrc.asp#Twelve

Child Rights Information Network (CRIN) (n.d.) 'Guiding Principles of the Convention', available at: www.crin.org/resources/treaties/CRC.asp?catName=International+Treaties&flag=legal&ID=6

Children's Workforce Development Council (CWDC) (2011a) *Common Assessment Framework*, link page available at: www.cwdcouncil.org.uk/caf

CWDC (2011b) *Newly Qualified Social Worker and Early Professional Development programmes*, available at: www.cwdcouncil.org.uk/social-work/nqsw-epd

Christiansen, Ø. and Anderssen, N. (2010) 'From concerned to convinced: reaching decisions about out of home care', *Child and Family Social Work* 15: 31–40.

Cleaver, H. (2000) *Fostering Family Contact*, London: The Stationery Office.

Cleaver, H. and Freeman, P. (1995) *Parental perspectives in cases of suspected child abuse*, Dartington Social Research Unit, London: HMSO.

Cleaver, H. and Nicholson, D. (2008) *Parental learning disability and children's needs: family experiences and effective practice*, London: Jessica Kingsley Publishers.

Collins, S. (2008) 'Statutory Social Workers: Stress, Job Satisfaction, Coping, Social Support and Individual Differences', *British Journal of Social Work* 38: 1173–93.

Colton, M., Drakeford, M., Roberts, S., Scholte, E., Casa, F. and Williams, M. (1997) 'Social workers, parents and stigma', *Child and Family Social Work* 2: 247–57.

Connolly, M. and Doolan, M. (2007) 'Child deaths and statutory services: Issues for child care and protection', *Communities, Families and Children Australia* 2(1): 26–38.

Cooper, A. (2005) 'Surface and depth in the Victoria Climbié Inquiry Report', *Child and Family Social Work* 10: 1–9.

Copello, A., Velleman, R. and Templeton, L. (2005) 'Family interventions in the treatment of drug and alcohol problems', *Drug and Alcohol Review* 24: 369–85.

Cronon, W. (1992) 'A place for stories: Nature, history, and narrative', *Journal of American History* 78(4): 1347–76.

Daguerre, A. and Taylor-Gooby, P. (2004) 'Neglecting Europe: explaining the predominance of American ideas in New Labour's welfare policies since 1997', *Journal of European Social Policy* 14(1): 25–39.

Dale, M. (1994) 'Learning Organisations', in Christopher Mabey and Peter Iles (eds) *Managing Learning*, London: Routledge/The Open University.

Dale, P., Green, R. and Fellows, R. (2002) *What Really Happened? Child Protection Case Management of infants with serious injuries and discrepant explanations*, London: NSPCC.

Dalgelish, L. (2003) 'Risk, Needs and Consequences', in Calder, M.C. and Hackett, S. (eds) *Assessment in Child Care*, Lyme Regis: Russell House Publishing.

Dalzell, R. and Sawyer, E. (2007) *Putting the analysis into assessment: undertaking assessments of need*, London: National Children's Bureau.

Day, C. and Leitch, R. (2001) 'Teachers and teacher educators' lives: the role of emotion', *Teaching and Teacher Education* 17(4): 403–15.

Delfabbro, P., Barber, J. and Cooper, L. (2003) 'Predictors of short term reunification in South Australian family care', *Child Welfare* 82: 27–51.

Dennett, D. (1991) *Consciousness Explained*, London: Penguin Press.

Department for Children, Schools and Families (DCSF) (2007) *National Statistics First Release, National Curriculum Assessment, GCSE and Equivalent Attainment and Post-16 Attainment by Pupil Characteristics in England, 2006/07*, DCSF, available at: www.education.gov.uk/rsgateway/DB/SFR/

DCSF (2009) *Joint Guidance on Development of Local Protocols between Drug and Alcohol Treatment Services and Local Safeguarding and Family Services*, London: Department of Health/DCSF/NHS.

DCSF (2010) *Working Together to Safeguard Children: A guide to inter-agency working to safeguard and promote the welfare of children* Ref: DCSF-00305-2010 Nottingham: DCSF available at: www.education.gov. uk/publications/standard/publicationdetail/page1/DCSF-00305-2010

DCSF (2011) Government website for *Every Child Matters* now accessed through the Department of Education website: www.education.gov.uk/childrenandyoungpeople/sen/earlysupport/esinpractice/a0067409/every-child-matters

Department for Education (DfE) (2010a) *(First) Serious Case Review 'Child A', November 2008*, London Borough of Haringey Safeguarding Children Board, available at: http://media.education.gov.uk/assets/files/pdf/s/first%20serious%20case%20review%20overview%20report%20relating%20to%20peter%20connelly%20dated%20november%202008.pdf

DfE (2010b) *(Second) Serious Case Review 'Child A', March 2009*, London Borough of Haringey Safeguarding Children Board, available at: http://media.education.gov.uk/assets/files/pdf/s/second%20serious%20case%20overview%20report%20relating%20to%20peter%20connelly%20dated%20march%202009.pdf

DfE (2011) *The Child Poverty Act*, available at: www.education.gov.uk/childrenandyoungpeople/families/childpoverty/a0066302/the-child-poverty-act

Department of Health (DH) (1995) *Messages From Research*, London: The Stationery Office.

DH (2000) *Framework for the Assessment of Children in Need and their Families*, London: The Stationery Office.

DH/Department for Education and Skills (DfES) (2007) *Good practice guidance in working with parents with a learning disability*, available at: www.dh.gov.uk/en/Publicationsandstatistics/Publications/PublicationsPolicyAndGuidance/DH_075119

Department for Work and Pensions/Department for Education (DWP/DfE) (2011) *A New Approach to Child Poverty: Tackling the Causes of Disadvantage and Transforming Families' Lives*, Cm 8061, London: The Stationery Office.

De Shazer, S. (1992) *Patterns of brief family therapy*, New York: Guilford.

Dewane, C. (2006) 'Use of self: A primer revisited', *Clinical Social Work Journal* 34(04): 543–58.

Dewey, J. (1916) *Democracy and Education: An introduction to the philosophy of education*, New York: Macmillan.

Dewey, J. (1976 [1938]) *Experience and Education*, London: Collier Macmillan.

Dickens, J. (2006) 'Care, control and change in child care proceedings: dilemmas for social workers, managers and lawyers', *Child and Family Social Work* 11(1): 23–32.

Dickens, J. (2007) 'Child neglect and the law: catapults, thresholds and delay', *Child Abuse Review* 16(2): 77–92.

Dickens, J. (2011) 'Social Work in England at a Watershed – As Always: From the Seebohm Report to the Social Work Task Force', *British Journal of Social Work* 41(1): 22–39.

Dingwall, E., Eekelaar, J. and Murray, T. (1983) *The Protection of Children: State Intervention and Family Life*, Oxford: Basil Blackwell.

Doka, K. (1989) *Disenfranchised Grief: Recognising Hidden Sorrow*, Lexington, MA: Lexington Books.

Donald, T. and Jureidini, J. (2004) 'Parenting Capacity', *Child Abuse Review* 13: 5–17.

Dorling, D. (2010) 'Axing the child poverty measure is wrong', *The Guardian* June 16, 2010.

Douglas, M. and Wildavsky, A. (1982) *Risk and Culture: An Essay on the Selection of Technical and Environmental Dangers*, Berkeley, CA: University of California Press.

Drake, B. and Jonson-Reid, M. (2007) 'A response to Melton based on the best available data', *Child Abuse and Neglect* 31: 343–60.

Durrant, J. (2006) 'From mopping up the damage to preventing the flood: the role of social policy in preventing violence against children', *Social Policy Journal of New Zealand* July 2006 Issue 28.

Dyke, M. (2006) 'The role of the 'Other' in reflection, knowledge formation and action in a late modernity', *International Journal of Lifelong Education* 25(2): 105–23.

Dyson, C. (2008) *Poverty and Child Maltreatment*, London: NSPCC, available at: www.nspcc.org.uk/ Inform/research/Briefings/povertyPDF_wdf56896.pdf

Eddon, G. (2009) 'Case Law', *Seen and Heard* 19(3) September: 15–116.

Edwards, J. (1995) '"Parenting Skills": Views of community health and social service providers about the needs of their "clients"', *Journal of Social Policy* 24: 237–59.

Eekelaar, J. (1986) 'The emergence of children's rights', *Oxford Journal of Legal Studies* 6: 161–82.

England, H. (1986) *Social work as art: making sense for good practice*, London: Taylor and Francis.

Erault, M. (1994) *Developing Professional Knowledge and Competence*, London: Falmer.

Erault, M. (2005) 'Editorial', *Learning in Health and Social Care* 4(2): 47–52.

Erault, M., Steadman, A., Maillardet, F. and Miller, C. (2007) *Early career learning at work: insights into professional development during the first job*, TLRP Research Briefing, available at: www.tlrp.org/pub/ documents/Eraut%20RB%2025%20FINAL.pdf

Etherington, K. (2007) 'Creation as transformation: parenting as a turning point in drug users' lives', *Counselling and Psychotherapy Research* 7(2): 71–8.

Eurostat SILC, available at: http://epp.eurostat.ec.europa.eu/tgm/refreshTableAction.do;jsessionid=9 ea7d07e30dd3b9116e8699b425ba9fa8fd4e07f9768.e34MbxeSahmMa40LbNiMbxaMaNuTe0?tab=t able&plugin=1&pcode=tessi120&language=en

Evans, T. (2011) 'Professionals, managers and discretion: critiquing street-level bureaucracy', *British Journal of Social Work* 41: 368–86.

Farmer, E. and Moyers, S. (2005) *Children Placed With Family and Friends: Placement patterns and outcomes*, Executive summary available at: www.rip.org.uk/qualitymatters/resources/summaries/%%20-%20 Summary%20of%20Family%20and%20Friends%20Placements.pdf

Farmer, E. and Owen, M. (1995) *Child protection practice: Private Risks and Public Remedies*, London: HMSO.

Farmer, E. and Parker, R. (1991) *Trials and Tribulations: Returning Children from Local Authority Care to their Families*, London: HMSO.

Farmer E., Sturgess W. and O'Neill T. (2008) *The Reunification of Looked After Children with their Parents: Patterns, Interventions and Outcomes*, Report to the Department for Children, Schools and Families, University of Bristol School for Policy Studies, DCSF Research Brief DCSF-RBX-14-08, available at: www.dcsf.gov.uk/research/data/uploadfiles/DCSF-RBX-14-08.pdf

Farmer, F. (1981) 'Recent Advances in Risk Assessment', *Annals of Occupational Hygiene* 24(3): 297–301.

Family Rights Group (2007) *Family Group Conferences: Where Next? Policies and Practices for the Future*, London: Family Rights Group.

Fargas, M., McSherry, D., Larkin, E., Kelly, G., Robinson, C. and Schubotz, D. (2010) 'Young children returning home from care: the birth parents' perspective', *Child and Family Social Work* 15(1): 77–86.

Farrington, D. (2002) 'Developmental criminology and risk-focused prevention', in Maguire, M., Morgan, R. and Reiner, R. (eds), *The Oxford Handbook of Criminology*, 3rd edn, Oxford: Oxford University Press, pp. 657–701.

Fawcett, B. (2009) 'Vulnerability: questioning the certainties in social work and health', *International Journal of Social Work* 52: 473–84.

Ferguson, H. (2003) 'Outline of a critical best practice perspective on social work and social care', *British Journal of Social Work* 33: 1005–24.

Ferguson, H. (2008) 'To protect children we must first protect social workers', *The Guardian* November 13, available at: www.guardian.co.uk/commentisfree/2008/nov/13/child-protection-social-care

Ferguson, H. (2009) 'Performing child protection: home visiting, movement and the struggle to reach the abused child', *Child and Family Social Work* 14: 471–80.

Ferguson, H. (2010) 'Walks, Home Visits and Atmospheres: Risk and the Everyday Practices and Mobilities of Social Work and Child Protection', *British Journal of Social Work* DOI: 10.1093/bjsw/bcq015 published online: February 26, 2010.

Ferguson, H. (2011) *Child Protection Practice*, Basingstoke: Palgrave Macmillan.

Ferguson, I. (2007) 'Increasing user choice or privatizing risk? The antinomies of personalization', *British Journal of Social Work* 37: 387–403.

Festinger, L., Riecken, H. and Schachter, S. (1956) *When Prophecy Fails: A Social and Psychological Study of a Modern Group that Predicted the End of the World*, Minnesota: University of Minnesota Press.

Field, F. (2010a) 'Poverty is about much more than money', *The Telegraph* June 5, 2010

Field, F. (2010b) *The Foundation Years: preventing poor children becoming poor adults*, London: The Stationery Office.

Flood, S. (2009) *Reunification: Supporting looked after children going home, key messages from research for social workers*, Dartington: DCSF/ Research in Practice

Fonagy, P., Gergely, G., Jurist, E. and Target, M. (2002) *Affect regulation, mentalization and the development of the self*, New York: Other Press.

Fonagy, P., Target, M., Steele, H., and Steele, M. (1998) *Reflective Functioning Manual, Version 5.0, for Application to Adult Attachment Interviews*, London: University College London.

Fook, J. (2002) *Social Work, Critical Theory and Practice*, London: Sage.

Fook, J. (2007) 'Reflective practice and critical reflection' in Lishman, J. (ed.) *Handbook for Practice Learning in Social Work and Social Care*, London: Jessica Kingsley Publishers.

Fook, J., Ryan, M. and Hawkins, L. (2000) *Professional Expertise: Practice, Theory and Education for Working in Uncertainty*, London: Whiting and Birch.

Forrester, D. (2010) 'Playing with fire or rediscovering fire? The perils and potential for evidence-based practice in child and family social work' in Ayre, P. and Preston-Shoot, M. (eds) *Children's Social Work at the Crossroads*, Lyme Regis: Russell House Publishing.

Forrester. D. and Harwin, J. (2006) 'Parental Substance Misuse and Child Care Social Work: findings from the first stage of a study of 100 families', *Child and Family Social Work* 11: 325–335.

Forrester, D. and Harwin, J. (2008) 'Parental Substance Misuse and Child Welfare: Outcomes for Children Two Years After Referral', *British Journal of Social Work* 38: 1518–35.

Forrester, D., Kershaw, S., Moss, H. and Hughes, L. (2008) 'Communication skills in child protection: how do social workers talk to parents?' *Child and Family Social Work* 13: 41–51.

Forrester, D., McCambridge, J., Waissbein, C., Emlyn-Jones, R. and Rollnick, S. (2007) 'Child Risk and Parental Resistance: the impact of training social workers in motivational interviewing', *British Journal of Social Work* 38(7): 1302–19.

Forte, J. (1998) 'Power and Role-Taking', *Journal of Human Behavior in the Social Environment* 1(4): 27–56.

Fortin, J. (2009) *Children's Rights and the Developing Law*, Cambridge: Cambridge University Press.

France, A., Freiberg, K. and Homel, R. (2010) 'Beyond Risk Factors: Towards a Holistic Prevention Paradigm for Children and Young People', *British Journal of Social Work* 40(4): 1192–210.

Fraser, C., McIntyre, A. and Manby. M. (2009) 'Exploring the Impact of Parental Drug/Alcohol Problems on Children and Parents in a Midlands County in 2005/6', *British Journal of Social Work* 39: 846–66.

Freeman, M. (1999) 'The Right to be Heard', *Adoption and Fostering* 22(4): 50–59.

Freeman, M. (2000) 'The Future of Children's Rights', *Children and Society* 14: 277–93.

Friere, P. (1972) *The Pedagogy of the Oppressed*, London: Penguin.

Gallagher, S. (2000) 'Philosophical conceptions of the self: implications for cognitive science', *Trends in Cognitive Sciences* 4(1): 14–22.

Garland, D. (1997) 'Governmentality and the Problem of Crime', *Theoretical Criminology* May 1(2): 173–214.

General Social Care Council (GSCC) (2002) *Codes of Practice for Social Care Workers and Employers*, available at: www.gscc.org.uk/codes/

Gerdes, K., Segal, E. and Lietz, C. (2010) 'Conceptualising and measuring empathy', *British Journal of Social Work* 40: 2326–43.

Ghate, D. and Hazel, N. (2002) *Parenting in poor environments: stress, support and coping*, London: Jessica Kingsley Publishers.

Ghate, D., Asmussen, K., Tian, Y. and Hauari, H. (2008) '*On Track' Phase Two National Evaluation*, London: DCSF.

Gillies, V. (2005) 'Meeting parents' needs: discourses of 'support' and 'inclusion' in family policy', *Critical Social Policy* 25(1): 70–90.

Gillingham, P. (2011) 'Decision-making tools and the development of expertise in child protection practitioners: are we 'just breeding workers who are good at ticking boxes'?', *Child and Family Social Work* advance access DOI: 10.1111/j.1365-2206.2011.00756.x

Godsall, R., Jurkovich, G., Anderson, L. and Stanwyck, D. (2004) 'Why some kids do well in bad situations: relation of parental alcohol misuse and parentification to children's self-concept', *Substance Use and Misuse* 39: 789–809.

Gordon, D. (2005) *Indicators of Poverty & Hunger*, at www.un.org/esa/socdev/unyin/documents/ydiDavid Gordon_poverty.pdf

Gordon, D., Levitas, R., Pantazis, C., Patsios, D., Payne, S. and Townsend, P. (2000) *Poverty and Social exclusion in Britain*, York: Joseph Rowntree Foundation, available at: www.jrf.org.uk/sites/files/jrf/185935128x.pdf

Gordon, J. and Cooper, B. (2010) 'Talking Knowledge – Practising Knowledge: A critical best practice approach to how social workers understand and use knowledge in practice', *Practice: Social Work in Action* 22(4): XX.

Gordon, J., Cooper, B. and Dumbleton, S. (2009) *How do social workers use evidence in practice?* PBPL paper 34 available at: http://oro.open.ac.uk/23097/1/cooper(9).pdf

Greybeal, C. (2007) 'Evidence for the Art of Social Work', *Families in Society* 88(4): 513–23.

Grimshaw, R. and Sinclair, R. (1997) *Planning to Care: Regulation, procedure and practice under the Children Act 1989*, London: National Children's Bureau.

Guggenheim, M. (2005) *What's Wrong with Children's Rights*, Cambridge, Mass: Harvard University Press.

Habermas, T. and Paha, C. (2001) 'The Development of Coherence in Adolescents' Life Narratives', *Narrative Inquiry* 11(1): 35–54.

Hagell, A. (1998) *Dangerous Care: Reviewing the Risks to Children from their Carers*, PSI Report 858, London: Policy Studies Institute.

Hardiker, P., Exton, K. and Barker, M. (1996) *The prevention of child abuse: a framework for analysing services*, National Commission of Inquiry into the Prevention of Child Abuse, London, HMSO.

Harker, R. (2011) 'Children in Care in England: Statistics', House of Commons Library: Social and general statistics, SN/SG/4470.

Harris, A. and Walton, M. (2009) '"Thank you for making me write this", Narrative skills and the management of conflict in urban schools', *The Urban Review: Issues and Ideas in Public Education* 41(4): 287–311.

Hawkins, J., Catalano, R. and Arthur, M. (2002) 'Promoting science-based prevention in communities', *Addictive Behaviors* 27: 951–76.

Hayden, C. (2004) 'Parental Substance Misuse and Child Care Social Work: Research in a city social work department in England', *Child Misuse Review* 13: 18–30.

Health and Safety Executive (HSE) (2009) *Improving health and safety performance in the health and social care sectors-next steps?* HSE Board paper no: HSE/09/84 23, Sudbury: HSE.

HSE (2011) Violence at Work, available at: www.hse.gov.uk/statistics/causdis/violence/scale.htm

Helm D. (2011) 'Judgements or Assumptions? The Role of Analysis in Assessing Children and Young People's Needs', *British Journal of Social Work* 41(5): 894–911.

Heron, B. (2005) 'Self-reflection in critical social work practice: subjectivity and the possibilities of resistance', *Reflective Practice* 6(3): 341-251.

Hester, M. (2011) 'The Three Planet Model: Towards an Understanding of Contradictions in Approaches to Women and Children's Safety in Contexts of Domestic Violence', *British Journal of Social Work* 41(5): 837-53.

Hirsch, D. (2009) *Ending Child Poverty in a Changing Economy*, York: Joseph Rowntree Foundation, available at: www.jrf.org.uk/sites/files/jrf/hirsch-child-poverty-changing-economy.pdf

HM Government (2008) *Drugs: Protecting Families and Communities: The 2008 Drug Strategy*, London: The Stationery Office.

HM Government (2010) *UK Government Drug Strategy 2010 Reducing demand, restricting supply, building recovery: Supporting people to live a drug free life*, London: HM Government, available at: www.parliament.uk/deposits/depositedpapers/2010/DEP2010-2217.pdf

HM Government (2011) *A Child-centred System: The Government's Response to the Munro Review of Child Protection*, available at: www.education.gov.uk/munroreview/downloads/GovernmentResponseto Munro.pdf

HM Treasury (2008) *Ending child poverty: everybody's business*, London: HM Treasury.

Hoghughi, M. (1998). Editorial. The importance of parenting in child health. *British Medical Journal* 316: 1545-1550.

Hoghughi, M. and Speight, A. (1998) 'Good enough parenting for all children – a strategy for a healthier society', *Archives of Disease in Childhood* 78: 293-96.

Holland, S. (2001) 'Representing children in child protection assessments', *Childhood* 8(3): 322-39.

Holland, S. (2009) 'Engaging Children and Families in the Assessment Process', in Horwath, J. (2009) *The Child's World: Assessing Children in Need*, (2nd edition) London: Jessica Kingsley Publishers.

Holland, S. (2010) 'Looked after children and the ethic of care', *British Journal of Social Work* 40(6): 1664-80.

Hood, C. and Miller, P. (2009) 'Public Service Risks: What's Distinctive and New?' in Economic and Social Research Council *Risk and Public Services*, London and Oxford: LSE/ Oxford University.

Horgan, G. (2007) *The impact of poverty on young children's experience of school*, York: Joseph Rowntree Foundation.

Horwath, J. (2006) 'The Missing Assessment Domain: Personal, Professional and Organizational Factors Influencing Professional Judgements when Identifying and Referring Child Neglect', *British Journal of Social Work* 37(8): 1285-1303.

House of Commons Health Committee (HCHC) (2009) *Health Inequalities Third Report of Session 2008–2009*, Volume 1, London: The Stationery Office, available at: www.publications.parliament.uk/pa/cm200809/cmselect/cmhealth/286/286.pdf

House of Lords (2009) *Child Poverty Bill 2009/10 Peers Information Pack December 2009*, House of Lords (now archived and available on request).

Howe, D. (1996) 'Surface and Depth in Social-Work Practice', in David Howe and N. Parton (eds.), *Social Theory, Social Change and Social Work*, London: Routledge, pp 77-97.

Howe, D. (1997) 'Psychosocial and relationship-based theories for child and family social work: political philosophy, psychology and welfare practice', *Child and Family Social Work* 2(3): 161-9.

Hoyle, E. and John, P. (1995) *Professional Knowledge and Professional Practice*, London: Cassell.

Humphreys, C. and Kiraly, M. (2010) 'High-frequency contact: a road to nowhere for infants', *Child and Family Social Work* 16(1): 1-11.

Humphreys, C. and Mullender, A. (2000) *Children and Domestic Violence: A Research Overview of the Impact on Children*, Devon: The Policy Press.

Humphreys, C., Regan, L., River, D. and Thiara, R. (2005) 'Domestic Violence and Substance misuse: Tackling Complexity', *British Journal of Social Work* 35: 1303-20.

Hyslop, I. (2009) 'Child protection policy and practice: a relationship lost in translation', *Social Policy Journal of New Zealand* 34: 62-72.

IASSW/IFSW (2001) *The International Definition of Social Work*, available at: www.ifsw.org/f38000138.html

Iowa Dept. of Human Services (2008) *Permanency for Children Returning Children Home Safely and Permanently*, Practice Bulletin September 2008, available at: www.dhs.state.ia.us/docs/Sept._Reunification.pdf

Ixer, G. (1999) 'There's no such thing as reflection', *British Journal of Social Work* 29(4): 513–27.

Jack, G. (2010) 'Place Matters: the significance of place attachments for children's well-being', *British Journal of Social Work* 40(3): 755–71.

Jack, G. and Gill, O. (2003) *The missing side of the triangle: assessing the importance of family and environmental factors in the lives of children*, Barkingside: Barnardo's.

Jackson, N., Oliver, N., Shaw, M. and Wisdom, J. (eds) (2006) *Developing Creativity in Higher Education: an Imaginative Curriculum*, London: Routledge-Falmer.

Jackson, S., Ajayi, S. and Quigley, M. (2005) *Going to University from Care*, London: Institute of Education.

James, W. (1890 [1983]) *The Principles of Psychology*, republished Cambridge, MA: Harvard University Press.

James-Hanman, D. (2011) 'Domestic violence: Why does she stay? A question loaded with assumptions', *Community Care* April 14, 2011.

Jarvis, P. (1992) 'Reflective Practice and Nursing', *Nurse Education Today* 12: 174–81.

Jenson, J. (2007) 'Evidence-Based Practice and the Reform of Social Work Education: A Response to Gambrill and Howard and Allen-Meares', *Research on Social Work Practice* 17(5): 569–73.

Johns, C. (2004) *The Development of Critical Reflection in the Health Professions*, edited by Sylvina Tate, and Margaret Sills, LTSN Centre for Health Sciences and Practice, available at: www.hsaparchive.org.uk/rp/publications/occasionalpaper/occp4.pdf/view

Jones, K., Cooper, B. and Ferguson, H. (eds.) (2008) *Best Practice in Social Work: Critical Perspectives*, Basingstoke: Palgrave Macmillan.

Joseph, K. (1975) 'The Cycle of Deprivation' in E. Butterworth and R. Holman (eds) *Social Welfare in Modern Britain*, Glasgow: Fontana, pp. 387–94.

Joseph Rowntree Foundation (n.d.) at www.jrf.org.uk/sites/files/jrf/930.pdf

Kellet, J. and Apps, J. (2009) *Assessments of parenting and parenting support need*, York: JRF

King, M, (2007) 'The Right Decision for the Child', *Modern Law Review* 70: 857–71.

Kirsh B. (1996) 'A narrative approach to addressing spirituality in occupational therapy: Exploring personal meaning and purpose', *Canadian Journal of Occupational Therapy* 63: 55–61.

Kolb, D. (1984) *Experiential Learning*, Englewood Cliffs, NJ: Prentice-Hall.

Kroll, B. (2004) 'Living with an elephant: Growing up with parental substance misuse', *Child and Family Social Work* 9: 129–140.

Kroll, B. (2007) 'A Family Affair? Kinship care and parental substance misuse: some dilemmas explored', *Child and Family Social Work* 12: 84–93.

Kroll, B. and Taylor, A. (2002) *Parental Substance Misuse and Child Welfare*, London: Jessica Kingsley Publishers.

Lamb, M. (ed.) (2010) *The Role of the Father in Child Development, 5th Edition*, New Jersey: Wiley and Sons.

Laming, Lord H. (2003) *The Victoria Climbié Inquiry Report, Cm. 5370*, London: TSO, available at: www.publications.everychildmatters.gov.uk/eOrderingDownload/CM-5730PDF.pdf

Laming, Lord H. (2009) *The Protection of Children in England, A Progress Report*, London: The Stationery Office.

Land, C. (2010) 2010 Child and Youth Wellbeing Index, Durham, North Carolina: Foundation for Child Development, Duke University, available at: www.fcd-us.org/resources/resources_show.htm?doc_id=126639

Laybourn, A., Brown, J. and Hill, M. (1996) *Hurting on the Inside*, Aldershot: Avebury.

Lazarus, R. and Folkman, S. (1984) *Stress, appraisal and coping*, New York: Springer.

Leeson, C. (2007) 'My Life in Care: Experiences of Non-Participation in Decision Making Processes', *Child and Family Social Work* 12: 268–77.

Leeson, C. (2010) 'The Emotional Labour of Caring About Looked After Children', *Child and Family Social Work* 15: 483–91.

Le Grand, J. (2007) *Consistent care matters: exploring the potential of social work practices*, Department for Education and Skills, London.

Lewin, G. and Lewin, K. (1948) *Resolving Social Conflicts: Selected Papers on Group Dynamics*, New York: Harper.

Lipsky, M. (1980) *Street-level Bureaucracy: Dilemmas of the Individual in Public Services*, Russell Sage Foundation.

Lombard, D. (2010a) 'Social care staff run high risk of assault, new figures reveal', *Community Care* Friday November 19, 2010.

Lombard, D. (2010b) 'Few social workers enrol for post-qualifying training', *Community Care* March 3, 2010, available at: www.communitycare.co.uk/Articles/03/03/2010/113937/few-social-workers-enrol-for-post-qualifying-training.htm

London Borough of Greenwich (1987) *A Child in Mind: Protection of Children in a Responsible Society*, London: London Borough of Greenwich.

London Borough of Haringey (2009) *Serious Case Review: Child 'A'*, London: Department for Education.

London Borough of Newham (2008) *Working with Violent and Aggressive Families, Newham LSCB Protocol 2008*, available at: www.newhamchildcare.proceduresonline.com/chapters/p_violent_fam.html#cpp

Lorenz, W. (2001) 'Social Work Responses to "New Labour" in Continental European Countries', *British Journal of Social Work* 31: 595–609.

Lundy, L. (2007) '"Voice" is not enough: conceptualizing Article 12 of the United Nations Convention on the Rights of the Child', *British Educational Research Journal* 33(6): 927–42.

Lupton, D. (1999) *Risk*, London: Routledge.

McConnell, D., Llewellyn, G., Matthews, J., Hindmarsh, G., Mildon, R. and Wade, C. (2006) 'Healthy Start: A national strategy for children of parents with learning difficulties', *Developing Practice: The Child, Youth and Family Work Journal* 16: 34–42.

MacDonald, A. (2008) 'The Voice of the Child: Still a faint cry?', *Family Law* 38: 648–53.

Macdonald, C. (2001) *Effective Interventions for Child Abuse and Neglect: An Evidence Based Approach to Planning and Evaluating Interventions*, Chichester: Wiley and Sons.

Macdonald, G. (1998) 'Promoting Evidence-Based Practice in Child Protection', *Clinical Child Psychology and Psychiatry* 3(1): 71–85.

McGaw, S. (2005) *What works with Parents with Learning Disabilities?* (2nd edition) London: Barnardo's.

McGaw, S., Beckley, K., Connolly, N. and Ball, K. (1998) *Parent Assessment Manual*, Truro: Trecare NHS Trust, available at: www.cornwall.nhs.uk/specialparentingservices/patientassessmentmanual.asp

MacGregor, K. (2011) 'What needs to change in the supervision of social workers? Towards better supervision: the Social Work Reform Board proposals', *Community Care* January 24, 2011, available at: www.communitycare.co.uk/Articles/24/01/2011/116159/what-needs-to-change-in-the-supervision-of-social-workers.htm

McIntosh, J. (2002) 'Thought in the Face of Violence: A Child's Need, The Way Forward', *Child Abuse and Neglect* 26: 229–41.

MacKay, S. (2008) *Measuring material deprivation among older people: Methodological study to revise the Family Resources Survey questionnaire*, Working Paper No. 54, Department for Work and Pensions, London: The Stationery Office.

McKeough, A. and Malcolm, J. (2011) 'Developmental Pathways to Interpretive Thought during Adolescence', *New Directions for Child and Adolescent Development*, Vol. 131 at http://onlinelibrary.wiley.com/doi/10.1002/cd.289/pdf

McLeod, A. (2006) 'Respect or empowerment? Alternative understandings of 'listening' in childcare social work', *Adoption and Fostering* 30(4): 43–52.

McLeod, A. (2010) '"A friend and an equal": do young people in care seek the impossible from their social workers?', *British Journal of Social Work* 40(3): 772–88.

McSherry, D., Larkin, E., Fargas, M., Kelly, G., Robinson, C., Macdonald, G., Schubotz, D. and Kilpatrick, R. *et al.* (2008) *From Care to Where?* Belfast: Institute of Child Care Research, Queens University, Belfast

McSherry, D., Weatherall, K., Larkin, E., Fargas, M., Malet, M. and Kelly, G. (2010) 'Who goes where? Examining young children's pathways through care in Northern Ireland', *Adoption & Fostering* 34(2): 23–37.

Magnuson, D., Patten, N. and Looysen, K. (2011) 'Negotiation as a style in child protection work', *Child and Family Social Work* online advance access DOI: 10.1111/j.1365-2206.2011.00780.x

Mahadevan, J. (2010) 'Local authority applications for care proceedings continue to rise', *Children and Young People Now* May 18, 2010.

Maluccio, A. and Fein, E. (1986) *Permanency Planning for Children: Concepts and Methods*, London: Routledge.

Mandell, D. (2008) 'Power, care and vulnerability: Considering use of self in child welfare practice', *Journal of Social Work Practice* 22(2): 235–48.

Manning, V., Best, D., Faulkner, D. and Titherington, E. (2009) 'New estimates of the number of children living with substance misusing parents: results from UK national household surveys', *BMC Public Health* 9: 377.

Mannion, K. and Renwick, J (2008) 'Equivocating Over the Care and Protection Continuum: An Exploration of Families Not Meeting the Threshold for Statutory Intervention', *Social Policy Journal of New Zealand* Issue 33, available at: www.msd.govt.nz/about-msd-and-our-work/publications-resources/journals-and-magazines/social-policy-journal/spj33/33-equivocating-over-the-care-and-protection-continuum-an-exploration-of-families-not-meeting-the-threshold-for-statutory-intervention-p70-94.html

Mansell, J. (2006) 'The underlying instability in statutory child protection: Understanding the system dynamics driving risk assurance levels', *Social Policy Journal of New Zealand* 28: 97–132.

Mantle, G., Moules, T. and Johnson, K. with Leslie, J., Parsons, S. and Shaffer, R. (2007) 'Whose Wishes and Feelings? Children's Autonomy and Parental Influence in Family Court Enquiries', *British Journal of Social Work* 37: 785–805.

Masson, J., Pearce, J. and Bader, K. (2008) *Care Profiling study*, Ministry of Justice Research Series 4/08, London: Ministry of Justice, available at: www.justice.gov.uk/publications/docs/care-profiling-study.pdf

Mattingley, C. and Lawlor, M. (2000) 'Learning from Stories: Narrative Interviewing in Cross-cultural Research', *Scandinavian Journal of Occupational Therapy* 7: 4–14.

May Chahal, C. and Kwong Har, M. (2010) 'Breaching Private Life with Authority', *Qualitative Social Work*, published online before print on June 7, 2010.

Mezirow (1991) *Fostering Critical reflection in Adulthood: A guide to Transformative and Emancipatory Learning*, San Francisco: Jossey-Bass.

Milan F., Parish, S. and Reichgott, M. (2006) 'A model for educational feedback based on clinical communication skills strategies: beyond the 'feedback sandwich', *Teaching and Learning in Medicine* 18(1): 42–7.

Minuchin, S. (1974) *Families and Family Therapy*, Harvard: Harvard University Press.

Morgan, R. (2007) Children's messages on care: A report by the Children's Rights Director for England, London: Ofsted, available at: www.rights4me.org/content/beheardreports/144/childrens_messages_report.pdf

Morgan R. (2011a) *Messages for Munro*, London: Ofsted, available at: www.ofsted.gov.uk/resources/messages-for-munro

Morgan, R. and rights4me.org (2011b) *Children on the Edge of Care*, available at www.rights4me.org/content/beheardreports/459/REPORT_Edge_of_Care.pdf

Morris, K. and Barnes, M. (2008) 'Prevention and social exclusion: New understandings for policy and practice', *British Journal of Social Work* 38: 1194–211.

Morrison, T. (2007) 'Emotional Intelligence, Emotion and Social Work: Context, Characteristics, Complications and Contribution', *British Journal of Social Work* 37(2): 245-63.

Morrison, T. and Wonnacott, J. (2010) *Supervision: Now or Never: Reclaiming Reflective Supervision in Social Work*, available at: www.in-trac.co.uk/reclaiming-reflective-supervision.php

Munro, E. (1999) 'Common errors of reasoning in child protection work', *Child Abuse and Neglect* 23(8): 745-58.

Munro, E. (2008) *Effective Child Protection*, London: Sage.

Munro, E. (2010a) *The Munro Review of Child Protection Part 1: A Systems Analysis*, London: Department for Education, available at: www.education.gov.uk/munroreview/firstreport.shtml

Munro, E. (2010b) *The Munro Review of Child Protection Part 2: The Child's Journey*, available at: www.education.gov.uk/munroreview/firstreport.shtml

Munro, E. (2011) *The Munro Review of Child Protection Final Report: A Child-Centred System*, available at: Department for Education, available at: www.education.gov.uk/munroreview/

National Evaluation of Sure Start (NESS) Research Team (2010) *The impact of Sure Start Local Programmes on five year olds and their families*, London: Department for Education, available at: www.ness.bbk.ac.uk/impact/documents/RB067.pdf

NESS (2011) *National Evaluation of Sure Start local programmes: An Economic Perspective*, Research Brief DFE-RB073, London: The Stationery Office.

National Institute of Social Work (NISW) *Social Workers: Their Role and Tasks*, London: Bedford Square Press.

NIDA (National Institute on Drug Misuse) (2009) *Prenatal exposure to drugs of misuse: a research update from the National Institute on Drug Misuse*, available at www.nida.nih.gov

National Treatment Agency (2009) Media Release: 'Moves to provide greater protection to children living with drug addicts', available at www.nta.nhs.uk/uploads/3_11_09_moves_to_provide_a_greater_protection_for_children_living_with_drug_addicts.pdf

Nevo, I. and Slonim-Nevo, V. (2011) 'The Myth of Evidence-Based Practice: Towards Evidence-Informed Practice', *British Journal of Social Work* 41: 1176–97.

Newman, T. (2004) *What Works in Building Resilience?* London: Barnardo's.

Noble, C. and Irwin, J. (2009) 'Social Work Supervision: An Exploration of Current Challenges', *Journal of Social Work* 9(3): 345–58.

NSPCC (2007) *Neglect*, available at: www.nspcc.org.uk/Inform/research/briefings/childneglectpdf_wdf51503.pdf

O'Brien, S. (2003) *Report of the Caleb Ness Inquiry*, Edinburgh: Edinburgh and the Lothians Child Protection Committee, available at: www.dundeeprotects.co.uk/guidance/external_pdfs/No%2017.pdf

Ofsted (2008) *Learning Lessons Taking Action, Ofsted's Evaluations of Serious Case Reviews*, available at: www.ofsted.gov.uk/resources/learning-lessons-taking-action-ofsteds-evaluations-of-serious-case-reviews-1-april-2007-31-march-2008

Ofsted (2009) *Learning lessons from Serious Case Reviews, Year 2*, available at: www.ofsted.gov.uk/resources/learning-lessons-serious-case-reviews-year-2

Ofsted (2010) *Learning Lessons from Serious Case Reviews 2009–2010*, available at: www.ofsted.gov.uk/resources/learning-lessons-serious-case-reviews-2009-2010

Ofsted (2011) *The Voice of the Child: Learning lessons from serious case reviews: A thematic report of Ofsted's evaluation of serious case reviews from 1 April to 30 September 2010*, Ofsted publication no. 100224, available at: www.ofsted.gov.uk/news/voice-of-child-learning-lessons-serious-case-reviews-0

Pajulo, M., Suchman, N., Kalland, M. and Mayes, L. (2006) 'Enhancing the effectiveness of residential treatment for substance abusing women: focus on maternal reflective functioning and mother-child relationship', *Infant Mental Health Journal* 27(5): 448.

Parton, D. (1998) 'Risk, advanced liberalism and child welfare: the need to rediscover uncertainty and ambiguity', *British Journal of Social Work* 28: 5–27.

Parton, N. (2008) 'Changes in the form of knowledge in social work: from the "social" to the "informational"?', *British Journal of Social Work* 38(2): 253–69.

Parton, N. (2011) 'Child Protection and Safeguarding in England: Changing and Competing Conceptions of Risk and their Implications for Social Work', *British Journal of Social Work* 41(5): 854–75.

Parton, N. and O'Byrne. P. (2000) *Constructive Social Work: Towards a New Practice*, Basingstoke: Macmillan.

Paster, A., Brandwein, D. and Walsh, J. (2009) 'A comparison of coping strategies used by parents of children with disabilities and parents of children without disabilities', *Research in Developmental Disabilities* 1337–42.

Pickett, K. *et al.* (2010) Professor Kate Pickett and 16 other representatives of universities, charities and other organisations in an open letter to *The Guardian*, 'Helping families in poverty now is vital to our economic future', March 24, 2010, available at: www.guardian.co.uk/society/2010/mar/24/helping-families-poverty-vital-economic-future

Platt, D. (2007) 'Congruence and co-operation in social workers' assessments of children in need', *Child and Family Social Work* (12): 326–35.

Platt, L. (2009) *Ethnicity and Child Poverty*, Department for Work and Pensions Research Report no 576, London: The Stationery Office.

Polanyi, M. (1967) *The Tacit Dimension*, New York: Anchor Books.

Public Law Outline (2010) *Public Law Proceedings Guide to Case Management*, London: The Judiciary of England and Wales, available at: www.judiciary.gov.uk/publications-and-reports/practice-directions/practice-directions-2009-date/public-law-procs-guide-to-case-management

Radford, L., Corral, S., Bradley, C., Fisher, H., Bassett, C., Howat, N. and Collishaw, S. (2011) *Child abuse and neglect in the UK today*, London: NSPCC.

Reason, J. (2000) 'Human error: models and management', *British Medical Journal* March 18, 2000 320: 768–70.

Reder, P. and Lucey, C. (eds) (1995) *Assessment of Parenting: Psychiatric and Psychological and Contributions*, London: Routledge.

Regehr, C., Bogo, M., Shlonsky, A. and LeBlanc, V. (2010) 'Confidence and Professional Judgment in Assessing Children's Risk of Abuse', *Research in Social Work Practice* 20(6): 621–28.

Rhodes, T., Bernays, S. and Houmoller, K. (2010) 'Parents who use drugs: Accounting for damage and its limitation', *Social Science and Medicine* 71: 1489–97.

Ridge, T. (2009) *Living with poverty: A review of the literature on children's and families' experiences of poverty*, Department for Work and Pensions Research Report no 594, London: The Stationery Office.

Riessman, K.C. and Quinney, L. (2005) 'Narrative in Social Work: A Critical Review', *Qualitative Social Work* 4: 391–412.

Rinaldi, C. (2006) *In Dialogue with Reggio Emilia: Listening, Researching and Learning*, London and New York: Routledge.

Rober, P. (2002) 'Constructive hypothesising, dialogic understanding and the therapist's inner conversation: some ideas about knowing and not knowing in the family therapy session', *Journal of Marital and Family Therapy* 28(4): 467–78.

Rose, W. and Barnes, J. (2008) *Improving Safeguarding Practice: Study of Serous Case Reviews 2001–2003*, London: Department for Children, Schools and Families.

Rossiter, A. (2005) 'Discourse analysis in social work: from apology to question', *Critical Social Work* 6(1): 1–6.

Rossiter, A. (2011) 'Unsettled social work: the challenge of Levinas's ethics', *British Journal of Social Work* 41(5): 980–95, DOI: 10.1093/bjsw/bcr004.

Rothstein, H. (2002) *Neglected Risk Regulation: the institutional attenuation phenomemon*, London: Centre for Analysis of Risk and Regulation, London School of Economics.

Rothstein, H., Huber, M. and Gaskell, G. (2006) 'A Theory of Risk Colonisation: the spiralling regulatory logics of societal and institutional risk', *Economy and Society* 35(1): 91–112.

Rowe, J. and Lambert, L. (1973) *Children who wait: a study of children needing substitute families*, London: Association of British Adoption Agencies.

Ruch, G. (2005) 'Relationship-based and Reflective Practice: Holistic Approaches to Contemporary Child Care Social Work', *Child and Family Social Work* 10: 111–23.

Ruch, G. (2007) 'Thoughtful practice: child care social work and the role of case discussion', *Child and Family Social Work* 12: 370–79.

Rustin, M. (2005) 'Conceptual analysis of critical moments in Victoria Climbié's life', *Child and Family Social Work* 10(1): 11–19.

Rutten, K., Mottart, A. and Soetaert, R. (2010) 'Narrative and Rhetoric in Social work Education', *British Journal of Social Work* 40(2): 480–95.

Rutter, L. (2009) Theory and practice within HE professional education courses – integration of academic knowledge and experiential knowledge, 6th LDHEN Symposium, 6th and 7th April 2009, Bournemouth University.

Rutter, M. and Taylor, E (2002) *Child and Adolescent Psychiatry* (Fourth Ed.), London: Blackwell.

Schein, E. (1997) *Organizational Culture and Leadership*, San Francisco: Jossey-Bass.

Schofield, G (2005) 'The voice of the child in family placement decision making: A developmental model', *Adoption and Fostering* 19(1): 29–44.

Schofield, G. and Beek, M. (2009) 'Risk and resilience in long-term foster care', *British Journal of Social Work* (2005) 35: 1283-1301, republished in M. Courtney and J. Thoburn (eds) (2009) *Children in State Care, Library of Essays in Child Welfare series*, Aldershot: Ashgate.

Schofield, G., Thoburn, J., Howell, D. and Dickens, J. (2007) 'The search for stability and permanence: modelling the pathways of long-stay looked after children', *British Journal of Social Work* 37(4): 619–42.

Schofield, G., Moldestad, B., Hojer, I., Ward, E., Skilbred, D., Young, J. and Havik, T. (2011) 'Managing loss and a threatened identity: experiences of parents of children growing up in foster care, the perspectives of their social workers and implications for practice', *British Journal of Social Work* 41(1): 74–92.

Schön, D (1983) *The Reflective Practitioner*, New York: Basic Books.

Schön, D. (1987) *Educating the Reflective Practitioner*, California: Jossey-Bass.

Scott, D. (2006) 'Towards a public health model of child protection in Australia', *Communities, Families and Children Australia* 1(1): 9–16.

Scottish Consortium for Learning Disability (SCLD) (2009) *Scottish Good Practice Guidelines for Supporting Parents with Learning Disabilities*, at: www.scld.org.uk/library-publications/scottish-good-practice-guidelines-supporting-parents-with-learning-disabilities

Scottish Government (2006) *Hidden Harm: Next Steps*, available at: www.scotland.gov.uk/Publications/2006/05/05144237/3

Sen, A. (2002) 'Positional objectivity', in: A. Sen (ed.) *Rationality and Freedom*, Cambridge, MA, and London: Harvard University Press, pp. 463–83.

Sharma, N. and Hirsch, D. (2007) *It doesn't happen here: The reality of child poverty in the UK*, London: Barnardo's.

Sheppard, M. (2006) *Social Work and Social Exclusion*, Aldershot: Ashgate.

Sheppard, M. (2008) 'How Important is Prevention? High Thresholds and Outcomes for Applicants refused by Children's Services: A Six Month Follow Up', *British Journal of Social Work* 38: 1268–82.

Sheppard, M. (2009) 'High Thresholds and Prevention in Children's Services: The Impact of Mothers' Coping Strategies on Outcome of Child and Parenting Problems – Six Month Follow-Up', *British Journal of Social Work* 39(1): 46–63.

Sheppard, M., MacDonald, P. and Welbourne, P. (2008) 'Service users as gatekeepers in children's centres', *Child and Family Social Work* 13: 61–71.

Sheppard, M. and Ryan, K. (2003) 'Practitioners as rule using analysts: a further development of process knowledge in social work', *British Journal of Social Work* 33: 157–76.

Sheppard, M., Newstead, M., Di Caccavo, A. and Ryan, K. (2000) 'Reflexivity and the Development of Process Knowledge in Social Work: A classification and empirical study', *British Journal of Social Work* 30: 465–88.

Simon, H. (1957) *Administrative Behaviour*, New York: The Free Press.

Sinclair, I., Baker, C., Wilson, K. and Gibbs, I. (2005) *Foster Children: where they go and how they get on*, London: Jessica Kingsley Publishers.

Sinclair, I., Baker, C., Lee, J. and Gibbs, I. (2007) *The Pursuit of Permanence: a study of the English care system*, London: Jessica Kingsley Publishers.

Sinclair, R. and Bullock, R. (2002) *Learning from past experience: a review of serious case reviews*, London: Department of Health.

Skinner, E., Kindermann, T. and Furrer, C. (2009) 'A motivational perspective on engagement and disaffection: Conceptualization and assessment of children's behavioral and emotional participation in academic activities in the classroom', *Educational and Psychological Measurement* 69: 493–525.

Skinner, K. (2005) *Continuing Professional Development for the Social Services Workforce in Scotland: Developing Learning Organisations*, Discussion Paper 1, Dundee: SIESWE.

Skinner, S. and Greene, T. (2009) 'Perceived Control: Engagement, Coping, and Development', in T. L. Good (ed.), *21st Century Education: A Reference Handbook*, Newbury Park: Sage Publications.

Skuse, T. and Ward, H. (2003) *Listening to Children's Views of Care and Accommodation, Report to the Department of Health*, Loughborough: Centre for Child and Family Research, University of Loughborough.

Slade, A, (2005) 'Parental reflective functioning: an introduction', *Attachment & Human Development* 7(3): 269–81.

Slovic, P., Finucane, P., Peters, E. and MacGregor, D. (2002) 'Risk as Analysis and Risk as Feelings: Some thoughts about affect, reason, risk and rationality', *Risk Analysis* 24(2): 1–12.

Smidt, S. (2006) *The Developing Child in the 21st Century*, London: Routledge.

Sneddon, H., Iwaniec, D. and Stewart, M. (2010) 'Prevalence of Childhood Abuse in Mothers Taking Part in a Study of Parenting their own Children', *Child Abuse Review* 19: 39–55.

Social Care Institute for Excellence (SCIE) (2005) Resource Pack on Learning Organisations 'Summary of Key characteristics of a social care learning organisation', available at: www.scie.org.uk/publications/learningorgs/files/key_characteristics_2.doc

Social Work Reform Board (SWRB) (2011a) *Professional Capabilities Framework for Social Work*, available at: http://media.education.gov.uk/assets/files/pdf/p/proposed%20capabilities%20framework%20 for%20social%20workers.pdf

SWRB (2011b) *Professional standards for social workers in England*, available at: www.education.gov.uk/ swrb/a0074240/professional-standards-for-social-workers-in-england

Social Work Task Force (SWTF) (2009) *Final Report of the Social Work Task Force: Building a Safe Confident Future*, Nottingham: DCSF, available at: www.dcsf.gov.uk/swtf

Söderström, K. (2011) 'Mental preparation during pregnancy in women with substance addiction: a qualitative interview-study', *Child and Family Social Work*, online publication September 2011, DOI: 10.1111/j.1365-2206.2011.00803.x

Søndergaard, D. (2002) 'Poststructuralist approaches to empirical analysis', *Qualitative Studies in Education* 15(2): 187–204.

Spicer, N. and Evans, R. (2006) 'Developing children and young people's participation in strategic processes: the experience of the Children's Fund initiative', *Social Policy and Society* 5(2): 177–88.

Staller, K. (2007) 'To Get Her Heart in Hand: Passing Words Between an Abused Child and Social Worker Practitioner', *Qualitative Inquiry* 13(6): 766–86.

Stanford, S. (2011) 'Constructing Moral Responses to Risk: A Framework for Hopeful Social Work Practice', *British Journal of Social Work* advance access published online March 24, 2011; DOI: 10.1093/bjsw/bcr030

Stanley, T. (2007) 'Risky work: child protection practice', *Social Policy Journal of New Zealand* 30: 163–77.

Stevens, I. and Cox, P. (2007) 'Complexity theory: Developing new understandings of child protection in field settings and in residential child care', *British Journal of Social Work* 38(7): 1320–36.

Strachan, G. (2010) 'Hundreds of Angus social workers assaulted', *The Courier* December 14, 2010, available at: www.thecourier.co.uk/News/Angus/article/8648/hundreds-of-angus-council-social-workers-assaulted.html

Strang, J. (2011) *Recovery-Orientated Drug Treatment: An interim report by Professor John Strang*, chair of the expert group, London: NTA, available at: www.nta.nhs.uk/uploads/rodt_an_interim_report_july_2011.pdf

Stratton, P. and Hanks, H. (1995) 'Assessing Family Functioning in Parenting Breakdown', in P. Reder, and C. Lucey (eds) *Assessment of Parenting: Psychiatric and Psychological and Contributions*, London: Routledge.

Strier, R. and Binyamin, S. (2010) 'Developing Anti-Oppressive Services for the Poor: A theoretical and organisational rationale', *British Journal of Social Work* 40 (6): 1908–26.

Suoninen, E. and Jokinen, A. (2005) 'Persuasion in Social Work Interviewing', *Qualitative Social Work* 4(4): 469–87.

Svensson, L. (2006) 'New Professionalism, Trust and Competence: Some remarks and empirical data', *Current Sociology* 54(4): 579–93.

Tate, S. (2004) 'Using critical reflection as a teaching tool', in S. Tate and M. Sills (eds) (2004) *The Development of Critical Reflection in the Health Professions*, London: LTSN Centre for Health Sciences and Practice.

Tate, S. and Sills, M. (eds) (2004) *The Development of Critical Reflection in the Health Professions*, London: LTSN Centre for Health Sciences and Practice, available at: www.health.heacademy.ac.uk/publications/occasionalpaper/occasionalpaper04.pdf

Taylor, A. (2005) 'Special Report: Sure Start Analysed' *Community Care* December 9, 2005, available at: www.communitycare.co.uk/Articles/2005/12/09/52106/Special-report-Sure-Start-evaluation-analysed.htm

Taylor, A., Toner, P., Templeton, L. and Velleman, R. (2008) 'Parental Alcohol Misuse in Complex families: The implications for engagement', *British Journal of Social Work* 38: 843–64.

Taylor, C. (2004) 'Underpinning knowledge for child care practice: reconsidering child development theory', *Child and Family Social Work* 9: 225–35.

Taylor, C. and White, S. (2000) *Practising Reflexivity in Health and Welfare: Making Knowledge*, Buckingham: Open University Press.

Taylor, C. and White, S. (2006) 'Knowledge and Reasoning in Social Work: Educating for Humane Judgement', *British Journal of Social Work* 35: 1–18.

Thoburn, J. (2008) 'Children in care in England: recent trends and policy debates', *Social Work Now* December 2008: 12–14.

Thoburn, J. (2009) *Reunification of children in out-of-home care to birth parents or relatives: A synthesis of the evidence on processes, practice and outcomes*, Germany: Bundesministerium fur Familie, Senioren, Frauern, und Jugen, available at: www.dji.de/pkh/expertise_dji_thoburn_reunification.pdf

Thomas, L. and Holland, S. (2010) 'Representing Children's Identities in Core Assessments', *British Journal of Social Work* 40(8): 2617–33.

Thomas, N. (2002) *Children, Family and the State: decision making and child participation*, Bristol: Policy Press.

Thomas, N. (2009) 'Listening to Children and Young People', in G. Schofield and J. Simmonds (Eds.) *The Child Placement Handbook*, London: British Association for Adoption and Fostering.

Thomas, N. and O'Kane, C. (2009) 'Children's participation in reviews and planning meetings when they are 'looked after' in middle childhood', in M. Courtney and J. Thoburn (Eds.) *Children in State Care*, Aldershot: Ashgate.

Thomson, J. and Thorpe, R. (2004) 'Powerful partnerships in social work: group work with parents of children in care', *Australian Social Work* 57(1): 46–56.

Timms, J. and Thoburn, J. (2006) 'Your Shout! Looked After Children's Perspectives on the Children Act 1989', *The Journal of Social Welfare and Family Law*, 28(2): 153–70.

TOPPS (n.d.) *National Occupational Standards for Social Work (England)*, available at: www.gscc.org.uk/cmsFiles/Education%20and%20Training/National%20Occupational%20Standards%20for%20Social%20Work.pdf

Townsend, P. (1979) *Poverty in the United Kingdom: A Survey of Household Resources and Standards of Living*, Harmondsworth: Penguin Books.

Tracy, E. and Johnson, P. (2007) 'Personal and social networks of women with Co-occurring substance misuse and mental disorders', *Journal of Social Work Practice in the Addictions* 7: 69–90.

Tracy, E. and Martin, T. (2007) 'Children's roles in the social networks of women in substance misuse treatment', *Journal of Substance Misuse Treatment* 32: 8–88.

Tregeagle, S. and Mason, J. (2008) 'Service user experience of participation in child welfare case management', *Child and Family Social Work* 13(4): 391–401.

Trevithick, P. (2003) 'Effective Relationship-based Practice', *Journal of Social Work Practice* 17(2): 163–76.

Trevithick, P. (2008) 'Revisiting the knowledge base for social work: A framework for practice', *British Journal of Social Work* 38: 1212–37.

Turnell, A. (2010) *Signs of safety: A Comprehensive briefing paper*, Resolutions Consultancy, available at: www.signsofsafety.net

Turnell, A. and Edwards, S. (1999) *Signs of Safety: A Solution and Safety Oriented Approach to Child Protection Casework*, Norton: London

Turnell, A. and Essex, S. (2006) *Working with 'denied' child abuse: The resolutions approach*, Maidenhead: Open University Press.

Unicef (2000) *Innocenti Report Card 1 A league table of child poverty in rich nations*, Florence: Unicef.

Unison (2008a) Unison survey of social work supervision, reported in 'Whatever Happened to Supervision?', *Community Care* April 23, 2008: 18–19.

Unison (2008b) Time for a change – UNISON Local Government Survey 2008, available at: www.unison.org.uk/acrobat/18055.pdf

Unison (2009) Still part of the job? Why history of violence against social care workers is repeating itself, available at: www.unison.org.uk/localgov/pages_view.asp?did=10913

United Nations (1998) *UN Statement of Commitment of the Administrative Committee on Coordination for Action to Eradicate Poverty*, UN Doc. E/1998/73, Geneva: United Nations.

United States Department of Labor (2004) *Guidelines for Preventing Workplace Violence for Health and Social Care and Social Service Workers*, available at: www.dangerousbehaviour.com/Disturbing_News/ Guidelines%20for%20PreventingViolence%20HSS.htm

Van IJzendoorn, M. (1992) 'Intergenerational transmission of parenting: A review of studies in nonclinical populations', *Developmental Review* 12: 76–99.

Velleman, R. and Templeton, L. (2003) 'Alcohol, Drugs and the Family: results from a long running research programme within the UK', *European Addiction Research* 9: 103–112.

Velleman, R. and Templeton, L. (2007) 'Understanding and modifying the impact of parents' substance misuse on children', *Advances in Psychiatric Treatment* 13: 79–89.

Velleman, R., Reuber, D., Klein, M. and Moesgen, D. (2008) 'Domestic misuse experienced by young people living in families with alcohol problems: results from a cross-European study', *Child Misuse Review* 17: 389–409.

Vygotsky, L. (1978) *Mind and Society: The Development of Higher Mental Processes*, Cambridge, Mass.: Harvard University Press.

Walsh, T. (2006) 'Two sides of the same coin: ambiguity and complexity in child protection work', *Journal of Systemic Therapies* 25(2): 38–49.

Watson, J. (2006) 'Addressing Client Resistance: Recognising and Processing In-Session Occurrences', *Vistas*, available at: http://counselingoutfitters.com/Watson.htm

Wattam, C. (1999) 'The Prevention of Child Abuse', *Children and Society* 13(4): 317–29.

Webb, S. (2001) 'Some considerations on the validity of evidence-based practice in social work', *British Journal of Social Work* 31: 57–79.

Weiss, I. and Welbourne, P. (2008) 'The Professionalisation of social work: a cross-national exploration', *International Journal of Social Welfare* 17(4): 281–90.

Welbourne, P. (2010) 'Twenty first century social work: the influence of political context on public service provision in social work education and service delivery', *European Journal of Social Work*, advanced access at DOI: 10.1080/13691451003706670

Wells, K. and Marcenko, M. (2011) 'Introduction to the special issue: Mothers of children in foster care', *Children and Youth Services Review* 33(3): 419–23.

White, J. (2008) 'Sustainable Pedagogy: a research narrative about teachers, creativity and performativity', *Transnational Curriculum Inquiry*, 5(1): 51–57.

Williams, S. (2009) 'Recovering from the psychological impact of intensive care: how constructing a story helps', *Nursing in Critical Care* 14(6): 281–88.

Winter, K. (2009a) 'Relationships Matter: the problems and prospects for social workers' relationships with young children in care', *Child and Family Social Work* 14: 450–60.

Winter, K. (2009b) 'Recent Policy Initiatives in Early Childhood and the Challenges for the Social Work Profession', *British Journal of Social Work* 39(7): 1235–55.

Woodcock, J. (2003) 'The Social Work Assessment of Parenting: An Exploration', *British Journal of Social Work* 33: 87–106.

Woodcock, J. and Dixon, J. (2005) 'Professional ideologies and preferences in social work: A British study in global perspective', *British Journal of Social Work* 35: 953–73.

Wulczyn, F. (2004) 'Family Reunification', *Children, Families and Foster Care* 14(1): 95–112.

Younghusband, E. (1978) *Social Work in Britain: 1950–1975*, London: George Allen and Unwin.

Index